THE SCIENCE OF A SLAP SHOT

ELLEN LABRECQUE

Published in the United States of America by Cherry Lake Publishing
Ann Arbor, Michigan
www.cherrylakepublishing.com

Content Adviser: Erik Zobel, Amherst High School Physics, Amherst, New York
Reading Adviser: Marla Conn, ReadAbility, Inc.

Photo Credits: © Aksonov/iStock.com, cover, 1; © SMI/Newscom,5; © Wickedgood | Dreamstime.com - Zdeno Chara Boston Bruins Photo, 6; © Jupiterimages/Thinkstock Images, 9; © Raytags | Dreamstime.com - Hockey Stick And Puck Photo, 10; © Ivica Drusany/Shutterstock.com, 11; © IHA/Icon SMI 524/IHA/Icon SMI/Newscom, 13; © Eric Fahrner/Shutterstock.com, 15; © Modestil | Dreamstime.com - Hockey Photo, 16; © Wickedgood | Dreamstime.com - Kostitsyn Checks Patrice Bergeron (NHL Hockey) Photo, 19; © Kevin Norris/Shutterstock.com, 20; © lsantilli/Shutterstock.com, 21; © Laszlo Szirtesi/Shutterstock.com, 22; © technotr/iStock.com, 25; © Jmweb7 | Dreamstime.com - Hockey Sticks Photo, 26; © Tumar/Shutterstock.com, 28

Library of Congress Cataloging-in-Publication Data

Labrecque, Ellen.
  The science of a slap shot/Ellen Labrecque.
    pages cm.—(Full-Speed Sports)
  Includes bibliographical references and index.
  ISBN 978-1-63362-584-6 (hardcover)—ISBN 978-1-63362-764-2 (pdf)—ISBN 978-1-63362-674-4 (paperback)—
ISBN 978-1-63362-854-0 (ebook)
  1. Hockey—Juvenile literature. 2. Sports sciences—Juvenile literature. I. Title.

GV847.25.L34 2015
796.356—dc23
                    2015005833

Cherry Lake Publishing would like to acknowledge the work of
the Partnership for 21st Century Skills. Please visit www.p21.org
for more information.

Printed in the United States of America
Corporate Graphics

ABOUT THE AUTHOR

Ellen Labrecque is a freelance writer living in Pennsylvania with her husband and two kids. She has written many non-fiction books and previously was an editor at *Sports Illustrated Kids* magazine. An avid runner, Ellen is always trying to figure out ways to become speedier.

TABLE OF CONTENTS

CHAPTER 1

ICE HOCKEY'S STRONGEST PLAYER

The score is tied 2–2 in a 2014 National Hockey League (NHL) game between the Boston Bruins and the New York Rangers. With just under nine minutes to play in the third period, Zdeno Chara of the Bruins winds up to take hockey's hardest shot, the slap shot. The slap shot is for ice hockey what a powerful swing is for baseball. A powerful slap shot can get an arena of fans on their feet, hoping for a goal.

Chara is the tallest player ever to be in the NHL. The 6-foot-9 (205.7-centimeter), 260-pound (118-kilogram)

Zdeno Chara has the fastest slap shot in the NHL.

Zdeno Chara winds up for a slap shot.

LOOK!

Look at how Chara has his legs and arms positioned. Do you think this will be a hard slap shot or just a little tap? How can you tell? Keep reading to see if you're right.

[21ST CENTURY SKILLS LIBRARY]

defenseman twists his upper body and reaches back with his stick. The stick lifts way up toward the rafters. As he swings, his stick moves so fast, you can barely see it. Chara transfers his weight from his back leg to his front leg and makes contact with the puck. *Whack!* The black blur goes flying toward Rangers goaltender Henrik Lundqvist at about 100 miles (161 kilometers) per hour (mph). After Chara fires his shot, he is knocked down to the ice, but the puck sails between Lundqvist's pads. *Goal!* While still on his knees, Chara pumps his fists in the air in celebration. The Bruins hold on to the lead and win, 3–2.

Chara holds the record for the hardest shot in the NHL. In 2012, during the Hardest Shot competition at All-Star Weekend, he fired the puck at 108.8 mph (175.1 kph)! This is even faster than Major League Baseball's fastest pitch record of 108.1 mph (174 kph).

How does Chara make the puck fly so fast? He follows the scientific rules behind the slap shot. Let's learn how to make the puck zoom at lightning speed!

CHAPTER 2

THE HISTORY OF THE SLAP SHOT

Ice hockey is the fastest-moving team sport. Players skate as fast as 30 mph (48 kph), and the puck flies at over 100 mph (161 kph). The first recorded indoor ice hockey game was on March 4, 1875, in Montreal, Canada. Nine players from each team took the ice, instead of six like in the modern game. They played with a wooden puck and wooden sticks. The National Hockey League was founded more than 40 years later, in 1917. The league included five teams, all from Canada.

Hockey has been popular in Canada for hundreds of years.

In the early days of ice hockey, sticks were made entirely of wood, which didn't bend or flex much. In the 1950s, manufacturers started making stick blades from plastic instead of wood. These sticks were stronger yet lighter than the wooden ones. They were also cheaper to make. Later that decade, players began to bend their stick blades before games, giving the blades a curved shape. Andy Bathgate, from the New York Rangers, is traditionally given credit for this. When a slap shot is

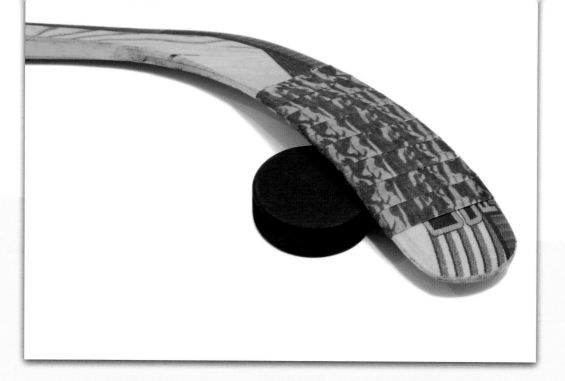

Wooden sticks, like this one, don't bend as easily as sticks made of composite material.

hit with a curved blade, the puck moves in unexpected ways. The **unpredictability** of puck movement makes it much harder for goalies to stop shots. Once stick manufacturers saw that the players were experimenting with curving their blades, they began to produce sticks this way. Modern sticks are made of a **composite material** that lets them bend or **flex** a lot.

Back when ice hockey was only played outside, some players made pucks of cow dung! The first rubber ice hockey pucks were made from rubber balls sliced in half.

Today, the NHL uses pucks made from hardened rubber. A puck is 3 inches (7.6 cm) across and 1 inch (2.5 cm) thick, and weighs about 6 ounces (170 grams), about as heavy as an apple. The NHL freezes their pucks before using them in games. Frozen pucks are less bouncy and easier to control than unfrozen ones. In an NHL game, the referees replace the puck with a newer, colder one after every couple minutes of gameplay.

Pucks need to be replaced several times per game.

Alex Shibicky of the New York Rangers is credited with inventing a version of the slap shot back in the 1930s. Now, the shot he used is considered more of a "snap shot," because he did not raise his stick higher than the knees. Still, Shibicky described his shot as moving "just like a bullet. Then, when you follow through, it's the most beautiful shot you'd ever want to see."

Fast-forward 15 years, and Bernard "Boom Boom" Geoffrion of the Montreal Canadiens is given credit for inventing the slap shot we are more familiar with today. He was the first to bring his stick far above his head

THINK ABOUT IT!

Before the 1950s, goalkeepers didn't wear masks. Now, all ice hockey goalies wear masks, as well as plenty of other padding to keep themselves safe. The thicker the padding, the more it can protect goalies against the **force** of a puck. (Imagine an airbag inflating to protect someone in a car accident.) Do you think the players should be able to choose for themselves how much safety gear to wear? What might happen if they wear too much or too little? How could this impact the game?

Jacques Plante developed an early version of a face mask for goalies.

when shooting. His nickname came from the sounds of his stick booming off the puck and then the puck booming off the boards.

Bobby Hull, of the Chicago Blackhawks, made the slap shot popular. Although technology at the time wasn't able to accurately record the speed, *Popular Mechanics* magazine estimated Hull could make the puck fly at speeds of over 100 mph (161 kph). In 1966, he became the first player to score more than 50 goals in a season. Many of these goals were the result of his fearsome slap shot.

SUPER SLAP SHOT SCIENCE

The game of ice hockey has gotten faster, and shots have gotten fiercer, over the years. Much of this advancement is due to better technology, training, and nutrition. But the scientific principles behind the slap shot have remained constant over the years. Why? Because they work!

The slap shot actually takes longer to execute than other shots. It also requires a lot of space for the player to perform it.

Players must have room to windup for a slap shot.

When a player takes a slap shot, the first step is the windup. In the windup, the player's shoulders and upper torso act like a **fulcrum**, or turning point. The hockey stick acts as the **lever** that is turned by the fulcrum. The player rotates his upper body backward until his stick reaches way over his head. Then, as he gets ready to strike the puck, he rotates his weight from his back skate to his front skate. This weight shift helps transfer the **momentum** he gained from

A hockey stick is full of potential energy as it comes in contact with the puck.

the stick and skating movement toward the puck. This also means a bigger and taller player would generate more force than a smaller and shorter one, if done correctly.

Before the player's stick strikes the puck, the blade slightly slides along the ice. This helps the stick flex, or snap back, and loads it with **potential energy (PE)**. When the stick slides along the ice, it is like pulling back on a slingshot before shooting it. The PE the flexed stick has, combined with the energy from the player, transfers to the puck to give it **kinetic energy**. The more energy that goes in, the more energy that comes out, and the more **velocity** the puck will gain.

The final step of the slap shot is the follow-through. Players follow through by pointing the stick where they want the puck to go. If they want to shoot high, they follow through high. If they want their shot low, they follow through low. *Goal!*

THINK ABOUT IT!

The NHL restricts the amount of curve on players' sticks. The league also restricts how long the stick and the blade can be. Why is this the case? If a player's stick is longer with more curve, will it generate more power? Why or why not? Go online to find out more.

CHAPTER 4

HARDER, FASTER . . . SCARIER?

Ice hockey can be a dangerous sport. After all, athletes wear sharp skates and swing long sticks at frozen pucks while skating on slick ice! Thanks to training and nutrition, athletes have also gotten bigger and stronger. This means they can **check** each other and hit the puck harder.

The good news about all this danger is that these same athletes have gotten smarter about protecting themselves. The first NHL player to wear a helmet was George Owen of the Boston Bruins. Owen had played

Andrei Kostitsyn slams Patrice Bergeron into the boards.

football in college. When he joined the NHL in 1928, he wore his leather football helmet during games.

The NHL didn't make helmets mandatory until 1979. After this date, every player who entered the league had to wear one. However, players who were already in the league were allowed to go without one if they wanted to. Today's hockey helmets have a hard outer shell with soft padding inside.

The NHL has also made it safer for fans to watch games rinkside. In 2002, the NHL put netting up

Nets above the boards protect fans from flying pucks.

[21ST CENTURY SKILLS LIBRARY]

Goalies wear helmets, leg pads, gloves, and other gear.

behind the goals and in the corners of the rink. The netting protects fans from **deflected** pucks flying off the ice.

Goalie equipment has changed the most over the years. When the slap shot started to be used more often, goaltenders needed more protection. Each goalie now wears 50 pounds (22.6 kg) of protection in every game! Wouldn't you want to be covered head to toe if you were trying to stop a puck flying at speeds of 100 mph (161 kph)? The biggest change for goalies

British goalie Stephen Murphy makes a save.

[21ST CENTURY SKILLS LIBRARY]

came when they started wearing masks in the 1960s. Today, plaster molds are made of a goalie's head. These molds help create the best helmet and mask for each player. The final product is made from a material called Kevlar. This is the same material used to make bulletproof vests.

"I don't know if I would play goalie without all this equipment," says Martin Brodeur, one of the NHL's best goalies. "If a player sent a slap shot toward me, I would only be thinking about survival, not stopping goals!"

GO DEEPER!

Read this chapter closely. What's the main difference between a "snap shot" and "slap shot"? Go online to watch videos of each. What do you notice?

CHAPTER 5

SKATING INTO THE FUTURE

Thanks to new training methods and equipment, learning to hit the slap shot at blazing speeds is easier than ever. One of the most useful modern technologies that help players improve their slap shot form is the Phantom cam. This is a high-speed camera that creates super slow-motion video clips of a player shooting.

"The high-speed camera is incredible," says Julie Chu, a forward on the United States women's ice hockey team. "We know that we are flexing the stick a bit when we take

24

a shot, but we would never know it bends that much without this technology."

Once a player watches himself on the Phantom cam, he can change his **mechanics** to make his shot better. He can twist his body a different way or shift his weight more to increase the power into his shot. This kind of information teaches ice hockey players the small tweaks they need to make to get off a better shot.

Not every goal scored comes from a slap shot.

*Players often have favorite sticks that they're
the most comfortable playing with.*

Even though it is still in the early stages, the NHL is
also experimenting with player-tracking technology.
During games, computer chips are placed in the jerseys
of every player, plus on the puck. These chips record the
player's speed, shot locations, and even how many miles
he skates per game. All of this information is sent to a
computer where the results are analyzed. These chips
help players improve each and every aspect of their

game. The league hopes to start widespread use of this equipment in the 2015–16 season.

One of the biggest equipment advancements for improving the slap shot is the invention of composite sticks. Composite sticks are made of a variety of materials including wood, aluminum, and plastic that combine to create more powerful and durable sticks. These sticks also have more flex in their blades. All of this results in some fast-moving pucks!

GO DEEPER!

In the 1990s, there came a new invention that wasn't for the hockey players, but for the fans. The FoxTrax puck had a computer chip inside to light up when shown on a television screen, which was supposed to make it easier for viewers to follow the action. But several commentators and journalists made fun of the glowing puck, and the NHL quit using it after a few seasons. Why do you think people complained?

Hockey fans love the game's fast pace.

Ice hockey is one of the world's roughest, fastest sports. Thanks to advances in equipment and technology, it continues to get even more physical and faster—but safer too. With each and every powerful slap shot you see in the future, you will know that science played the biggest role in its success!

TIMELINE

A TIMELINE HISTORY OF HOCKEY

1875	First indoor ice hockey game is played.
1889	First women's ice hockey game is played.
1893	The first Stanley Cup is awarded to Montreal Hockey Club.
1917	The National Hockey League is formed and consists of five teams: the Montreal Canadiens, Toronto Arenas, Ottawa Senators, Montreal Wanderers, and Quebec Bulldogs.
1920	Ice hockey makes its debut at the Summer Olympics.
1924	Ice hockey makes its debut at the Winter Olympics; the NHL expands to the United States with the founding of the Boston Bruins.
1930s	Alex Shibicky invents the slap shot.
1945	The Hockey Hall of Fame inducts its first members.
1966	Bobby Hull becomes the first player to score more than 50 goals in a season. Many of these goals were the result of his slap shot.
1980	The United States defeats the USSR in the semifinal and Finland in the final to win the Olympic gold medal. The win over the USSR is called "the miracle on ice."
1980s	Aluminum sticks are used, the first that are completely non-wooden.
1990s	Sticks made of composite materials become popular.
1998	Women play ice hockey at the Winter Olympics for the first time.
2012	Zdeno Chara of the Boston Bruins sets the NHL slap shot record with a speed of 108.8 mph (175.1 kph).

THINK ABOUT IT

Think about what you knew about the slap shot and ice hockey before reading this book. Does the slap shot seem harder or easier to do now that you know the science behind it?

In chapter 3, you learned about potential energy. In ice hockey, the potential energy is loaded in the stick when it is flexed back. Can you think of other examples of potential energy in sports like baseball or tennis?

Do you think the NHL should regulate how long and how much bend a player's stick should have? Why or why not?

Do you think ice hockey is more dangerous to play than baseball? Think about the differences in equipment. Why or why not?

LEARN MORE

FURTHER READING

Frederick, Shane. *Hockey: The Math of the Game*. North Mankato, MN: Capstone Press, 2012.

Levine, Shar, and Leslie Johnstone. *Sports Science*. New York: Sterling Publishing, 2006.

Napier, Matt. *Z is for Zamboni: A Hockey Alphabet*. Ann Arbor, MI: Sleeping Bear Press, 2003.

WEB SITES

International Ice Hockey Federation
www.iihf.com
This site has information about the worldwide governing body for ice hockey and in-line hockey.

National Hockey League
www.nhl.com
Find lots of different articles, photos, and videos on the official NHL web site.

PrintActivities: Hockey Printables
www.printactivities.com/Theme-Printables/Hockey-Printables.html
Try your hand at some hockey-related games and worksheets.

GLOSSARY

check (CHEK) to use shoulders to block the progress of another hockey player

composite material (kuhm-PAH-zit muh-TEER-ee-uhl) a substance made of materials that are stronger together than they are apart

deflected (di-FLEKT-ed) made something go in a different direction

flex (FLEKS) to bend

force (FORS) an influence that causes an object to change its speed or direction of movement

fulcrum (FUL-kruhm) the pivot point where something turns

kinetic energy (ki-NET-ik EN-ur-jee) energy associated with the movement of an object, such as a hockey puck that has been shot

lever (LEV-ur) a rigid piece that transmits force or motion when a force is applied

mechanics (muh-KAN-iks) a player's movement and technique when performing an action in sports

momentum (moh-MEN-tuhm) the property that a moving object has because of its mass and its motion

potential energy (puh-TEN-shuhl EN-ur-jee) the energy that something has because of its position or the way its parts are arranged, such as a hockey stick in a windup position ready to strike the puck

unpredictability (uhn-pri-DIK-tuh-BIL-i-tee) behavior that makes it hard to say what will happen in the future

velocity (vuh-LAH-si-tee) rate of speed in a particular direction

INDEX

[21ST CENTURY SKILLS LIBRARY]

} Introduction

Ableton Live 5 Power! is a comprehensive guide to making music with Ableton's revolutionary live performance and studio software, Live 5. Written for all Live users, from digital audio beginners to seasoned pros, this book explores each fundamental feature within Live and provides power-user tips and insider tricks for integrating Live into your home or professional studio. But Live's in-studio capabilities are just the beginning. Every last feature, button, fader, instrument, and effect in Live 5 was also designed with the live performer in mind. *Ableton Live 5 Power!* is a book written for musicians by a musician who uses and discusses the software daily. Whether you use Live for producing, composing, DJing, or film and television, *Ableton Live 5 Power!* will help you put the fun back into making music with computers.

What You'll Find in This Book

* Step-by-step instructions for creating, producing, and mixing music in Live.
* Definitions of key digital audio concepts such as: What is a sample? What is a loop? How do my loops and samples become music?
* Music-making ideas and tips.
* Full explanation of Live's Devices and how to use third-party plug-ins in Live.
* Audio-interface and MIDI-controller tips and recommendations.
* Simple yet complete explanation of MIDI and its many uses in Live.

* Recommendations for choosing and using an audio editor for optimizing your loops and samples.

* In-depth guide to editing, recording, performing, and paint 'n play composing with Ableton Live.

* Expert tips, tricks, and interview excerpts with world-famous Live power users and performers.

* Specialized hardware considerations to help musicians feel at home performing with Live.

* How Live will reinvent your own music and attitude about making music with a computer.

* How ReWire makes Live the hub of your software studio.

* Carefully edited and labeled screenshots, giving you a first-person view of how experts work in Live.

* Companion CD-ROM with example Sets and samples, plus a few excerpts from the *Live 5 CSi* movie tutorial from Thomson Course Technology.

Whom This Book Is For

This book is for people who want to make music using the power of their computers. Ableton Live 5 sews the seams that exist between digital audio, MIDI files, live performance, software synchronization, musicality, and fun on a Mac or PC. If you've heard of Live's "magical" audio and loop dexterity, let this book be your guide to unlocking that power; or, if you have already discovered Live and want to take your performing and composing skills to the next level, *Ableton Live 5 Power!* is written for you.

How This Book Is Organized

Ableton Live 5 Power! is divided into 14 chapters and an appendix. Each chapter contains targeted direction and thoughtful notes about every aspect of Live. The chapters can be used as a reference, but I strongly suggest that you read through them sequentially. There are many concepts at work in Live and learning some will require the mastery of others. The chapters in this book are therefore arranged in such a manner that each chapter builds on concepts from the previous one, providing you with knowledge needed to move forward at each step. This book is not intended to replicate the *Ableton Live User Manual*. This book is designed to turn you into the ultimate master of Live, where you no longer need to think about what to do and how to do it, but you simply *do it*.

❊ **Chapter 1, "Live 5"**: I will begin with a brief introduction to Live, the concept behind its development, and a basic overview of how you might use Live both on stage and in the studio.

❊ **Chapter 2, "Back to School"**: If you're brand new to the realm of MIDI and digital audio, this chapter's for you. MIDI messages, controllers, sample rate, bit depth, digital glitches and peaks—it's all here.

❊ **Chapter 3, "Getting Live Up and Running"**: To get you up and running, this chapter will provide key PC- and Mac-related recommendations for MIDI hardware, choosing an audio interface, installing and running Live, and basic MIDI setup.

❊ **Chapter 4, "Live Interface Basics"**: This chapter will take you through Live's two main interfaces—Session and Arrangement—point out key controls, talk about how to get help, and instruct you on how to set up your first song. Live Interface Basics will also teach you about Live's Control (transport) Bar, song settings, customization, and general maneuvering in Live. Although the chapter is an overview of Live, experts may still pick up tricks in this chapter.

❊ **Chapter 5, "Making Music in Live"**: Live is used by many different types of people for several different applications. "Making Music in Live" outlines the four most common ways to make music with Live, unveils key working methods for each group, introduces common sections of the Clip View, and dives deeper into the Live composition process. Whether you are a DJ, producer, film/television composer, or live musician, this chapter is packed with intermediate level tips and will warm you up for what is to come.

❊ **Chapter 6, "The Audio Clip"**: Clips are the building blocks in Live. Every musical idea takes the form of a clip. This chapter will delve into the world of Audio Clips, covering topics such as Warp Markers, Warp Modes, Clip Envelopes, and audio recording. Everyone should learn this chapter inside and out to get the most from Live.

❋ **Chapter 7, "The MIDI Clip"**: The MIDI features of Live will be discussed at length in this chapter. You'll learn about overdub recording, quantizing, editing a performance, importing and exporting files, as well as MIDI control envelopes. This stuff is hot information for everybody.

❋ **Chapter 8, "Using Effects and Instruments"**: Here, I will explore the Track View and methods of using effects and virtual instruments within your projects. I'll also explain Live's signal routing possibilities and plug-in automation functions.

❋ **Chapter 9, "Live's Virtual Instruments"**: Live includes three virtual instruments: Simpler, Impulse, and Operator. This chapter takes each instrument apart, explains its workings, and gives you some great tips along the way. If you're coming from the world of hardware synthesizers, you'll love seeing and hearing what your computer can do now!

❋ **Chapter 10, "Live's Audio Effects"**: This chapter is the definitive reference for all of Live's built-in Audio Effects. Here, every dial and button is explained in detail and tips are provided for tweaking your effects into oblivion.

❋ **Chapter 11, "Live's MIDI Effects"**: Another reference chapter for Live's MIDI Effects. Here's where to find out how the power of these simple tools can be harnessed in your songs.

❋ **Chapter 12, "ReWire"**: ReWire is the key to linking Live with other powerful applications. The good news is that you already own it (once you own Live). Now make it swing. Both ReWire Master and ReWire Slave will be covered.

❋ **Chapter 13, "Playing Live...Live"**: Now that you're familiar with how music is made in Live, it's time to start playing. Learn how to set up your system for various types of gigs, methods for MIDI control, as well as some of the most detailed tips for importing and looping audio.

❋ **Chapter 14, "Live 5 Power"**: Chapter 14 is pure fun. This chapter is loaded with all sorts of juicy information, including more Warp Marker trickery, methods for destroying beats, creating templates, editing samples, and the amazing Follow Actions. Keep some water handy in case your head catches on fire.

Keeping the Book's Content Current

I have remained in close contact with Ableton throughout the writing of this book to ensure that each instruction, recommendation, and tip works with the most recent version of Live 5.0.1 at the time of this writing. (I work for M-Audio, which distributes Live in the United States.) If you should find any errors or have suggestions for future editions, please contact me via the Course Technology Web site:

www.courseptr.com

At this site, you can also find updates, corrections, and other information related to the content of the book. You should also regularly visit the Ableton Web site (www.ableton.com) for software updates and helpful advice found in Ableton's "user forum."

1 } Live 5

Every so often, a new piece of technology or software application makes an indelible mark on the way things are done. Be it the arrival of the electric guitar, a new kind of synthesizer, or the invention of digital audio recording—the impact on musicians and the artistic world can be both major and long lasting. Once conceived, technology can take on a life of its own, inspire a range of other complementary technologies, or even spawn a whole new school of thought. Ableton's Live has instigated a revolution in the audio software world by transforming computers into playable musical instruments, real-time remix stations, and the world's most dexterous audio environment. Live is the culmination of years of studio software development and the infusion of DJ and electronic music-making instincts. Live is also a labor of love born out of the desire of a few software-savvy musicians who wanted to take their elaborate computer-based recording studio on the road.

While Live has been on the market for many years, new ideas are still emerging. From the laptop tech-house stylings of musicians such as Gauss Control, Monolake, and Akufen to the soundtrack work of Steve Tavaglione and Klaus Badelt, Live's user base is made up of professionals who demand the most from their tools. Former Nine Inch Nails keyboardist and television music composer Charlie Clouser said this of Live: "With Nine Inch Nails, it took us two years to finish a record. Today, I finish cues in seven minutes. Without Ableton, it simply couldn't happen. Within eight seconds of downloading the demo, I knew I had to have it—at any price." The ease and skill with which Live can handle audio is a natural for film and TV work.

With its expanded recording and MIDI functionality, Live is a full-blown music production environment suitable for any artistic style. You'll find all the features you'd expect from other digital audio workstations, such as multi-track audio and MIDI recording, non-linear editing, quantization, pitch shifting, freezing, delay compensation, and more. Live's advantage is that all these common features are implemented within its unique sequencing interface.

Live is also a digital DJ performance tool and has begun to replace MP3-based DJ units, CD spinners, and turntables. It is also becoming increasingly common to see laptop performing artists

❈ ❈ ❈

employing computers as their primary sound source or record collection. This makes perfect sense when you stop to think that—for the last couple of years—synthesizers, samplers, and their sounds have been purchased en masse via Web download or e-mail, instead of as a separate hardware component or sound module. In the next couple of years, more and more musicians, bands, and solo artists will be using Live's technology to realize their artistic vision from the comfort of their own laptop.

What Is Live?

In January 2000, Berlin-based Ableton knocked the audio software world on its ear by releasing Live 1.0 Since its inception, Live has evolved into a real-time music production system, allowing users to integrate samples, MIDI, effects, and live audio data quickly and musically enough for a live performance.

Similar to modern software MIDI-sequencers or production suites, Live (Figure 1.1) allows you to create and modify musical elements, such as guitar riffs, bass lines, and piano parts, which can be arranged and played from a large, customizable grid. The grid can be thought of as both a music organizer and sonic palette. Once these elements have been placed into a cell on the grid, you may designate MIDI or computer keyboard triggering options for these pieces, alter their playback parameters, add effects, and more. After enough cells for the song are filled, it is time for "the take" or live performance.

Figure 1.1

Here is a quick peek at the Session View grid in Live 5. The rows make up musical sections called scenes, while the columns function as virtual mixer channels.

This grid/sonic palette makes up the improvisational sequencer component of Live and can be used to trigger groups of musical elements, like sections of a song. For instance, during a live performance, you might want to progress from the verse to the chorus back to the verse—something you'd never done in practice. You can do so by triggering a specified row in Live's grid matrix that, in turn, directs Live to play the second group of elements (the chorus) and cease play of verse parts. To go back, you would merely click on the preceding row. The song arrangement is under full real-time control. This makes it easy to jump around through various subsections of the song, break down important song sections, and come up with new possibilities. In addition, any individual piece contained within a grid cell can be played independently in similar fashion to an "old school" phrase sampler (like Roland's Dr. Sample). It is quite possible to make new parts and original ideas by playing these parts as one-shot samples or to overdub a previously made arrangement. Keep in mind that these pieces can be tweaked to oblivion, much like the sounds in a hardware sampler or synthesizer, only more flexibly with Live.

The true power housed within Live is the software's ability to play, or play with, sound. Live can be played in a "jam" situation or simply used as a creative tool for building a song in layers. Live specializes in stretching audio alongside MIDI to any desired tempo or pitch. What's more, Live can bend audio within itself so that a sound may start at one tempo or pitch and end up in an entirely different place (all within the same performance). The editing possibilities are nearly infinite. Ableton has made recording and editing the performance a main function of Live, so that a single software application turns your laptop (or desktop) PC/Mac into a live performance system, a multi-track audio and MIDI recording studio, a powerful loop and song editor, and a full-blown remix factory. Live enables you to map the cells of your grid-palette (full of musical parts) to a MIDI controller or computer keyboard. In essence, you can record a live improvisation or band performance for later editing, further arranging, overdubs, and added automation. If the final mix isn't to your liking, you can always take another pass. To get an idea of what I'm talking about, look at Figure 1.2, which features a screenshot of Live's Arrangement View.

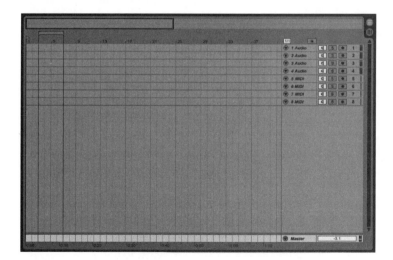

Figure 1.2

If you are familiar with desktop audio, Live's Arrangement View may remind you of many different programs. However, Live's feature set is sure to raise a few standards for many years to come.

Musically speaking, Live is a one-two punch whose focus is spread equally between live performance and recording/editing, all in one application. As you learn how to play (jam) in Live, you will also be gradually setting up your song's arrangement and learning new tactics to apply to your live performance. In other words, Live is quite unlike any other software application currently on the market and fills a certain void that has been overlooked by the majority of developers—the needs of the performing and recording musician.

Why Was Live Developed?

One of the greatest advantages for musicians employing Live is that it is a program written for musicians by musicians—they actually use the very software they create. Initially, Robert Henke and Gerhard Behles (paired in the Berlin-based electronica group Monolake) were looking for a better way to create their own music through the use of a computer. Both were experienced sound designers and had spent time working for Native Instruments, one of the industry's chief authorities on virtual or "soft" synthesizers and sound design software. At the time, the industry lacked a user-friendly software application conducive to creating music as a musician would: intuitively and spontaneously. There were plenty of "loop-friendly" applications and more than a couple live jamming programs, but most audio software was built for studio use and lacked the interface necessary to create music the way a musician does: *live*.

Since the drawing board days of development, Behles, Henke, and the Ableton team honed Live's interface and functionality with the performing artist in mind. While complex, build-your-own software suites such as Native Instruments' Reaktor and Cycling '74's Max/MSP are powerful sound-generators, they often prove too complex for the performing musician who may be contending with any number of distractions—including lighting, sound system woes, fog, etc. Live, on the other hand, was developed (and has been continually improved) to be the best possible live recording and performance system available on a computer. It contains professional-grade audio tools and software compliance such as VST and Audio Units effect plug-ins and instruments, plus ReWire software-studio synchronization. These tools will be discussed in greater detail as I progress. For now, recognize Ableton's commitment to the performing artist and to the end user. Don't just take my word for it; jump on out to Ableton's closely monitored user forum at www.ableton.com, where you can anonymously enter your own wish list of ideas for future development of Live. Don't be too surprised if Ableton CEO Gerhard Behles, Conceptualist Robert Henke, or any of the other Ableton developers chime in to discuss how your idea might better the world of Live.

The World of Live

Over the last several years, the idea of music creation and live performance on a PC or Mac has become increasingly attractive. With the increase in processing power and audio storage capacities, even relatively inexpensive computers have become powerful audio editing and recording studios. Producers using audio software have enjoyed exponential improvements in performance and the number and types of tasks performable by a computer. Also, the customization and potential for add-on software/hardware as new technology emerges has made it less intimidating to jump into the fray. For less than $2000 (US), you can acquire a decent laptop, a sound card, and Live, the most powerful and flexible music creation and performance software on the planet. For just a bit more, it is quite possible that your bedroom studio could compete with the pros, not to mention the fact that an investment in an Ableton Live performance rig is cheaper and easier to maintain than a stack of hardware samplers, rack-mounted sound modules, outboard mixers, and, well, you get the point.

How Does It Work?

Live allows you to sort your music into easy-to-define sections, called *scenes*, while maintaining all the flexible effects and routing options made possible only via PC- or Mac-based software. These scenes, which are spread horizontally across the screen, look like the rows of a spreadsheet or graph. The columns that are formed correspond with mixer channels. Within each column, only one sound—be it a MIDI sequence or audio sample—can play at a time. So to play through your song, you can literally run down the rows, letting each row represent a musical section. Live also enables you to trigger sequences, loops, and samples; tweak effects; and change mix settings from a MIDI controller, MIDI keyboard, or computer keyboard. You can preview any audio loop in real-time at any tempo from within your project. You can even record new pieces into your song without ever stopping playback. Enhancements in Live empower users to handle different kinds of musical parts specific to their content. For example, a drum beat can be handled differently than a synthesizer or vocal take. A drum loop typically contains several short sounds, such as hi-hat, snare, and kick drum hits, while a synthesizer or vocal part will most often sustain or consist of longer sounds. Since Live analyzes the audio's contents, it is necessary for Live to "look" at each loop in a different way to achieve the best results.

You may also turn off Live's time-correcting warp feature to make your loops behave more like standard multi-track recording software. Live also encourages plenty of manipulation in terms of feel, tempo, and pitch, but how Live really works is up to you. Never before has software been so dependent upon its owner's proficiency, and never before has software been so intuitive and musical after a few basic principles are understood. Live works with your audio loops, MIDI sequences, hardware synthesizers, recorded material, and other software applications to make music. You can create new music from scratch or build a "remix" from previously recorded material. When it comes to making music in Live, the creative possibilities are limitless.

What Sets Live Apart

If you are an audio software enthusiast, you've certainly heard of powerful digital multi-track studio applications such as Digidesign's Pro Tools, Emagic's Logic Audio, MOTU's Digital Performer, Cakewalk's Sonar, and Steinberg's Cubase (and Nuendo). These programs, and their hardware counterparts, are often referred to as *DAWs*, or *Digital Audio Workstations*. Their main task is to ensure that music is recorded and played back properly in a studio situation. Other, more loop-oriented, products such as Propellerhead's Reason, Arturia's Storm, Sonic

Foundry's Acid Pro, Cakewalk's Project5, or Sonic Syndicate's Orion Pro are also touted in the media for their originality and have become popular along with the self-contained studio paradigm. Each of these programs allows for using the computer as a stand-alone music composition center and loop factory. Like the aforementioned products, Live can operate by itself, record multiple audio and MIDI sources, integrate loops, and handle other basic studio functions. But Live also introduces the idea of performing with software and editing your improvisation afterwards, and automating has never had a better platform.

To fully understand why Live is such an innovative program, it helps to take a look at Live 5's feature-set.

* First, Live works on both Mac (OS X 10.2.8 or later) and PC (Windows 2000 and XP) platforms and takes advantage of all current industry standards, such as ASIO drivers, VST and Audio Units effect plug-ins and instruments, and ReWire synchronization technology.

* Live is among the first programs for the Mac that allow loops to be previewed at the project tempo independently from pitch. Other programs have tried, but none have succeeded in bringing the Mac this kind of efficiency. As for PCs, Acid Pro and Sonar do a nice job of time stretching, and as long as you have Rex files, ReCycle can also help out, too. But Ableton could definitely make a case that Live "sounds" better, provides more types of stretching algorithms, and can recalibrate tempos in an instant, which is important if you consider that some time-stretching may need to be done in front of an audience.

* In addition to generating MIDI Time Code and MIDI Beat Clock, Live can also be synched to another program's MIDI clock.

* As mentioned previously, MIDI-note information can be used to trigger sounds or MIDI-controller info for knobs and sliders. Even your laptop computer keyboard can trigger parts. Better still, all MIDI-controller and keyboard-triggering information can be assigned while Live is in playback mode, so the music doesn't have to stop.

* In terms of routing, Live is constrained only by the limitations of your sound card and MIDI interfaces. And as we've alluded to, ReWire-compatible software applications (such as Reason, Max/MSP, FL Studio, and ReBirth) can be directed through Live's mixer in a variety of ways. Live's output may also be ReWired to another program's inputs. You can record audio from an outside source straight into Live or render (record) Live's own output to a fresh track (for later use) while you play.

* Another distinguishing feature of Live is the DJ-style crossfader built right into the performance mixer. Just like the DJ mixer pictured in Figure 1.3, you can assign mixer channels to A, B, or both channels and mix between the two with a MIDI- or mouse-controllable crossfader, or even the arrow keys on your computer's keyboard. This subtle tool enables

Figure 1.3
DJ mixers have evolved over the years to the point at which software counterparts can barely keep up. Live can be set up to function as a DJ system that will blow the doors off what a standard mixer can do, as you'll see in Chapter 14.

gradual song and loop transitions, along with more flexible performance options, not to mention DJ-style fader-flipping and cross jags.

❋ And while all of these elements make Live sound attractive, Ableton's not-so-secret weapon, the "Warp Engine," is the feature that has caused many a jaw to drop. Aside from being able to quickly quantize an audio loop's start and end points at the current project tempo, Live uses what's called "elastic audio" to wrestle WAV (or AIFF) files into submission. How is this done? Live has the ability to elasticize audio to any degree the composer would like and with greater accuracy and fidelity than ever before. I will dive into this in greater detail in subsequent chapters, but for now, be aware that Live makes a living out of dividing samples into sections, much in the way Propellerhead's ReCycle would. The difference with Live is that you are able to move slices (called *Warp Markers*), thereby stretching (or compressing) the loop's contents. This may seem minor, but consider for a moment that in Live, any sound within a given sample can be played at any time within itself.

❋ Confused? Here is an example: Live can speed up a 25-second sample so that it will play in 5 seconds or vice versa (slowing down the 5-second sample to take up more time). Taking it a step further, you could chop up this sample and resize select portions of the sound, thereby causing the first half of the sample to play faster than the last, for example. Amazingly enough, Live can do this with just a couple of mouse clicks, while you monitor the results. More common examples include matching up bass and drum loops, using select portions of a long performance, correcting sloppy takes, fixing near-perfect ones, humanizing a drum machine part, and the list goes on. For more on the power of elastic audio, see the section on Clip View in Chapter 5, "Making Music in Live." You can also truncate the loop's end points, move the loop reference (starting point) anywhere you like, and fine-tune the pitch in either half-step or cent increments.

❋ The elastic audio concept has been expanded in Live to the "elastic song." Global groove and swing templates allow us to apply subtle shuffle feels to all MIDI and audio parts in a project—all in real-time. Have you ever wondered what Kraftwerk's "Trans Europe Express" would sound like swinging? You can now find out within seconds. This will be extremely helpful for DJs who want to mix from a track with a straight feel to one with a triplet swing feel. The straight song can be gradually swung until it matches the second track without ever stopping the beat!

❋ Thanks to the crafty implementation of *clips*, Live lets you treat MIDI sequences with the same flexibility and control of their audio brothers. MIDI parts can be recorded, quantized, and edited on the fly (just like audio), plus MIDI overdub recording allows you to build musical elements, such as drum parts, in layers. Live hosts VST and Audio Units virtual instruments, commonly referred to as *soft synths*, and can also drive external MIDI hardware such as samplers, synthesizers, or even light and video installations. The MIDI effects work just like their audio counterparts allowing transposition, volume scaling, and more—all in real-time.

Because Live's design has been engineered for live performance, Ableton has created a powerful studio ally, almost by accident. After all, if Live makes it so easy to handle music in front of a stadium audience, it will be able to keep pace with the creative flow in a studio session easily. Placing television and movie cues is a natural fit for Live. Let's face it: Even the best-equipped recording studio would be doing itself a disservice by not integrating at least one computer running Live to handle some of these tasks. While most applications are focused on a specific task, such as sound design or the recording process, Ableton has zeroed in on the concept of making music, from the first iota of inspiration to the perfected performance, while still catering to the studio all the way.

Possible Applications

Before you jump in and start making music with Live, consider for a moment why this software was developed. Perhaps you have been lucky enough to spend some time in a recording studio using analog tape or a digital medium (such as ADAT or Pro Tools). If not, you have most likely seen pictures of a decent-sized studio and can imagine a fairly large mixer console (desk), accompanied by several pairs of different-sized monitor speakers, power amplifiers, racks of outboard effects, and the inevitable patch bay full of cables. Now imagine the last concert you attended. You may have seen a band complete with a cocky lead guitarist sporting shiny effects pedals; a keyboardist with bigger and shinier effects gear; or even a DJ with two-plus turntables, DJ mixer, and crate upon crate of back-breaking vinyl. Can you see where I'm going with this? Live eliminates the messy patch bay, the nightly setup and teardown of elaborate effects and amplifiers, and the need to carry your vinyl. Live can even save your entire performance for later editing. To say Live is a replacement for tried-and-true analog studios (or a substitute for your obnoxious guitar player) is to miss the point entirely. What is certain is that Live can not only survive in today's music making environment, but thrive. What's more, Live is only beginning to realize its full potential.

Super New York session drummer Shawn Pelton (The Saturday Night Live Band, House of Diablo) has taken to using Live both onstage and in the studio for creating music in ways he had only dreamed of previously. His live setup is shown in Figure 1.4. DJ superstar Sasha uses Live in his CD *Involver* and for his DJ sets—he's even gone so far as to make a custom MIDI controller for Live! Electronic music is a natural beneficiary of a program such as Live, as sample- or loop-based dance music has proven to drive the audio software world in some fascinating ways. Thankfully, Live offers this power and wealth of tools to all musicians, not just DJs and remixers, allowing them to develop their music with the same free-form approach.

FIGURE 1.4
Shawn Pelton incorporates a laptop running Ableton Live by triggering additional loops with foot pedals and a controller. This is but one imaginative way to use Live.

Here are some other possible Live scenarios:

❋ **Stage**—If your band plays with a sequencer, and your drummer is used to playing with a click track, you could easily incorporate live loops into your music. Some bands use phrase samplers to add in a layer of percussion, noise or effects loops, or even backup vocals.

❋ **Studio**—I have already mentioned why Ableton Live would be a perfect addition to any studio. It can function as a high-power drum machine, a flexible loop remixer, or versatile musical sketchpad. While some may use Live as their only studio application, bigger Pro Tools studios may simply enjoy Live for its ability to take bits of a project and let artists, producers, and engineers hear some different arrangements quickly and easily.

* **Bedroom**—With a nice audio interface and a decent computer running Live, platinum hits can be fashioned while you're still in your shorts. If professional studios can benefit from the power of Live, a solo musician can reap the rewards ten times over. Recording a simple guitar and vocal demo or producing a full-blown masterpiece is all within the scope of Live's capabilities.

* **Club**—The laptop DJ trend has been building steam for several years now. The benefits included less wear and tear on your vinyl, lightweight transport, the many possible software tricks for enhancing the sound, and more. To be fair, there are a few compromises to recognize, such as the time it takes to digitize vinyl and the look and feel of the performance. While paradigm shifts are always tricky, one thing is for sure: My vinyl weighs a ton (and so does yours).

Goals of This Book

Like Live, *Ableton Live 5 Power!* is written by a musician—a drummer, in fact—but don't let that scare you. I've spent plenty of time performing with Live and have been recording and remixing in Live for years. Live is built to be musical, and this book will aspire to be the same. It is my hope that you have many long hours of enjoyment using Live while creating some interesting new music. Although this book is designed to be a "power user" book, don't be deterred if you are new to Live, new to music, or new to computer-based production. This book will serve as a basic guide to interfacing with Live and an advanced tips and tricks collection for taking advantage of Ableton's industry-rocking technology.

Many sections in this book are not specific to Live but are included as a reference for novice and intermediate digital audio studio owners. Topics such as wave editing, loop making, and sample manipulation are broken down so that you won't have to seek out this information somewhere else. General audio computing tips, such as configuring your PC for audio, will help you make the most of any audio application you currently use and will only bolster your basic working knowledge of computer-based (digital) audio as musicians should understand it.

If you are already familiar with Live, this book should feel like a souped-up reference manual with some powerful tips and musical ideas for you to incorporate into your Live vocabulary. This book should help you optimize Live's settings for speed and sound, which should translate into maximum musical output. *Ableton Live 5 Power!* covers some sticky but rewarding topics, such as Live's MIDI implementation, editing Live's mix automation, and using virtual EQs and compressors for professional audio results.

The CD-ROM

To get you going as quickly as possible, a CD-ROM is included with this book. The CD-ROM, titled "Live 5 CSi LE," contains excerpts from the Live 5 CSi Master CD-ROM, as well as custom-built

Live Sets and presets (by me and my cohorts) to illustrate the topics as you read about them. After all, what fun is it to read about music? It's much more fun to *hear* music.

One of the new features in Live 5 is the Ableton Live Pack file format, which is a special file that contains presets, waveforms, and other goodies, which will be installed into your Ableton Library by simply double-clicking the file. Ableton has been kind enough to pack the example Sets and presets for this book into this new format to make installation as painless as possible.

To install this supplemental material, make sure you've first installed Live on your computer (see Chapter 3, "Getting Live Up and Running," for installation directions). Insert the "Live 5 CSi LE" CD-ROM into your computer and find the folder titled "Resources" on the CD. Open this folder and double-click the "AL5P.alp" file found inside. Live automatically begins to load if it's not running already. Live will then ask you if you want to install this pack. Click "Yes" to proceed. Live will automatically extract all the data from the file and place it into your Ableton Library. That's it! I think you'll agree that installation can't get much easier than that.

2 Back to School

When I was a child, "back to school" was one of the most dreaded statements I could possibly hear. It signaled the time of the year when the carefree summer was over. No more fun—time to work. The first couple of days back were always torturous. I could see the beautiful day rolling by outside while I was forced to listen to the dribble of my new history teacher. Some of my friends were in other classes on different schedules, meaning we were not able to eat lunch together or fool around anymore. It was horrible.

As you read the title of this chapter, the same feelings of dread may begin to crop up inside you. Some of you may even be suffering from flashbacks of studying endless pages of technical jargon for chemistry finals right now. Fear not! This book is not a boring compendium of scientific babble. I will keep the mood lively, fun, and interesting; yet in order to be a skilled Live user, you need to understand a few basic concepts. Knowing these concepts will improve your creativity with Live, help you develop your own working methods, and give you a true appreciation for everything this extraordinary software can do.

If you've used computers for music before, you may already be familiar with these subjects. But I still encourage you to read these brief sections, even if it's only to reinforce what you already know. Those of you who are new to the world of computer music production and Live should study these next sections very closely.

While a lot of technical information, including computer number theory, is about to be dumped on you, you will not be expected to know or remember specific details from this text or perform tedious number crunching. The most important thing you should walk away with after reading this chapter is an understanding of the concepts—insight into what's happening "under the hood" of your computer. For example, you may not be able to solve 453×78.34 off the top of your head, but you still understand the concept of multiplication. That's the level I'm shooting for here.

MIDI Primer

If you've read the first chapter, you've no doubt stumbled across the term "MIDI" a few times. In fact, if you've been even slightly involved in music electronics over the last two decades, you've probably had to deal with MIDI at some point along the way. Live is no exception. While MIDI was used only as a means of remote control in previous versions of Live, Live 5 uses MIDI as a core element of music and sound creation. This opens up a whole new set of doors for Live users by offering an expanded creative pallet to work from. I know that sounds exciting, but you may still be wondering what MIDI really is. To answer that, here is a brief history of MIDI development.

Why Was MIDI Developed?

During the dawn of musical electronics in the 60s and 70s, there were no rules or standards for building instruments. Back then, the workings of every electronic instrument created were determined solely by the manufacturer. Some devices had traditional keyboards; others used resistive strips for playing tones. Heck, one of the first electronic instruments, the Theremin (Figure 2.1), was played without even touching it! Indeed, many companies had wonderful and unique products, but there was no interconnectivity between them. If a musician wanted to layer the sounds of two separate synthesizers, like a MiniMoog and a Prophet 5, or drive a synth with a sequencer, it required enlisting the services of a borderline mad scientist to create a unique, one-of-a-kind connection interface. These interfaces were usually handmade, fragile, expensive, and extremely temperamental.

Figure 2.1
The Theremin is quite an esoteric instrument, but one with a distinct sound. You've probably been propelled through the stars in some of your favorite old sci-fi flicks by sounds from the Theremin.

As the technology of electronic instruments continued to grow into the 80s, digital circuitry began to find its way into these devices. With that, a solution for a standardized interconnectivity protocol was realized and Musical Instrument Digital Interface (MIDI) was born. Nearly every synth manufacturer from then up to the present has included MIDI protocol and connections on their hardware. This allows information to be passed back and forth between instruments, regardless of type, model, or manufacturer. Keyboards can be connected together and connected to sequencers, which can be connected to more sound modules and drum machines. The possibilities are endless.

Remote Control

You have probably used a TV set with a remote control (another gift of 80s technology) at some point in your life. Many of these remote controls can actually perform functions not possible with the physical controls mounted on the TV set. For example, the only way I can control brightness, contrast, hue, and color on my living room TV is with the remote. Programming the VCR, navigating satellite TV and DVD menus, titling my MiniDiscs, and managing active channels are all performed solely with the remote.

You probably have a fair understanding of how a remote works, too: It sends a special infrared signal at the TV, which the TV interprets as a command. If you want to change the channel, you press the "channel up" button on the remote and the remote sends the "channel up one" infrared signal. The TV picks it up and interprets it, then changes the station up one channel just as if you'd pressed the "channel up" button on the TV itself. This happens within a split second.

MIDI happens to function in the same way. An action on one device is translated into a signal that is transferred to another device. The receiving device decodes the message and takes the appropriate action. This way, if a keyboard is connected to a sound module by MIDI, the sounds from the sound module can be played with the keyboard. When a key is pressed, say middle-C, the keyboard will send the "play middle-C" message to the sound module. When the sound module receives the message, it will produce the proper sound. This happens instantaneously, just like the changing of TV channels.

❇ WHAT IS THIS GEAR?

Typical MIDI gear can be divided into a few categories: keyboards/workstations, sound modules, controllers, and sequencers. Keyboards and workstations are all-in-one musical solutions. They will have a keyboard for you to play and an internal sound generator to create the sounds you play. Quite often, these keyboards will also have built-in sequencers, allowing you to compose and arrange entire songs from one convenient unit.

Sound modules are basically just the guts from a keyboard/workstation—without the keyboard. Since all the hardware (plastic keys, springs, sensors, etc.) necessary to make a keyboard can present a great cost to the musician, sound modules offer you the tonal flexibility you'd achieve with a workstation without the extra hardware costs of the keyboard. These units are controlled completely via MIDI messages.

Controllers are the exact opposite of sound modules: They are keyboards that output MIDI messages but have no sound-generating capabilities of their own. While a silent device may seem like a worthless hardware category, controllers are actually extremely useful. They're much lighter than a keyboard/ workstation, making them perfect choices for musicians on the go. They also come in a much greater variety of sizes and configurations. See Chapter 3, "Getting Live Up and Running," for examples of control surfaces that are especially suited for Live.

Finally, a sequencer is a device with neither a keyboard nor sound generating capabilities. The sequencer's purpose is to record, edit, store, recall, and play back MIDI data to other MIDI devices. Usually, the sequencer contains all the data to play your song, while the sound modules and keyboards generate the sounds.

Live can be thought of as a workstation—without the keyboard.

The most powerful application of MIDI is the *sequencer*. A sequencer is a device that records MIDI messages and plays them back—like a tape machine for MIDI data. A sequencer can take the form of a hardware box with controls, while some synthesizers have sequencers built right into them. You can also use a computer as a sequencer (which is exactly what you'll be doing when using Live). By recording a list of MIDI messages transmitted from a keyboard while being played, the sequencer can then play the messages back to the keyboard at the same speed, causing the keyboard to re-create the original performance. As you delve into the program, you'll see that Live is a full-fledged MIDI sequencer. Actually, Live is more like hundreds of little sequencers inside one big one, but I'll get to that a little later.

You may ask, "If I'm going to record a performance and play it back, why do I use a sequencer? Why don't I just record the performance directly to tape?" The reason is that after you've recorded the MIDI messages into the sequencer, you can change (edit) them to improve the performance. Imagine playing a melody into a sequencer. As you're playing, you hit one wrong note about two-thirds of the way through. This performance, including the wrong note, is now stored as a list of messages in the sequencer. Before you play the melody back, though, you change the wrong note message to the correct pitch so the melody will be correct. This type of edit is not possible on tape since the tape does not contain notes—it contains sound. If you were using tape, you'd have to rewind the tape and re-record the whole melody over again until you got it right or try to "punch in" at that location to re-record the bad section.

Aside from fixing pitches of notes, you can change how loud they are, their timing, and their duration, as well as a myriad of other parameters, such as pitch bend and aftertouch. Groups of MIDI messages can be copied and pasted elsewhere in the list, so you can repeat sections of your composition without recording the same thing again. This allows you, for example, to take a chorus and repeat it later in the song.

As you can see, the benefits of MIDI are intriguing. Being able to meticulously edit a performance is a level of power that can save some serious time. It's also welcome news to those of us who don't happen to be as technically accurate with our instruments as we'd like. Some of you may even be learning a new instrument right now! One could even argue that we're *all* learning a new instrument—Live—thanks to the innovative minds at Ableton.

What Is the Language of MIDI?

As the name Musical Instrument Digital Interface implies, MIDI messages are comprised of numbers. These numbers are used to represent functions within synthesizers, such as "turn up the volume," "change the sound," and "play a note." This makes MIDI work very much like your TV's remote control.

Though I wrote the text you're reading on a computer, the letters of the words I typed are not what are stored on my computer's disk drive. Instead, numbers are used to represent the letters I typed. In fact, everything a computer does—whether it's writing an e-mail, watching a DVD, playing a video game, or writing music—is all done and represented by numbers. It would then come as no surprise that MIDI messages are represented by numbers, too. That sounds like a whole lot of numbers, right? It definitely is, and it's mind boggling that the computer can manage all of this while using only two digits.

Binary Numbers

Binary (bi- meaning "two") is the numbering system used by all computers and digital devices. It consists of only two digits, 0 and 1, whereas our standard decimal system (deci- meaning "ten") consists of ten digits: 0, 1, 2, 3, 4, 5, 6, 7, 8, and 9. Does that mean that the computer can't count any higher than one? Of course not. You can count higher than 9 using decimal, can't you? The way it's done in decimals is that digits are grouped together and given unique multipliers to their values to attain greater values (Figure 2.2). For example, the number 37 is equal to 37 because there is a 3 in the "10s" column and a 7 in the "1s" column. When you add 3×10 to 7×1, you get 37.

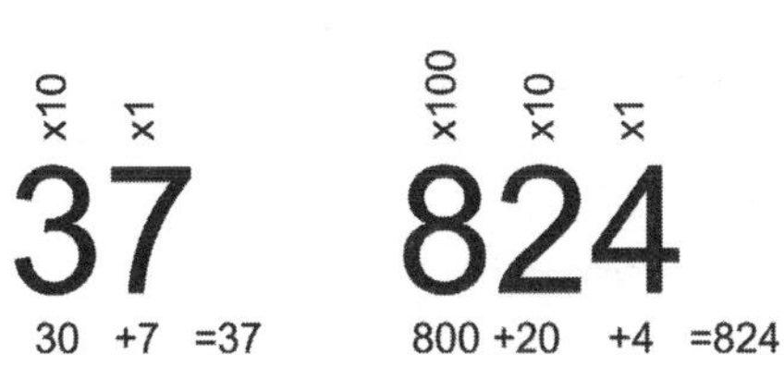

$$\overset{\times 10}{\underset{30 \ +7 \ =37}{3}}\overset{\times 1}{7} \qquad \overset{\times 100}{\underset{800 \ +20 \ +4 \ =824}{8}}\overset{\times 10}{2}\overset{\times 1}{4}$$

Figure 2.2
This figure shows the value of each column in a decimal number. Multiply each digit by the value in each column and then add the results together to find the value.

While the previous example may be seen as some sort of circular reasoning, it will make sense when you examine the same number, this time represented in binary. In Figure 2.3, you can see the binary representation of the number 37 is 100101. Of course, you don't need to know the ins and outs of binarycomputation in order to use Live effectively.

Figure 2.3

This figure shows the number 37 represented in binary form. You'll see that the columns in a binary number have different values than those in a decimal number.

While the column multipliers in a decimal number are easy to remember (1, 10, 100, 1000, etc.), the column multipliers for a binary number are different. Instead of being based on powers of 10, binary multipliers are based on powers of 2. So, the first column (on the left) is worth 1, since 2 to the power of 0 equals 1. The next column is 2 to the power of 1, which equals 2. The next column is 2 to the power of 2 (which equals 4), and so on. This means that the multipliers for an 8-digit binary number are: 128, 64, 32, 16, 8, 4, 2, and 1. When you apply the formula from the decimal example using these new multipliers, you get $1 \times 32 + 1 \times 4 + 1 \times 1 = 37$. And, since you'll never be multiplying any value with a number higher than one while using binary, you can just add up the values of the columns containing 1s; thus, $32 + 4 + 1 = 37$. Easy! Want to try another one? How about 11011010? Again, you just add up the values of the columns that contain a 1. The result is: $128 + 64 + 16 + 8 + 2 = 218$.

Bits and Bytes

In computer language, each digit of a binary number is referred to as a *bit*. Binary numbers are usually expressed in groups of eight bits, therefore 00100101 would be the correct notation for 37. These groups of 8 bits are referred to as a *byte*. If you've used a computer for more than two seconds, you're probably familiar with bytes; it's how file sizes are expressed on a computer, although they are usually measured in larger amounts known as *kilobytes* (1,024 bytes) and *megabytes* (1,024 kilobytes). And no doubt you've heard the word "bit" thrown around, too, when discussing video game consoles, such as 32-bit and 64-bit systems. If you pay attention, you'll find these terms permeating conversation everywhere these days.

What's in a MIDI Message?

A MIDI message is, on the norm, composed of three bytes, meaning each message is 24 bits (24 binary digits) in length. Each of these 3-byte MIDI messages describes one *event*. An event is when something changes in a device, such as pressing a key, twisting a knob, moving a slider, or stepping on a pedal. The TV remote has events, too, like turning on the power, adjusting the volume, and choosing channels.

Let's talk about the TV remote for a moment. When you press the Power button on the remote, the TV turns on. The TV will stay on, even if the line-of-sight between the remote and TV is obstructed. This is because the TV remote is not sending out a constant signal to keep the TV on. Instead, the remote only sends a signal when the power state of the TV should change. So, when the TV receives another "power" message from the remote, it turns itself off.

The same is true for MIDI. When you press a key on a keyboard, that action generates an event known as "note on." Along with the note on message, the keyboard will send the number of the key that was played (note number) in addition to a number representing how hard the key was struck (velocity). This comprises the three bytes of a MIDI message. The receiving sound module or device then follows that MIDI instruction and plays the note represented in the message at the indicated volume. At this time, the note will continue to play indefinitely. In fact, one can disconnect the MIDI connection between the keyboard and sound module, and the module will continue playing its sound. Just like the TV, the sound module is waiting for a command directing it to turn the sound off. So, when you release your finger from the keyboard, the keyboard generates another event, a "note off." Attached to the command is the number of the key released and the strength at which it was released. The module then responds in kind by stopping the sound.

❋ **MAXIMUM VELOCITY**

In music, it is a common technique to vary the loudness at which notes are played. On the piano, you can play quietly by pressing the piano keys gently. The harder you strike the keys, the louder the sound. In MIDI language, this striking force is known as *velocity*. Velocity is expressed as a number (big surprise) from 0 to 127. A note on message with a velocity of 127 means the key was struck with full force.

After note on and note off messages, the most common MIDI command sent is a *control change*, which is usually generated by moving a controller (knob, slider, button, etc.) on your MIDI device. Examples of controllers include the mod wheel, foot pedal, breath control, volume, and pan. Let's look at the mod wheel a little closer. When the mod wheel is in its lowest position, the value output by the wheel is zero. When the wheel is moved up, its output value increases. Moving the wheel downward causes the value to decrease. Just like the MIDI note events, the mod wheel, or any other controller for that matter, will only output a message when its position changes. So, when the wheel is moved to its full upward position, it will output its full value. The wheel won't output another value until you start moving it back down again.

Putting It All Together

I've talked about binary numbers and I've talked about MIDI messages, so how are they related? As I mentioned earlier, a MIDI message consists of three bytes of data (see Figure 2.4). Each byte can be a status byte or a data byte. A status byte is the first byte sent when a new event is triggered. The status byte contains a couple pieces of information, but most importantly, it includes the MIDI command name, such as note on, control change, poly aftertouch, etc. The two following data bytes will contain information regarding the command. As previously stated, a note on message will have two additional values: the note played and the force used to play it. The purpose of the data bytes will change, based on the status byte. If, for example, the status byte signaled a control change, the following two data bytes would contain the number of the parameter to change, such as 7 for volume or 10 for pan, and the value to which you want to change it.

Figure 2.4

This MIDI message contains 3 bytes: 1 status byte and 2 data bytes. The status byte is signified by a 1 in the far left column of the byte while the data bytes contain a 0 in the far left column.

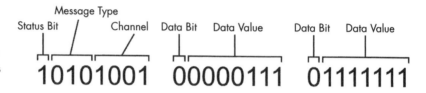

The status and data bytes are distinguished from one another by looking at the first bit in the byte. When the first bit is a 1, it is a status byte. A data byte will begin with a 0. This means the remaining 7 bits of the byte contain the actual values of the message.

Let's decode the message shown in Figure 2.4. As you can see, the first byte has a 1 in its far left position, meaning this byte is a status byte. When decoding a status byte, you look at two groups of numbers. The first group is the three bits just to the right of the status bit. These three bits will determine the type of event being processed. You decode the value by treating these bits as their own binary number. In this case, 010 decodes as the number 2, which is the number for a control change.

The remaining four bits of the status byte indicate the *MIDI channel* intended to receive this message. This is extremely useful if you want to control two different MIDI devices, such as a sound module and a drum machine, from the same source, such as a sequencer. The sound module can be set so it receives only MIDI messages set to channel 1. The drum machine could similarly be set to receive only on MIDI channel 10. This way, a note sent to the sound module won't simultaneously trigger a sound in the drum machine. The MIDI channel is determined by treating the last four bits as their own binary number, just like decoding the MIDI command. In this case, 1001 decodes as 9, which is actually MIDI channel 10. Why? The reason is that with four bits, it's only possible to count from 0 to 15. So, the MIDI specification adds 1 to the decoded MIDI channel, so the channels become 1 through 16 instead.

OK, you now know that the event you're decoding is a control change intended for a device set to MIDI channel 10, just like the drum machine above; however, you still need to know some more information before you can complete the control change command, which is what the remaining data bytes are for.

The second byte in Figure 2.4 is a data byte because its first bit is set to 0. You then find the value of the remaining seven bits to get the control being changed by this message. 0000111 decodes as 7, which is the MIDI number for volume. The last data byte, 1111111, decodes as 127. So, your complete MIDI message is: "Change control 7 on MIDI channel 10 to 127." This message will cause the volume of the drum machine to be turned to its maximum.

✳ **ROUND NUMBERS**

Have you ever wondered why such stupid numbers are used when it comes to computers? Why does RAM come in megabyte sizes such as 128, 256, and 512? It seems like nice round numbers such as 125, 250, and 500 would be a lot easier to remember, don't you think?

It turns out that those numbers actually are round numbers, at least they are for the computer. The reason for this can be seen when you fill all the bits of a binary byte with 1. The value of 11111111 is 255 (128 +64+32+16+8+4+2+1=255), meaning 100000000, which looks pretty round, actually equals 256. This is the equivalent of 99 in decimal language, where adding another digit gives you 100. I like to think of 255 in binary as being similar to 99 in decimal and 256 in binary being similar to 100 in decimal.

In the case of MIDI, the first bit of a byte is always used to indicate status or data which leaves you with only seven bits of information to use. Filling up the seven bits of a data byte with 1 yields a value of 127 (64+32+16+8+4+2+1=127); therefore the largest transmittable value with a data byte is 127. You'll find that almost all MIDI parameters are adjustable between 0 and 127 for this very reason. So, next time you go to turn up the volume or crank up some modulation, remember that MIDI goes beyond 100 up to 127.

Benefits and Pitfalls of MIDI

While throwing messages around between your gear will prove to be amazingly powerful, there are still a few quirks with MIDI you should be aware of. First, MIDI is not audio. It is impossible to hear MIDI. The only way to hear what is being transmitted is to have a device receive those messages and act on them. Since MIDI is only information about what pitches were played, what knobs were moved, etc., the sound of your MIDI information will be based entirely on the synthesizer that's being controlled by the messages. This means that if I write a piano piece on my Brand X keyboard and record it as MIDI, it will sound slightly different when played back on my friend's Brand Y keyboard. The melodies will still be the same, as well as all the timing of the performance, but the sound and tone of the piano will be different. It's exactly the same as playing a piece on an upright piano and then playing it again on a grand piano. The musical piece is the same, but the instrument sounds different. While this may be an annoyance when collaborating with another artist who has different equipment than you, it can be a powerful production tool. For instance, if you write a bass part using a fretless bass sound on your keyboard, you can change that sound to something else (like a slap bass) to hear what another instrument sounds like when playing the same part without having to re-record. Perhaps you'll discover that the bass part actually sounds best when played by a bassoon sound. This type of experimentation is possible only through MIDI.

Another useful quality of MIDI is that you can alter the pitch and timing of the MIDI messages independently of one another. This allows you to record a part at one tempo and then play it back faster without changing the pitch—handy when you're doing some intricate parts. This doesn't work in the analog world, because recording something to tape and then playing it back faster will cause its pitch to rise, possibly altering the tonal quality of the recording. Also, you can move the pitches of the MIDI messages without changing their timing, allowing quick transposition of parts or fixing bad notes. Furthermore, you can fix rhythmic timing issues without altering the pitches that were played.

What makes MIDI truly appealing is its file size. The amount of MIDI data necessary to reproduce a musical performance is only a fraction of the amount needed to play back a digital audio file of the same length. Therefore, projects that rely heavily on MIDI programming and control will be much smaller in size than one dependent on audio files.

Digital Audio Primer

If MIDI data is so small and efficient, why would you even concern yourself with digital audio? One reason is that you may want to incorporate non-MIDI instruments such as vocals, acoustic guitar, sitar, didgeridoo, and bagpipes into your compositions. Since you can't program these instruments (yet?), your only option is to record the real thing or use gigantic sample playback libraries. Another reason to use digital audio is that its recordings capture the exact nuances of a performance far more accurately than MIDI.

For decades, major recording studios have been relying on analog tape machines for recording audio. Indeed, the sound of analog tape is amazing, but it comes at quite a cost. These professional multi-track tape machines are grossly expensive, extremely sensitive to environmental changes, a chore to maintain and operate, and just plain huge. Moreover, the quality of the recording begins to degrade from the moment it is made and is helped further along by replaying the tape over and over, which is a necessary evil of overdub and mixdown sessions. Editing tape requires that a skilled professional make cuts (splices) in the tape with a razor blade, rearrange the pieces, then retape them together, something that needs to be done right the first time—there's no "undo" in the analog world.

Fortunately, with the increase in speed of computer processors and the expanding capacity of affordable storage media such as tape and disk drives, it is now possible to digitize sound waves so they may be recorded as a series of 1s and 0s. While this method has numerous benefits, some experts still dispute the quality of digital sound. To explain why, let's take a closer look at how the digital audio process works.

What Is Sound?

Before you can start recording and digitizing sound, you must first understand what sound is. Basically, sound is the repeated rise and fall of air pressure. When these repetitions, or *cycles*, fall within a particular rate, or *frequency*, your ears pick them up and send impulses to your brain. Your brain then decodes the impulses, allowing you to "hear." Your ears are most sensitive to sound falling within the frequency range of 20 to 20,000 cycles per second. *Hertz* is the term used to indicate cycles per second, so you'll commonly see these frequencies listed as 20Hz to 20kHz. (Hz is the abbreviation for Hertz; k is a prefix that means "×1000.") Frequency and pitch are directly related to one another; when the frequency of a sound rises, its perceived pitch rises as well.

Another quality of sound, besides its frequency, is its volume, or *amplitude*. The amplitude of a sound is measured as a *sound pressure level (SPL),* which is notated with units known as *decibels (dB)*. The quietest sound the average person can hear lies at the threshold of hearing, which is where they set the 0dB SPL mark. As the volume of the sound begins to rise, the decibels also rise. At some point, the sound is going to get so loud that you will start to feel physical pain in your ears. This is known as the *threshold of pain* and lies somewhere around 130dB SPL. While some concerts may well exceed this loudness, it is recommended that musicians (or anyone who enjoys being able to hear) keep their listening levels somewhere in the middle ground, around 80dB SPL. Remember: Without your ears, Live is no fun at all!

One final element of sound is the color or tone of the sound, called the *timbre* (pronounced TAM-ber). This quality is what allows you to differentiate between the sounds of a piano, trumpet, clarinet, guitar, or any other instrument, even if they're all playing the same pitch. The timbre of a sound is analogous to its *waveform*. In Figure 2.5, you'll see three different waveforms. All are at the same frequency and amplitude, but they have different shapes. Thus, while the sounds will have the same pitch, they will sound distinctly different.

The waveform drawings in Figure 2.5 were created by mapping sound pressure levels on the vertical axis of a graph while mapping time along the horizontal axis. An increase in air pressure is shown by the waveform being above the 0dB line, and a decrease in pressure is shown by the waveform being under the 0dB line.

Figure 2.5
Pictured are three elementary waveforms of the same pitch: a) sine wave, b) sawtooth wave, and c) square wave. Though their shapes repeat at the same rate, they will each sound different to your ears.

How Is Sound Represented in the Computer?

By now I'm sure you've anticipated that the computer must represent sound with numbers—the name "digital audio" gives it away. The computer must use numbers to represent not only audio, but other forms of media, such as movies (digital video) and pictures (digital imagery). Interestingly, the processes of digitizing an image and digitizing audio are remarkably similar, so I'll compare them both in this discussion. The digitizing process is known as *analog-to-digital conversion (ADC)*.

You've probably heard the term "analog" before, and you may feel it has a "vintage" or "old school" connotation. You'll find numerous artists and engineers who, when looking for "that fat, analog sound," reach immediately for old equipment. While many engineers prefer old analog circuitry, "old" is not what the word analog really means. Analog simply refers to something that has infinite variations and degrees. You can see the difference when you compare an analog thermometer with a digital thermometer (Figure 2.6). The analog thermometer can show temperatures between 70 and 71 degrees. As temperature rises, the mercury will slowly rise from 70 to 71. The digital counterpart, however, can only show 70 or 71 degrees—it can't show any value in between—so, when it's actually 70.6528 degrees outside, the digital thermometer rounds up to 71 degrees. Pretty close, right? Perhaps, but some people may want a more accurate reading. So, to get a more accurate temperature reading, you get a digital thermometer with the ability to display 10ths of a degree. Now, you see that instead of 71 degrees, it's actually 70.7. That's closer than 71, but it's still and always will be an approximation of the actual temperature, which could be varying at an unmeasurable level.

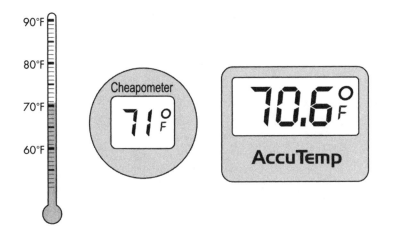

Figure 2.6
Here are three thermome-
ters measuring the outside
temperature. The digital
thermometer on the right
can provide a more accu-
rate reading than the one in
the middle.

When you digitize audio or images into the computer, the computer is similarly making approx-
imations of the original. Actually, the computer is making thousands, if not *millions,* of approxi-
mations, which are used collectively to approximate the original.

Sampling Process

When you want to get an image into a computer, you use a scanner. This device usually looks
like a super-thin photocopier and has a cable that connects it to your computer. To record audio
into the computer, you use an audio interface (see Chapter 3 for examples of these), which is, in
essence, a scanner as well, but one made for audio. Therefore, the processes of digitizing an
image and digitizing audio are very similar, and the same parameters that affect image quality
will affect audio quality. Since you're reading about all of this, I'll give you the visual example
first.

In Figure 2.7, you see a black-and-white photograph. You want to scan this image into your
computer using a scanner, so you place the image on the scanner and press "start." You see
some light moving around under the scanner lid, and after a few moments, your image magically
appears on your screen.

Not bad, right? Perhaps, but when you look closer at the photograph, both the original and the
one on the screen (Figure 2.8), you'll start to see that the computer version is "blocky." What's
that all about? Why doesn't the computer image look sharp like the original? The reason for this
is that the computer uses assortments of colored blocks, known as *pixels,* to create an image. The
computer creates the pixels by looking at tiny areas of the picture and approximating the color
there. The approximated colors are then laid out side-by-side and line-by-line on the computer
screen. When you stand back from the screen, you see the image. When you get closer, you start
to see the individual pixels.

Figure 2.7
This is a photograph that has been captured by a scanner.

Figure 2.8
An enlarged version of the photograph (left) and computer screen (right) shows that the computer image is not as sharp as the original.

This phenomenon can be experienced at a sports game when a huge group of people in the stands hold up individually colored cards to make a sign. When you're standing right next to them, all you see is people holding huge crimson and gold squares. But when you're on the other side of the stadium, all those little cards form a colossal sign that reads "Go Trojans!" This means that when the pixels, or blocks, used to make an image are small and close enough together, your brain will cease to see the individual pieces and will construct instead a single image. The trick is to record and store only as many pixels as are necessary to create an acceptable reproduction. After all, it's wasteful to record a whole bunch of tiny pixels if you'll never zoom in far enough for it to be an issue.

The process of digitizing audio is the same. The computer takes "pictures" of the incoming audio waveform and stores them in a list (Figure 2.9). Each of these little pictures is known as a *sample* and is analogous to the pixel used in images. A sample represents the approximate amplitude of an audio signal over a brief amount of time. When it's time to play back the audio, the individual amplitudes are lined up side by side to re-create the waveform.

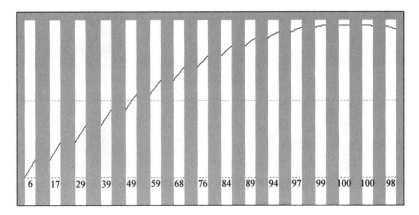

Figure 2.9
Here, an audio signal is broken into tiny little pieces so they may be numerically approximated by the computer.

If audio digitizing and image digitizing are so closely related, you can probably anticipate the next problem. When you zoom in on your digitized audio wave and compare it to the original (Figure 2.10), you can see that the computer's version is again very rough and blocky. Does that mean that it sounds rough and blocky, too? You bet. The good news is that there's a solution.

Figure 2.10
When looking at the digitized waveform in detail, you can see it is broken into steps similar to the way an image is broken into blocks (pixels).

Sample Rate

One thing you can do to improve the quality of your images and sounds immediately is to capture more information when digitizing. If you use an even greater number of smaller pixels to generate an image, the resulting picture will appear to be much crisper in detail (Figure 2.11). You have just increased the *resolution* of the image and have therefore packed a greater number of pixels into the same amount of space as your previous image. As a result, you can zoom in further to these higher resolution images before you start to notice the pixels.

If you can increase the number of pixels used to compose an image, can you increase the number of samples taken for a sound wave? Absolutely! By taking more samples of the audio every second, you are increasing the *sample rate* of the recording, therefore producing a more refined waveform with a less pronounced blocky effect upon playback (Figure 2.12). Sample rate is defined as the number of amplitude readings taken every second and is expressed in Hertz.

Figure 2.11
The picture on the right was scanned at a higher resolution (sample rate) than the one on the left, and therefore still looks decent after zooming in.

Figure 2.12
Here, the waveform with the higher sample rate preserves the shape of the original waveform much more accurately.

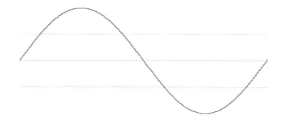

While increasing the sample rate will have advantageous effects on audio quality, it is only doing half the job. In essence, you're taking more measurements per second, but you're still using a cheap thermometer.

Bit Depth

At the beginning of this section, you looked at thermometers and the added accuracy of having additional digits to read. The first thermometer only had two digits and could therefore only show values from -99 to +99 degrees (we're assuming that the minus sign doesn't constitute a digit). The second thermometer had an additional digit, so it could accurately show readings from -99.9 to +99.9 degrees. Does that mean you only gained 1.8 degrees in range? That doesn't sound impressive.

❄ DOES IT REALLY SOUND THAT BAD?

Here I am telling you that low sample rate and low bit depth sound bad. Don't take my word for it, try it out for yourself! Included with Live is the Redux Device, which specializes in reducing, decimating, or otherwise destroying audio by using sample rate reduction and dithering techniques. Check out Chapter 9, "Live's Virtual Instruments," for a walkthrough of Redux to hear this phenomenon firsthand (or is that first ear?).

While you haven't increased the range of your thermometer by much, you have increased its accuracy immensely. The name of the game here is not to get an expanded operating range. What you want is more sensitivity, more response to subtle changes in temperature. By taking this increased accuracy analogy and applying it to the scanner, it means the computer can make a closer approximation of color for each pixel since it is now more sensitive to subtle differences in shades (Figure 2.13). So, increasing the resolution of an image increases the number of pixels used, therefore creating a sharper image. By increasing the accuracy of each pixel, you've improved the color tone and depth to provide a more natural appearance.

Figure 2.13
By allowing each pixel to represent a larger number of shades, you can achieve a smoother tone across your image.

But how do you do the same thing with sound? In order to increase the accuracy of your samples, each sample will have to be capable of representing a larger number of amplitudes. In essence, you need to use more digits for each sample. In the thermometer example, a digit was added to the right side of the temperature readout. This gave the thermometer the ability to register smaller changes in temperature. You can also add some digits to the sample value to achieve the same results. Since each digit in a binary number is called a *bit*, the number of bits used to represent a sample is called the *bit depth*. Increasing the bit depth will increase recording accuracy just as it did for the thermometer (Figure 2.14). Just as adding digits to the thermometer had a negligible impact on its range but a profound impact on accuracy, increasing the bit depth doesn't really let you capture louder sounds. Instead, the computer can now maintain a more accurate waveform at lower amplitudes.

❄ **QUANTIFY THIS!**

I've been speaking in general terms so far, so I'm now going to apply some numbers to all of this. As I mentioned, a lot of samples are needed in a short amount of time to yield quality audio. The standard CD format calls for 44,100 samples to be taken each second for both the left and right channels of audio. That's 88,200 samples a second being read from the CD. Furthermore, the CD specification also calls for samples to be 16 bits long. This means it takes two bytes of data to represent one sample of audio (8 bits equals 1 byte, right?). The binary number 11111111 11111111 (that's 16 ones) happens to be equal to 65,535, so that means a 16-bit sample can represent 65,536 different amplitudes. That's a pretty good number.

While CD standard is what most of us are used to hearing, audio professionals regularly use even higher sample rates and bit depths to attain even more accurate audio recordings. A common recording format is 24-bit/96kHz. This means that the computer is now recording 96,000 samples every second for each channel of audio. On top of that, a 3-byte number is used for each sample, enabling the computer to represent 16,777,216 different amplitudes!

Figure 2.14
You can see that the wave-form with the higher bit depth maintains detail even as the sound gets quieter.

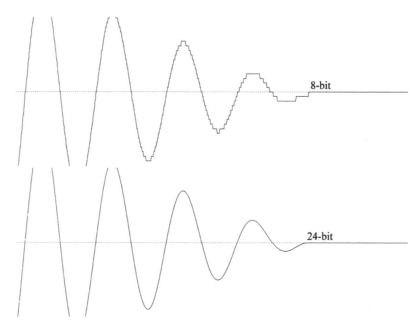

The point of increasing the sample rate and bit depth when recording audio is exactly the same as increasing the resolution and color depth when scanning an image. Just as the image grew sharper and more vibrant with the increase, the audio will also become smoother, deeper, and more detailed. Just as your eyes blend the tiny pixels into a large, crisp image, your ears will blend the tiny samples into a smooth, continuous waveform.

Benefits and Pitfalls of Digital Audio

Digital audio definitely has advantages over its analog counterpart. The recording media for digital audio, be it CD, digital tape, or hard disks, are cheaper than professional analog tape, and these digital mediums have significantly higher capacity than tape. Also, once audio (or any data for that matter) has been stored as digits, it will suffer no loss of quality. The audio data can be played again and again for months, and the last play will still sound identical to the first. This also means that copies can be made with no loss of quality since the computer merely transcribes the numbers (samples) from one location to another.

Since digital audio is just numbers, it's also easy to transport and distribute. Portable hard drives make it possible to take entire albums of working material from studio to studio with ease. CDs and DVDs are super thin, yet hold hundreds of megabytes (that's 1,024 kilobytes) of data. Audio can also be distributed over the Internet, allowing instantaneous collaboration between artists, even when they're on opposite sides of the world.

Of course, the ease with which digital audio can be copied and distributed is also a pitfall. Although illegal, it is quite common for music files to be traded over the Internet between users. While this does wonders for spreading the work of artists, they receive no money for their efforts. Fortunately, a number of companies such as Apple and Napster have created online stores where you can buy songs individually at a fraction of the CD price and have them transferred (aka *downloaded*) immediately to your computer's hard drive. Since there are no CD production, packaging, or distribution costs involved, the price is reasonable for the consumer, and the artists still get their share. There's one small catch, though—the downloaded files have a sound quality that is slightly inferior to that of a CD.

Why would these companies only allow you to download inferior quality files? The reason is simple: Digital audio files are huge. Consider how many numbers are being recorded for every second of audio. At CD rates, there are 88,200 16-bit samples taken every second. That's 176,400 bytes of data per second. Multiply that out over a four-minute song, and you'll get 42,336,000 bytes—roughly 40 megabytes of sample data. Downloading 40 megs of data can be quite an undertaking, especially if you're confined to a dial-up Internet connection. So, to make transferring files easier, the files are *compressed* before being sent. The process of compression can vary from protocol to protocol. The most popular format, MPEG-1, Layer-3 (MP3), is what is called *lossy compression*. In an effort to reduce the file size, an MP3 *encoder* will remove what it considers to be extraneous data and will compact the remaining audio data into a file that is roughly a tenth the size of the original. Clearly, downloading 4 megabytes is much preferred to 40 megs. When the file is uncompressed after download using a *decoder*, an approximation of the original audio is produced, which is usually acceptable for most intents and purposes. Some people are still unsatisfied with the quality of MP3, so additional compression formats have popped up, including WMA, AAC, and Ogg Vorbis (is that a cool name or what?).

The last thing you should consider when working with audio is that the pitch and speed of the audio file are directly related to one another. This means that slowing down the playback rate of an audio file will also cause its pitch to drop. The opposite is also true—increasing the pitch of an audio file causes it to play back faster. Think of a record on a turntable. If you turn off the motor while the record is playing, it will begin to slow down. As it does, you'll hear the song also start dropping in pitch until the record finally makes a complete stop. DJs use this phenomenon to create new pitches and melodies by manipulating the record's speed while scratching.

I mention the relation of pitch and speed last because it is a barrier that has been broken—by Live. You will see throughout the rest of this book how Live has turned digital audio data into complete goo, allowing you to repitch and morph the tempo of these files at will *in real time*. This capability is one thing that makes Live stand out from all the music applications available today. By removing this crippling limitation, Live has "opened up" audio for complete experimentation and creativity.

3 } Getting Live Up and Running

If you are accustomed to buying studio gear (hardware), you are probably like me—get the sucker home, tear open the box, and start making noise. Manuals are for other people after all and, well, who's got the time? When it comes to software, however, there is one fundamental difference: It is almost always up to you, the end user, to set up and configure the hardware properly, install the software the way it was designed, and set up the preferences so that the new application won't interfere with any legacy applications, cause strange hardware issues, or impair general functionality. In short, you become the final manufacturer. It is this sort of engineering control that is both the advantage and disadvantage of personally transfiguring your computer into a recording studio, a performance sampler, or a Live sequencing instrument.

Before you dive in and start producing hits, it is important to take a moment to verify that your computer system is up to speed and to install Live properly to ensure maximum performance potential. This chapter will provide more than a few recommendations to help you through the lonely installation process and a few rarely mentioned tips for fine-tuning your Ableton Live studio. I will cover both Mac and PC setup and talk about several methods for optimizing your system. Also, remember that Ableton's technical support is an excellent way to get to the bottom of anything not covered in this book, as is Ableton's online user forum (go to www.ableton.com and click on Forum), which is usually rich with tips, tricks, and advice (see Figure 3.1).

System Requirements

Listed below are Ableton's posted system requirements, dependent upon system make, and followed by my recommendations. For the record, I've tested and composed music using Live on several different makes of Windows PCs and Macs running OS X. Still, as mentioned above, every computer is customizable, and this can lead to unforeseen problems. If Live is acting strange—for example, if the audio is stuttering or if each edit is taking a very long time—try running Live completely by itself. Make sure you are not running any other applications in the background, such

Figure 3.1

Ableton's user forum is packed with good information. Make sure you take full advantage by logging on (selecting a username and password), so that you can receive private messages, converse with other members, and be notified when any of your posts have been responded to. Also, by using the forum's search window, you can usually find some reference to the problem you are facing and eliminate needless inquiries to commonly asked questions.

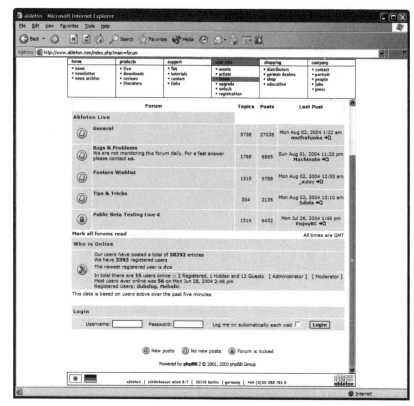

as MP3 players, office suites, or third-party plug-in effects (as I will cover in Chapter 8, "Using Effects and Instruments"), which can cause CPU performance problems.

Keep in mind that the vast difference in *requirements* versus *recommendations* could mean the enviable difference between functioning and flourishing with your Ableton product.

Ableton Live's System Requirements for Macintosh

* Any G3 or faster
* 512MB RAM
* Mac OS X 10.2.8 or later

Ableton Live 5 Power!'s Mac Recommendations

* G4 1GHz or faster
* 1GB RAM

- ❋ Internal SCSI, ATA/IDE, or external 7200RPM FireWire drives only (USB hard drives tend to be slower and less reliable)
- ❋ Mac OS X 10.4.1 or later
- ❋ Sound card with MIDI interface

Ableton Live's System Requirements for PC

- ❋ 600 megahertz CPU or faster
- ❋ 512MB RAM
- ❋ Windows 2000 or XP
- ❋ Windows-compatible sound card (preferably with a DirectX or ASIO driver)

Ableton Live 5 Power!'s PC Recommendations

- ❋ 2GHz CPU or faster
- ❋ 1GB RAM
- ❋ Windows 2000/XP
- ❋ No USB 1.1 hard drives
- ❋ ASIO-compliant sound card with MIDI interface

Installing, Running, and Updating Live 5

If you are brand new to Live and haven't yet picked up your copy or have never installed audio software before, then this section is for you. Sometimes a little background information helps make for a more rewarding software experience. Here are a few general tips for installing, running, and updating Live 5:

- ❋ Live can be purchased via the Ableton Live Webshop or by ordering the packaged version through an Ableton distributor (M-Audio in the U.S., www.m-audio.com) or retail outlet (Guitar Center, Sam Ash, and others). No matter where you get it, Live 5 can run on Mac OS X 10.2.8 and up, as well as PCs running Windows 2000 and XP. Note: If you have downloaded the Ableton Live 5 demo, you should still check to see that your version is the latest update when you decide to buy the program. To check this, simply go to www.ableton.com and click on "downloads" to see the latest version.

- ❋ To begin making music in Live, you will need samples, recorded music, or an audio interface that will enable you to record into your computer. If you picked up the boxed version of Live, you already possess over 600MB of royalty-free loops from Big Fish Audio. If you are anxious to get your hands on some more rights-free loops, please see "Where to Get Loops" in the FAQ (Appendix B). Also, there are literally hundreds of Web sites and other sources of free and inexpensive loops, as well as a couple hundred professional grade companies that make high-end sounds, such as Ilio Entertainment, PowerFX, E-Lab, QupArts, and Zero-G.

❋ In terms of audio, Live supports ASIO and DirectX for PC and Core Audio for Mac OS X. If you don't have an ASIO- or WDM-compatible sound card, be prepared to hear some audio latency when recording and playing back recordings made in Live. For a more detailed explanation of audio and MIDI latency and a discussion of all their trappings.

❋ Also, aside from the infallible book you hold in your hand, it won't hurt to take a look at Ableton's Live 5 manual. All versions of Live contain a PDF version of the manual that can be viewed by going to the Help menu and choosing Read the Live Manual. The boxed version of Live includes an analog (printed) owner's manual, which is still worth referring to, even though you have wisely purchased *Ableton Live 5 Power!* It is worth noting that Ableton frequently updates Live, and when they do, Live's PDF manual is always updated.

Live Installation Tips (Mac OS X 10.2.8 and Up)
Due to Ableton's foresight and Live's minimal dependency upon an operating system, Live was the first multi-track audio application on the planet available for Mac OS X! As you might expect, installing Live 5 (like all previous versions) on OS X is a breeze. Insert the Live installation disc, open the disc dialog, and drag the Live 5.x folder to the Applications folder on your hard disk. All pertinent files, including Live 5's manual, will be contained here. For quicker access to Live, you may want to install a shortcut onto the OS X dock (if you are using it). This makes Live easier to open and a little more fun—you can watch the bouncing Live icon as the program loads. To do this, simply open your Applications folder or the location on your drive where you decided to install Live and drag the program icon to the dock. An instant shortcut is made. To remove the item from the dock, drag it to the trash or to the desktop and watch it go "poof."

Live Installation Tips (Windows 2000 and XP)
Installing Live onto a Windows machine is much like installing any other Windows-based application. After you click on Setup and follow the instructions, Live's installer will ask you where you would like to place the Ableton folder and its files. I recommend using the installer's default setting, which will place Live in an Ableton folder in your computer's Program Files folder. You will want to pay special attention to where your VST plug-in folder exists. It is common practice to keep all VST plug-ins stored in one common location so that every VST-compatible application will be able to use them. For instance, if you have Steinberg's Cubase SX installed on your computer, you can instruct Live to look for plug-ins in the Steinberg shared VST folder, which is commonly located at Program Files → Steinberg → VST plug-ins. After the installation, you will want to customize your preferences (see the "Setting Preferences in Live" section later in this chapter).

MAC USERS TAKE NOTE

The centralizing of plug-in folders is useful in both Windows and OS X, although OS X audio applications typically take care of this for you by installing VST plug-ins at the location Library → Audio → Plug-ins → VST.

Updating Live

To check what version of Live you are currently running under Mac OS X, click on Live → About. On a PC, go to Help → About Live. Both the version and serial number will be displayed (see Figure 3.3). Click anywhere on the pop-up screen to close this window. To see if there is an update for Live, you will need your serial number. Visit www.ableton.com and click on Downloads; then simply follow the instructions for downloading and installing the latest version. Or you can use Check for Updates in the Live Help menu if your computer is currently online. I recommend checking for updates as often as your time and interest allow. Updates seem to be posted approximately once a quarter. Ableton remains ambitious about tracking down even the smallest bugs in Live and posting software updates. Their user forum (click on Forum) is also of value and is a great place to pick up new tips, suggest ideas to Ableton, trade songs, and network with other Live users. (See Figure 3.2.) Be sure to sign up for Ableton's newsletter to be alerted to all major updates and general Ableton news and events.

Figure 3.2
This screen will confirm in which version of Live you are currently working. After you update your copy of Live, follow the steps described in the "Updating Live" section of this chapter to make sure that the new version is running properly. You may need to swap out old desktop or dock shortcut icons because they will continue to point to (launch) the old version of the product.

Copy Protection

Ableton uses a challenge-response authentication system to protect Live from the ills of software piracy. Many companies are employing this method now because of both its effectiveness in deterring illegal copying and its ease for the customer. I like it because you really don't even need to rely on the original system disk, which can become scratched or broken. With this system, you could be in the middle of a tour, notice a new update online, click on Live's About menu, and jot down your serial number. You can then use this number to download and authorize the newest version. Live keeps track of all challenge and response codes internally, as does Ableton's database.

Here's how it works. After installing and launching Live you will be asked to enter a serial number. Live will then generate a unique (specific to your machine) number that coincides with your serial number. This new number is your challenge number. If you're connected to the Internet, simply click Unlock Online, and Live will handle all of the challenging and responding invisibly behind the scenes. Authentication can also be done via e-mail. In fact, you have 10 days to complete this authentication procedure before Live will cease to operate. If you don't have access to the Internet (if, for example, the computer with Live on it does not have a modem), you can obtain this information via fax or phone. Then you can manually plug Ableton's response number into Live when the authentication dialog box emerges. Note that Live will only ask for this information immediately after the first installation, after major hardware upgrades, or until the information is provided within the first 10 days.

Should you encounter problems authorizing Live, write a kind note to support@ableton.com and you will get an answer soon.

Basic Computer Specifications

When buying a computer, you're often faced with a dilemma centered around brand, timing, processor speed, and a ridiculous number of options. You can spend your entire life chasing processor speeds and faster CD-R drives. My feeling is that it is more important to get a functional machine rather than bending-edge technology that may or may not be 100 percent stable. Here is a list of the most important considerations when buying a PC, Mac, or laptop for using Ableton's Live software.

Processor Speed

It is in our very nature to want the fastest and most efficient processor available. Business folks want to spend less time waiting for massive data crunching, and musicians want to hear fewer digital "hiccups" in their music. Two or three years ago, a case could be made that Pentium III may have completely out-clocked a Pentium II, or now that the 1.67GHz G4 PowerBooks have arrived, they should be light years ahead of last year's 800MHz. This is not always the case, however, and although faster may be better, don't spend all of your time chasing processor speeds. Trust me, it can be an expensive proposition. Instead, set your sights just below the industry top dogs. For example, at the time of this writing, the 3.8GHz PC chips and dual 2.7GHz are the PC and Mac (respectively) top performers. Ableton Live doesn't necessarily require this kind of processor speed to perform basic functions. Sure, there are limitations, and contrary to popular belief, there always will be. So instead of spending $3,500 (or more) on your next industry champion, take a step back, save several hundred dollars, and invest in a quality sound card and a pair of professional speakers. Your music will be better for it.

Hard Drives

Fast hard drives, on the other hand, are essential. Say what you want about processor speeds, but when recording audio, your hard drive spin and data throughput are terrifically important. Most drives run at 7200 RPM these days, but be wary of buying one of those 5400 RPM internal or USB hard drives. As for seek time, 9 milliseconds or less is the maximum I would tolerate. Superfast SCSI hard drives are the best option if money is no object, but I find that 7200 RPM FireWire or internal ATA/IDE and SATA drives are plenty fast enough for most mono and stereo recording and overdubbing.

Laptop users should be especially aware of their hard drive specs, particularly if you want to buy a new laptop for use with Live. In an effort to conserve energy, most laptops ship with extremely slow internal hard drives, usually in the neighborhood of 4200 RPM. This slow hard drive speed will limit the number of Audio Clips that you will be able to play simultaneously in Live. If the laptop manufacturer doesn't offer any hard drive upgrades at the time of purchase, you can usually have a third-party drive installed after the purchase. Just recently, 7200 RPM hard drives have become available for laptops, so these can offer nearly the same performance as a standard hard drive in a desktop computer. The downside is that these higher power drives will usually drain your laptop's battery faster.

RAM

In Live, most of your short samples (less than 5MB) will sit in RAM, as opposed to on the hard disk. Any samples used in your virtual instruments must also occupy memory space. I think that 1GB should be plenty for any serious computer musician, although more is always better if you've got the cash. You can make it with 256MB for a short while, but more RAM will help to ensure stability during live performances, as well as help if you have other applications or plug-ins running in the background or in concert with Live.

Cache

Cache is generally thought of as ultra-fast RAM that handles mission-critical data even closer to the hardware level of a computer. The amount of cache and speed of the motherboard can enhance overall system performance. Laptop users want to be particularly careful not to get jilted out of their cache. Since it is pricey, many resellers will diminish its importance. Most of Macintosh's Titanium G4 PowerBooks now ship with Level 3 cache. When talking about cache, you will also hear talk of bus speed, which refers to the speed limits of your CPU's circuitry. Most

Mac laptop motherboards these days are clocking in at around 133 to 167MHz, while the PCs clock in at 533 to 800MHz, which is plenty fast enough for Ableton Live.

Audio Interface Specs

No piece of hardware is more important in determining the audio quality of your work than your audio interface. Almost invariably, the audio capabilities that come standard with your PC or Mac are lacking. Depending upon your needs and budget, you will want to either replace your computer's audio hardware or add a second interface to your system. Audio interfaces can connect in several different ways. PCI cards for desktop computers and PCMCIA (CardBus) cards for laptops are thought of as internal sound cards, while USB, FireWire (IEEE 1394), USB 2.0, and FireWire 800-connectable sound cards can be thought of as external cards. Pro Tools TDM interfaces, in which the internal and external hardware are integrated, can be thought of as a combination of the two. Here are some items to consider.

What Kind of Audio Interface Should I Get?

Desktop computer users have the greatest number of choices when shopping for audio interfaces. These computers can normally accept PCI and PCI-X audio cards, external USB and FireWire connected interfaces, and hybrid internal/external audio solutions. PCI and PCI-X cards, which fit into slots inside your computer, will offer the best performance of any format available. PCI offers high bandwidth and bus speeds, which allow greater amounts of data (digital audio) to be passed back and forth between the CPU and interface.

The increase in speed and reliability of laptop computers has made them very attractive candidates for hosting Live. By running live from a portable computer, you have the convenience to take your instrument wherever you go, just like guitar, bass, saxophone, and harmonica players can. Also, since Live is a robust multi-track recording environment, a laptop gives you the ultimate remix and recording studio for the road or bedroom studio. I also like the fact that the laptop allows for and encourages spontaneous creativity, since your studio is never far from reach.

Laptops, due to their compact size, do not have room to accept PCI and PCI-X formatted audio interfaces. Instead, laptops are equipped with a PCMCIA, or CardBus, slot that allows small format cards to be added when necessary. Laptops also sport USB and, commonly, FireWire ports to facilitate the connection of external audio devices. FireWire and USB 2.0 are currently your best choices for low-latency audio. PCMCIA comes in second, while USB 1.x comes in a distant third. External sound cards are portable and efficient, but many feel that USB 1.x is just not fast enough. This is due to the fact that USB 1.x can transmit only up to 12 megabits per second (Mbps), while FireWire and USB 2.0 cards push up to 400 or more Mbps per second (called *throughput*). Playback is usually decent on USB cards because you are often just listening to a stereo mix (two channels), but when recording multiple tracks (more than three or four), USB 1.x can have some problems keeping up. You should consider carefully which applications (besides Ableton Live) you plan to use and then decide upon the best hardware platform. USB 1.x is fast enough for typical Ableton Live use, where "typical" is one or two inputs and a stereo output mix. Power users will want to take advantage of Live's multiple ins and outs (routing) to employ hardware mixers and outboard effects and will therefore need an interface to support it.

How Many Outputs Do You Need?

The advantage to multiple outputs is an increased amount of control over your project. With Live, you may want to send drum and percussion tracks to outputs 1 and 2, while sending the vocals to output 3. These outputs are often routed through a hardware mixer (separate and apart from the computer). All sound cards that I am aware of provide at least two outputs as a stereo pair. Other common specs include 4, 6, and 8 outputs, and many provide outputs in other kinds of formats, such as S/PDIF (Sony/Phillips Digital Interface) and AES/EBU (Audio Engineering Society/European Broadcast Union) digital formats, analog XLR, RCA, and others. There are many different digital formats available, so always be sure the interface you get will work with the gear you currently have. If you have a keyboard with a coax S/PDIF connection, you won't want to buy an interface with an optical digital input—the two are not compatible.

How Many Inputs Do You Need?

Like outputs, the number of inputs you need will narrow the list of interfaces to consider. Generally, sound cards have a minimum of two input channels, a right and left input, used together as stereo. These can be RCA, XLR, digital (S/PDIF or AES/EBU), or others (such as ADAT Lightpipe). Keep in mind that for more than two channels of input, FireWire, USB 2.0, and internal PCI and CardBus cards will be a more efficient means than USB 1.x in delivering the large amount of multi-track audio data to your hard drive.

Selecting the Right Sound Card

Road-worthy components, great sounding analog-to-digital converters, and responsive tech-support are the three most important qualities to consider when selecting your most vital piece of hardware outside of your computer—the sound card. Here is a short list of tried and true sound cards with quality, precision, and portability in mind.

M-Audio (www.m-audio.com)

M-Audio's Delta series has proven that professional specs can be affordable (see Figures 3.3 and 3.4). All of M-Audio's Delta series cards connect via PCI and support the leanest audio drivers (ASIO and Core Audio); however, M-Audio's latest (2004) devices introduce FireWire connectivity (see Figure 3.5). FireWire is an excellent solution for laptop users, as it offers an expanded bandwidth while maintaining the convenience of USB. Mobile users can now take advantage of multi-channel audio for previewing tracks or routing outputs to a mixing desk. M-Audio is a company committed to Live like no other; they are Live's U.S. distributor.

Figure 3.3
The Delta series of M-Audio audio cards are made with a variety of input, output, and MIDI options. They are both affordable and well supported. The Audiophile 2496, pictured here is the Honda Civic of audio cards.

Figure 3.4
The Delta 1010 pictured here is a powerful professional audio card that can handle eight analog inputs and outputs and an additional stereo input via S/PDIF. The pictured front and back rack-space portion of the unit, like many breakout boxes of this type, connects to the additional PCI card inside your computer (seen on top of rack unit).

Echo Audio (www.echoaudio.com)

With their newly revamped product line, Echo has its eye on the pro-audio crowd. With 24-bit/96kHz sampling, the Layla line of desktop and laptop sound cards has garnered some excellent reviews. Echo's Layla24 and Gina24 are similar in design to M-Audio's Delta 1010 (seen in Figure 3.5), with professional hardware drivers and plenty of input/output options. If these boxes are too expensive for your budget, you might want to take a peek at their newest product line, the Indigo series (see Figure 3.6.), which is an inexpensive ($129 and up), high-end prosumer level PCMCIA card that could easily support small clubs or informal editing sessions. The Indigo DJ is specially suited for use with Live, since its additional output allows you to preview clips before sending them to the dance floor. The Indigo I/O ("I/O" means the card handles both input and output) swaps the second output pair from the DJ for an analog input pair.

Figure 3.5
The new FireWire Ozonic is the perfect solution for Live. It is not only a 4×4 audio interface, it's also a 37-note velocity- and after-touch-sensitive keyboard with knobs, buttons, sliders, and a joystick for control.

Figure 3.6
Echo Audio's Indigo series audio cards provide consumer level audio support that is both inconspicuous and simple. No MIDI or digital transfer is supported, but what do you want for less than $200 bucks?

RME Hammerfall (www.rme-audio.com)

As I prepped to write *Ableton Live 5 Power!*, Hammerfall's Multiface (Figure 3.7a front and 3.7b back) turned up again and again as the sound card most preferred by laptop aficionados. It has too many capabilities to list here, but if you are looking for a solid, professional solution, you will not be disappointed. The Digiface and Multiface breakout boxes (external audio interfaces with multiple inputs and outputs) add an exceptional level of professional audio support and flexibility to laptop producers, and they connect via the RME's CardBus connection. For stand-alone PCs and Macintosh, RME offers a PCI interface, so that you can transfer either of the above two breakout boxes to laptop or to your home/studio computer. RME has done a commendable job of making sure all possible digital formats are covered.

Figure 3.7a
RME makes the most flexible, and possibly the most professional, laptop audio card on the market.

Figure 3.7b
The back of the Multiface. There are connections for eight inputs and outputs, S/PDIF, ADAT, word clock synchronization, and more. Multiface is your top-of-the-line studio on the go.

Digigram (www.digigram.com)

The "Pocket" series by Digigram is a family of pro-level cards that, as the name says, are small enough to fit in your pocket, although you really should just put them in your laptop card slot. Newer Digigram units feature on-board processing, which can really take the load off of a strained processor and free up headroom for more audio content. One other advantage to Digigram's products is that the CardBus design (pictured in Figure 3.8), like Echo Audio's hobbyist-oriented Indigos (see Figure 3.6), is contained inside the laptop. There is nothing else to carry, power-up, or break, as the case may be. Digigram's less expensive "Pocket" series cards are known to sound great and are simple enough to use.

Figure 3.8
Digigram makes several similar-looking card slot pro-audio sound cards for laptops. The PCXpocket 440 supports on-board effects, which can take a good deal of the audio effect processing load off the laptop CPU. Extra reverb, anyone?

Aside from the above-mentioned sound cards, Emu (www.emu.com), Aardvark (www.aardvarkaudio.com), and Edirol (www.edirol.com) all make professional-level sound card products. It almost goes without saying that times change quickly and new technology emerges. So keep your eye on the latest reviews in magazines such as *Computer Music, Remix, Mix, Electronic Musician, Keyboard, EQ,* and non-biased Web sites such as Harmony Central (www.harmonycentral.com) for fresh product info. Also, it is extremely important to continually check your sound card manufacturer's Web site to be sure you have the latest audio drivers. Current and correct audio drivers can make a world of difference in how your software performs in your system. Depending upon your hardware vendor, drivers may be updated as frequently as once a month or more. Don't just trust that the included CD that ships with your soundcard has the most recent drivers. These CDs are usually packaged well before the final tweaks to driver software are finished, and well in advance of software innovations.

What Do You Need to Know About ASIO Drivers?

ASIO (Audio Stream Input/Output) was first invented by German software-slinger Steinberg (www.steinberg.de or www.cubase.net). Originally, ASIO drivers were created to help musicians and producers using Cubase to digitally record multi-track audio with a minimal amount of time lag within their digital system. This time lag can be a real buzz-kill and is called *latency*. Latency occurs because the sound you are recording is forced to travel through your operating system, your system bus, and host application to end up on your hard drive. Like bad plumbing, the signal may be coming down the pipe, but there are unnecessary clogs and corners that must be navigated along the way. The gist is that your computer is performing calculations (remember, it's all numbers for the computer) and, though they are blazingly fast, it takes a moment for the processor to do so, and the result is latentcy.

Live 5 supports ASIO on PCs (ASIO is unnecessary on Mac OS X, thanks to Core Audio). You'll be happy to know that most popular consumer and professional grade audio cards support the format, too. It has become an industry standard and can cut latency down to barely detectable levels. Properly installed, ASIO drivers will make Live as responsive as a hardware instrument, with less than eight milliseconds of audio delay. ASIO helps Live users hear the instantaneous results of MIDI commands, audio input/output, mouse moves, and keyboard commands. Someday, we'll all look back and laugh that latency was ever an issue, but for now, count your blessings that there is ASIO. See the "Setting Preferences in Live" section later in this chapter for more on the infamous "L word."

❋ **ASIO 4 All**

If you're stuck with the internal sound processor of your PC or have an audio card that doesn't support ASIO, there still may be hope for you. Michael Tippach has programmed a freeware driver called "ASIO4ALL," which is available at www.asio4all.com. I've tried this driver on a couple of machines, and it worked flawlessly every time. If you use it, you will have solved your latency problem, but you'll still want to consider a new audio interface because the converters in a pro interface will sound much better than those used in standard sound cards.

Choosing a MIDI Interface

Nothing makes playing Live more rewarding than cranking real knobs and watching virtual faders move (or perhaps I should say *hearing* them move). You can move virtual faders, adjust the amount of effects and their settings, modify the tempo, and do just about anything else you can imagine, all by using a MIDI interface. Those wishing to exploit the power of Live's MIDI sequencing features will also require a good MIDI control device. In the next section, I will take a look at several portable, affordable, yet full-featured MIDI controllers—a product category that has grown exponentially over the last couple of years.

One controller commonly found in use by Live users is the Evolution X-Session controller (Figure 3.9). This compact device is especially suited for Live, as it sports a DJ-style crossfader among its 16 other controls. The 10 programmable buttons also function perfectly as scene select and launch controls. You'll find it extremely easy to map filters, delays, feedbacks, and other parameters to the knobs for instant tweaking; plus, it will fit just about anywhere. Take a look at the setup of either Junkie XL or Sasha, and you'll see the X-Session staring back at you.

Figure 3.9
The X-Session is the choice for anyone seeking to dominate Live's crossfader.

Encore Electronics, www.encorelectronics.com, makes several basic MIDI controllers. The two shown here, Knobby Control in Figure 3.10 and Slidemate in Figure 3.11, are perfect for small stage setups, tight budgets, and minimizing programming hassle. Both the Knobby and the Slidemate can be programmed via a computer and can also send SysEX (system exclusive) messages—a great asset for those hard-to-reach MIDI parameters.

German-based Doepfer, www.doepfer.de, makes a mean blend of quality controllers with customizable parameters and a small footprint for inconspicuous fader-flippin'. The Pocket Dial's (see Figure 3.12) endless rotary knobs make tweaking Live a blast. You can grab or turn a knob and not have to worry about its previous placement. Knobs that have a range of 1 to 10 or 0 to 10 can limit the creative possibilities in a program such as Live by causing unwanted spikes in whatever parameter you are adjusting. Endless rotary allows you to pick up wherever the value is at a given time and modify it from that point. Of course, endless faders are not really an option, but Pocket Fader, pictured in Figure 3.13, helps to migrate software-based remixes to your desktop.

Figure 3.10
Knobby Control features what else? Knobs! Eight to be exact. These come in handy with a program like Live, and just like Live, Knobby can be updated on the fly.

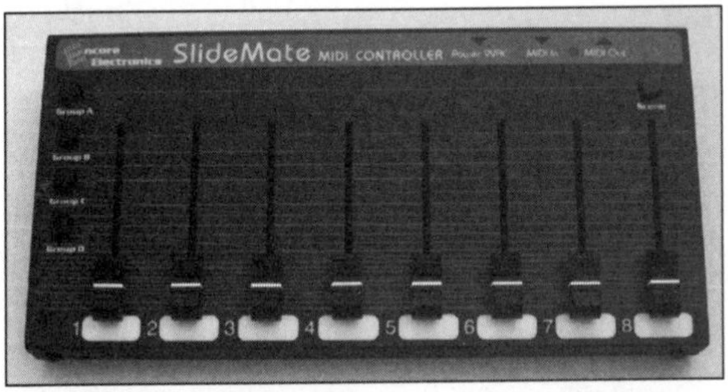

Figure 3.11
Slidemate's eight live pro-grammable sliders will comfort those missing their old analog desks (mixers). Slidemate programming is nearly identical to Knobby above, although some Live tweakers may want both.

Figure 3.12
My personal experience with Pocket Dial has been nothing short of a joy. Its small footprint and 16 knobs times 4 banks for 64 accessible presets make Pocket Dial one of the best all-around options where inexpensive MIDI-controllers are concerned.

Figure 3.13

Fade-outs and volume swells never really feel that great on a mouse, not to mention that it is hard to control multiple tracks (unless you are creating an aux bus). Pocket Fader is specifically designed to handle these kinds of tasks.

The FaderFox controllers are so compact and functional you'd think they came from James Bond's arsenal of gadgets. No larger than a guitar stomp box, the Micromodul LV1 and LX1 (see Figure 3.14) are designed specifically with Live in mind, allowing control of the Session Mixer and Clip Slot Grid (both of which are discussed in Chapter 4, "Live Interface Basics"). These self-powered units use standard MIDI connections, so you'll need a MIDI interface. A one-port interface will suffice, as the modules can be daisy-chained together. These controllers may soon be distributed in the U.S., but in the meantime, you can order one directly from the manufacturer at www.faderfox.de.

Figure 3.14

There's obviously some Ableton Live fans over at FaderFox.

Finally, I must do a little self-promotion here and introduce you to the M-Audio Trigger Finger (see Figure 3.15). As a Product Manager at M-Audio, this was my first project, and what an amazing success it has been! You Live users can take heart that I designed this controller with Live first and foremost in my mind—I even slipped in a preset for controlling two Impulse drum machines simultaneously. Along with the 16 velocity- and pressure-sensitive pads, you get 8 knobs and 4 sliders that can be used to control Live's mixer or sound parameters within Impulse. You will find me making reference to this controller time and time again throughout this book, so why not pick one up for yourself?

Figure 3.15
It's my baby—16 pads for you to bash upon to your heart's content.

The above MIDI controllers begin to give you an idea of what is available for just a couple hundred bucks (or less). Virtually any MIDI controller, including MIDI-based mixers, can work with Live. You can assign sliders, knobs, or faders in an infinite number of creatively rewarding ways. In Chapter 5, "Making Music in Live," I'll explore specific ways of making a MIDI map. There are literally millions of possibilities. Imagine mapping these controllers to adjust panning, effects, tempo, crossfader, frequency filters, EQ settings, and on and on.

MIDI Connectivity

MIDI controllers usually connect to your computer in one of two ways: either via USB or through your audio interface (if MIDI input is supported). Earlier, when I discussed USB for audio, I suggested steering clear of USB and recommended FireWire, PCI, or PCMCIA (on a laptop) when looking for a reliable audio card. With MIDI, however, USB is a safer route because MIDI information is much less cumbersome than digital audio when traveling over your system bus. MIDI information is so small that it can even be transmitted over a serial port, but in recent times, we have become accustomed to pairing MIDI controller information and digital audio through the same card. If your sound card does not support MIDI, USB is an efficient means to interface. Several companies, including Edirol and M-Audio, make simple little single-input MIDI connectors, such as the UM-1S and MIDISport (pictured in Figures 3.16 and 3.17, respectively).

Figure 3.16
UM-1S is a simple USB MIDI port that will quickly route your new sassy MIDI controller or MIDI keyboard into Live.

Figure 3.17
M-Audio has been making MIDI connectivity devices for as long as I can remember—well, at least since around the time MIDI was invented.

One of the most popular combination MIDI keyboard/controllers to hit the market was M-Audio's Oxygen8 (Figure 3.18). The original unit was cheaply made, with less than optimal controller knobs, but it represents the merging of two similar worlds (keyboard and MIDI controller) and has inspired competitors like Edirol to release their own knob-and-fader keyboard conglomerates, the PCR-30 (Figure 3.19) and the PCR-50. In response, M-Audio has attempted to outdo itself by releasing an improved version of the Oxygen8, called Ozone, which also features a mic preamp and audio interface. As you can see, the only thing certain about the future is change.

Figure 3.18
The design and release of Oxygen8 created quite a splash among laptop studio owners and other MIDI-happy musicians concerned with overall space.

Figure 3.19
Edirol's hybrid PCR-30 sports keys, faders, and knobs and is really made for musicians who think small, at least in terms of their desk (studio) size.

Setting Preferences in Live

Optimizing Live's preferences is essential for smooth operation. You see, preferences are more than merely your personal whims about how you would like Live's interface to be colored or where your files are automatically saved. Preferences are your primary control center for fine-tuning Live's ability to actually work in your customized computer/audio environment. From the Preferences menu, you will be able to control default loop traits, audio and MIDI interface settings, and audio/MIDI latency settings. Sound like too much to manage? Read on, and let's tame this beast. To call up the Preferences dialog box on a PC, select Options → Preferences; on a Mac running OS X, select Live → Preferences. The emerging dialog box contains six tabs: Audio, MIDI/Sync, Plug-in, Defaults, Misc, and Products. I will discuss these in order, so click on the Audio tab if you are not already there.

The Audio Tab

The first section you will likely get to know is the Audio tab in Preferences seen in Figure 3.20. This tab's pulldown menus and options will depend largely on what kind of sound card you have, whether it is correctly installed, and the operating system you are using. In Figure 3.20, you will see that I am using an M-Audio Ozonic with ASIO drivers on the PC. It says M-Audio FW ASIO because it is using the M-Audio FireWire audio driver.

Figure 3.20
Audio preferences will be revisited often as you seek out the perfect latency settings and audio interface setup.

Driver Type and Audio Device

The first menu in this section allows you to choose the Driver Type you want to use for your audio interface. On the PC, options will include MME/DirectX and ASIO; Mac OS X will feature Core

Audio. Once you select the Driver Type you want to use, you will have a selection of audio devices to choose from in the second menu.

You may not find the audio device you want to use when using certain driver types. For example, the built-in audio cards on laptop computers don't support ASIO, so you'll only find these cards listed when MME/DirectX is selected for Driver Type.

Please note that Live will always seek out the audio interface last saved in Preferences each time the program launches. If Live cannot find the sound card, such as when you have unplugged or swapped it out, Live will still launch, but with no audio enabled. In this instance, you will see a small warning message mentioning that Live cannot find the audio card and that audio will be "disabled" upon startup. You will also notice a second red warning on Live's actual interface (after the program launches) that says, "The audio engine is off. Please choose an audio device from the Audio Preferences." After you do this, you will again be ready to set up Live for audio.

Buffer Size

You may or may not be able to adjust your sound card's Buffer Size from this Preferences menu. Most ASIO and other sound cards need to be accessed directly through their own driver interface, which can be launched with the Hardware Setup button. If you are using a standard or consumer-level audio interface, such as Apple Core Audio or DirectX, you will see a buffer slider here. The lower your Buffer Size setting is (in samples), the less latency you'll experience, but more potential problems can arise. In other words, too much buffer will increase the amount of undesirable latency, yet too little latency will most often result in your system choking and wheezing in the form of digital pops, audio dropouts, and the like. In the next section, I will take this latency discussion up a level and give you a couple of ideas for possible workarounds.

Latency Settings

Latency—there is that dirty word again. Here is how to approach optimizing your Live software to work with your computer and sound card to achieve the least amount of audio latency. First, recognize that there is output latency, input latency, and MIDI latency. Each type of latency imposes a different kind of problem, and while there are some ways to combat these timing issues, zero-latency is still not really a viable option for applications reliant upon an operating system (such as Windows or Mac OS 9, OS X). Realize also that latency is designed to be a buffer for when you put extra strain on your system and your CPU is having trouble keeping up with all of the required processes.

Output latency is the amount of lag time between when you trigger a sound or action and when you hear it. Or if you add an effect, such as distortion or reverb, the extra time that it takes to actually hear that sound is output latency. Do not confuse this output latency with Clip Update Rate, described below. For instance, if your Clip Update Rate is set for 1/4 note, you may hear a small (1/4 note or less) pause before hearing many of Live's clip effects, even with output latencies of only a few milliseconds. This can be remedied in ways I'll discuss later.

WHO DUNNIT?

Many people blame their software for their latency problems, and this is just simply not the case. Another tip for hunting down latency issues is to make sure your audio interface (sound card) has been adjusted to the best possible settings, which can be done via the sound card's Control Panel on a PC or the Preferences within Live on the Mac. Try lowering your buffer settings to reduce the audible latency until you experience dropouts, digital pops, or other system-related problems. Then raise the buffer to just above the level where the problems occur and record your track. You may need to increase the buffer again when starting the editing/mixdown process.

You can stress test your system for latency and alleviate the above mentioned confusion. Here are the steps for the stress test:

1. Click the Misc tab and turn your Clip Update Rate to 1/32 (1/32-note timing).

2. Load a decent size audio clip, preferably a stark drum loop, into the Session View.

3. Load several Live effects and audio clips until your CPU meter in the upper right-hand corner reaches about 70 percent of capacity.

4. Then, while slowly reducing the Output Buffer Size, listen for pops or clicks in the audio. Adjust your final setting to a comfortable level above the popping level. Note that this buffer size may need to be adjusted from your sound card's settings or, if it is not grayed out, can be set in the Preferences' Audio tab.

Don't be surprised if you get your latency time extremely low and detect no discernible latency. It is there all the time, but often miniscule when using ASIO, WDM, or Core Audio drivers, which is why these driver types are preferred.

Input latency arises for the same reasons as output latency. Audio is buffered on the way in to the computer, so Live receives this audio a little later than it should. Fortunately, Live knows it's behind, and it takes this into account when recording. The result is a take that is recorded in time. When input latency starts becoming a problem, though, is when you try to monitor audio *through* Live. Now the audio has to pass through the input buffers, through Live and any potential effects that may be loaded, and back to the output buffers before it can reach your ear. Keeping your buffer settings as low as possible will keep this "double" latency to a minimum.

Most professional audio cards, like the ones mentioned above, feature "direct monitoring," which helps alleviate some of the problems of recording with latency. Instead of having Live blend your input signal with its output signal and buffering it to the audio card, the audio card will blend your input signal with the output from Live so the input signal doesn't have to travel all the way through the computer and back out again. The result is instantaneous monitoring of your input signal—no latency. The drawback is that you will not be able to use effects on a direct monitored signal since the audio signal is not being sent from the computer. The audio interface simply routes the input right to the output.

Audio interfaces are designed to report their latencies to Live so it can offset its operations properly. However, in the case that a device reports its times improperly, Live gives you the option to add or remove time from the overall latency calculation by changing the value in the small data entry box.

MIDI latency can be divided into two camps: synchronization problems and MIDI triggering delays. The latter has nearly disappeared with wide adaptation of Steinberg's ASIO technology and the recent integration of Windows WDM drivers in Windows 2000 and XP, plus the advent of AMS in Mac OS X. MIDI sync issues will be covered in section "The MIDI/Sync Tab" below.

Sample Rate

The Sample Rate setting in the Audio Preferences tab will determine the recording quality of both Live's output and recorded input. A good basic sample rate to start out with is 44,100, or 44.1kHz. As you learn more about digital audio, or if you are pro already, the Sample Rate dropdown box will give you a multitude of friendly choices. I never recommend using anything lower than 44,100, but if you are long on system resources (including hard drive space), you might experiment with 96,000 or 192,000 so long as your audio interface can handle it.

Channel Configuration

When you make music in Live, you have to send it to the outside world somehow. For simple audio interfaces, Live will automatically set this up for you by sending a stereo master output to your audio interface's master output; however, if you have the good fortune to have an audio interface that supports multiple outputs, then you can take advantage of that here. In Chapter 13, "Live Playing...Live," I will talk about how to capitalize on Live's cueing ability via sound cards with multiple outputs. Also, if you have the option of digital or analog output, this is the place to set up that output.

The MIDI/Sync Tab

This brings me to the second Preferences tab, shown in Figure 3.21, the MIDI/Sync tab. This is where you will specify which of your MIDI devices will serve as remote controls, MIDI inputs and outputs, and sources for synchronization; however, if you are not planning on synchronizing Live to work with a hardware or software MIDI sequencer, then some of the MIDI/Sync parameters will not be of much interest. The tab is divided into three subsections: MIDI Control, MIDI Synchronization, and MIDI Timecode. Beginners will want to step right up and tackle the MIDI Control box, which is the place to assign any of the toys discussed in the "Choosing a MIDI Interface" section earlier in this chapter.

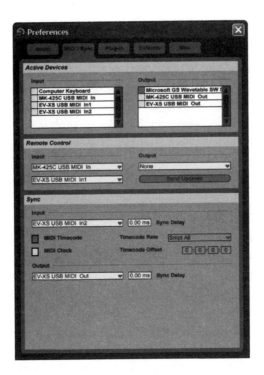

Figure 3.21
The MIDI/Sync tab found in Live's Preferences box. This is the logical place to handle how Live works with MIDI and syncs to the outside world and to resolve MIDI timing issues.

Active Devices

These two tables show a list of the MIDI input and output devices available on your computer. The tables have columns for the names of each MIDI port found by Live, plus columns named Track, Sync, and Remote. In order for a MIDI device to be usable, it will have to be enabled as a Track input or output, as a Sync source, or as a MIDI Remote Control.

Enabling Track for a MIDI input device (the top table) means that you can use it as an input to a MIDI track, available in the Input/Output Routing Strip. This would be enabled for something like a control keyboard that you used for playing notes on a virtual instrument.

The Sync option enables the port as a MIDI Sync source. This will have to be enabled for at least one port for any of the Sync functions, described in a moment, to work.

MIDI Remote Control refers to using a MIDI controller to control Live itself—things such as the Session Mixer controls (Pans, Volumes, Sends, Mutes) and Effect parameters (Delay, Wet/Dry Mix, Rate, etc.). Enable this option for any device you may want to use as a Remote source. And, yes, you can have all three options selected for one port at the same time.

On the output side of things (the lower table), the options are the same. Enabling Track on a MIDI port sends MIDI data from a MIDI track out to an external piece of hardware via the Input/Output

Routing Strip. If you're transmitting MIDI Beat Clock (still to come—you're almost there!), it will be copied and sent out of every port with Sync enabled.

The last column, Remote, is especially nifty. Live provides the ability to send feedback messages to MIDI controllers with motorized MIDI knobs and faders, or those with light-up encoders, buttons, and so forth. If you have a control surface with these types of controls, you can enable Remote in the Output table for that device. Once you map a fader or knob to a MIDI control, Live will move the control anytime its value or position changes on-screen.

Sync

MIDI synchronization is a two-way street. Live can either drive or be driven. To drive Live from an external device, you will want to send it either MIDI Timecode (MTC) or MIDI Clock (also called *MIDI Beat Clock*—MBC). The difference between MIDI Timecode and MIDI Clock is simple: MIDI Timecode is location information expressed in hours, minutes, seconds, and frames, while MIDI Clock is tempo, measure, and beat information, such as beat 1 of measure 5, moving at 120 beats per minute. MIDI Clock is best for interconnecting sequencers. It is also most useful when synchronizing two or more Live users, as the tempo and beat location will be matched between all of the computers.

Most often, MIDI Timecode is used when syncing to an external hardware (or occasionally software) video device. While Live can do this type of work, it may be best used when run in tandem with any one of a number of programs adept at video work. In other words, I would recommend syncing Live to that application, also called running Live in slave mode. This is not to be confused with running Live in ReWire mode, which is a form of audio and MIDI synchronization that runs transparently between two ReWire-enhanced software applications. For more info on this, see Chapter 12, "ReWire."

Use the menus to select whether Live will receive either MIDI Timecode or MIDI Clock. If you choose MIDI Timecode, you'll need to specify the Timecode Rate by choosing from the menu. You can also add a Timecode Offset, if needed.

If you decide to use Live as the master clock source (other devices will receive their clock positions from Live), you'll need to choose at least one MIDI output port for the MIDI Clock (see above). Unlike the incoming Timecode options, Live can transmit only MIDI Clock.

In both cases, you may experience a slight misalignment when using Sync. The Sync Delay value may be adjusted to bring Live and the external device into accurate sync with one another. For the best results, synchronize one machine at a time, using a process of elimination to figure out the hardware or software (usually the problem) culprit. Also, don't forget to try swapping out MIDI cables. They can easily go bad and will make you crazy if you don't check on them.

Also, it is worth noting that when syncing machines, I usually have to give the second machine a negative value for its Sync Delay. The best result I have found after much trial and error is to activate the click tracks on both machines, with the Preferences open, and then reduce the one machine's Delay Sync into negative territory. With luck on your side, you should hear the click tracks begin to flange or sound out of phase. This means they are sitting virtually on top of one another, or they are right in sync.

Recently, when attempting this with a friend, we used two Mac PowerBooks, one with no sync delay (the master) and the slave with a sync delay of about –100ms. If you are attempting to sync hardware, you will want to adjust Live's delay, as many machines won't have a similar Sync Delay function.

The Plug-In Tab

Pictured in Figure 3.22 is the Plug-In tab. Here you can set preferences for displaying plug-ins and mapping out Live's VST and Audio Units plug-in folders.

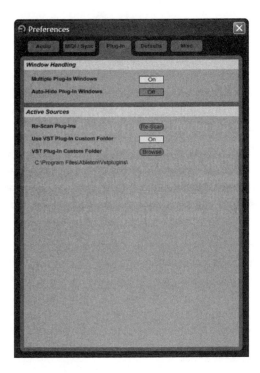

Figure 3.22
The Plug-In Tab allows customization of window handling and plug-in location.

Active Sources

The VST and Audio Units (Mac OS X only) plug-in folders can be set to any folder on your machine that holds VST or Audio Units effects and instruments compatible with Live. The only sure way to know if Live is compatible with a plug-in is to try it out. To do this, place the plug-in in the appropriate folder and click the Re-Scan button. If you can see the new device listed in the plug-in section of Live's Browser, then chances are that Live will at least be able to load the plug-in.

Live will occasionally not work with some plug-ins, possibly because they are incompletely developed. If this occurs, please do everyone a favor and send in a quick bug report to both Ableton and the third-party plug-in developer. Each time Live is started, the program scans your system for new VST and Audio Units' plug-ins in the designated locations. If you notice an unusually long startup time (an extended view of Live's splash screen), you may have added a large number of new plug-ins or unintentionally added an incompatible device that is having trouble "talking" to Live.

Performance

This is a new setting in Live 5, which sets the buffer size used when Live passes audio to and from external plug-ins. Normally, this option should be left on As Audio Buffer. Setting this option lower will result in your plug-in responding a little more quickly but can easily overburden your CPU. Make sure to save your work before changing this value in case you choose a setting too low for your computer to handle.

Window Handling

These three options determine how Live will display a plug-in's custom display window. When Multiple Plug-in Windows is activated, it will be possible to open more than one plug-in window at a time. When this is off, open plug-in windows will be closed anytime a new one is open. Keeping this option off can help minimize screen clutter.

The second option, Auto-Hide Plug-In Windows, will make plug-in windows appear only for those plug-ins loaded on a selected track. For example, if you have a MIDI track loaded with an instance of Native Instrument's Battery and another MIDI track with LinPlug Albino, Battery will be hidden when the Albino track is selected, and Albino will be hidden when the Battery track is selected. This can also help minimize screen clutter, which is especially useful for laptop users.

The third option here is the Auto-Open Plug-In Windows box. When active, the plug-in's window will be opened immediately after the plug-in is loaded onto a track. This makes perfect sense as you'll usually need to make some modification to the plug-in after you load it.

The Defaults Tab

Preference's Defaults tab (seen in Figure 3.23) will likely be a place you visit as you discover your own preferences for working in Live.

Live Set

The Save button is used to save the current Live Set as the default or template Set that will be loaded each time Live is launched. This can be helpful for preconfiguring commonly used settings, such as MIDI assignments, input and output routing, and common effect patchwork (such as EQs on every channel). Note that at this time, you can save only one template in this Preferences tab. For additional templates, I recommend that you create a Live set folder called "templates," and save empty, yet configured, Live sets there.

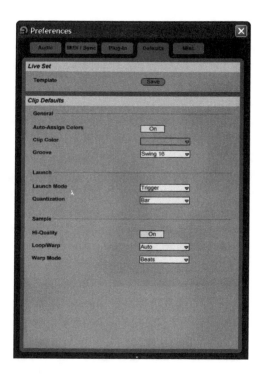

Figure 3.23
Live will automatically open loops the way you like once you tame the Defaults tab in Live's Preferences. Your settings in this tab will likely change as you experiment with how you use Live most often.

Clip Defaults

The remainder of the Defaults screen determines the settings applied to a new clip when it is created in Live. As you begin performing with Live and have a chance to build a few practice Sets, take note of how you tend to configure your clips. Are you always setting them to Tones mode? Do you prefer 1/4-note quantization? You can specify any of these parameters as defaults in the following sections.

GENERAL

First, you'll find the Auto-Assign Colors toggle switch and the Default Clip Color selector. With Auto-Assign Colors on, Live will randomly choose a color for each new clip or recording. These colors can be changed at any time in a screen called Clip View, which will be covered later in the book. If Auto-Assign Colors is off, the Default Clip Color comes into play by determining which color Live will default to for all new audio. Of course, color will not affect the sound and is strictly a matter of preference.

The last option determines the Groove template associated with a clip. Groove templates produce subtle or drastic requantization of audio and MIDI by offsetting certain beats to create different feels. See Chapter 6, "The Audio Clip," for a detailed explanation of how to get your groove on.

LAUNCH

When triggering a clip to play, Live gives us some options known as *Launch modes*. The full rundown on these modes can be found in Chapter 5. For now, I recommend leaving the mode on Trigger or Toggle.

The idea of launch quantization is to force your performance to fit into the time grid of the current piece. Any time you launch a clip in Live, you have the option of launching it on the "one" of the next bar, or every second bar, every fourth bar, every eighth bar, or by picking a note quantifier to begin playback on the very next 1/32, 1/16, 1/8, 1/4, or 1/2 note after you trigger the clip. Of course, this is a grand selection of choices, and the right selection can depend upon the type of sound you are launching. For instance, an orchestral or ambient guitar sound might not need as strict a quantization as a conga or cowbell loop. You can also opt to turn Quantization off by default by selecting None from this dropdown dialog box, or the safest bet for novice or careful Live musicians is to select Global, which will assume the same quantization setting as the project—a good way to keep every sound in line.

SAMPLE

You will also want to pay attention to the Hi Quality default toggle button, which (when activated) will make Live use a more complicated algorithm when calculating Live's loop warping attributes. The reason not to use Hi Quality is simple—it demands a bit more system resources, and when applied to all of your loops, can really create a noticeable CPU spike. You can also opt to leave Hi Quality off as a default setting yet still use it on select loops by double-clicking a clip and adjusting its settings. More on this subject is found in Chapter 6.

The Loop/Warp Short Samples menu is used to determine the default state of a new Audio Clip, be it a loop or a one-shot sound. The Auto setting will cause Live to try and determine the nature of an imported loop on the fly and set its loop and warp settings accordingly.

The next option relates to Live 5's new Auto-Warp feature. When this option is on, Live will attempt to determine the tempo of the imported audio file and will place Warp Markers into the Audio Clip automatically. This will only happen on long samples—files that Live assumes to be complete songs. This is extremely helpful when DJing as Live can automatically synchronize two songs with little or no assistance from you.

Warp Mode, the next and last item on the Defaults tab list, is another story entirely. In Live 5, there are five Warp modes. The original product, Live 1.5, treated every loop as a beat, which can be problematic when treating melodies, basses, drones, ambient textures, and, well, just about anything without a well-defined percussive texture. Here is a DJ-style breakdown of the five Warp modes in Live. This is a topic central to understanding how Live works and will be revisited in chapters to follow. Remember, these are merely the defaults; all can be changed after the clip is loaded in Live.

❋ **Beats:** Beats mode is the original Live Warp mode. The program automatically breaks up the loop into sections determined by the Transients settings. For instance, Live can divide a loop into 1/32 notes, 1/16 notes, 1/8 notes, 1/4 notes, 1/2 notes, and full measures. As long as the sound is rhythmic and fairly short in duration, Live does an impeccable job of making the loop sound as though it were recorded at your project tempo. Drum loops, dance grooves, and percussive instrument loops (bass, short synth, turntables, or funk guitars) can all be stretched convincingly in Beats mode.

❋ **Tones:** This is the mode for bass and keyboard lines, melodies, and pitched sounds that are not necessarily grooving in perfect time with a metronome, such as a legato horn line or harmonic chord progression or even vocals.

❋ **Texture:** For sounds more complex than melodies and rhythms, Ableton has brought us Texture mode. This is the mode to use for ambient effects, atonal pads, and indefinable sounds. Texture mode bears the distinction of further tweaking possibilities with Grain Size and Flux (fluctuation) controls. These two new parameters determine the intensity, severity, and randomness of Live's slicing. This can be an excellent sonic deconstructing tool for any kind of loop, in addition to the ones mentioned.

❋ **Re-Pitch:** For loops that just can't be sliced, or for samples that offer the right attitude only when they are sounding their fattest, Ableton's Re-Pitch mode defeats all pitch correction, yet still corrects the loop's tempo to fit into the piece at hand. Some loops may sound funny at their new pitch, but this is a sure-fire way of eliminating strange artifacts that can sometimes appear when retiming and re-pitching a loop simultaneously.

❋ **Complex:** This fifth mode is new in version 5. It utilizes a phase-vocoding algorithm for warping. The benefit of this mode can be heard best when warping a fully mixed song. The downside is that the algorithm can be somewhat CPU intensive. This mode was added to version 5 primarily for those using Live to DJ. Matching an entire MP3 file to your set will sound best when using this Warp mode.

Also, Live 5 turns any of the above five modes off entirely. This means that the sample/loop is played back exactly as is, at its original tempo and pitch. This no-warping mode can be achieved by deselecting the Warp button at the bottom of the Audio Clip View.

Audio Recording

Anytime Live attempts to record audio, either through resampling or from a live input, it will use the record parameters you set here. While it doesn't matter so much these days, it is worth noting that a PC's native format is WAV and a Mac's is AIFF. You can invert these settings, but if you want to have these files available in native applications, you may run into problems. I also recommend setting the bit depth to 24 when recording (the Record Bit Depth option), so long as your audio interface supports it. This ensures the maximum detail for newly recorded sounds. You

❋❋❋

can always render a file downward (to 16-bit), but you cannot really go up to add detail that is not there. Think of it this way: a color photo can be degraded to black-and-white easily, but the reverse—changing black-and-white to color—is much more difficult and requires some special technology.

The Temporary folder is the folder into which Live places all WAV and AIFF audio files once recorded. You will find that once you save a file (song), you can choose to place all corresponding audio into a designated (aka less confusing) location. So think of this folder as a temporary scrap heap from which you can retrieve old files, browse for hidden gems, or just flush periodically.

The Misc Tab

Just because this tab is titled Misc, don't assume these parameters are extraneous. Each of the five subsections, Appearance, Behavior, Samples, Library, and Decoding Cache, is important in creating a smooth Live environment.

Appearance

The Appearance section (seen in Figure 3.24) chooses the skin for Live. There are 33 skins provided with Live 5, and artists such as Monolake (www.monolake.de) are developing new ones all the time. To test out which scheme you like best, simply click on the Load Skin menu in the Preferences dialog box and use the up and down arrows on your keyboard to scroll through the options. If you download a new skin or two, place these inside the Skins folder. For PCs, the skins are located in the Resources folder in the Live directory. For Macs, skins can be found in the Ableton Content/Skins folder. To add skins to OS X, Ctrl + click the Live 5 application icon, select Show Package Contents, and then open the folder Contents → App-Resource → Skins. Then place the newly downloaded skins here.

> **THE SKIN I'M IN**
>
> Many GUIs (graphic user interfaces) have customizable color schemes called skins. Just as Windows and Mac screens can be altered via Preferences, Live can be given a face-lift by loading a new skin. This feature will have no bearing on the performance or sound of Live, but it can make for an inspiring change of scenery.

Also, it may be of interest to point out that Live's internal language settings, which affect its internal help menus, interface text, and informational messages, can be set to read in French, Spanish, and German, as well as English. Ableton offers a separate version of Live that supports Japanese if you need it. If you do not see one of these languages, you can visit the Ableton Web site and click on Download to find the Ableton Live application file with the languages you need.

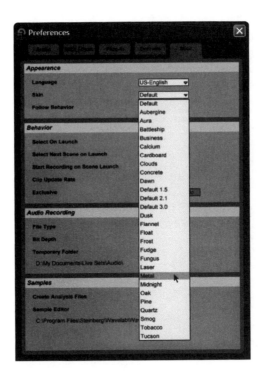

Figure 3.24
Live's Appearance section.
With these two menus, you
can customize Live's Skin
and Language settings.

The third option, Follow Behavior, determines the graphical style used when following the cursor (Now Line) in the Arrange and Clip Views. When set to Scroll, the Now Line will stay in place while the window moves smoothly under it. When set to Page, the window will stay stationary while the Now Line moves. When the Now Line reaches the right edge of the screen, the window jumps ahead so the Now Line appears again on the left. The Scroll option is much harder on your CPU, so if you are experiencing dropouts or sluggish response, set this option to Page.

The final option, Hide Labels, is new to Live 5. When set to Show, the Live interface will look normal. When set to Hide, all of the little labels on the interface (such as Track Delay and Audio To) will disappear. This will buy you a little more screen real estate once you've memorized all of Live's components.

Behavior

The second section, Behavior, (Figure 3.25), determines how Live handles clips once they are loaded (dragged or recorded) into Live. Select On Launch will cause the Clip View of a newly added clip to be displayed immediately when it is played. This is useful in the creation stage of your song because you'll probably need to modify the new clip to match all of your other pieces; however, when performing with Live, it may be more valuable to turn this option off. During the performance stage, you've probably made all the adjustments necessary for a clip and may want to maintain a view of effects that are loaded, instead.

Figure 3.25

The Behavior section is for specifying Live's treatment of audio files.

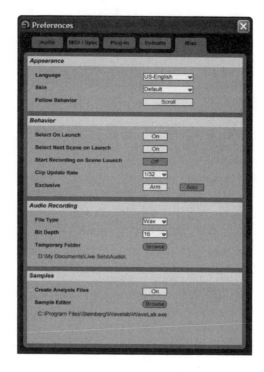

Select Next Scene on Launch greatly simplifies the performance of Live Sessions. Any time a scene is launched by keyboard or remote control, Live will automatically advance the scene selector to the one below it. If you've already laid out the sections of your song in a top-to-bottom arrangement on the Session Grid, you can progress through the song with just one button.

Start Recording on Scene Launch determines if clips will begin recording when launched by a scene. Having this option off will allow you to play an instrument live (track is armed for recording) while navigating through scenes. If this option is armed, a clip will begin to record in an armed track when the scene is launched. This can be powerful when used live by triggering a recording at a particular point in a piece. The recorded part can be looped instantly for building compositions in real-time.

Clip Update Rate is the frequency with which Live recalculates changes to the clip. For instance, if you transpose a clip in Live while the Clip Update Rate is set to 1/32 note, you will hear nearly instant changes to the pitch of the loop in the clip. Conversely, choosing a Clip Update Rate of 1/4 note, or the even slower rate of Bar (meaning one update per measure), will result in changes occurring more slowly. This is meaningful during a live performance, in which changes may need to be heard as they happen, instead of after the fact. For example, if you are working in the studio with Live, or if you're editing and noticing slow performance, turn down the Clip Update Rate to

1/4 note (its default setting), as seen in Figure 3.26. When performing, go for broke at 1/16 or 1/32 note settings.

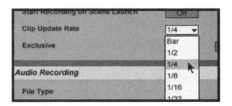

Figure 3.26
By adjusting the Clip Update Rate, Live can change loops (per your direction) more quickly, which is an excellent advantage for the live laptop loopist.

The Exclusive buttons are used to determine the Live Mixer's behavior when engaging solos and arming tracks for recording. For example, when Solo Exclusive is on (green), only one track may be soloed at a time. If you click the Solo button of another track, the previous track will have its solo status turned off. The same is true for Arm Exclusive. Only one track can be record-enabled when this button is active. To solo more than one track at a time in Live, simply hold down the Ctrl (⌘) key and click away. You can also arm more than one track at a time for recording by using the very same method.

The last option in this section is Count In. This is also a new feature in version 5. When set to None, Live will begin to record immediately when the transport is engaged. If you select a value here, such as 1 Bar, Live will provide one bar of count-in time (the metronome will sound but Live will not be running) before it begins to record. This is useful if you're recording yourself and you need some time to get to your instrument after you've engaged recording.

Samples
The Create Analysis Files option states whether Live will save its graphical display of audio waveforms for quick loading in the future. The first time an audio file is used in Live, the program will create a waveform display for use in the Clip View. When this option is enabled, Live will store the graphical analysis as a file on your computer's disk. The file has the same name as the sample it is associated with and has .asd as its extension. The next time the audio file is used in a Live Set, you won't have to wait for the graphical display to be rendered again.

The Sample Editor setting is for defining the location of your favorite wave editor, such as Sonic Foundry's Sound Forge, Steinberg's Wavelab, Bias Audio's Peak, or Syntrillium's Cool Edit Pro. Your preferred editor will launch when you press the Edit button in an Audio Clip. For a more detailed look at wave editors, please refer to Chapter 14, "Live 5 Power."

Library
New to Live 5 is the Library. This is Ableton's ingenious way of collecting all of its necessary support files into one place that can easily be accessed by you. The Library is installed

automatically when you install Live, and this setting will already be pointing to its location on your hard drive. If you decide to move the Library to a new disk or folder, you'll need to update this preference to reflect the new location. If Live is unable to find the Library, it will not be able to load any of the plug-in presets in the Browser or any of the Lessons, to name a few.

Decoding Cache

Ableton has really made Live 5 DJ-friendly. One of the enhancements made to the program is the capability to import MP3 files directly into your Set. In order for Live to play the MP3, it must first be decoded/decompressed into a standard WAV file. The resulting file is then stored in the Decoding Cache. Live is quite good at doing its own housekeeping, and keeping the Decoding Cache tidy is no exception. The parameters in this section determine how Live will handle the creation and cleanup of the decoded files.

The first option, Minimum Free Space, is the amount of free space that you always want available on the hard drive. If you set this to 500MB, Live will stop increasing the size of the cache once there is only 500MB available. This can be extremely important if you only have one hard drive on your entire computer system (frequent for laptop users). Usually, the operating system will need some amount of free space on the drive for swapping files and other housekeeping tasks. This setting will ensure that the space is free.

The last option here sets the maximum size for the Decoding Cache. Every time you add an MP3 into a Set, it will be decoded and stored. The more MP3s you use, the more files will be stored in the cache. After the maximum size is exceeded, Live will begin to delete the oldest decoded files in order to make room for new ones.

You'll notice that if you add an MP3 to your set and Live decodes it, Live will not have to decode the file again if you drag the same MP3 into a set at a later time. This is because the decoded file is still in the cache. When you keep adding newer and newer MP3s, the old files may be deleted. When this happens, you'll have to wait again for the previously decoded MP3 to be decoded again. The larger your cache is, the less this will happen.

The goal of Chapter 3 has been to get you up and running with Live and to give you a general idea about how the Preferences settings will affect your workflow. As you move through the book, I will again and again direct you back to the Preferences discussion in this chapter. In Chapter 4, I will proceed with the rest of your introduction to Live's two primary views.

4 } Live Interface Basics

One of Ableton's software development team's crowning achievements is the creation of Live's simple, but elegant, interface. Only two views are needed to accomplish everything in Live: Session View and Arrangement View. Session View is geared for live performance, loop experimentation, and a quick multi-track recording sketchpad, while Arrangement View better facilitates studio editing, audio and MIDI sequencing, and song arranging. Each subsection of Live's paired-down interfaces is intuitive, easy to maneuver, and contains built-in help to remind you of any on-screen buttons or features that might be unclear in the heat of a mix. Ableton's Zen-like approach to audio software provides solid relief in a world full of gargantuan multi-track applications, with gaggles of resizable pop-up windows and confusing setup and routing schemes. Instead, Live is a breath of fresh air, boasting streamlined controls with easy-to-read menus and discernible mixer and effect settings. Even with the fog machine blowing and lights down low, Live lets you get into the mix, rather than trying your patience with unnecessary system customization.

In the next few sections, I will break down each section of Live's two primary landscapes, as well as point out some timesaving ways to maneuver in Live. Later in the chapter, I'll look at some of Live's more customizable viewing features, a few pertinent file saving schemes, and the permanent parts of Live's screen real estate. Feel free to skip around if you need help in a particular area. If you are a Live user but are new to version 5, you will want to pay extra attention to the new Browser and Preset organization.

Session View

Live's Session View (see Figure 4.1) is where you will spend the greater part of your performing and composing time. With some practice, Session View can take on a musical life of its own and may well be the software world's first "jam-friendly" songwriter's sketchpad. Even better is that after the jam, Live permits an infinite amount of additional recording, editing, and arranging, which I will get to later in this chapter. There are four main sections contained within the Session View:

* The Clip Slot Grid
* The Scene Launcher
* The Session Mixer
* The Input/Output Routing Strip

The grid-like screen in the upper-right corner of your monitor is the actual Session View, while the side and bottom retractable rectangle views (such as Browser Info and Track/Clip View) are present in any view when you want them to be. Session View is where most people experience the creative spark in Live, so if you should create something worth saving while you are working through this chapter, go to File → Save Live Set As and name your new sketch. I also want to point out that while I will cover each element in the interface, the Browser and Info View will be explained later in the chapter, while Track and Clip View will be saved for Chapter 5, "Making Music in Live."

Figure 4.1

Pictured above is Live's Session View. This is the window used for live performance. Each Clip Slot (represented as rectangles beneath the Track Title Bar) is a placeholder for audio samples, loops, and MIDI sequences.

This ordinary-looking grid will be the launchpad for many a Live jam. Each cell—Ableton calls them *Clip Slots*—can contain a clip. A clip is a musical part that can be triggered to play or stop via the mouse, computer keyboard, or MIDI-controller, depending upon your settings. Each clip can even be played in similar fashion to an Akai MPC, drum machine, or similar phrase sampler. For example, artists such as Shawn Pelton may lay out several sampled drum hits across the 16 pads of a Trigger Finger and then play them with the comfy rubber pads. Live's Clip Slot Grid, which I will explain in detail below, is similar in design and can house an unlimited number of loops, samples, one shots, and MIDI parts.

Clip Slot Grid

Session View's Clip Slot Grid (see Figure 4.2) is actually the first tool you will use to organize your musical parts (clips) into a song. Live uses these rows and columns, referred to as "scenes" and "tracks," respectively, to give you different levels of control. What's important is that you begin to think of Live's Clip Slot Grid as a palette upon which to place your sonic colors (in this case musical parts composed of audio files and MIDI data) for later sonic "painting" and further color exploration (sound combining).

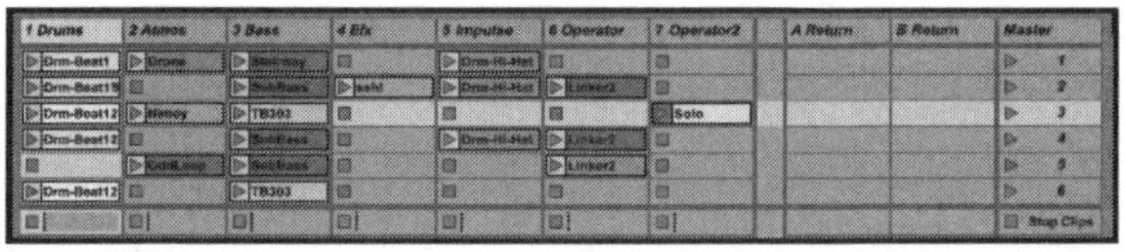

Figure 4.2
The Clip Slot Grid with a few clips loaded in some slots.

Along the bottom of the Clip Slot Grid are the Clip Stop buttons. Clicking the square in one of these slots will cause any clip playing on that track above it to stop. Also, there is another box labeled Stop Clips in the Master Track at the right. This button, as its name implies, will stop all clips—both audio and MIDI—when triggered.

 SPACE OUT

The spacebar starts and stops audio in Live as it does in most other audio software applications.

By loading clips into the Clip Slot Grid, you are arming Live with musical ammo. Next steps range from firing off parts in a live performance to creating new musical combinations (songs) to switching to the Arrangement View for more editing.

KNOBBY DIGITAL

To adjust any of the virtual knobs found in Live, click on the knob and move the mouse forward and backward just like moving a fader. In other words, sideways mouse moves are a waste of time. Don't feel silly practicing how this feels; after all, it's your "sequencing instrument."

Some Live users prefer to build their entire song in Live by using several small, yet simple loops, and then utilize Live's Session View to organize, improvise, or compose. Other artists may show up to the gig with a blank slate, along with a stash of well-organized clips, and practice building their mix from the ground up in a more gradual, yet still improvisational way.

The Scene Launcher

As mentioned previously, the rows in the Clip Slot Grid are referred to as scenes. Since Live can play only one clip at a time in each track, it makes sense to put each one you want to play in a horizontal line across the grid. Live then offers you a way to launch all of the clips in the scene using the Scene Launchers (see Figure 4.3) found on the right side of the Clip Slot Grid in the Master Track. As you get deeper into the program (especially in the next chapter), you'll see how using scenes offers you a quick way of arranging and performing a song.

Figure 4.3

Click the triangle to launch all the clips in the scene (row).

The Session Mixer

Live's Session Mixer, seen in Figure 4.4, approximates a hardware mixer in both concept and design, but since it's a software mixer, it is also completely automatable, MIDI-mappable, and expandable. Similar to its hardware cousin, Live's Session Mixer utilizes a set of individual channel controls and a master section.

Figure 4.4

Live's Session Mixer looks similar to most other virtual mixers. Each vertical strip represents a channel with individual values for volume, panning, and routing.

Audio Tracks and Their Controls

The track shown in Figure 4.5 is an Audio Track. This type of track has been with Live since the beginning. You can use Audio Clips and Audio Effects (both described in detail later) on this type of track as well as record new Audio Clips.

The Audio Track outputs an audio signal that is fed into an audio channel of the Session Mixer below it. The audio channel controls give you control of the output volume, pan position, and effect sends for the track. The buttons include the Track Activator (the large button containing the track's number), which enables the track when it's green, and can also be used to mute the

Figure 4.5
The Audio Track can house Audio Clips and process them with Audio Effects. The controls available on Audio Track are Volume, Pan, Mute, Solo, Record Arm, and Sends.

track; the Solo/Cue button, which routes the track to the Pre-Listen Bus; and the Record Arm button, which enables the track for recording as well as monitoring for tracks set to Auto (monitoring will be explained in a few sections).

MIDI Tracks and Their Controls

A MIDI Track without a virtual instrument (Figure 4.6) does not output audio; thus, there are no Volume, Pan, or Send knobs for them in Session Mixer. You still have the Track Activator, Solo/PFL, and Arm buttons, which function the same as their Audio Track counterparts. When a virtual instrument is loaded onto the track (see Chapter 8, "Using Effects and Instruments"), the full Audio Track controls explained previously will appear instead.

Figure 4.6
The MIDI Track does not have a Volume or Pan control if there is no virtual instrument loaded into its Track View.

> **P.F. WHAT?**
>
> PFL stands for Pre-Fader Listen. This is a function found on many mixers that allows the user to listen to the sound on a channel without letting the audience hear it. The process is "pre-fader," meaning that you listen to the channel before the sound enters the volume fader. You will therefore be able to listen to a channel that is muted or has the volume turned all the way down.

Return Tracks and Their Controls

The Return Tracks (see Figure 4.7) output audio, but unlike their Audio Track cousins, they can't hold any clips. What good is a track that can't hold clips? While they may not add new parts to your song, they can still hold effects and can receive input from both the Send knobs and Audio Output routing. These can be used for send-style effects like reverbs and delays or can be used to group tracks together by routing the individual track outs to the Return Track. Since clips can't be used on Return Tracks, there is no Record Arm button. See Chapter 8 for a full explanation of Return Tracks and their uses.

Figure 4.7
The Return Track is basically an Audio Track without Clip Slots.

> **STEREO ON THE GO**
>
> All channels in Live are both stereo- and mono-capable, depending upon the source that is playing. Panning works similarly for both stereo and mono tracks (as you would imagine), but keep in mind that stereo signals may sound noticeably weaker when panned. Mono signals, on the other hand, will provide more "presence."

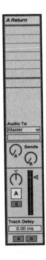

Your computer's first eight function keys (F1 through F8) double as channel mute shortcut keys for Live's Session Mixer. F1 works for channel 1, F2 for channel 2, and so on up to channel 8. This is an exceptionally handy tool for live performance when you are looking to mute and un-mute parts in a hurry—a technique employed by many DJs and Electronica artists. For those using Mac PowerBooks, you need to hold the "Fn" key while you use the function keys.

Master Track and Its Controls

The Master Track, shown in Figure 4.8, is the granddaddy of them all. All tracks outputting to Master will pass through this track on their way to your speakers. You can't make or destroy the Master Track, and it, like the Return Tracks, cannot house clips. In place of the Clip Slots are the Scene Launchers explained earlier. The Master Track provides you with one final point to treat your mix since it has a Track View that can be loaded with effects such as mastering EQ and compression. You'll also find the Solo/PFL volume knob here, which adjusts the pre-listen level while browsing audio files and also sets the volume of the metronome.

Figure 4.8
Your entire mix will generally pass through the Master Track, so it's a nice place to add final effects to your song.

❋ SOLO/CUE

Here in the Master Track is the Solo/Cue volume knob and Function button. The knob controls the volume of all pre-listen functions such as soloing tracks and previewing audio files in the Browser. If you've selected unique outputs for your pre-listen bus (see the Audio Tab in Chapter 3 , "Getting Live Up and Running"), the Solo button above the knob may be switched to Cue. When Cue is active, the Solo buttons on the Audio Tracks will turn to Cue buttons (little headphone icons). When you press one of these Cue buttons, that track will be routed to the pre-listen output without muting the other tracks. You can use this feature to listen to a track before switching on its Track Activator—a helpful performance tool.

Track Delay

New to Live 5 is the Track Delay (see Figure 4.9), which is a godsend when synchronizing loops and external MIDI gear. With this feature, you can manually nudge entire tracks ahead or behind the current play location. This is handy if, for example, you've got a piece of external MIDI gear that responds sluggishly (this is more common with older MIDI devices). If you dial in a negative Track Delay value for the MIDI Track, Live will send the MIDI data to the external device just a little earlier than normal. The result is that you'll hear the external device play in time instead of sounding a little late. This can also be handy if you have a drum loop that feels a little out of sync—just adjust this parameter to move the track back into alignment. In order to hear the effects of Track Delay, Delay Compensation must be activated under the Options menu.

Figure 4.9

The Track Delay feature is a handy way to compensate for sluggish MIDI gear.

Track Delay	Track Delay	Track Delay	Track Delay		Track Delay	Track Delay		Track Delay
3.00 ms	-4.00 ms	0.00 ms	0.00 ms		0.00 ms	0.00 ms		0.00 ms

The Crossfader

Live features a weapon like none I have ever seen in audio software—the MIDI-mappable DJ-style crossfader. (Live calls it just a plain old *crossfader*.) For over 20 years now, analog crossfaders have been making magicians out of DJs by enabling them to mix two or more tracks together, juggle those mixes, and break up monotonous loops with one simple gesture. Scratch DJs have also taken crossfader technique to incredible levels. The Live adaptation of the analog crossfader (seen in Figure 4.10) is the humble-looking horizontal slider just below the Master Volume section described in the preceding section.

Figure 4.10

Live's crossfader adds a whole new set of performance (and mix) tools to Live's Session View. The A and B buttons assign their respective tracks to one side of the crossfader or the other.

To use the fader, you will have to assign Session Mixer channels to either A or B sides of the crossfader. If you are new to crossfaders, think of it as a double-sided volume fader. As you move to B (to increase the volume of all channels set to B), you decrease the volume of all channels set to A. The reverse holds true when you come back to A—A channels get louder, while B channels get quieter.

Here are a few tips for jumping into Live's crossfader feature:

❋ **Assign a couple of channels to A or B sides of the crossfader:** When selecting your Session Mixer channels to A or B, you don't have to designate all of your active tracks (to A or B). By not assigning a track to A or B, you have, by omission, selected both. This means that you will hear any non-specified channels all of the time regardless of the crossfader's position. DJs often like to bring in a different groove under the same music bed and vice versa. Simply leave all of your tracks as they are and make one drum groove A and the other B. Now gradually flip back and forth on the crossfader.

❋ **Get your MIDI on:** By assigning a MIDI controller to control Live's crossfader, you can add a whole new performance element to Live. To do this, you will need a MIDI controller or MIDI keyboard set up for your computer (see the X-Session controller in Chapter 3). Then all you need to do is press the MIDI button on the upper right-hand side of Live's screen. Click once in the middle of the crossfader, and then move a knob or keyboard wheel (the modulation wheel works well). For scratch-DJ style transforming controls (fast fades from the far left to the far right of the crossfader), you can assign MIDI notes to the left and right sides of the crossfader as well.

❋ **Dry up the mix trick:** You can quickly "dry" up your mix (remove all audible effects) by routing each of your effect Returns to one side of the crossfader. To do so, simply route all effect Returns to B, and leave all other Crossfader Assigns alone (no assignment). Assuming you have effects on your Aux Returns (I will describe how to do this in the following sections), moving the crossfader to position A will have no effects, while the B position will have full effects.

❋ **HIDEAWAY**

Live can feel a little constrictive with its profusion of virtual controls. You can hide sections of the Session View by clicking the small icons to the right of the Master Volume slider. You can also turn the same sections on and off by selecting them in the View menu.

Track Input and Output Routing

Live's Session Mixer is even more flexible once you get under the hood. The Input/Output Channel Routing is capable of routing any input imaginable into a Live track from external audio and MIDI sources, ReWire clients, and other Live tracks by merely clicking the menus (see Figure 4.11) and picking your source. Any multi-channel input, such as an eight-channel sound card or multiple-output software such as Propellerhead's Reason, can have inputs routed to correspond with any given channel. If, for example, you want microphone input number one to be recorded on Session Mixer channel one (or any other), the dropdown menus will accomplish this.

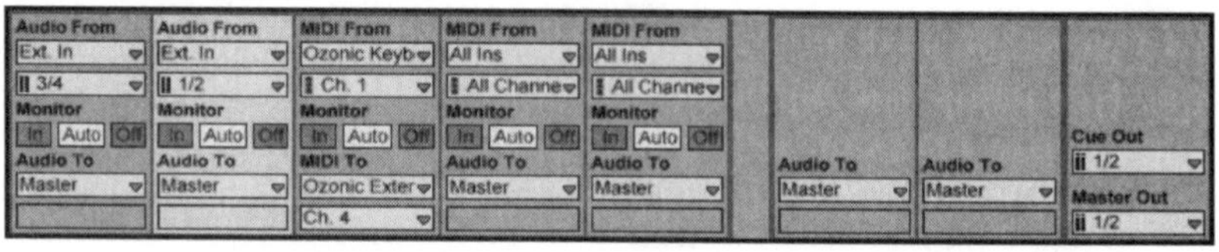

Figure 4.11

The Input/Output Routing strip. In Live, you have the choice of configuring Input Type and Channel, as well as Output Type and Channel for audio and MIDI Tracks. Return Tracks only have the output options.

Any ReWire applications currently existing on your computer will also be seen in the Input dropdown menu. (ReWire is a software linking technology invented by Propellerhead that allows Live to run, control, or be controlled by programs such as Reason, Sonar, Cubase, Project5, Storm, and many others. See Chapter 12, "ReWire," for the lowdown.) By routing a ReWire application through Live's inputs, you will be able to monitor and record that application's audio output as you would another audio source.

You will also see "Resample" in the inputs section. This is available in case you want to send Live's own output to itself, for instance, when you have finished a track and want to render your song in real-time, or if you want to make a quick submix of more than one track. These various inputs and methods will be covered in the next three chapters.

> ### CLONING AND GROUPING TRACKS
>
> Live's Input/Output section uses data from one track to feed other multiple tracks. This is especially useful with MIDI Tracks since you can trigger multiple instruments from one clip, creating colossal layers. It is functionally the same as cloning your track, clips, effects, and all, and adding another instrument. However, this way controls it all from only one set of clips.
>
> When performing this type of routing, your first instinct may be to set the output of your controlling track to multiple destinations. However, the Output section of each track only allows one destination to be selected. Instead, you'll need to set the inputs of the other tracks to the control track. If you're feeding

multiple tracks into one, such as when grouping Audio Tracks, the process is the opposite—you choose the destination track for all the control tracks.

Arrangement View

Beginners may think of it as merely Live's "other" window, but Arrangement View (seen in Figure 4.12) is the place for recording and editing your Live Session View jams, performing overdubs, automating additional effects, and rendering your final track. If Session View is the spontaneous right-brain-tickling creative screen, Arrangement View is the analytic, left-brain-stimulating, "finishing touches" side of Live. You may notice that Live's Arrangement View closely resembles many other multi-track applications' "Arranger" screens. Programs such as Acid Pro, Sonar, Cubase, Logic, Pro Tools, and many others are based on horizontal, left-to-right audio arrangers (also called *linear-based arrangers*). If you like this method of working, you will be right at home making music in Live, Arrangement-style.

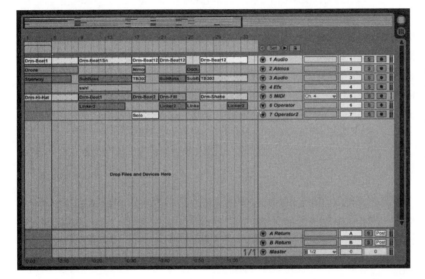

Figure 4.12

Live's Arrangement View will contain the results of your recorded Session View songs. Each horizontal line in Arrangement View represents a track that will correspond to a vertical channel in the Session Mixer.

For those who didn't read the figure caption, here it is again: Each track in Session View corresponds precisely with its track counterpart in Arrangement View. If you have eight tracks in Session View, you will have eight tracks in Arrangement View. You can add a track in either view, and it will appear in the other as if you are working on the same project—because you are.

There is, however, a very important distinction between Session View and Arrangement View. Once you record your music from Session View into Arrangement View, you will hear your new arrangement (playing from Arrangement View) until you override it by executing a control in Session View or by actively moving a previously automated control.

This is actually a great feature, but it can baffle those making the switch from a traditional linear-based sequencer application. The idea rests on Session View being a palette for your musical "painting" in Arrangement View. You can record a single run-through (a take) and then move to Arrangement View to edit your song to completion. Or you can do multiple takes or punch-ins by again activating Global recording and "overdubbing" additional song parts into Arrangement View from Session View. This is also a great method for touching up previously recorded automation data.

This is an extremely important concept to grasp, so let's look at it a bit more closely by loading up the example Set titled Automation.als. After you have loaded the file, which will be found in the (AL5P Examples) → Chapter 04 folder in the Ableton Library, follow the steps below.

1. When you load Automation.als, you will be looking at a simple song in Live's Arrangement View. Press Tab to switch to Session View.

2. Take a look at the Session Mixer and notice all the red markings. These markings mean that the knob, fader, or button has associated automation data in the Arrangement View. (Automation data consists of the recorded movements of every fader, knob, or button you moved when you did your Live recording.) Press the spacebar and watch all these controls move automatically as the song plays.

3. Now move the volume slider on Track 2. Notice that the red blip on this control turns gray, and the red light on the Back to Arrangement button (in the Control Bar) lights up. You have now told Live to ignore that specific fader's automation and use your manual setting. This fader will no longer move automatically as you play the song.

4. To reinstate the automation—so you can listen to the song's original recording settings—simply press the red Back to Arrangement button on the Control Bar to the right of the Record button. Notice how Track 2's fader level jumps back to its original position.

> ※ **SESSION OR ARRANGEMENT?**
>
> Important: Any time you move a control that has been automated, Live ceases playback of that particular control's automation. By overriding the control, Live assumes that you would like to temporarily listen to that particular control (or group of controls) as you have set them in Session View. In any given project, you can only be sure that you are hearing the mix from Arrangement View when the Back to Arrangement button is dark (Figure 4.13). If the Back to Arrangement button is on, you are likely hearing a mix of both your Arrangement and Session View clips and controls. If you launch a clip in the Session View, this will override playback of the corresponding track in Arrangement View. If you flip to the Arrangement, you'll see that the corresponding track is faded out, symbolizing its inactivity. When you press the Back to Arrangement button, all of the Session View clips will stop instantly (this does not wait for the Global Quantization setting or anything like that), and the Arrangement clips will play. This is true for fader movements or manually changing the state of any control with automation. Your new moves

interrupt what should be playing from the Arrangement's automation tracks, so the Back to Arrangement button lights signal the divergence. Therefore, you should always double-check exactly which side you are hearing (either your programmed automation or manual mix settings) if Live seems to be "misbehaving."

Back to Arrangement

Figure 4.13
Whether you are in Arrangement View or Session View, you can always revert to the Arrangement View's mix settings, which usually contain automation, by pressing the Back to Arrangement button.

This view-dependent mixer settings concept is a drastic difference from other applications you may be used to; the reasoning is simple: You will want to hear entirely different settings on your improvised remix or jam than you will on a finished piece of music. It can be handy to remove the automation or, if you are in Session View, to hear the automation at a moment's notice. For this reason and others I will delve into later, remember that Arrangement and Session View track settings are not always the same mix—hence they will not necessarily sound the same.

✼ **ICON FLIP**

In the upper-right corner of the Live window are two icons: one with three vertical lines and one with three horizontal lines. These icons can be used to switch between the Session and Arrangement Views. The Session View is accessed with the icon with the vertical lines (the Session View has its tracks oriented vertically), while the other icon with its horizontal lines represents the Arrangement View.

Track Settings and Contents

The Arrangement View's track settings are located on the right side of the screen and take up about one-third of the working portion of the Arrangement View, as seen in Figure 4.14. To maximize (view) a track, click the downward-pointing triangle. Any clips on that track will reveal their contents and several hidden track settings.

Each Arrangement track is still bound by the same rules as the tracks in Session View. Only one clip can be playing at a time in an Arrangement track. Clips can be added to Arrangement tracks in the same manner used to add them to the Session View. Simply drag the desired file from the File Browser into an Arrangement track. The clip will appear, and you will be able to

Figure 4.14

Each track in Arrangement View has the same controls as the tracks in Session View. This makes sense since the Arrangement tracks and Session tracks are actually the same.

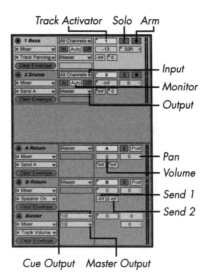

move it, copy it, lengthen or shorten it, and perform other editing features described in the Arrangement section of Chapter 5.

Volume, Panning, FX sends, Solo, Mute, Arm for Recording, and the same track routing features found in the Session Mixer are still accessible in Arrangement View. The only difference is visual: The controls have been turned on their sides and are represented by values instead of graphical controls. The Session Mixer's Master Settings are located on the bottom line of Live's Arrangement View.

Relation to the Session View

Though the Arrangement and Session Views seem like two different sections in the Live environment, they are actually closely related to one another. In Live, there are two places to arrange and play clips: the Arrangement View and Session View; however, there is only one mixer in Live, and that is the Session Mixer. This means that the Arrangement and Session need to share this mixer. Just like only one clip can be playing on a track at a time, only one track—either from the Session or Arrangement—can be fed into a Session Mixer channel at a time.

If you are playing clips on a track in the Session View, they will override any clips in the associated track of the Arrangement. When you press the Back to Arrangement button, the tracks in the Arrangement will take over, and all clips in the Session View will stop.

This relation between the two views means that you can arrange a song in the Arrangement View, but can begin improvising in the Session View. When your improvisation is done, press the Back to Arrangement button and your preset Arrangement will take over.

Overview

Standing tall above Live's Arranger/Session Views and just below the Control Bar is the Overview (of your Live Arrangement). The Overview, which resembles a musical staff, is there purely for navigation and reference to show you where you are in your Arrangement. So long as you have clips in Live's Arrangement View, it offers a bird's-eye view of your entire composition. You will see tiny colored lines representing your clips in the Arrangement View. The Overview (Figure 4.15) can be seen in Session View, but is a permanent fixture in Arrangement View. You can hide the Overview (in Session View) by pressing Ctrl+Shift+O on a PC, or Option+⌘+O on a Mac.

Figure 4.15
Live's Overview is quite literally a view from above.

To use the Overview to move to a new location, hover the mouse over the portion of the Overview bar you want to move to; the magnifying glass icon will appear; click once and you will be moved to the corresponding location in the Arrangement. To zoom in and out, hover over the Overview bar, depress the mouse button (left on PC), and move the mouse forward and backward to zoom in and out (respectively). You can skip quickly from the beginning to the end with one click of the mouse—though I should point out that you will still need to place your cursor in the desired location and then press your spacebar to start playback. Try this a couple of times; it takes some getting used to.

> ❋ **TAB = FLIP**
>
> To see Live's other screen, simply strike the Tab key; for example, if you're in the Session View, press Tab, and the Arrangement window will appear. Press Tab once again to return to Session View and then just for fun, hit F11, to see Live's full screen view (or F11 again to go back to Live's previous dimensions).
>
> Mac OS X users with Exposé enabled will not be able to use the F11 key for controlling Live's view since that key is used by Exposé. Enter your Exposé settings (in the System Preferences) and reassign the F11 function to another key. F11 will then control Live's full screen view.

The Live Control Bar

Headlining each one of Live's two different working views (Session and Arrangement) is Live's own version of a transport bar. Typically, transport bars function as the start/stop mechanism and song position finder all in one. Although transport bars are often free-floating in many other applications, in Live, the Control Bar (see Figure 4.16) is fixed to the top of your screen. Still, most "power-users" default to keyboard shortcuts such as the spacebar for starting and stopping playback, rarely using the icons at the top of the screen. Also, many Live aficionados map Live's Control Bar functions to MIDI or computer keyboard controls. I will cover this in detail later in this section.

Figure 4.16
Live's Control Bar remains constant at the top of both of Live's main views. Here you will find standard symbols for Stop, Play, and Record, as well as time/ tempo information and other project parameters.

In the Control Bar, you will find pertinent song information, such as time signature, tempo, and processor load (a vital stat for the computer-based musician). The Control Bar will also help you pinpoint your exact location within the song and determine Live's master quantize settings, and a Tap Tempo and metronome make recording your Live projects from scratch just a tad more manageable.

Tempo, Time Signature, Groove, Metronome, and Sync

On the left side of the Control Bar, you will find settings for song parameters (see Figure 4.17). The buttons are (from left to right) Tap Tempo, Tempo, Time Signature, Groove Amount, Metronome, External Sync Switch, and External Sync Indicators.

The Tap Tempo button is a handy song-starting feature in Live. For a quick test drive of one of Tap Tempo's features, click the button four times, and your project will begin at that tempo. This is a handy feature if you need to sneak in while another DJ is playing, synch up with your drummer, or match another device such as a turntable or CD player. You can also use Tap Tempo to help map out songs and align groove clips better. Sound confusing? Chapters 5 and 6 will clear it up.

Figure 4.17
This subsection of the Control Bar is devoted to time, including MIDI sync, tempo, and time signature.

Next up are Live's project Tempo and Time signature settings, which are found just to the right of the Tap Tempo button. Live can handle tempos ranging form 20 to 999 BPM (beats per minute) and time signatures with numerators ranging from 1–99 and denominator choices of 1, 2, 4, 8, and 16—a huge range of possibilities.

Moving to the right of time signature, you will come upon Live's Metronome button. This feature/function works in a complementary fashion to the Tap Tempo. When engaged, you will hear a customizable click track (metronome) that can serve as a guide for new recordings and help with loop editing. The volume of the click can be adjusted by using the Solo/Cue volume knob in Live's Master Track (the same knob you use for adjusting the preview volume when browsing for samples).

Finally, the External Sync button and the External Sync monitoring lights show how Live handles the job of synchronizing to an external device. Provided that Live's Preferences have been set correctly (to synchronize playback with another MIDI source), the External Synch Switch engages or disengages Live's MIDI-synchronization to an outside source, while the monitoring lights announce that the MIDI sync signal is being sent or received.

Follow, Play, Stop, Record, MIDI Overdub, Quantize, and Pencil

Most starting and stopping in Live is best handled with the spacebar (tap it once to start, tap it again to stop); however, the second area of Live's Control Bar (Figure 4.18) sports official Start and Stop buttons. You will also find the Arrangement Record, MIDI Overdub, and Back to Arrangement buttons here, which you will use during the track editing process.

Figure 4.18
Here is the second element of Live's Control Bar. Keep your eye on the Quantization menu. This is the key to sounding like a pro when you fire off your loops.

Other points of interest include the Arrangement Position box and the global Quantization menu. The Arrangement Position box provides a continuous readout—in measures, beats, and subdivisions—of where you are in the song, whether you're listening or recording. You can manually enter a start time value into this box or drag up and down with the mouse to change the setting.

The global Quantization menu, to the right of the Record button, sets the triggering timing for Clips in Live's Session View that are set to Global quantization (more on this in Chapter 5). The global Quantize setting also determines the step size of the Nudge buttons (found in the Clip View, which will be explained in the next chapter). You have the option of selecting 1/32, 1/16, 1/8, 1/4, 1/2, and multiples of the full measure (called *bars*). What this means is that each clip triggered in the Session View will "fire" at the very next subdivision you have selected. For instance, at the Bar setting, your "fired" clip will not begin to play until the first beat of the very next measure. If your setting is 1/16, your clip will begin playing at the next 1/16 note. You can imagine how this quantitative correction tool will clean up your performance. This can be a huge help and a very cool trick for guiding rapid-fire sample sections, or just ensuring that your next scene launches right on the first beat.

If quantization sounds sterile to you, and you want your music to breathe more, you can also set this menu to None for no quantization of any sort. Any clip (set to Global) you fire while None is selected will sound the instant the sample is triggered.

Punch In/Out and Loop

Live provides several features that are built for both the (self-engineering) recording musician and the mad loop concocter. Punch In and Punch Out is just that type of tool. Using it, you will be able to record a select length of audio or create a submix of Live's output. Recording in small segments like this can be an excellent way to make original loops for your collection or add in just the right bit of music to your song. I will cover recording in detail in later chapters, so don't worry if this description seems a little overwhelming. The third set of tools in Live's Control Bar section, seen below in Figure 4.19, includes controls for two loop points, the start and the end. If the Loop button is depressed, then Live's playback will loop (the defined start/stop length) continuously, as opposed to playing though to the end of the song. If the two punch points are activated, Live can be set to record in typical multi-tracking get in/get out fashion. This tool is meant to provide a quick way of recording for a specified amount of time.

Figure 4.19

Live's Punch In and Punch Out functionality makes recording Live's output or tracking some additional input a breeze.

Computer Keyboard, Key and MIDI Assigns, System Performance, and MIDI I/O

The fourth segment of the Control Bar (see Figure 4.20) is the system-monitoring and Key/MIDI setup area. The first icon on the left turns the computer keyboard on and off (this is a feature that allows you to use your computer's keyboard as a MIDI input device, which can be handy when working on a laptop on the go). I will cover the many ways to configure MIDI and computer keyboard triggering and controls in Chapters 5, 6, and 7; however, I want to point out that the Key (Key Map Mode Switch) and MIDI (MIDI Map Mode Switch) buttons are your entrance points to controlling Live with an outside hardware controller. Ableton was ingenious enough to make sure that all MIDI and Keyboard mapping could be done on the fly, without ever stopping playback—no small feat.

Figure 4.20

Pictured is the fourth segment of Live's Control Bar. From here, you can monitor your hardware (CPU load and MIDI input/output action) and set up your Key and MIDI controls.

Knowing how much gas is left in the tank—or whether you're running on fumes—is important in the computer world. Here to help, Live's CPU Load Meter continuously shows the amount of strain on your system for a given set of audio processing or loop playback. If, for any reason, this bar is beginning to approach 100%, you may begin to experience performance degradation or audio dropouts. The D (Hard-Disk Overload Indicator) button just to the right of the CPU meter will begin to flicker red if your hard drive is not able to stream all the necessary audio files playing in the song quickly enough. This will also result in dropouts.

> ❄ **MIDI PROGNOSIS**
>
> The last two indicators, just right of the Disk Overload Indicator, represent MIDI Input and MIDI Output signal presence by lighting up (turning colors) when Live is sending or receiving MIDI signals.
>
> The two similar indicators between the MIDI Map Mode and Key Map Mode buttons will illuminate when an incoming message is assigned to a MIDI Remote function.

Live's Custom Views

Live also hosts several concealable windows accessible in both Session and Arrangement Views. These secondary windows enable you to explore your loops and files, Live's devices, plug-in effects, and Live's integrated Info menu. Unlike most configurable software applications, these windows pop up or close with the click of a single triangle-shaped icon (see Figures 4.21a and 4.21b). For instance, if you are working on a song arrangement, you will not need to have the File Browser open; or, if you are familiar with Live, you can close the Info View to give more space to the Clip and Track Views. After some experimentation, you will discover your favorite working views in Session or Arrangement View. The idea is that you may want to hide collapsible windows in order to maximize screen real estate.

Figure 4.21a
Live's Session View with the Browser, Info, and Clip View (Chapter 5) maximized (open).

Figure 4.21b
With Browser, Info, and Clip View closed, Live's screen is wide open. You'll be able to see a greater number of tracks and clips this way.

The Browser

The Browser window (see Figure 4.22) provides the means to access all of the prefab elements you will add to a Live Set. It provides quick access to three different locations on your hard drive for finding samples and MIDI files; it houses the collection of 22 Live devices and their presets; and it provides a listing of all external plug-in devices located by Live. The Browser is retractable and located in the upper left section of either the Session or Arrangement View. By clicking the leftward-pointing, triangle-shaped arrow, you can hide this window. Conversely, if the arrow is pointing toward the right, simply click once to view the Browser.

Figure 4.22
Located on the far and upper left-hand side are Live's internal device, plug-in effects, and file browsers.

File Browsers

Warning! Do not underestimate the power of Live's Browser. With it, audio and MIDI can be previewed in real-time at the project tempo. Cakewalk's Sonar and Sonic Foundry's Acid Pro both do this for the PC, but most other programs require some preformatting before this can be achieved. Auto-previewing, or as Ableton calls it, "pre-listening," can be toggled off and on by clicking on the miniature set of headphones to the uppermost left of the Browser. When pre-listening is on, simply click on a file in the Browser, and Live will preview it on the next downbeat.

❋ **CUEING THE MIX**

You can adjust the volume of loops heard via Live's pre-listening feature by rotating the virtual solo/pre-listening volume knob on Live's mixer. In Session mode, you will see this control near the bottom of the master channel in the lower right corner of your mixer. In the Arrangement View, you will need to maximize the master channel (at the bottom of the track display) and adjust the pre-listening level in the box in the lower right-hand corner.

Drag and Drop

If you happen to like the sounds you are hearing when previewing loops, simply drag and drop the part(s) into either the Session or Arrangement View. You can place it in a Clip Slot in Session View or onto a track (at any point you like) in Arrangement View. The sound file can then be accessed immediately in Live's Clip View.

Conversely, if you like a clip that you've created using Live's clip settings and effects, you can drag the clip from Live back into the Browser to store a new *Live Clip* there. You will then have access to this new clip in any project you work on in the future. When you drag it back into an empty track in another project, the original effects and instruments associated with the clip will automatically be loaded into the track. You can also perform this same trick on multiple clips simultaneously. If you select a group of clips and drag them over to the Browser, Live will create a new Live Set in this location with tracks for all the clips you're saving.

Another new feature of the File Browser is the ability to drag portions of Live Sets, or even entire Live Sets, into your current project. When you see a Live Set in the Browser (indicated by the Live icon and the file extension .als), there will now be a small triangle in front of it, just like you see in front of the folders. You can click this triangle to "unfold" the Live Set so you can see the individual tracks in the Set. Each of the tracks will also have a triangle in front of it, which will let you unfold the track to see the individual clips in the track. You can drag the clips, tracks, or the entire Set right into your current project. Additionally, if you drag these new elements into empty tracks or into the empty space in the Session or Arrangement View Live will reload all of the effects and instruments associated with the parts.

On top of all this, the Live Browser works almost identically to Explorer (on the PC) or Finder (on the Mac). You can drag and drop files from one location into another, use the Copy, Cut, and Paste commands (Ctrl⌘+C, Ctrl⌘+X, and Ctrl⌘+V, respectively), as well as rename and delete files.

Navigating the Browser

The default position of Live's File Browser will be the same position that you were searching when you last closed Live. To facilitate faster manual searches, Live enables you to set up shortcuts within three different File Browser placeholders (seen in Figure 4.23). These will save you time as well as aid in the time-consuming process of organizing your loops for a live show.

At the top of the Browser, just below the tap, tempo, and time signature information, are five key icons. They will be just to the left of the name of your current folder (Figure 4.24). You will see a set of headphones (Live's Pre-Listening button) and two separate arrow markers—one hooking

Figure 4.23
The File Browser placehold-ers. They may be tiny, but they are a mighty big time-saver.

up (the Move Up button), the other pointing down (the Root button). The Move Up and Root buttons help you locate the file you are looking for and then designate the Browser position, to save you time.

Figure 4.24
The Pre-listening, Move Up, Root, Library, and Search buttons.

Earlier, we touched on the importance of pre-listening to your sounds in the Browser before bringing them into your project. The Pre-listening (headphone-shaped) icon will engage or dis-engage Live's loop preview function. You will generally leave this on while you're composing and experimenting and then turn it off when it is time to go to the gig. The logic is simple in that you don't want to accidentally preview (hear) the wrong loop during a performance unless you are routing your pre-listening output through a separate sound card. Generally, when prepping for a live performance, your loops and samples will be organized and named descriptively enough that you will not have to hear them before importing them into your project.

The next two icons, Move Up and Root, will help you by place-setting or bookmarking your location in Live's Browser so that each time you open Live you can begin looking in the same folder. (The fourth icon will provide one-click access to the Ableton Library folder on your hard drive.) Since you have three separate File Browser Choosers, you can set three different book-marked locations. Here's how to do it:

1. Open Live's Browser and click one of the File Browser Choosers (the file folder icons num-bered 1, 2, and 3).

2. Next, click into the folder you would like to browse sounds from by cycling down the file folder tree. You may need to click through several folders to get to the one you are after.

3. Now click once on the folder you would like Live to default to (your new desired bookmarked location for this File Browser).

4. Press Root (the downward-pointing arrow-shaped icon in the Browser). After you click Root, the Browser will move that folder to the top (starting position) for all future browsing. If you change your mind or want to go back to a folder that you cannot see, click the Move Up

button (the upward-pointing arrow-shaped icon). The Move Up button simply moves your Browser's view up one folder level at a time.

Searching for Files

New to Live 5 is the Search function, which is accessed with the fifth icon in the Browser title bar. This will allow you to find files in your collection by typing in key words for your search. When you click Search, Live will search only within the selected root folder. So, if the Browser's Root is set to a folder titled My Samples, Live will only search within that folder for your desired sounds. This can help speed up or narrow your search by limiting the scope.

The first time you try to search for something, it will take Live longer than usual because Live will be building an index of your files. On subsequent searches, Live will reference the index file, making the search faster. Additionally, Live will also keep this index up-to-date as files are added and removed from the search area.

Organizing Your Files

In an effort to keep workflow smooth, you can rename your clips and sample inside the Browser. This can be an enormous time saver and creative tool when composing in Live. To rename a loop, simply highlight the loop in the Browser (shown in Figure 4.25) and then press keyboard shortcut keys Ctrl+R. You may also do this via the menu by highlighting the loop and selecting Edit → Rename or by right-clicking on the file and choosing Rename from the context menu.

Figure 4.25

By highlighting a file in Live's Browser, you can rename the file. Simply press Ctrl+R and begin typing the new filename. If you change your mind at any point while typing, press Esc (escape).

Develop a system of organizing your loop/sample collection that works for you. It is important that your naming scheme is informative and promotes creativity. For instance, if you name every drum loop sequentially, drumloop1, drumloop2, drumloop3, etc., this may be definitive, but ultimately not inspiring to work with. I try to come up with short titles that give me a brief idea of what I was thinking when I first made a given group of loops. For instance, bigloudDR1 and bigloudDR2 would be a couple of big loud drum loops. This brief but apt description can limit long searches through your mounds of loops and help you to better find the sonic character you are seeking. Also, if you stumble across a sound you are particularly fond of, you can take a look at some others in that same batch.

A trick I like to use is to create folders for each category of samples and MIDI clips I have. I have folders titled Bass, Drums, Keys, Pads, Effects, Vox, etc. Some of these folders, such as the Drums folder, have additional subfolders, such as Snares, Kicks, Hi-Hats, Loops, etc. This makes it a snap to find parts I'm looking for. Organizing these folders from Live's Browsers is also possible—you can drag and drop files between various folders just like you would normally in your operating system. Even the standard Cut, Copy, Paste, and Delete commands are supported here.

The Device Browser

Live's Device Browser (see Figure 4.26) contains Ableton Live's own brew of effects and instruments. Each device type has its own folder in the Browser, one each for instruments, MIDI Effects, and Audio Effects. Each device also has its own folder(s) containing presets. The Device Browser is accessed through the button with the "box" icon at the left edge of the Browser window.

Figure 4.26

Live's Device Browser. To add an effect or instrument, highlight the track you want to receive the device, and then double-click the device in the list.

I will explain each of Live's wonderful devices and how to incorporate VST (which stands for Virtual Studio Technology) effects and instruments in Chapter 8. For now, it's enough to know that when you double-click on one of Live's devices, you'll instantly add (or plug in) an instance of the selected device into the channel you have highlighted.

The Plug-in Browser

Plug-ins have become wildly popular in the last few years as a result of the efficiency that VST and Audio Units plug-ins are capable of delivering (in terms of system performance) over DirectX and Soundmanager plug-ins. One reason VST development is so rampant is that the development information remains free to download from the Steinberg Web site. While this open source philosophy sounds fantastically carefree, be forewarned: Free code can spell danger. There are some incredibly smart, well-intentioned, software developers who are building innovative and interesting audio software (even for free), but with only the smallest of beta test pools. That means you should be wary of any plug-in, regardless of how expensive it is, until you have tried it on your system with your sound card and your Live song in several different situations/combinations. I will recommend some safe plug-in tips in Chapter 8, but for now, recognize that Ableton's "house" plug-ins are capable of handling most common audio situations (and they do an excellent job at it). Unless you are absolutely certain there is a plug-in available that you "need" or have thoroughly tested, don't assume all external plug-ins are trouble free.

All of your VST plug-ins need to be in the VST folder that Live searches at each startup. If you've been following along, you set this folder up during the Preferences chapter. I recommend giving Live its own VST folder and simply copying all VST plug-ins you would like to run in Live into that folder. Any Live-compatible plug-ins in this folder will be visible by clicking on the small "power plug" icon to the left of the Browser window, as shown in Figure 4.27. See Chapter 8 for the rundown on using external plug-ins in Live.

Figure 4.27
The Plug-in Browser will look different for everybody since it reflects your own unique collection of effects and instruments.

Saving Your Work

If you are new to audio software, that is a good thing. This means you come without preconceived notions of how difficult it can be just to organize all the files necessary for a given audio project. If you are a Pro Tools or Logic veteran, you know that calling up last week's session from a CD you burned that night might not be so simple. Live features an enhanced file-saving scheme sure to reduce at least some of the frustrating missing file searches and "which version am I working in?" blues.

Saving the Live Set

Live offers four ways to save project files: Save Live Set, Save Live Set As, Save a Copy, and Save Set Self-Contained. If you are familiar with common computer documents, such as word processor applications, Save and Save As work in exactly the way you'd expect. Save, which can be done by pressing Ctrl+S, saves the document (in this case a Live song file called a *Set*) in its present state, under its present filename. This is the most common way you will save while you are working on new song, especially when you like the results.

Save Live Set As, done via Ctrl+Shift+S, is the command for saving the current song file in its current state under a *different* name and is usually done only when you want to begin a new song or modify an existing song without changing the original version. To do this, select File → Save Live Set As, select the location where you would like to place the file, and type the song's newest name.

If you are modifying a song but would like to preserve the original, or if you would like to make a backup just for safety's sake, File → Save a Copy will automatically add the word copy to the end of your filename.

Saving the Set as Self-Contained

The greatest save method is undoubtedly Save Set Self-Contained. If the very idea of a self-contained file makes you smile, you are no stranger to computers. It is a terrible inconvenience (to put it mildly) to lose a file. Save Set Self-Contained eliminates this problem by guaranteeing that all related audio files, as well as Live's proprietary analysis files (recognizable by the file extension .ASD), are stored in a single folder (called *Sounds*) as a brand spanking new copy of the original. Note: Save Set Self-Contained will *not* make your song into a single file (such as a Word document or text file) but will create a single folder for all of your sound and sound-analysis files. To play/load your song, you will need this folder (automatically labeled *Song Name* Sounds by Live) *and* the Ableton Live Set (.ALS) song file that contains all of your song-specific information.

Sounds great, doesn't it? Imagine never ever having a problem again locating a file, opening a song on a different computer, e-mailing a track to a buddy, or just coming back two days later and not having any trouble recalling your song just as you had left it.

To save your Live set as self-contained, select File → Save Set Self-Contained and then navigate to the folder where you would like to place the song (and all of its related audio files).

SAVING FACE—KEEPING YOUR FILES INTACT

When saving as self-contained, Live saves the song file in the designated folder and then creates a corresponding Sounds folder just beneath it (one folder level down). For instance, if your song is called "Eye of the Tiger," you will notice that Live will create a folder with all of the sounds for your song and automatically title it Eye of the Tiger Sounds.

Even though saving as self-contained does sound all-encompassing, and it does work wonders for keeping all your audio files in the same easy-to-locate folder, there are still some items to keep in mind.

- **VST and AU plug-ins:** While Save Set Self-Contained can be an effective way of keeping all of your audio files together, any external plug-ins (VST and AU) used in a given song will not be saved inside your file. This means that if you transport your song to a different computer or uninstall any effect or instrument plug-in that is present on the song you are saving, the plug-in will be missing upon load-up. If this is a free plug-in, this isn't too big of a problem; simply download a new version from the site where you originally got it; however, a shareware or store-bought plug-in is an entirely different matter—keep your installation CDs and registration numbers in a safe place!

- **Multiple copies:** Long (large) audio files will eat up a lot of hard drive space, so be conscious of how many copies you make when saving as self-contained. This can be a real problem on smaller laptop hard drives or if you are planning on sending a song over the Internet or even setting up FTP downloads for collaboration. I recommend burning any song worth saving to a CD or DVD once you have saved all pertinent files via Save Set Self-Contained.

❀ **Don't forget the song file:** When you are making a backup of your song, you will need to save both the song file *and* its associated folder full of sounds. This fact is critically important when transporting, backing up, or otherwise relocating your Ableton Live song files. Remember that the song file will never be placed into the Sounds folder (created by the Save Set Self-Contained feature), only the sounds, samples, loops and recordings go into the Sounds folder. Repeat: You must have the Live song file *and* the folder full of sounds to open up your complete song.

One other nice thing about Live's Save Set Self-Contained feature is that upon subsequent saves, Live will make sure that all files in the Sounds folder are being used. For instance, if you delete a clip and are no longer using its sound file in the project, Live will notice this and, the next time you save, will ask:

Remove unreferenced sample x, y, and z (whatever your files are called).wav or .aif? This sample is contained in the Sounds folder "C:\your directory\your folder\song name Sounds\" but the Set doesn't use it anymore. Please consider the sample might be accessed from other Sets.

What to answer at this point depends on what you've done since the very moment you began working on this Set. Throughout your creative process in Live, you may be creating new audio files, possibly from recording an external audio input or resampling Live's output. What Live is telling you in the above message is that it can *technically* play this Live Set when you reload it if it deletes the unreferenced samples, which is true. After all, if there are no clips in the Session or Arrangement View, nor samples in Impulse or Simpler that need the audio file in question, the file would never be played even when playing the whole set in its entirety. Live's question may sound like a no-brainer (who would want files taking up space on their hard drive if they won't be used?), but you may still want to keep them. Consider this:

❀ If you deleted a clip from your Session or Arranger *assuming* you could always drag it back from the Browser (that is a normal work method in Live, after all), this is one point where answering "Yes" to the above question will have you screaming "No! No!" later on. Answer "No" and Live will leave the (temporarily) unused audio files where they belong so you'll find them there the next time you need them.

❀ If you've been having a heyday with effects and doing multiple layers of resampling in the process, you've probably achieved a copious assortment of interim audio files—building blocks in your quest for the perfect sound—but are only using the final few in your Set. If you still want to keep these files as a pseudo-Undo, answer "No" to keep them safe.

❀ Multiple takes on vocals and instruments are usually edited into one "super take" and are the result of using small sections of various files. While you may have achieved what is thought to be the perfect edit now, you may want to revisit some of the other takes, possibly to create vocal doubling or a natural chorus (playing nearly identical takes simultaneously). This vault of archived audio will come in handy for that. Answer "no" if you want to keep this stuff on hand.

Saving as self-contained is the best method for saving any Live song. You can try just saving the file and keeping your audio where it is, but my experience and that of many expert audio users is that if you do so, you will inevitably be referring to the section that follows.

Finding Missing Samples

It's going to happen. You can count on it. No, I'm not psychic, but if you work in Live over an appreciable length of time, you will lose a beloved audio file, loop, or sample. This usually happens when files are moved, saved quickly (using the standard quick save, Ctrl+S), or after adding audio from a sample CD or temporary hard drive (and then ejecting/detaching the disc).

Here is what to do (if you are unsure of where you moved the file):

1. Click on your Mac or PC desktop.

2. For Mac OS X, Press +F. For Windows select Start → Search → For Files or Folders.

3. Type the filename you are looking for and make sure you are looking on all possible hard drives.

4. If the file is located, jot down its location so you will be able to direct Live to the correct folder.

5. If you cannot find the file, pray that you have backed up your sounds to CD/DVD and will find it there. If not, well...back to the old drawing board.

Working with Multiple Versions

By now you can guess that I'm going to heartily recommend that you save multiple versions of every song, creation, loop, or other chunk of digital data that is near and dear to your heart. Every time you do this, you feel just a little bit of reassurance that your creative work is safely documented and will not be lost by some idiotic press of a button or some random Bill Gatesian infection, etc.

To do this in the most effective and least confusing manner, set up a folder entitled *Backup*. Copy your files into the Backup folder. Don't change their names or anything else. Sounds simple enough, doesn't it? It is, but many people create elaborate backup filenames that can be hard to remember.

If you have a multiple partition hard drive, make sure to put your Backup folder and files on a different partition (a different drive letter) than the original song and sounds files. Or you may want to back up to a different hard drive altogether. This will ensure the safety of your files if your original partition gets corrupted.

Getting Help

The software world is big on searchable help menus, online help files, and gazillion-page PDF manuals. Between Google.com and online forums (such as Ableton's), the challenge is in the sifting.

The Info View

Are you having trouble locating what you need quickly enough? Once again, Ableton has anticipated the needs of their end user—this time in the form of many methods to seek out help in Live. Built into the very interface of Live is the "Info View," which is a retractable and informative window in the lower-left corner of the Live window that will discuss whatever topic correlates with the control your mouse is hovering over. (See Figure 4.28.) This won't always provide enough information to satisfy the power user you are becoming, but in a pinch or sudden memory lapse, it is the perfect thing to remind you of, "oh yeah, that's what this button is for."

Figure 4.28
The Info View can be hidden or expanded to give you quick bits of pertinent Live wisdom. In this case, the mouse is hovering over a Track Activator.

Feel free to pop this baby open any time you are unsure about a specific element of Live. You can easily hide it again, to protect your reputation, when your friend looks over your shoulder.

Getting Help Online

We all know the Internet holds an amazing amount of random and erroneous content. Finding precisely what you are after can be more elusive than Elvis's ghost. Thankfully, Ableton knows this better than most and remains faithful to its customers by providing the Live user forum and reliable technical support. You can also feel free to drop corporate headquarters a note and tell them what a great job they've done.

All you need to do is click on Live's Help menu, and you will see these options:

❋ **Lessons Table of Contents:** This will open up the Live Lessons View and will present you with a list of all the inclusive interactive tutorials. As with using the Live Sets provided with this book, playing around with Live using real sounds will open your eyes much more quickly than reading about it ever would.

* **Read the Live Manual:** The new manual is in Adobe PDF format and only takes up about five megabytes of hard drive space. Most of the information is expanded upon in this book, but sometimes a point in the right direction may do the trick. Go to the Help menu and choose Read the Live Manual to automatically open the document.

* **Visit Ableton.com:** Ableton's Web site is easy on the eyes and full of neatly organized goodies. If you are looking for some helpful distraction, the Artist page hosts scores of interviews, loops to download, and insightful hardware and setup tips. You'll also notice that Ableton prides itself on acknowledging bugs as they are reported instead of denying their existence. After all, bugs are a part of software, and Ableton's admissions and frequently provided workarounds will tell you that you are not alone with your problem.

* **Join the User Forum:** Ableton Live users are some of the more savvy audio software heads on the planet. Try posting your question and set the option for e-mail notification. (You'll get an e-mail message when someone responds to your post.) Nearly all sensible inquiries are answered, even if they are repeats or misnomers. In fact, once in awhile, real live Ableton employees will jump in on the discussion. Now that's team spirit.

* **Get Support:** Every so often, the user board isn't fast enough, or a problem is just plain weird enough that you really need a direct line to the author. Realize that Ableton, like most specialized software houses, is small, and they may need a couple of days to get back to you.

* **Check for Updates:** How handy is that? Ableton puts a shortcut right to their download section of their Web site so you can check if you have the latest version of Live. For added convenience, Live will automatically enter your serial number into the Web site, saving you the tedium of tracking down the serial number and typing in the string of hexadecimal values.

❋ WHO'S USING LIVE?

Sound Tribe Sector 9

Sound Tribe Sector 9 (www.sts9.com) is a five-piece group from Santa Cruz, California, comprised of Hunter Brown on guitar, Jeffree Lerner on percussion, David Murphy on bass, David Phipps at the keyboards, and Zach Velmer on drums. Many have dubbed the group a "jam band," possibly because their music borrows elements from so many other styles. However, their arrangements and production are a little too well thought out, which pushes the group beyond the genre of jam band into a realm all their own. The band has just released ARTiFACT, their first studio album in five years, and I got a few moments to ask them some questions about Live.

Give me a brief introduction to the band. You have five members—where did you all meet? What are your creative influences? How does Live fit into your process?

We met in Atlanta, Georgia. We're influenced by all things creative, mostly music, people, culture, and life in general. We were drawn to Live by its simplicity of design, ease of use, and the fact we're able to do a lot of things in one place. We use Ableton Live in all of our musical applications: sampling, composing songs, throughout album production, and in our shows. It has become a crucial tool in our music from creation to performance.

How does Live help you maintain the organic feel of your music? Most people would probably assume that incorporating computers and sequencers would make music rigid and sterile. Is this the case?

No, it doesn't have to be. Some rigid music is incredible, so it's just dependent on what you like. In our case, most of our recordings that we arrange and sample from come from ideas written on our instruments or played on a sampler. Whether it's from a chord progression on the piano or guitar or a beat, we maintain a live feel by playing almost all the parts we use. With Live and the right controller, we're able to set up really efficient sample banks with easy hands-on access to each clip in order to best compose, trigger, and perform songs. The endless possibilities of using any sound and doing anything we want with that sound, plus being able to trigger it in a number of ways, is the reason we've been doing things the way we do. As a five-piece band, this adds a priceless sixth member with infinite sounds and instruments at its disposal. We're able to use sequences and samples as actual instruments that don't have to be synched to a clock. That allows for tempo variation and a human feel. It also lends itself to some interesting mistakes!

When you use Live, what kind of computer system do you use? Mac or PC? Laptop or desktop?

We run Live on a Mac. We have laptops and have a desktop in the studio.

What kinds of controllers and interfaces do you use with Live?

The Korg MicroKontrol, Novation X-Station, M-Audio Trigger Finger and Oxygen8, Akai MPD16, Minimoog, a Juno, MS-2000, Digidesign M-Box, Digi002, and a Roland HandSonic.

Do you have any tricks or secrets about Live that you'd like to share with the readers?

I like to make two MIDI Tracks and assign both of them to the same Impulse instrument. I make a beat on one track and then draw custom rolls and fills on the other one, which I then assign to MIDI notes for triggering on the fly. It's like having a roll button for the Impulse.

5 } Making Music in Live

At last, the time has come to begin making music in Live. In this chapter, I'll cover how to analyze and prepare files for use in Live. I will explain the common areas of Clip View and, through practical examples, discover some of the most common ways music is made in Live. I'll also take a look at software configuration and general working methods for the Live musician.

Whether you are playing a popular hotspot or working in the privacy of your own home, the basic Live configuration and performance concepts are the same. Before writing this book, I spent a good amount of time interviewing Live "power-users," the Ableton Live team, and conceptualists Robert Henke and Gerhard Behles. Through these discussions, and my own practice, I have discovered that nearly everybody is using Live just a little bit differently, depending upon their musical style and live performance needs. DJs demand different things out of Live than do producers working in studios. Film and television composers may be looking for different kinds of sounds than a musician playing Live in a band. As you read this chapter, think about how you want to use Live and focus on the areas that make sense for your situation. After all, there is no reason a DJ can't borrow techniques from a film composer and vice versa. As I proceed through the various ways to work in Live, take a minute to try some of the provided examples. As with learning any musical instrument, discovery will lead to inspiration, additional detail will bring delight, and a little practice never hurt, either.

I will warn you now that this is a long chapter—I will be covering a lot of information. You'll find it interesting, though, as each concept I explain will introduce the next. This parallels the way Live's working process is based on a hierarchical structure of principles, starting from small musical pieces up to a finished masterpiece. The basic procedure goes like this:

❋ **Create individual musical parts**: Record bass parts, guitar riffs, keyboard lines, drum grooves, MIDI instruments, or import samples and MIDI sequences. These become *clips*.

❋ **Create song sections**: Arrange the clips side by side in the Session View to make *scenes*. Each scene represents a section of your song, such as intro, verse, chorus, bridge, and outro.

❋ **Record an arrangement:** Live will record your actions in the Session View while you trigger the scenes on the fly to record your song into the Arrangement View.

❋ **Finalize the song:** Edit the arrangement, add effects to the mix, layer additional parts, finalize the automation, and render the song to disk.

Each element of Live's interface is optimized for one of these tasks. You'll see that clips are manipulated in the Clip View, scenes in the Session View, song arrangements in the Arrangement View, and mixes in the Session Mixer and Track Views. This logical approach and use of only one window makes Live a streamlined composition environment. Furthermore, the same tools you use for writing are available for performing—there's a blurry gray line between composing and performing in Live.

You'll notice that the steps above are not numbered. This is because the creation process can always be in flux when using Live. You can record multiple layers of a part in the Arrangement View and bounce the results to a clip in the Session View. You may begin mixing the song as you're composing it. In any case, Live is flexible enough to suit your style.

Working Methods

One of the remarkable things about Live is that no two people use it the same way. Some musicians come to use Live as a quick and flexible multi-track recorder that allows them to explore their own music in deep and original ways. Other artists use Live as a way to integrate their samples and loops quickly into a performance or group environment. Some will use Live for the entire production process—concept to mixdown. DJs like Sasha and Gabriel & Dresden are using Live to play their favorite tracks, as well as to integrate their own material and pre-produced loops. In other words, DJs are producing and remixing full-length tracks on the fly; while producers are acting more and more like DJs all the time by mixing unusual textures, rhythms, and styles into a single track. On that note, one of the most popular users of Live will be remix and dance music producers, who take a pre-produced track, break it down, and rebuild it in another musical style. Let's take a closer look at each of these methods, to understand better each one's perspective and see why Live is the perfect application for each approach.

Using Live to DJ

Today, DJs make music using CDs, MiniDisc players, MP3 players, turntables, and computers. Their artistry involves selecting their own mix of music or musical components (beats, samples, etc.) to entertain, explore, or make something altogether new. Live fits into the DJ world perfectly, as it allows for songs to be synchronized to other tracks and other playback devices. Additional parts, such as beats and basslines, can be made on the fly using MIDI instruments, which also lock perfectly to the beat. Many of the DJs I've talked with use Live in conjunction with turntables, CD players, and other computers. Often, they will spend a good deal of time configuring their songs for use in Live. This can involve editing tracks in a wave editor, mapping any necessary

Warp Markers (see Chapter 6, "The Audio Clip") in Live's Clip View to time-align the track, or merely cropping their favorite portion of a larger track to be used as one in a collection of many time-synced loops. The bottom line is that DJs are benefiting from the flexibility and choices Live offers. DJs can use different parts of the same song looped against one another at the same time or take advantage of multiple tracks (as opposed to being limited to a finite number of turntables, CD players, or mixer channels). Besides, a digital DJ doesn't ever have to worry about wearing out precious vinyl and irreplaceable acetates or scratching a CD surface.

Using Live with a Band

The organic nature of bands may seem like an unfit environment for computers. Every gig has a different energy, and playing to the same old backing track every time could end up sucking the life out of a stage performance. Many bands have a freeform approach that doesn't follow a preset number of bars in a song arrangement. Whatever the case, Live has some exciting news for you: The parts from the computer *can* be different every time and can be placed under full control of the band.

❋ Live performers, especially jazz musicians, may feel that using a sequencer removes a level of freedom that is essential for improvisational music. Many times throughout this book (with more to come), I've referred to Live as a sequencing *instrument*. Live can be played in a live setting, and it leaves the musical arrangement completely under user control. Perhaps your band always practices a song with an 8-bar solo section for your guitarist. When you are playing the show, your guitarist basically "catches on fire," and you all feel that the solo needs to be longer. By having the song arranged as scenes in the Session View, you could extend the solo section by *doing nothing*, thus, allowing the solo section clips to loop, naturally extending the section. You finally trigger the next section once the guitarist signals to move on.

❋ The Tap Tempo features of Live will keep Live playing to the band, rather than the band playing to the sequence. A drummer could assign a trigger pad or footpedal (anything that outputs MIDI) to the Tap Tempo button and could tap out quarter notes from time to time to keep Live in time with the band. Starting a song is also under the drummer's control as he can issue four taps while he counts off the song, resulting in the band and Live starting together.

❋ When playing a gig, it may be necessary for some of the musicians to hear a click track from Live, possibly when the song calls for two bars of silence with everyone (including the computer) then coming in together. Live can provide this by means of its cue and multi-channel output functions (see the following Note).

> ❄ **CLICK TRACK**
>
> A click track is nothing more than a metronome that a band or musician plays along with, just like the one in Live's Control Bar. Usually, the click is piped into the headphones of the person(s) who is recording. By playing along with the click track, the musician performs the musical parts in synch with parts of the track that have been previously recorded. In the studio, click tracks are often replaced by percussive loops, which are less monotonous and generally more musical. This can easily be accomplished with Live by assigning a track with a fitting loop to Cue (see "Audio Tracks and Their Controls" in Chapter 4, "Live Interface Basics").

Multi-Tracking

Crafting songs by multi-tracking can be one of the most rewarding and creative activities a song-writer can take part in. Whether you are a solitary artist composing a demo in your bedroom or a band with limited input channels, multi-track recordings can allow you to add many layers of music to the same piece without erasing previous tracks. In today's age of unlimited audio tracks, you might take for granted the power of layering ideas on top of one another and auditioning different digital arrangements. Live can be a perfect composition tool or arrangement-auditioning tool. I have shown several songwriters Live's ability to easily and musically rearrange a song (whether it was recorded to a click or not). Often, their eyes are wide with disbelief. While Pro Tools, Logic, Cubase, and other multi-track studio applications are powerful, their audio flexibility cannot match Live's instant audio warping ability. In the next few years, watch for your favorite songwriters to be employing Live instead of their ratty old tape decks.

Producing and Remixing Music

Since the beginnings of computer-based music, remix and dance music producers have been the driving force behind many of the industry's most impressive innovations. Of course, "producer" is a loose term that usually refers to any remix artists, consultants working with bands or vocalists, or musicians with a penchant for hard disk recording and editing. Whether they are set up in a fancy studio or holed up in their college dorm room, producers using Live may be the largest and most feature-savvy group of them all. Many producers have already tapped into the exciting prospect of remixing another artist's work, as well as creating new music, when using Live's instant time-stretching and unprecedented sample manipulation ability. Producers want to compose, make music, put together unusual elements, find the "right" hook, etc. Live allows them the creative freedom to stick to the task at hand while keeping the process simple enough to remain focused on the music.

Scoring for Video

They say timing is everything. Nowhere is this more evident than in scoring music for the moving image. Whether you are attempting to add sound effects or mood music or creating a complete soundtrack, Live's ability to stretch audio in sync with MIDI is the perfect tool for the job. As we begin to discuss Live's unique "elastic audio" ability in the next few sections, you will see how

Live is built to make sound behave in ways that were simply not possible before. Film and television music composers often run into problems when trying to synchronize audio and video. For instance, the audio track may need to speed up and then slow down; the music then must reflect this tempo change. Movie and TV music also need to be done quickly, and Live's ability to be played, rather than just programmed, is a huge advantage.

While I have pointed out some of the typical ways creative people like you are making use of Live, I have by no means covered it all. New uses for Live continue to emerge. In fact, you will invent a few of your own. As an example, check out this brief excerpt from an interview with film composer Klaus Badelt (taken from the Ableton Web site).

✳ **FAIR USE**

New ways to use Live are popping up all the time. Here are a couple of ideas by film music maestro Klaus Badelt.

"Ever since Live came out, it changed my life. It enabled me to use our whole library of percussive loops. I'm not talking about loops (only) in the sense of just electronic loops, but all kinds of orchestral or ethnic percussion loops. I'm finally able to use them all very quickly and try them out in tempo. It makes it possible to work much faster, especially when you only have a few days to write a whole score.

"I don't actually use (Live) in the way it was originally intended. I'm playing it from my sequencer. I trigger the program from the other computer as Live runs on its own machine. It holds the library. I drag in the loops I'm using and trigger them from the keyboard. I use the effects in there, but basically submix and then send to the mixer. I basically use it as a synthesizer."

—Klaus Badelt is credited with The Thin Red Line, Mission Impossible 2, Hannibal, Pearl Harbor, Pirates of the Caribbean, *and many other award-winning films. (Taken from www.ableton.com.)*

In the next section, I am going to take a brief but important sidestep to explore the more practical side of Live's interface, Clip View and Track View, as well as several tips for working with loops and samples. Later in the chapter, I will return to the idea of working methods and different approaches for using Live. The combination of both practical knowledge and tried and true examples should put you well on your way to discovering your own particular way of harnessing the power of Live.

Live's Musical Building Blocks: The Clip

Within a musical composition, the parts involved can be broken into smaller pieces, such as "verse 1 bassline," "chorus backing vocals," "intro percussion," or whatever terms you might use. Each of these pieces is suited perfectly for a *clip*—the musical building block in Live. Everything in Live is based on the creation, editing, arrangement, and playing of clips. By having the pieces of your song assembled in clips, you can then arrange the song on the fly and intermix different sections, whether for a live performance or as a means for programming the Arrangement View.

The Clip

Clips are the colored rectangles scattered throughout the Session View (see Figure 5.1a) and the Arrangement View (see Figure 5.1b). Each one plays an audio file or MIDI sequence. Playing clips in the Session View is done by clicking the small "play" triangle at the left side of the clip. Clips in the Arrangement View will be played when the Now Line passes over them.

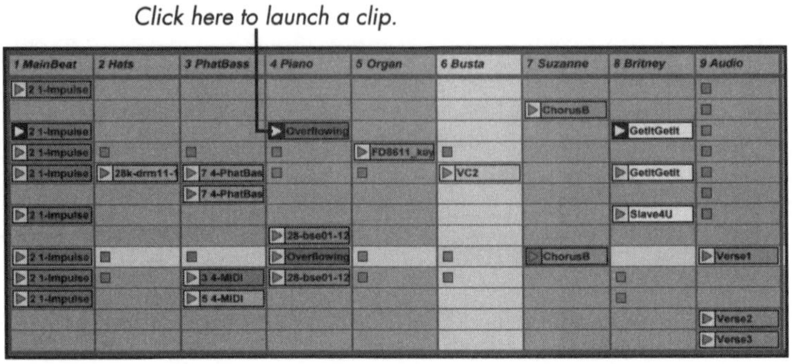

Figure 5.1a

Clips, as they appear in the Session View.

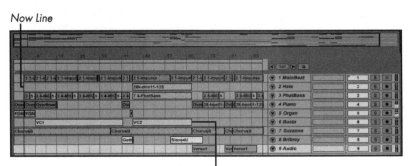

Click here to launch a clip.

Figure 5.1b

Clips in the Arrangement View can be resized to change how long they will play.

Now Line

Click and drag to resize.

Clips can be thought of as small, independent MIDI sequencers and audio samplers that all play in relation to one another. This is similar to pattern-style sequencing, except that the patterns can all be different lengths from one another. This offers the convenience of creating anything from small musical units to larger evolving parts and using them in any combination together.

While a clip can be copied from one place to another, either by copying it from the Session View to the Arrangement View (or vice versa) or by creating multiple instances in both views, each resulting clip is independent from the others, even if they contain the same musical data and share the same name and color. This means that a clip that was recorded into the Session View can have its parameters modified in the Arrangement View, while leaving the original Session View clip intact. This separation will become clearer as you look closer at the Session and Arrangement Views later in this chapter.

What Do Clips Contain?

Clips come in two forms: Audio and MIDI. Audio Clips (see Figure 5.2a) contain references to audio files, while MIDI Clips (see Figure 5.2b) contain MIDI data for playing MIDI instruments (either virtual or hardware instruments).

Figure 5.2a

An Audio Clip plays an audio file on the computer. A graphical representation of the audio can be seen in the Clip View waveform window.

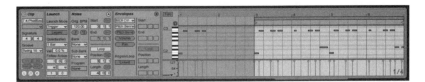

Figure 5.2b

MIDI Clips contain sequences of MIDI notes and data, which can also be seen in the Clip View.

❄ **WHAT AUDIO CLIPS DON'T CONTAIN**

While you can easily think of all the little clip boxes as containing audio loops and such, it should be remembered that the audio file used in those clips is not actually part of the clip or Live Set. A clip merely contains the information necessary for Live to play an audio file from disk—it is a pointer to your sample.

Should that file (sample) become altered by another application, such as a wave editor, each clip that used that file will now play with the same alteration. If you delete the sample that is referenced by a clip, the clip, and any other clips that used that file, won't play any more! See Chapter 4 on how to save your Set as self-contained to keep the audio files you use in a safe location.

Where Do Clips Come From?

Clips are created in two ways: By adding an audio or MIDI file from disk to the Session or Arrangement View and by recording new audio and MIDI performances into Live. When learning the first concepts of Live, you'll more than likely begin with Audio Clips created from audio files on your computer. Live comes with a library of loops for this purpose, and you'll also find sample libraries from companies such as East West, Big Fish Audio, Power FX, M-Audio, and more, to arm you to the teeth with audio loops for musical inspiration. Of course, Live can work with audio files that aren't loops—any audio file (in WAV, AIFF, SDII, MP3, Ogg Vorbis, Ogg FLAC, or FLAC format) on your computer is fair game for manipulation in Live.

What's also great is that new clips can be made by recording audio from external sources. If you've found a drum loop and bass loop that you want to use as the foundation for your song, you can plug in your guitar and record your own riffs on top, which are instantly turned into clips.

The same is true for MIDI Clips. Tracks from MIDI files can be added from File Browsers, or new performances can be recorded directly into the Session or Arrangement. Unlike Audio Clips, the MIDI information in a MIDI Clip is saved in the Live Set file itself. Even MIDI Clips created from MIDI files will be independent from the original files.

Because the methods for recording Audio and MIDI Clips are different, they will be covered separately in the next chapters. What's important to understand at this point is how clips work and how they integrate into the production process in Live. Whether they came from a sample CD, your own voice, a General MIDI file, or from your MIDI controller, both Audio and MIDI Clips behave the same; most importantly, once you have a full understanding of using clips, you'll be able to record better clips yourself.

The Clip View

While there are two distinctly different types of clips in Live (MIDI and Audio), there are a number of behaviors and settings that are common to both types of clips, all of which will be discussed next. The common behaviors of MIDI and Audio Clips help blur the line between audio and MIDI in the Session and Arrangement. After all, when you're performing, you don't really care if a piano part is coming from an audio file or being triggered from a MIDI instrument. When you launch the piano clip, you expect to hear the piano part with nothing else to worry about.

Obviously, your understanding of clips will have a tremendous impact on your ability to use Live. If clips are not set up properly, many of Live's other functions, such as the ability to play multiple clips in sync, will be compromised. The settings determining clip behavior are accessed and edited through the *Clip View* (see Figure 5.3), which appears at the bottom of the Live window whenever you double-click a clip.

Figure 5.3

The Clip View contains multiple sections that can be shown and hidden using the icons at the bottom-left corner of the window. Turn them all on now so that you can see all the options in Clip View.

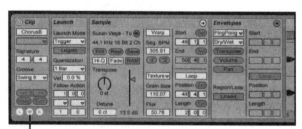

These buttons show and hide the Launch, Sample, and Envelopes windows.

There are different sections within the Clip View that can be accessed with the icons in the lower-left corner of the window. A few of these sections are common to both MIDI and Audio Clips. Those common properties will be explained in this chapter, while the type-specific parameters and features will be explained in detail in their own chapters (see Chapters 6 and 7, "The MIDI Clip").

The sections you'll be concerned with at the moment are the Clip and Launch sections, as well as the Loop settings found in the Sample window (for Audio Clips) or Notes window (MIDI Clips).

Clip Name and Color

The first two settings in the Clip section (see Figure 5.4) are purely cosmetic—they have no impact on the behavior or sound of the clip. The first field is the Clip Name, which can be any name and as many characters as you want. You'll only see about the first nine letters in Session View clips when using the default track width, but you may see more of the name if you widen the track or extend the clip in the Arrangement View.

Figure 5.4

Give your clips useful names, like synth1 or vrs1Vox. You can also give similar clips the same color to help organize your Views. Live 5 also allows you to change the width of tracks in the Session View, giving your clips greater visibility.

Clips are automatically named when they are created (they're also given a color based on your Preferences). If you create a clip by dragging a file in from the Browser, the clip will be named the same as the file. When you record a new clip, it will be given the name of the track it is created in. To help keep multiple takes (recordings) in order, Live tacks a number on in front of the clip (and file) name as each new one is created.

You can change the name of a clip by selecting it in the Session or Arrangement View and clicking the Name field at the top-left corner of the Clip View. New to Live 5 is the added ability to simply click a clip and press Ctrl(⌘)+R. If you forget, you can also right-click the clip, or Ctrl-click on the Mac, to select Rename from the context menu. Using this technique, you'll be able to rename the clip right within the Session and Arrangement Views, speeding things up tremendously.

When changing the name of an Audio Clip, you should be aware that the name of the associated audio file is not changed. If you drag a file from the browser called DnB Loop07 (168 BPM) into the Session View, the resulting clip will have the exact same name. If you change the clip name to something more useful, like MainBeat, the original audio file on your hard drive will still be named DnB Loop07 (168 BPM).

Time Signature

The clip's Time Signature determines the numbering of the grid markers and quantizing grid (discussed separately in Chapters 6 and 7, respectively). It also affects the Launch Quantizing behavior, which I'll explain in a moment.

Groove Template

The Groove section is probably one of the most mind-blowing features you'll ever witness in an audio program. Using Groove Templates and the Global Groove Amount value in the Control Bar, you can add a shuffle or swing feel to the individual clips in your songs. The idea of morphing between straight and swing feels is not new. Many classic drum machines, like Roland's TR-909, have a shuffle control. The shuffle control delays certain beats of a sequence to create a swing or triplet feel—the further the control is turned, the more dramatic the effect.

While a swing control on a drum machine isn't news, swinging audio tracks is unheard of, or should I say, was unheard of. Since Live already has the whole time-stretching thing down pat, it's not really surprising that it can make such a surgical change on the fly to an audio file. After all, if MIDI sequencers just delay certain beats, Live can similarly delay portions of an audio file (using short expansions and compressions of time) to yield the same results. Indeed, Live can swing your audio and MIDI performances in perfect sync with each other.

Choosing your Quantize Template within the Clip View will determine which beats get delayed. The Global Groove Amount (see Figure 5.5) will set the intensity of the shuffle from 0 to 99. For example, the Swing 8 setting is for 1/8-note swings and shuffles. Setting the Global Groove Amount to 50 will cause a straight 1/16-note groove to morph into a 6/8 feel. The Swing 16 setting will take a straight sixteenth feel and delay the even-numbered 1/16 notes, resulting in a nice swing to get everybody dancing. Any clip with Straight selected for the Groove will be impervious to the Global Groove Amount setting. Of course, you don't have to set the Global Groove Amount to 50. Smaller amounts will make the swing less pronounced and less machine-like at the same time. For the swing timing found in most dance music, dial in a Global Groove Amount of 65. Going beyond 65 will give your clip a crazy hip-hop "over-swing" that you'll want to hear for yourself!

❋ ONE OF THESE CLIPS IS DOING ITS OWN THING

While the Global Groove Amount value sets the intensity of the swing applied by Live to your clips, remember that each clip has its own Groove setting. If you're increasing the Global Groove Amount but are getting weird results, be sure that all of the playing clips are set to the same template. If some clips

---

are set to Swing 8, while others are set to Swing 16, the time shifts will not be in sync with each other, which can result in strange polyrhythms (of course, if this is what you're after, don't mind me).

It may seem strange that Ableton didn't just use a global Groove setting; however, by having each clip follow its own Groove settings, it's possible to have part of the song (perhaps clips at the beginning) in Swing 8, while another section of the song (maybe the bridge) is in Swing 16.

The inconspicuous Global Groove Amount.

Figure 5.5
The Global Groove Amount is the tiny, unlabeled number in the left section of the Control Bar. Click and drag, type in a number, or assign it to a MIDI control to change it.

Clip Offset Controls

New to the Live 5 Clip View are the Clip Offset Controls, which are comprised of four buttons in the lower-left corner of the fully opened Clip View. These controls were primarily added to assist DJing with Live, allowing you to nudge the timing of the clip a little earlier or later to make it sync up tighter with the other clips that are playing. Of course, non-DJs will still have a use for this, as just about everybody runs across a clip that's slightly offset from time to time.

Pressing the two arrow buttons (the Nudge buttons) will perform the shift (the clip should be playing when you do this). Each time an arrow is pressed, the start and playback positions of the clip will be altered by an amount determined by the Global Quantize setting (don't confuse this with the clip's Launch Quantization, which will be explained next). If the Global Quantize is set to 1 Bar, the clip's start location will be shifted by 1 bar with every click of the Nudge buttons. If you want to offset by a smaller amount, select a smaller Quantize value. When you offset the clip's start position, an orange dot will appear in the timeline of the Clip View. This orange dot shows the temporary starting location for the clip.

❋ **CHANGES AHEAD**

At the time of this writing, Ableton is experimenting with some other methods for handling the Clip Offset. While the new Clip Transport features in Live 5 allow you to do more things than were possible in previous versions, such as being able to jump to any location within the clip, many old-school Live users have been less than impressed with Live 5's handling of Clip Offset. Most notably, the old Sample Offset Marker has been removed, which many power users previously used as a performance tool. Because Ableton truly listens to their users, you may find that release versions later than 5.0.1 may behave and look differently than described in this book.

Of particular interest is the behavior of the Nudge buttons when a Global Quantize value of None is selected. In this case, clicking the Nudge buttons will offset the clip by extremely tiny increments. This small offset is what you'll use for aligning songs while DJing or bringing loose loops into sync with the rest of your clips.

After you've nudged the clip into alignment, you can click the Keep button. This will move the clip's Start Marker to the new location created with the nudge (the position occupied by the dot). Now, whenever this clip is launched, it will play in sync with the others. If you find that you don't like the amount you nudged the track, click on Revert instead to cancel all nudging you'd performed up to that point.

 THE FIFTH CONTROL

While it looks like the Offset controls are limited to only four buttons, there is a fifth offset control that can be accessed only through MIDI assignment. When you enter the MIDI Map mode Ctrl(⌘)+M, you'll see a tiny box appear between the offset arrow buttons. Click on this box and twist a knob on your MIDI controller. Now you can twist the knob to perform the nudge. I would recommend using an endless encoder knob for this, allowing you to offset the clip over a wide range of time.

Quantize

There are two types of quantizing that can be performed with Live. One method will line up stray notes in a MIDI Clip. This is called *Note Quantization*, which will be explained in Chapter 7. The other method is *Launch Quantization*, which is the topic of this section.

Launch Quantization determines when a clip will start playing or recording after it has been triggered. Proper Launch Quantization settings will ensure that clips will start on time and in sync with each other, even if they are triggered a little early by us sloppy humans. The default setting for this value is set in the Preferences. Most people choose either Global or Bar as the default values.

The available choices for Launch Quantization range from 1/32 notes up to 8 bars and are selected from the dropdown menu shown in Figure 5.6. There are also two additional settings, Global and None, which will cause the clip to follow the Global Quantize setting (in the Control Bar) or ignore quantization, respectively. Any clips set to Bar will only start playing on the downbeat of a measure, even if they were triggered before that. This means that you can click (launch) a number of new clips, but they won't start playing until the next measure. You can therefore launch a new bassline, drum part, and guitar riff halfway through the bar and Live will wait until the downbeat before playing them all.

Figure 5.6
The Quantize settings for a clip.

When you trigger a clip before its Quantize setting will allow it to start, its green "play" triangle (the *fire button* or *play button*) will start to blink, indicating that the clip is standing by to play. Once the beat for the Quantize setting is reached, the play icon will turn solid green and the clip will begin playing. It's at this point that the previous clip playing in the track (if there was one) will be cut off in favor of the new one.

Of course, you may not always want to start a clip on the downbeat of a measure. In these cases, a smaller Quantize setting can be selected. A setting of 1/4 will force a clicked clip to start on the next beat rather than waiting for the bar. Any clip set to None will start playing the instant it is launched.

✳ **BAR LENGTH**

Bar is another term for measure, which is the length determined by the time signature. In the case of 4/4 time, a measure (bar) is four beats long with the 1/4 note equaling one beat. 12/8 is 12 beats long with the 1/8 note equaling one beat. This means that the length of time determined by a Bar Quantize setting is dependent on the time signature.

If the time signature is 3/4 and your Quantize is set to Bar, you'll be able to launch new clips every three beats (each measure is three beats long). When the time signature is 4/4, you'll be able to launch the clips every four beats.

A special condition can arise when you're using clips with time signatures different than the Live Set. If your project is set to 4/4, but your clip has a time signature of 3/4, a setting of Bar in the Clip View will allow the clip to launch every three beats. This means that while 4/4 clips will launch on the downbeat, the 3/4 clip will launch on bar 1, beat 1; bar 1, beat 4; bar 2, beat 3; and bar 3, beat 2. In this case, the length of the Bar setting is determined by the clip's time signature.

If, on the other hand, the 3/4 clip has its Quantize set to Global, the Quantize setting in the Control Bar will be used. If this value is set to Bar, the 3/4 clip will launch every four beats (on the downbeat with the other 4/4 clips) because the length of the Global Bar setting is determined by the project's time signature (4/4 in this case).

Launch Controls

To add more creative possibilities when using clips, Ableton has given you four Launch modes (see Figure 5.7) to add extra control to your performances. In all of my descriptions so far, launching a clip has caused it to start playing (once the quantize time has been reached), at which point it continues to play indefinitely (if looped) or through its entirety (when unlooped). This is the default behavior for clips, and one that makes quite a lot of sense, but times may arise when you want a different level of control.

Figure 5.7
Launch modes: Choose, but
choose wisely...

Launch modes will change not only the clip's playback state when the clip is launched (either by clicking with the mouse or pressing an assigned key or MIDI note), but will also determine the action taken (if any) when the mouse or key is released. The four available Launch modes are as follows:

❋ **Trigger:** The most common Launch mode for use in most performance situations is Live's Trigger mode. Each time you fire a clip, it will launch. Once a clip is launched and playing, you will be able to stop its playback only by pressing one of the Clip Stop buttons located in the same track. This mode ignores the up-tick (release) of the mouse button, computer keyboard key, or MIDI note. Each clip can be fired as rapidly as the Quantization will allow, and each time the clip is fired, it will restart the clip from the beginning, even if it was already playing.

❋ **Gate:** When triggering a clip in Gate mode, you will only hear the sound for as long as your mouse or keyboard key is depressed. This is an excellent setting for dropping in snippets of sound without playing the entire clip. In short, holding your left mouse button (or MIDI/computer-keyboard key) down will continuously play the clip until released.

- ❄ **Toggle**: With Toggle mode engaged, the fire button basically turns into an "on/off" switch for the clip. If you "launch" a clip that is playing, it will stop. Launch the stopped clip, and it will begin playing. This also works at the scene level if you trigger a scene with clips set in Toggle mode. Each time you trigger the scene, clips that are playing will stop, and stopped clips will start. It is this functionality that makes Toggle mode my personal favorite since each Clip Launch button can now have two functions: start *and* stop.

- ❄ **Repeat**: Repeat mode is a way of re-triggering a clip by holding down the mouse or assigned key/MIDI note. Any time the mouse or key is held, the clip will continuously restart itself at the rate specified by the clip's Quantize setting. If the setting is 1/4, holding the mouse/key will cause only the first beat of the clip to play over and over again. When the mouse or key is released, the clip will play through its entirety like normal. This mode can create fun stutter effects, but should be used sparingly. This mode is probably not a good choice for default behavior.

Velocity

Just below the Quantization box is the Clip Velocity scale setting (see Figure 5.8). This value only works for clips launched by MIDI. It uses the incoming velocity level of the MIDI note to set the playback volume of the clip. At 0%, the velocity has no effect on clip playback volume—it plays at its original level. At 100%, the clip will respond as a velocity sensitive clip. For settings in between, lower velocities will have less of an attenuating (quieting) effect. This works for both Audio and MIDI Clips.

Figure 5.8
Velocity scaling based on the MIDI velocity of the clip's trigger note.

Follow Actions

Live's Follow Actions allow an amazing level of automation to be achieved within the Session View. Basically, using Follow Actions, you can set rules by which one clip can launch another. Any particular clip can launch clips above and below it, replay itself, or even stop itself—all based on odds and a time period that you can program. I like to think of Follow Actions as a virtual "finger" that presses Clip Launch buttons for me. While that may not sound that impressive yet, it's just another example of Ableton's ingenuity in bringing simple, generalized tools to its users that can unleash the imagination. In fact, Follow Actions open up so many creative possibilities that you'll find a long list of possible applications listed in Chapter 14, "Live 5 Power."

Follow Actions work on groups of clips, which are clips arranged above and below one another in the same track (see Figure 5.9). If an empty Clip Slot is between two clips, they are in separate groups. Follow Actions will allow automatic triggering of other clips in the group and cannot be used to trigger clips in different groups or tracks.

Figure 5.9

The track on the left features one group of clips, while the track on the right has two groups.

The time and conditions for a Follow Action are set in the three sections at the bottom of the clip's Launch window (see Figure 5.10). The first section, the Follow Action Time, determines how long the clip plays before it performs the Follow Action. If the time is set to 2.0.0, the clip will play for two bars before "clicking" on another clip.

Figure 5.10

These parameters determine the Follow Action behavior of the clip.

Instead of just doing the same action over and over again, Ableton gives you the ability to create two different possible Follow Action scenarios for each clip. Live will randomly choose between the two actions selected in the dropdown menus in Figure 5.11 (one on the left and the other on the right). The possible Follow Actions and their effects are:

❋ **No Action:** The empty menu selection refers to No Action, and it is the default Action for all new clips. In fact, clips are always performing Follow Actions; however, with No Action selected in both menus, Live will never trigger any other clip.

❋ **Stop:** This action will stop the clip. This can be used to make a one-bar loop play for eight bars every time you trigger it, for example.

❋ **Play Again:** Essentially re-triggers the clip just as if you'd clicked on it again with the mouse.

❋ **Previous/Next:** These options will trigger the clip either above or below the current one. If the clip at the top of a group triggers the Play Previous action, it will "wrap around" and trigger the bottom clip of the group and vice versa.

❄ **First/Last:** These will trigger the top or bottom clip in a group, no matter how many clips are in the group. If the top clip in a group triggers the Play First action, it will re-trigger itself.

❄ **Play Any:** This Action will trigger a randomly chosen clip from the group. It is possible for Live to re-trigger the same clip with this option.

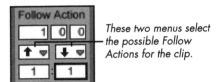

These two menus select the possible Follow Actions for the clip.

Figure 5.11
The left Follow Action will trigger the clip above this one, while the right Follow Action will trigger the clip below this one.

Which Follow Action Live chooses to perform is based on the odds set in the numerical boxes below each Follow Action. By default, the odds are 1:0, meaning that the Follow Action in the left menu will always be performed. Odds of 0:1 will cause the right Follow Action to always be performed. Odds of 1:1 will give you a 50-50 chance of either the left or right Follow Action being performed. You can put in any values you like, such as 2:3 or 1:200.

❄ **PLAYING THE ODDS**

It should be noted that odds are calculated fresh every time a Follow Action is performed. If you have a clip with Follow Action odds of 1:1 and Live chose the left Action the first time, it does not mean that Live will choose the right Action the next time. Just as it is possible to roll the same number on a die time after time, it is quite possible for Live to choose the left Follow Action five times in a row, even with 1:1 odds.

When looking at the Follow Action choices, some of you may be scratching your heads at the Play Clip Again selection. What is the point of this one? To explain, let's look at a practical example.

You have two drum loops; one is the standard beat while the second is a variation of the first. You really like the standard beat, but from time to time, you want the variation thrown in to keep things from getting too repetitive. Consider Figures 5.12a and 5.12b. Both may appear to be the proper setups for this situation, but one has a flaw.

Figure 5.12a
Here, if the left Follow Action is chosen, the clip will loop indefinitely.

Figure 5.12b

In this example, when the left Follow Action is performed, it will relaunch this clip, causing the Follow Action to be performed again after the specified time.

Follow Actions are performed only after the specified time has passed since triggering the clip. Thus, in the case of Figure 5.12a, after one bar, the clip performs the Follow Action. If the option on the left, "do nothing," is chosen, no Follow Action will be performed, and the clip will keep playing (infinitely if set to loop). In Figure 5.12b, when the left option is performed, the clip will be retriggered, causing the Follow Action time to start counting down again. After the specified time, odds will be calculated and the appropriate Follow Action will be performed. By using Play Clip Again, you have basically looped the Follow Action.

> ❄ **QUANTIZE STILL RULES**
>
> When triggering other clips with Follow Actions, the target clip will still follow its Launch Quantize setting. If a clip has a Follow Action time of one beat and triggers a clip with a Bar Quantize setting, the new clip will still wait for the downbeat before playing. If the clip is set to Global or None, the clip will begin playing immediately when the Follow Action triggers it.

Tempo Settings

A clip's tempo is used to determine the timing grid for the clip. This timing grid affects the Grid Markers and Warp Markers in an Audio Clip and the playback speed of a MIDI Clip. This tempo is also what Live uses to keep clips in sync with each other (if Live doesn't know the original tempo, it won't know the proper amount to speed up or slow down the clip to match the rest of your project).

The tempo settings work a little differently in the Audio and MIDI Clip Views. For one, tempo is only available in Audio Clips (see Figure 5.13) when the Warp feature (see next chapter) is engaged. If Warp is off, Live will simply play the audio at its original speed and perform no time-stretching on the clip, therefore its original tempo is irrelevant; however, with it engaged, Live will be able to warp the audio as necessary to match the tempo of the Set. Secondly, the clip's tempo and the position of the Grid and Warp Markers are related. As you make timing adjustments with the Warp Markers, you may notice the Seg BPM change slightly (or drastically) to compensate for the change in file playback speed. I will delve into this further in Chapter 6.

Figure 5.13
A clip's tempo setting is crucial to the proper operation of Live. Without the proper value here, the clip will not match the speed of other clips in the project.

MIDI Clips do not have Warp Markers, so the original tempo is solely controlled by the user. When a new MIDI Clip is created, it will take on the current tempo of the Live Set. This is usually sufficient, and you probably won't need to change it; however, if you do (perhaps an imported MIDI Clip is playing at the wrong speed), changing the Tempo value will scale all of the MIDI data in the clip accordingly to make it play back faster or slower.

Below the Tempo value are two icons. The left "divide by 2" and right "multiply by 2" buttons will quickly double or halve the playback speed of both Audio and MIDI Clips. If the original tempo was 120 BPM, pressing the "divide by 2" button will result in a new tempo of 60 BPM. If the tempo of the Live Set is 120, Live will play the clip twice as fast to bring the 60 BPM up to 120 BPM. The "multiply by 2" button will effectively cut playback speed in half. Reset will erase all Warp Markers and return the clip to default values. I find myself using this all the time when writing drum and bass tracks, which are usually in the 170 BPM range. When I drag in a drum loop at that tempo, Live often mistakes the loop as being a half-tempo loop, thus importing at 85 BPM. A simple click of the *2 button brings the tempo of the drum loop back up to 170 BPM.

Clip Start/End

The size of the data in a clip versus the size of the portion that you actually choose to use can be vastly different. In other words, you may have a four-bar clip but decide to use only the first bar of the part. You may have a five-minute song from which you isolate a great drum fill in the middle. Clip Start/End defines the area and length of the sound that is played within a clip. In the example in Figure 5.14, I am using only a portion of a larger sample. To do this, I constrained the length of the loop by setting the Clip Start and End Markers (shown as markers with little triangular flags) to the locations I wanted. Note: You can make these adjustments while you are listening, or even recording, in Live.

Remember, Live is streaming audio files from disk, as opposed to playing them from RAM. This means that using 10 seconds of a 10-minute file is no different than using all 10 seconds of a 10-second file. Don't worry about chopping off the ends of an audio file that you're not using—those sections are never loaded into RAM (like a sampler would do), and you may want to use

Figure 5.14

You can define a smaller section of a clip to use by setting the Clip Start and End Markers.

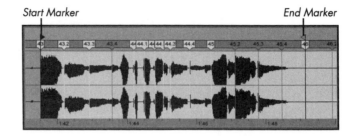

those parts in another song in the future. Moving the Start and End Markers around your desired section is all that's necessary.

Loop Settings

Looping of clips has changed significantly in Live 5. Previous to version 5, the Loop Start and End points were the same as the clip's Start and End points. Now, in Live 5, the use of Start, End, and Loop Markers in a clip matches the use of the same markers in the Arrangement View. This is excellent news because it means that you can now start a clip playing from one point in time, have it enter a loop at another point in time, and then proceed beyond the loop to the end of the clip.

While the clip's Start and End Markers are shown as small left- and right-facing triangles, the Loop region is shown with a pair of connected markers (see Figure 5.15). If a clip's Loop button is on, the clip's play position will jump to the Loop Start every time it reaches the Loop End Marker. When Loop is turned off, the clip will be allowed to pass the Loop End Marker and play until it reaches the Clip End Marker.

Figure 5.15

There are four markers in a clip now: Clip Start, Loop Start, Loop End, and Clip End.

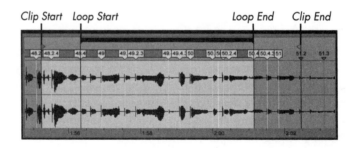

This new loop methodology means you can have a clip that plays normally through its first three bars before it begins to loop infinitely on its last bar (see Figure 5.16). I find this to be particularly useful with drum loops that begin with crash cymbals. Instead of looping the entire clip, resulting in the crash cymbal sounding every time the clip repeats, I can specify a loop area after the crash cymbal. This way, I'll hear the crash the first time I trigger the clip, but I won't hear it again until I relaunch the clip.

The clip starts here...   ...and loops here.

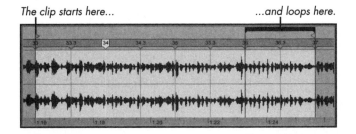

Figure 5.16
You can now loop a sub-section of a clip.

As you'll discover, this new loop procedure is quite handy when DJing. This is because Live not only lets you set these loop points by hand within the Clip View, but because Live also lets you define these loop points on the fly by pressing the Loop Position Set and Loop Length Set buttons (see Figure 5.17) while the clip is playing. This makes the clip behave like a DJ CD player where you can instantly grab perfect loops out of songs or other types of clips.

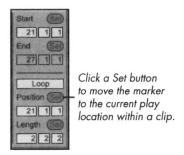

Click a Set button
to move the marker
to the current play
location within a clip.

Figure 5.17
The Set buttons will cause the associated markers to jump to the current play position.

RED DIGITS

When loading new clips, you may find that some of the numbers in the Loop Settings display are red. This means that the number being displayed is not exact. For example, if a clip length is listed as 1.4.4 with the last 4 in red, it means that the clip is not exactly that length and may actually be 1.4.45 beats long. Since Live cannot display values smaller than the sub-beats, the digits show up red when there are further numbers that can't be seen. Resetting the Warp Markers (next chapter) will fix these red digits by defining the exact size and timing of the clip.

Loop Start Offset

Like a sentence, the point from which you start a musical phrase can make a huge impact on getting your meaning across (so says my editor). Because the clip's Start and End points are now completely independent of the clip's Loop points, it is entirely possible to start a looped clip from a point other than the beginning. If you place the clip's Start Marker after the Loop Start, the clip will begin playing in the middle of the loop when launched. In fact, it's possible to set the clip's

Start Marker to a position after the Loop End Marker. In this case, the clip will never loop (even if the Loop is turned on) because the clip starts from a location after the Loop End Marker (see Figure 5.18).

Figure 5.18
Even though this clip is set to loop, it won't because it begins playing after the Loop Marker.

The clip begins after the loop points.

❄ **CLIP TRANSPORT**

Another new feature in Live 5 is the ability to start a clip playing from any point you choose without having to move the Start Marker. To do this, simply hover your mouse over the waveform or MIDI data of the clip until it turns into a speaker icon (this will happen in the lower-half of the waveform). When you click the waveform, the clip (as well as everything else in Live) will begin playing from this location. This is great when you're Warp Marking a long track and need to check different places quickly. You can also use this as a performance technique that allows you to jump to different locations in the clip at will while all the other clips in your Set play normally. Best of all, the jumps are based on the Global Quantize setting, so if you wanted to go immediately to the "break-down" in a Warp-Marked track, with Clip Transport and the proper Global Quantization setting, it's easier than ever.

Editing Multiple Clips

New to Live 5 is the ability to edit multiple clips simultaneously. In previous versions of Live, selecting two or more clips would make the Clip View disappear. Now, only part of the Clip View will be hidden from view. The controls that remain are those that can be changed for all of the selected clips.

Some of the options, such as Clip Name and Clip Color, will be set identically for all clips—if you change the Clip Name to "Hot Drums," all of the selected clips will take on the same name. This same behavior is true for nearly all of the available fields when editing multiple clips.

There are a couple of settings, however, that aren't copied identically to all of the clips. These would be the Transpose, Detune, Velocity, and Volume settings. Changing these controls will change all of the selected clips by the same relative amount. For example, if the Transpose setting of one clip is -2 and another is +3, turning up the Transpose knob 2 ticks while selecting both clips will result in the first clip being set to 0 while the second clip is set to +5. This is extremely handy because you can select multiple clips and transpose them all at once while maintaining their relative tunings. If you decide to change the key of your song or need to create a section that is modulated a full step higher, you can do it in a snap.

> ✳ **WHAT THE ****?**
>
> When selecting multiple clips, you may see that some of the fields contain an asterisk (*) instead of a value. This means that this value is different for each of the clips selected. (This is more than likely what the Clip Name and Clip Color fields look like, as most clips have different names and colors.) When you change one of these settings to a specific value, all of the selected clips will inherit the same value and the asterisk will disappear.

The Track

Moving up the totem pole from the clip is the *track*. The track is a pathway for signals, audio or MIDI, to enter a channel of the Session Mixer and is also a place to arrange related clips for playback. There are four different types of tracks in Live (see Figure 5.19), and each one serves a specific purpose in the way audio flows through your Live project.

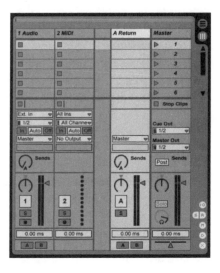

Figure 5.19
The Session View with one of each type of track.

The Audio Track

An Audio Track (the leftmost track shown in Figure 5.19) is where you will place Audio Clips so they can be routed through effects and fed into the Session Mixer. As I've mentioned before, only one clip can be playing at any time on a track, therefore it is wise to place similar clips that won't need to play simultaneously on the same track. For example, "Verse Gtr" and "Chorus Gtr" are two guitar parts from different sections of the song. They won't be played at the same time, so putting them on the same track makes sense. You can trigger the verse guitar part, and it will play until you trigger the chorus part. This gives you instant control of the arrangement since you can switch between the verse and chorus parts with a click of the mouse (or push of a button, if you've assigned external control).

To create a new Audio Track, choose Insert Audio Track from Live's Insert menu. You can also press Ctrl(⌘)+T for the same results. Double-clicking an Audio Track will display its Track View. It is here that you'll place plug-in effects for processing the clips as they're fed to the Session Mixer (Chapter 8, "Using Effects and Instruments," explains the use of effects in Live).

The MIDI Track

A MIDI Track is the same as an Audio Track, except it holds MIDI Clips, MIDI Effects, and virtual instruments. When you create a MIDI Track (Insert → Insert MIDI Track or Ctrl(⌘)+Shift+T), it will output MIDI information, which can't be fed into the Session Mixer directly. Instead of seeing the normal volume and pan controls in the Mixer, you'll only see a status meter. These MIDI Tracks can send their data to external devices, such as sound modules, or to other MIDI Tracks using the Input/Output Routing section.

Double-clicking a MIDI Track displays its Track View. MIDI Effects can be added to this view for performing operations on the incoming MIDI data. More importantly, virtual instruments, such as Live's built-in Simpler, Impulse, and Operator, can be placed on the track to convert the incoming MIDI data to audio. Once an instrument has successfully been added, you'll see that the MIDI Track now has audio controls in the Session Mixer. This essentially turns the MIDI Track into a hybrid MIDI/Audio Track, one that functions as MIDI from track input through the Clip Slots and into the Track View, but functions as an Audio Track from instrument output through the Session Mixer. This means Audio Effects can be added to the Track View any place to the right of the virtual instrument.

The Return Track

A Return Track does not hold any clips, audio or MIDI, but can host Audio Effects. Each Return Track is fed by a mix of the Send knobs corresponding to the Return Track (see Figure 5.20). As you'll discover in Chapter 8, the Return Tracks allow you to add additional effects to multiple tracks without overly taxing your CPU.

By default, there are two Return Tracks in a new Live Set. You can add more, up to 12, by choosing Insert → Insert Return Track from Live's menu, or by pressing Ctrl(⌘)+Alt+T on your computer keyboard.

The Master Track

The final track, the Master Track, is created automatically with every new Live Set and cannot be deleted. This track does not feed into the Session Mixer. Instead, the Session Mixer outputs its

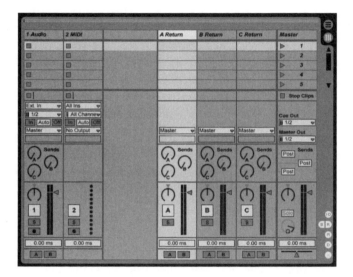

Figure 5.20
The Return Track has a corresponding Send knob in each audio channel of the Session Mixer. Here we have three Send knobs for three Return Tracks.

audio into this track to give you one last chance to add effects and adjust output volume and position.

The Master Track has its own Track View, and this is a fitting place for master compression or EQ to put the final touches on your mix (see Chapter 8). Also, the Master Track will not hold clips but instead houses the Scene Launchers, which are explained in a moment.

Track Freeze

Here's a lifesaver new to Live 5. The Track Freeze function will help you manage your CPU load by "freezing" tracks such that they can still be launched but don't require all their processing to be performed. Live does this by rendering the clips on the track through all its instruments, effects, or whatever else is on the track and placing these clips back onto the track. To do this, simply right-click or Ctrl+click the name of the track you want to freeze and select Freeze Track from the context menu. You'll have to wait a moment while Live processes all the clips through the tracks effects—longer clips will obviously make this process take longer. When finished, the track will turn an ice-blue color. Now, when you launch one of these frozen clips, you'll be playing an audio file from disk as opposed to the CPU-intensive instruments and plug-ins that were running before.

What's so great about this is that, after rendering the new clips, Live automatically disables all the plug-ins on the track, thus freeing up valuable CPU resources. It does not, however, delete or remove these plug-ins—they merely lie dormant.

So what's the catch? Saving CPU must come at some sort of cost? Indeed, it does, but a manageable one. Since Live has rendered the clips into temporary Audio Clips, you can no longer make any real-time tweaks of your sounds. The only thing you can do is launch the various clips in the track, which is still pretty cool because you keep real-time control of the song arrangement even when the tracks are frozen. Additionally, you will still be able to alter the mixing controls on frozen tracks, such as Volume, Mute, Pan, Solo, and In/Out routing.

If you find that you do need to make a tweak to the sound, you can unfreeze the track (again, right-click or Ctrl+click the track and select Unfreeze Track), at which point Live will discard all of the temporary Audio Clips and will re-enable all of the plug-ins on the track. You can now use the track as normal. When you've completed your tweaks, you can re-freeze.

This means you can make more parts in your song than would normally be possible by running everything in real-time. Furthermore, it means slower computers now have the ability to create more complex compositions, using sounds from instruments and effects that normally wouldn't be able to run simultaneously.

The Session

You'll quickly find the Session View to be the most spontaneous section of Live. It is here that tracks are arranged side-by-side and broken into tiny cells called *Clip Slots*. This Clip Slot Grid (see Figure 5.20) becomes a huge organizer for our musical ideas (all nicely encapsulated in clips) where you can begin to create the structure of your songs, as well as perform live arrangements.

> ### CLIP STOP BUTTONS
>
> In Figure 5.21, you'll see that only some of the empty Clip Slots have small squares in them. These are the Clip Stop buttons. If you click or trigger one of these buttons, it will stop the clip playing on that track. The clip will stop according to the Global Quantize setting.
>
> Removing Clip Stop buttons from a scene will leave any playing clips on the track untouched when the scene is launched (no new clip will start, and any playing clip will continue). You can toggle a Clip Stop button on and off by selecting it (or a group of them) with the mouse and pressing Ctrl(⌘)+E.

Adding Clips to the Session

Adding new clips to the Session is as easy as dragging a file from the Browser into one of the Clip Slots. Audio files are dragged into the Clip Slots of Audio Tracks and MIDI files into the Clip Slots of MIDI Tracks. You can also grab multiple samples from the Browser (hold Shift to select an area or Ctrl (⌘) to select individual files) and add them as a group to the Session View. By default, the clips will be created on the same track. In fact, you'll see transparent versions of the clips as you drag them into the Session. To have Live arrange the samples in the same scene, press and hold Ctrl (⌘). You'll see the transparent clips change their arrangement into a horizontal fashion, and you can then choose their final destination.

Clip Stop button

You can also drag parts from the Browser and drop them onto empty areas of the Session View (where there are no tracks). When you do this, Live will automatically create the appropriate type of track and will place the new clip there.

New clips can also be created directly in the Session by recording your performances, either audio recordings or MIDI recordings. Recording new clips is covered in the Recording sections of Chapters 6 and 7.

Drag-and-Drop Techniques

Clips can be added, moved, and duplicated in the Session View using a variety of key and mouse combinations. A clip already on the grid can be moved to other slots just by clicking and dragging it and then releasing the mouse button once the clip is over the desired location. A group of clips can be moved by first selecting the area of clips you want to move and then dragging the group to a new location in the grid. Groups can be selected by dragging an area around the clips with the mouse. If there isn't any room around the clips, you can click one corner of your desired area (selecting the clip) and then click the other corner while holding the Shift key. By defining the corners of the area you want, all clips within that area will be selected.

You can also duplicate a clip by selecting it (click once); then drag the new copy to the desired location while holding the Ctrl (Option) key. By holding the Ctrl (Option) key when you click and drag, the original clip will stay in its original location. This is the same as selecting a clip, choosing Edit → Copy from the menu, clicking the destination, and choosing Edit → Paste. This duplicating technique also works with groups of clips like above.

Editing Commands

The clips in the Session View (and Arrangement View, for that matter) all respond to the standard Cut, Copy, Paste, and Delete editing commands. You can select a group of clips, choose Cut Ctrl(⌘)+X to remove them and then paste them Ctrl(⌘)+V in a new location. You can also copy Ctrl(⌘)+C clips and paste new versions elsewhere in the Session. If you merely want to create a new copy of some clip to be moved later, you can use Duplicate Ctrl(⌘)+D to instantly create a copy of your clips below the originals. Of course, you can always select clips and press Delete to erase them.

Using Scenes

Scenes are horizontal rows of clips in the Session View that can be triggered all at once, meaning that several clips can be triggered with a single action. Musical arrangements in Live often work best if you think of your music as starting in scene 1 (the top row) and then progressing downward, scene by scene (row by row). In other words, scene 1 may be an intro section, scene 2 may be a verse, scene 3 may be a chorus, and so on. Of course, don't get caught up in the idea that your song has to work this way—you can set up and skip scenes in any manner you see fit. As you read on, this concept will begin to make sense.

Notice that in Live's Session View, the Scene Launcher is located just to the right of the Clip Slot Grid. By pressing the sideways triangles in the Scene Launch strip (under the Master Track column), called *Fire buttons* in Live, you can launch simultaneous playback for all clips in the given scene. If there are any Clip Stop buttons in the scene, they will stop any clip in their track. Fire buttons prove useful when composing live, on the fly arrangements, during which you may want to jump from one song section to the next and then back again. Figure 5.22 shows a single scene (row) in Live's Session View.

Click here to launch all clips in this scene.

Figure 5.22

Scenes can be used as song sections, such as the verse, chorus, or bridge.

> ❄ **TWO SCENES ARE BETTER THAN ONE**
>
> One of my favorite shortcuts is the one for duplicating scenes. This command will insert a new scene directly below the scene you are working in and copy all present loops—a huge timesaver! To do this, press Ctrl(⌘)+Shift+D. By using this technique, it is easy to build basic song progressions for a more varied sounding musical composition. Incidentally, you can duplicate the contents of a single Clip Slot by pressing Ctrl(⌘)+D.

Different Live users will explore their own creative ways to use Live's interface. For the laptop DJ, scenes may represent complete songs or pieces of music (as opposed to short loops), in which one Clip Slot could contain a clip that is really an entire song. In this instance, a "scene" change is more like swapping vinyl than moving to a new part of the song. Back in Figure 5.21, you can see eight Clip Slots in a single row, all playing a separate clip at the same time. These all happen to introduce the section of the song known as "Act II." These new clips are launched with the simple click of the "Act II" Scene Launcher.

INSERT SCENE

To insert an additional scene (row) in Session View, or to insert a scene at a given point, select the scene above the desired location where you would like the new scene to appear and press Ctrl(⌘)+I. Additional scenes can also be added by choosing Edit → Insert Scene. If you create a new scene in the wrong place, see the "Moving Scenes" Tip.

MOVING SCENES

To move a scene, simply grab the scene's title with the mouse and drag it up or down to the preferred location. All clips in the scene will be included in the move.

It is worth repeating that triggering any clip or Clip Stop button will halt the playback of any other clip on the same track. Figure 5.23a shows an example of eight clips in a column, while Figure 5.23b shows eight clips in a row. Note: In Figure 5.23a, you can play only one of the clips at a time, while in Figure 5.23b you can play all eight at once.

Figure 5.23a
Eight clips in a column, aka track. Each track is a channel in Live's virtual mixer.

The fact that a track can play only one clip at a time, rather than being a limitation, is actually a tool that can be used to your advantage in a couple of different ways. For instance, by using variations of the same drum loop—each in its own Clip Slot, stacked in the same track—you can

Figure 5.23b

Each row can house whole musical sections, new song directions, or merely a slight modification in the piece currently playing. Many Live users think of their songs from top to bottom, advancing their song as they move down the grid, one row at a time.

make more realistic-sounding, or at least more interesting, drum fills, "breakbeats," and rhythmic turnarounds. This is also a great method for organizing other instrument tracks that change parts when moving from scene to scene (such as two different bass guitar loops: one for the verse, the other for the chorus). By dedicating a single track for variant clips of one particular instrument (one track for drums, one for bass, one for piano, etc.), you will create a more common mixer setup, one that will feel more like an actual recording studio.

CHANNEL STRIP

Live's Session Mixer approximates its analog cousin in a couple of important ways. For starters, any mix, panning, or effect settings on a given channel will be applied to any sound on that channel. If you plan carefully, you can take advantage of this fact by keeping similar instruments on the same track. For instance, if you apply an EQ to Track 1 and boost the highs, all highs on all clips on this channel will be boosted. As you move from scene to scene, verse to chorus, the settings remain the same. You will see in later chapters that Live's Arrangement View allows you to automate effects, toggle them on and off in the middle of a song, etc.

You can therefore set up Live's Session Mixer to resemble an analog studio mixer: Track 1 is designated for drums, Track 2 is designated for guitar, etc. The difference is that you will have several drum clips vertically aligned on the same track in each scene. Here is a more complete song (see Figure 5.24). Notice how the same loop is copied multiple times on each track (in multiple scenes).

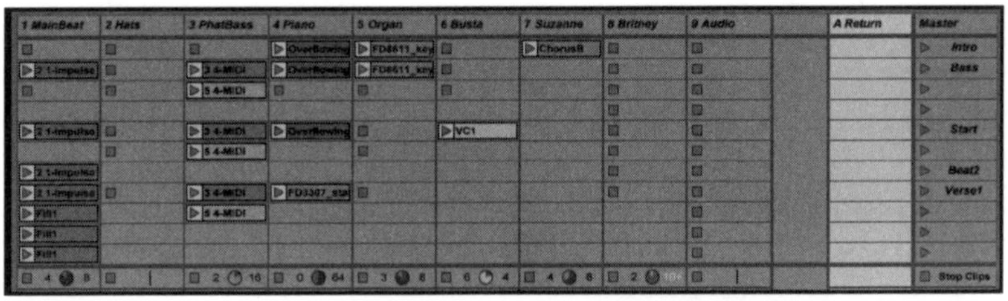

Figure 5.24
This more complete-looking Clip Slot Grid shows how a more developed song might work. You will move through the song sections by clicking the scenes, which are named in the Master column. As you can see, you don't need to use every row—scenes can skip rows if you like.

❊ **RAM TOUGH**

All of these copied loops will not strain your CPU more than the one instance of the loop playing. Live "knows" that the clips all reference the same file for playback.

In order to move downward easily, row-by-row, you can take advantage of the Scene Launcher in the Session View. Scenes can be triggered by pressing one of the Fire buttons in the Scene Launch vertical strip (with mouse, computer keyboard, or MIDI keyboard) on the right-most side of Live's Clip Slot Grid (see Figure 5.25). You can also trigger a scene by pressing the Enter (Return) key so long as the scene number/name is highlighted. Changing the highlighted scenes can be done with the arrow keys and then triggered again with the Enter (PC) or Return (Mac) key. Live also features a Preferences setting (see Chapter 3, "Getting Live Up and Running") that will automatically advance the scene highlight down to the next scene every time the Enter key is pressed. Note: If you select another Clip Slot or parameter on the mixer, you will need to highlight the scene again to begin triggering with the Enter/Return key.

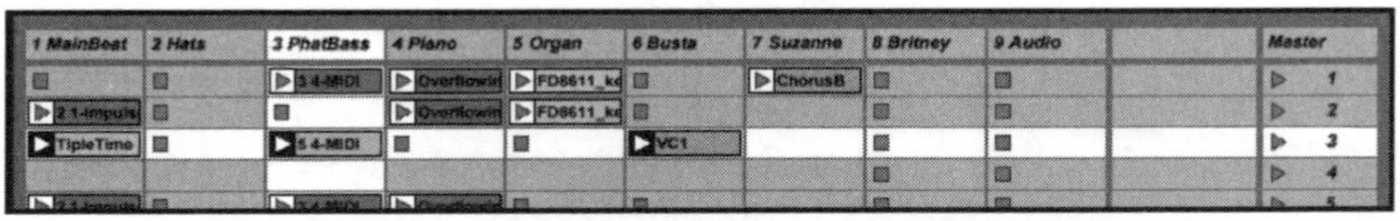

Figure 5.25
Live's Scene Launch strip (titled Master) appears to be just another column in the grid, yet these are the triggers for firing multiple clips at once. Here, scene 3 is triggering three loops.

Capturing Scenes

When experimenting with random combinations of clips in the Session View, you'll come across combinations that work well together. You can press Ctrl(⌘)+SHIFT+I, or select Insert → Capture and Insert Scene, to create a new scene that is populated with the currently playing clips. You can quickly build a collection of potential scenes this way that you can experiment with to build a song arrangement.

Naming Scenes

Scenes can be named and renamed as many times as you like (the default name is simply a number). Many Live users label their scenes by song section, such as "verse," "chorus," "bridge," or "breakdown," in order to remind them of what section they are triggering. To rename a scene, click on its current name or number, press Ctrl(⌘)+R, or choose Edit → Rename; then type in whatever you like. Press Enter, or the Return key, to accept the new name or Esc (escape) to leave it as it was.

Programming Scene Tempos

From time to time, you may want to make instantaneous jumps to different tempos while in the Session View. By naming a scene using a special convention, you can cause Live to change tempo when the scene is triggered. To switch the tempo to 85 BPM, name the scene "85 bpm" and launch it. The scene can be empty; you don't need to trigger any clips when you launch this scene if you merely want to change tempos. You can remove all the Clip Stop buttons (select them and press Ctrl⌘+E) so that none of your clips are stopped.

One instance where programming scene tempos is particularly helpful is when organizing a large batch of clips into a Set so that a single Live Set contains multiple songs. One group of scenes may belong to one song at a given tempo while another group of scenes represents a different song and tempo and so on.

MIDI and Computer Keyboard Control

There sure is a lot of mouse clicking going on in Live. Thankfully, you can offload a lot of these tasks to a much more intuitive interface, such as your MIDI keyboard or your computer's keyboard. Once you get Live under external control, you'll really be able to feel the musical power at your fingertips.

Controlling Live from external devices is called *Remote Control*. Before you start, select your desired control devices in the Remote Control section of the MIDI/Sync Preferences pane (Chapter 3). Live will remember these settings, but loading Live without one of your devices connected will require you to re-select it when it's available again.

First, click the MIDI Assignment button in the upper-right corner of the Live window or press Ctrl (⌘)+M (see Figure 5.26). You'll see a bunch of blue squares and rectangles appear above Live's Clip Slot Grid, Session Mixer, Effects, and a variety of other parameters, such as Tempo and Groove in the Control Bar.

Click here to enable MIDI mapping.

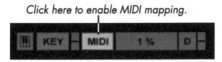

Figure 5.26
Clicking the MIDI Assign-
ment button exposes the
MIDI layer where control
can be assigned to ele-
ments of Live.

The superimposed blue squares indicate controls that can have a MIDI message assigned to them. If you click on one of your clips in the Clip Slot Grid and press a key on your MIDI keyboard, you'll see a white box appear in that Clip Slot showing the MIDI channel and note assigned to that slot. Clicking the MIDI Assignment button again will exit Assignment mode and return Live to normal. Now, when you press the assigned key on your MIDI keyboard, the clip will launch, just as if you'd clicked it with the mouse.

You can also assign knobs and sliders on a MIDI controller to the knobs and sliders you see on Live's screen. If you like, you can assign a knob to control a slider and vice versa—whichever suits your style. To assign MIDI controllers, press the MIDI Assignment button, click on the dial or fader you want to control, and then twist or move the control you want to use. Exit MIDI Assignment mode, and you'll be ready to go.

 WITH THE PUSH OF A KNOB

Live will allow you to assign MIDI knobs and sliders to its buttons, as well as assign MIDI buttons to its sliders and knobs. In the first case, the button in Live will turn on when your MIDI control passes 64. It will switch off when you move the control back under 64. If you assign a MIDI button or key to a slider or knob, pressing the button or key will make the slider or knob toggle back and forth between its lowest and highest settings.

Just to the left of the MIDI Assignment button is the Keyboard Assignment button. This works the same way as the MIDI button, except it assigns Live's controls to keys on your computer keyboard instead of the keys on your synthesizer or other MIDI control device. Press Key (or Ctrl⌘+K) and orange highlight boxes will appear. Click and press a key to assign; then exit Key mode.

 MIN/MAX

New to Live 5 is the ability to constrain the movement of MIDI knobs to a smaller range of values. Normally, the relationship between a MIDI knob and a knob in Live is 1-to-1. This means the knob on-screen will follow the same exact movements of the associated MIDI knob.

This can prove troublesome from time to time, however, if you only wish to make minute changes to a parameter. For example, if you assign a MIDI control to the volume of the track, you may not want the track ever to pass a certain volume because it would overpower your mix. To prevent this, you can assign minimum and maximum values to a control while making a MIDI assignment. After you've clicked on the knob while in MIDI Map mode, you'll see two number boxes at the bottom of the screen. Here, type in the minimum and maximum volumes you desire. When you leave MIDI Assignment mode and attempt to crank up the volume of the track using the MIDI control, you'll find that the volume only goes up to your maximum value when the MIDI control is moved to its maximum position.

For even greater creativity, Live will allow you to place a higher number in the Minimum field and a lower number in the Maximum field. This will essentially switch the polarity of the MIDI control, where turning up the MIDI control makes the value of the control in Live turn down, or vice versa.

Also note that these minimum and maximum values only affect the way in which a MIDI knob or slider controls a value in Live. If you use your mouse on the Live control, you'll still have full range of motion.

Key and MIDI assignments are saved in each Live Set, so every song can have a different control scheme. If you find yourself always making common assignments, such as buttons for the transport, you can assign them and save them as part of your Live template (see Chapter 3).

WHO'S YOUR RELATIVE?

When assigning knobs to control Live's on-screen dials, you may use a MIDI controller that features endless knobs, also known as *rotary encoders*. These knobs are unique in that they will spin around and around without stopping like a normal potentiometer would.

Rotary encoders transmit a special form of MIDI message known as *relative control*. Instead of transmitting an exact value like the mod wheel on a keyboard, they simply transmit how far they've been turned and in what direction.

Unfortunately, there is no standard in the MIDI specification for relative control, so many different schemes have popped up from various manufacturers. Live does, however, read a variety of different relative control schemes.

When you assign a control to a slider or a knob, a menu will appear at the bottom of the Live window. It will be set to Absolute, but you can change it to one of the relative schemes listed. If you don't know what scheme your device uses, you'll have to experiment.

The Arrangement

Even though I've been touting Live's unique on-the-fly arranging style possible in the Session View, you still have the Arrangement View to consider. I've hinted a few times at what the Arrangement View does and how it shares channels on the Session Mixer with the Session View, but how does the Arrangement View augment your compositional workflow in Live? Some of you may think that the Arrangement View is a step in the opposite direction from Live's real-time capabilities; however, because of the unique interrelationship between the Session and Arrangement Views, you'll find the Arrangement View is just as creative a space to work in as the Session View, and it can be used to enhance a live performance.

LOOK BOTH WAYS

You can zoom and scroll through the Arrangement View using the same method as navigating the waveform display of the Clip View.

Anytime your mouse turns into a magnifying glass, you can click and drag to change your view: Dragging up and down changes the zoom setting, while dragging left and right pans the view.

You can also use the condensed Overview, located at the top of the Arrangement View, to locate sections of your arrangement. You can drag the left and right edges of the Overview box to choose the area you want to view.

What Is an Arrangement?

Briefly, an arrangement is a predetermined playback scheme of clips and mix automation (to be explained in a moment). The Arrangement View (see Figure 5.27) has horizontal tracks (unlike the vertical track layout of the Session View), and clips are placed in these tracks so they can be played in order from left to right. The Arrangement View is almost exactly like the timeline views of other sequencer packages such as ProTools, Logic, Cubase, etc. For those with experience in those programs, the Arrangement View will be instantly familiar.

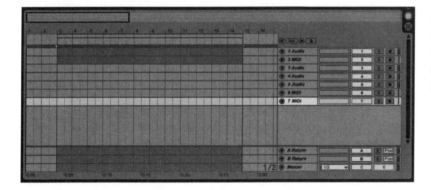

Figure 5.27
The Arrangement View is where you can start putting the arrangement of your song into stone.

Just like other sequencer programs, the Arrangement View has a *Now Line* (the thin vertical line that moves from left to right when Live is running) that shows the current playback location of the arrangement. When you press the Play button in Live's Control Bar, it will start the arrangement running. In fact, *anytime* Live is running, even when just playing clips in the Session View, the arrangement will be running as well.

Controlling where you'd like to begin playback within the Arrangement, as well as starting and stopping it, is handled a little differently in Live 5 than its previous versions. First, when starting Live's transport, the Arrangement will start playing from the beginning of the song. If you want to start from a different position, click anywhere in the Arrangement to place the Start Marker (see Figure 5.28). Now, when you start the transport, Live will begin playing from the Start Marker. If you press Stop and then press Play (or if you press the spacebar once to stop, followed by another press to start again), the Arrangement will restart from the Start Marker. If you double-click Stop, the Start Marker will be removed, and the Arrangement will play from the beginning. If you want to have the Arrangement restart from the point where you stopped it, you'll need to hold down Shift while you press the spacebar. The Shift + spacebar command means "continue" instead of "start."

Figure 5.28
The Start Marker is signified by the small orange
triangle at the top of the
Arrangement View.

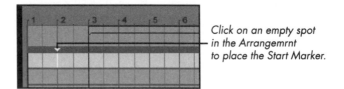

Click on an empty spot in the Arrangemrnt to place the Start Marker.

Another method for changing the start location of the Arrangement is to type in a new start time in the Control Bar. Also, if you click on a clip in the Arrangement, the Arrangement will start playing from the beginning of that clip the next time you start the transport.

The final method for controlling the Arrangement transport involves hovering your mouse in the marker lane of the Arrangement (see Figure 5.29). When your mouse turns into a speaker icon, you can click, and Live will immediately begin playing from this location. You can even do this while the transport is already running to jump to a different position in the Arrangement.

Figure 5.29
Click in this lane to make
the Arrangement jump to
that location.

Click in this area to jump to different places in the Arrangement.

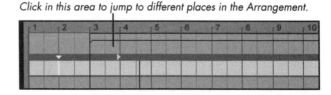

Recording from the Session into the Arrangement

Because the Session and Arrangement Views are so closely related, it's possible to program the Arrangement by recording your performance from the Session View. With the Session View open, press the Arrangement Record button in the Control Bar and then perform your song as usual. When you're finished, press Stop and take a look at the Arrangement View (press Tab). It will now be filled with an arrangement of clips (see Figure 5.30). Press Play, and the Arrangement will begin to play. You'll hear your entire performance played back for you exactly as you recorded it, including all control movements, such as tempo changes, volume adjustments, and effect tweaks. Easy!

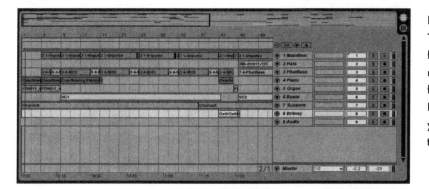

Figure 5.30
The Arrangement View is filled with clips after you record your performance from the Session View. Pressing Play will play back your performances just like the original.

❈ **BACK TO ARRANGEMENT**

Since the Session and Arrangement Views share the same channels in the Session Mixer, it is possible to override what has been programmed into the Arrangement by launching clips in the Session. These newly launched clips will play in place of what is programmed into the Arrangement. When this happens, the Back to Arrangement button (see Figure 5.31) will light up red. Clicking this button (turning it back to gray) will stop any clips playing in the Session View and will re-engage the tracks in the Arrangement. If you're working on an Arrangement and find you're hearing something different than what you see in the Arrangement View, check this button and be sure it's gray.

In the case of an empty Arrangement View, *anything* you do in the Session View will cause the Back to Arrangement button to light. This is because you're hearing something different from the Arrangement, which is silence. You'll see that if you click the Back to Arrangement button in this situation, all of your clips will stop in order to "play" the silence programmed into the Arrangement.

If you find you like a different selection of clips in the Session View better that what you'd programmed into the Arrangement, you can press the Arrangement Record button, and the Session clips will begin replacing the contents of their Arrangement tracks. This is just another way Live makes it easy to experiment and capture our ideas quickly without stopping the flow of music.

Adding Clips to the Arrangement

While recording from the Session View is one way of quickly filling the Arrangement View with clips, you can create new clips manually by using the same methods employed in the Session View. You can either drag files from your Browser to create new clips, or you can record new clips from external sources.

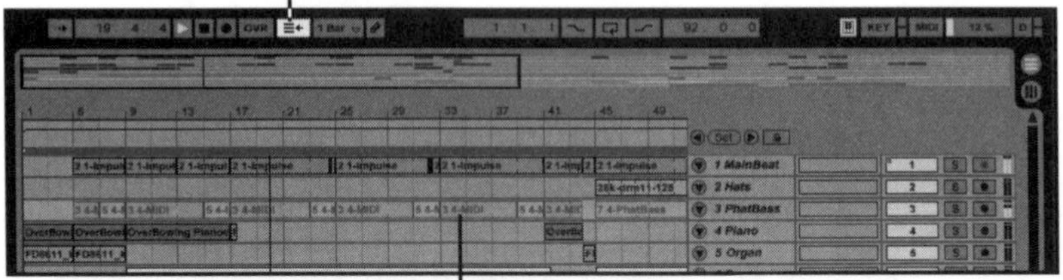

Figure 5.31
You can see that the Back to Arrangement button is lit. You can also see that Track 3 of the Arrangement is not playing because the track is slightly transparent. Clicking on the Back to Arrangement button will make Track 3 solid again so you can hear it.

Back to Arrangement

This track is being overridden by something in Track 3 of the Session View

Drag a file from the Browser into an Arrangement track. *Voila!* A new clip appears. This is exactly like dragging a file into one of the Clip Slots in the Session View. You can double-click this clip to see its Clip View where you can make all of your adjustments just like in the Session View. Indeed, clips in the Session View and Arrangement View are identical. One does not have more functions than the other; however, one thing you can do with an Arrangement clip is determine its play length. When a clip is added from a file, it will appear as only one repetition of the file (i.e., a one-bar drum loop will appear as a clip that is one bar long). By clicking and dragging the right edge of the clip, you can lengthen it, which will cause the clip to repeat as it's played. This will only work for clips with Loop engaged. If your clip is not extending past a certain point, check the Clip View and make sure Loop is enabled.

Editing the Arrangement
By editing the contents of the Arrangement, you can fix mistakes you may have made while recording your performance. Perhaps you launched a clip a bar early when recording from the Session View. Maybe you coughed during the middle of a vocal take. You can remedy these mishaps using the techniques explained below.

You can also use the tools of the Arrangement View as a step in the creative process as well. The meticulous editing and manipulation that can be achieved at this level can be used as a stylistic element of your music. In fact, the Arrangement View is often used as a "cutting table" for assembling new clips for use in the Session View. Beats can be spliced together and combined into new clips, or multiple vocal takes can be assembled into one perfect take.

Cut, Copy, Paste, Duplicate, Delete
The standard Cut, Copy, Paste, Duplicate, and Delete commands work as expected in the Arrangement View. Copy Ctrl(⌘)+C will copy the selected clip(s) to the computer's "clipboard," which is a temporary memory location for items being copied. You can then place a copy of the clip(s) at a new location on the timeline by first clicking the destination location for them in the

desired track. A flashing red line will appear, indicating where the new clip(s) will be added. Use Paste Ctrl(⌘)+V to copy the clip(s) from the clipboard to this new location. The clip(s) will still be in memory, so you can paste additional copies anywhere you like. The clip(s) will remain in the clipboard until replaced by other ones, or until you quit Live.

The Cut command Ctrl(⌘)+X works like the Copy command, except that it removes the selected clip(s) when copying to the clipboard. You can then use Paste to place the clip(s) to a new location in the Arrangement. Duplicate Ctrl(⌘)+D will simply take the selected clip(s) and make a new copy directly to the right of the selection. This is handy for repeating a section. If you simply want to remove a clip or clips without copying to the clipboard, select the clip(s) and press the Delete key.

Dragging Techniques

You can move a clip or group of clips from one location in the Arrangement to another by simply clicking the middle of the clip and dragging it to a new location. Select a group of clips and click-drag one to move the whole group. You can even drag the clip(s) to a different track if you want. Furthermore, you can change the length of a clip by moving your mouse to the right end of the clip. When your mouse turns into a bracket (it looks like "]"), click and drag the clip to your desired length. You'll be able to extend the clip beyond its original length only if the Loop button for the clip is on.

Using Copy and Paste, explained above, to create multiple clips is a technique that you will probably use a lot. Because of this, Live gives us a simple way to copy clips without using the multiple keycommands. If you click on a clip while holding the Ctrl (Option) button on your keyboard, you can drag the clip to a new location and release the mouse button. A new copy of the clip will be made while the original stays in place.

Splitting Clips

You can break a clip into smaller clips using the Split function. Perhaps your guitarist recorded the verse part and the chorus part all in one take. You'd like to split that clip so you'll have one containing the verse part and another containing the chorus. To do this, you'll need to view the contents of the clip in the Arrangement View by pressing the Track Unfold button, which looks like a downward-pointing triangle just before the Track Name. Once the track is unfolded, you can find the point at which you want to split the clip. Click (with the Pencil tool turned off) the location for your cut and press Ctrl(⌘)+E. The clip will be split into two clips (see Figure 5.32). These new clips are completely independent of one another, meaning they can have their own unique Transpose, Gain, Warp, Loop, and Envelopes.

Because the resulting clips are all independent, you can modify each clip at will. If you want your clip to change from Beats mode to Tones mode at a certain point in the song, Split the clip and set the second clip to Tones mode. If you want to do a slew of effects on tiny slices of audio, Split the clip into tiny pieces and retune each one with different Transpose, Gain, and Loop settings.

Figure 5.32
Just click and split to break clips into smaller ones for independent editing.

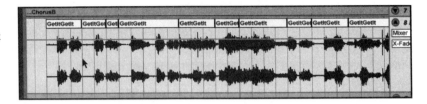

Consolidating Clips

After breaking clips into smaller ones for editing purposes, you can rejoin the clips into one clip for easier use. Select the clips that you want to join and select Consolidate from the Edit menu, or press Ctrl(⌘)+J. Live will quickly render a new clip containing all the parts you had selected (see Figure 5.33).

Figure 5.33
Consolidating all the "micro edits" from the previous figure gives us one single clip to work with.

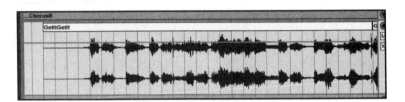

When Live consolidates a clip, it is creating a new audio file on your hard drive. This new file is what Live will use when playing the new clip. The pieces that were used to assemble the new clip are removed from the Arrangement View. If these audio files are not used anywhere else in the Live Set (either in the Session or Arrangement View), Live will ask if you want to delete them when you save or exit. If you know you'll never use those smaller clips again, go ahead and delete them; however, if you plan to assemble some more clips from the same pieces in the future, you'll want to keep them on hand.

Another good use for the Consolidate command is to trim a larger file down to just the section you actually want to use. This isn't necessary to do since Live is streaming audio from your hard drive, but I find that it can be a good way to clean up files on your hard drive. For example, let's say you record a 10-minute vocal recording but decide that only five seconds of the entire take are worth using. In the Arrangement View, simply select the five-second region of the clip that you would like to keep and then consolidate that portion of the clip. After you delete the larger portions of the clip from the Arrangement, Live will ask if you would like to delete these files since they are no longer in use.

Cut, Paste, Duplicate, Delete, and Insert Time

While copying and manipulating clips are achieved with the Cut, Copy, Paste, and Delete functions, you can use the Cut Time, Duplicate Time, Delete Time, and Insert Silence commands to make broad edits to the whole Arrangement. When using these commands, it is only necessary to select (by click-dragging) the area of time you want to manipulate. These commands work on all tracks simultaneously, selected or not.

The Cut Time command Ctrl(⌘)+SHIFT+X works like the regular Cut command, except that it cuts a section of the Arrangement away and stores it to the clipboard. An eight-bar chorus can be chopped to four by selecting the last four bars and choosing Cut Time. You can place the cut time in a new location, if you wish, by clicking the desired insert point in the Arrangement and selecting Paste Time (Ctrl⌘+SHIFT+V).

Duplicate Time (Ctrl⌘+SHIFT+D) works the opposite of Cut Time: Extend an eight-bar chorus to 16 bars by selecting the first eight bars and using Duplicate Time. The selected time is duplicated and inserted directly to the right of the original area. Delete Time will remove a section from the Arrangement without copying it to the clipboard.

Insert Silence Ctrl(⌘)+I will insert an amount of silence where you click-drag an area. Selecting the first two bars of an Arrangement and executing Insert Silence will shift the entire Arrangement to the right by two bars, thus giving you two bars of silence before the song starts.

Automation

Along with the clips in the Arrangement are tracks of *automation*. Automation is programmed or recorded movements for controls in Live's Session Mixer, devices, and plug-ins. For example, if you want to fade out the volume at the end of your song, you would *automate* the Master Volume so Live will perform the fade every time the end of the song is reached.

Just about every parameter in Live can be automated. One rule of thumb: If you can control a parameter by MIDI Remote, you can automate it in the Arrangement View. If you're wondering if a particular control can be automated, click the MIDI Assignment button in the upper-right corner of the Live window. If your control gains a superimposed blue square, it can be automated.

Recording Automation

The simplest and most intuitive means of automating your Arrangement is by recording the desired control movements in real-time while the song plays. For example, to program the fade-out I explained above, you'd activate the Arrangement Record button in the Control Bar and press Play. When the song reaches the point you want to start fading out, start moving the Master Volume control downward. You can either click and drag with the mouse or use an external MIDI controller—both methods will be recorded the same way. When you're done with the fade, press Stop. You'll now see a red dot in the Master Volume control. This red dot appears over any control that has recorded automation in the Arrangement. You can go back and repeat the recording process as many times as you like to build your automation in layers. For instance, you can control the volume of a synth part on the first pass and then make another recording to automate the pan. Live will perform the previous pass of volume automation while you make the new recording of pan movements.

Viewing Automation

You can see the automation for a track by first unfolding the track (click the downward-pointing triangle next to the track's name) and then selecting the parameter you want to view. The parameter is selected by using the two menus in the track: The first menu selects the general category of automation, such as Mixer, Send, or any plug-in that is loaded onto the track. The second menu selects a specific parameter from the general category selected. For example, to see the track's volume automation, you'd select Mixer in the first menu and Volume in the second menu. If an Auto Filter effect is loaded onto the track, you can view its Cutoff automation by choosing Auto Filter and Cutoff Freq.

Automation is displayed as a line graph superimposed over the clip's data (see Figure 5.34). The meaning of the line shown in the automation track is determined by the parameter being controlled. In the case of level controls such as Volume or Send, volumes increase as the line moves toward the top of the track. For other controls, such as Pan, a line in the center of the track represents a center pan position. Lower values cause the pan to move left, while higher values cause the pan to move right.

Figure 5.34
You can see the final fade-out of the song represented by the downward-sloping line in the Master Track of the Arrangement.

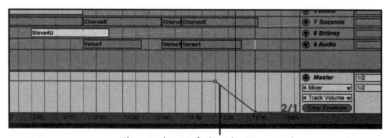

This envelope is fading the Master Volume.

Editing Automation

You can change the shape of the automation graph by using two techniques. When the Pencil tool is off (toggle the Pencil tool with Ctrl⌘+B), you will be using the *Breakpoint Editor* (see Figure 5.35). The automation will be displayed as lines with little circles at each "elbow," known as a *breakpoints*. You can click and drag these breakpoints to new locations to reshape the graph. You can double-click a circle to delete it, or you can double-click a line to create a new breakpoint in that location. You can also select an area of the automation graph (click and drag the desired area) and then move a whole section of automation around with the mouse.

❄ **MAINTAIN CTRL**

When editing automation curves, you'll frequently be making only small modifications, such as increasing volume by 1dB or making a mute happen a little sooner. By holding the Ctrl (⌘) key while moving points of the graph, your mouse movements will be minimized, allowing you to make subtle and specific changes with ease.

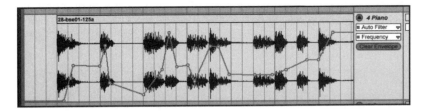

Figure 5.35
The Breakpoint Editor is great for creating smooth ramps between values.

By switching the Pencil tool on, you will be working with Live's Step Editor. By drawing with the Pencil in the automation graph, you'll create flat "steps" that are each the same width as the current Quantize setting (see Figure 5.36). This will allow you to create tempo-synched automation effects, such as volume gates or timed effect sends. The Pencil will overwrite any ramps that may have been made in the Breakpoint mode in favor of its flat step style.

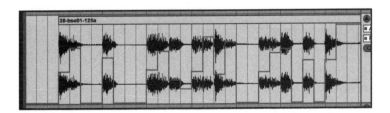

Figure 5.36
Using the Pencil tool, you can create tempo-synched steps in your automation graphs.

❋ **QUANTIZE KEYS**

You can change the value used for the quantize grid with these keystrokes:

Ctrl (⌘) + 1: Makes the quantize units smaller.
Ctrl (⌘) + 2: Makes the quantize units larger.
Ctrl (⌘) + 3: Toggles triplet mode on and off.
Ctrl (⌘) + 4: Toggles the quantize grid on and off. When the grid is off, you will be able to draw values anywhere.

Locators

Locators are a welcome addition to the Live Arrangement View. In simple terms, Locators can be used to mark different sections in an Arrangement, such as flagging the start of a verse, chorus, or bridge. However, Ableton did not stop there—they have given you the ability to jump around to different Locators in your Arrangement, thus allowing you to perform custom arrangements right within the Arrangement View.

Creating Locators

Creating a Locator is about as simple as it gets: Click the Set button in the upper-right corner of the Arrangement at the point where you want to drop the marker (see Figure 5.37). Like all things in Live, the Locator will be placed at the nearest bar automatically. You can create as many Locators as you'd like by pressing Set every time you need another Locator.

Figure 5.37

Every time you click Set, a new Locator will be created at the current play position.

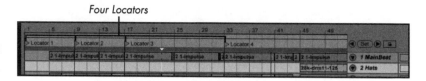

Four Locators

Moving and Renaming Locators

Each time you make a Locator, it will be given the name "Locator" followed by a number. To give the Locator a more useful name, right-click (Ctrl+click for Mac) on the Locator and choose Rename. You can also click the Locator to select it, and then press Ctrl(⌘)+R to rename.

You can also change the location of Locators after you've made them by clicking the Locator and dragging it to a new location in the timeline. If you want to remove the Locator, click it to select it and then press Delete.

Jumping to Locators

The best part about Locators, however, is the ability to jump between them seamlessly while the Arrangement is playing. All you have to do is click on a Locator (it will begin to flash green) and the Now Line will jump to that location on the next downbeat. You can also use the two arrow buttons to the left and right of the Set button to jump to the previous or next Locator.

Ableton really hit the mark, though, by allowing you to assign MIDI notes and computer keys to these Locators. Just like all other assignments in Live, enter the MIDI or Key Map mode (either Ctrl⌘+M or Ctrl⌘+K, respectively), click on the desired Locator, and then press the MIDI note or key for assignment. When you exit the Map mode, you'll be able to jump to the Locator by pressing the MIDI note or key.

This means that the Arrangement is now nearly as flexible as the Session View in that you can repeat sections of the song at will or jump to other areas as you see fit. Even the most complex of Arrangements is now opened up for your experimentation, thanks to these Locators.

Loop/Region Markers

The Loop/Region Markers, found in the Arrangement View, serve two purposes. They function as loop points, and they also mark the start and stop points for automatic recording.

Creating a Loop

You can loop, or repeat a section of the Arrangement, by placing the Region Markers around the desired area and clicking on the Loop button in the Control Bar (see Figure 5.38). You can start the Arrangement anywhere you like, but if playback ever reaches the right Region Marker, playback will jump back to the position of the left Region Marker. If you switch the Loop button off while the Now Line is between the Region Markers, playback won't be affected except that the song will continue after it reaches the right marker instead of repeating.

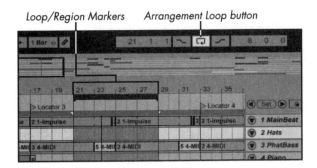

Loop/Region Markers   Arrangement Loop button

Figure 5.38
Playback will loop repeatedly between the Region Markers while the Loop button is engaged.

You can move the loop region while the Arrangement is playing. Playback will not follow the Region Markers as you move them, but the song will begin to loop again once it reaches the new location of the right marker. This means you can loop one section and then just move the markers to the new location once all the desired repetitions are played. After Live reaches the next region, it loops. This can help you to zero in on problem spots, automate mix settings, or merely give a section a good listen. If you happen to move the loop region to a position to the left of the Now Line, playback will continue until the end of the song. The Now Line will not jump backward to the location of the markers.

❊ **INSTANT LOOP**

Often, you'll be working on settings for a particular clip in your Arrangement and will therefore want to loop the entire Arrangement around this clip. To do so, simply click the clip(s) to select; then press Ctrl (⌘)+L, which is the shortcut for Loop Selection. This will automatically move the Loop/Region Markers to the nearest bar markers surrounding the selected clip(s).

Auto-Punch

In the next two chapters, I will discuss recording audio and MIDI into Live. The process is nearly identical for both Audio and MIDI Clips. I will cover how to record both into the Session View and the Arrangement View.

However, when recording to the Arrangement View, Live can be set so that it automatically begins recording at a specified point in the Arrangement and stops at another. This is the second function of the Region Markers. This auto-recording function is referred to as *auto-punching* and is controlled by the two buttons on either side of the Loop button (see Figure 5.39). Punching-in is when you start recording; punching-out is when you stop. Normally, punching is used when you need to replace only a section of a recording. Perhaps your bassist put down an amazing take but happened to rush an intricate part leading into the last chorus. You can use the auto-punch feature to begin recording right where the bad part is and then stop right before the chorus.

Figure 5.39
I've placed the Region Markers around the bar right before the last chorus. With the Punch-In and Punch-Out buttons, I can start playback before the bad measure, but Live will only record the section in between the markers.

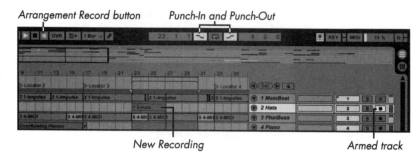

Arrangement Record button   Punch-In and Punch-Out

New Recording   Armed track

As you can see, the Punch-In and Punch-Out buttons can be set independently. This means you can have Live start recording at a specific point and continue until you stop it. This will allow you to punch-in partway through the song and record until the end. You can also have Live stop recording in the same spot every time. This is helpful when trying to nail down a tricky intro part.

Render to Disk

After you have finished your Live song—and you are liking the way it sounds—it is time to get it out of your computer, burned to CD, and onto the streets. Although Live cannot burn CDs, it can help you prepare your song with an intermediary step called *rendering*. Figure 5.40a shows the Render to Disk menu that appears any time you press the Render command Ctrl(⌘)+R. Note that Figure 5.40b is the same menu in the Arrangement View with one exception. Since you manually select the length of the section to be rendered, you will not see the top Length [Bars.Beats.16th] settings.

In both the Session and Arrangement View Render to Disk menus, you have several important decisions to make. To begin, you will need to know the exact length of the section of audio you are rendering. If you are rendering from Session View, then you are likely only rendering a 4-, 8-, or 16-bar section; whereas in the Arrangement View, you may well be rendering an entire song and can select the amount of desired rendering time by click-dragging on any track to highlight the desired length of your render. For instance, if you want to render a four-minute

Figure 5.40a
The Render to Disk menu in Session View.

Figure 5.40b
The Render to Disk menu in Arrangement View.

song, simply drag (highlight) the entire length of the song on any track. Explicit directions for rendering are found in the "Rendering Techniques" section later in this chapter.

Normalize
When the Normalize setting is set to On, Live will raise the level of audio to the maximum level possible without distortion. I recommend leaving this setting Off for full songs and relegating all mastering/normalizing tasks to your wave editor. Most wave editors, such as Sonic Foundry's Sound Forge, Bias' Peak Audio, and Steinberg's Wavelab (to name a few), have a good deal more flexibility than Live in the matter of normalizing; however, if you are merely rendering a quick loop or small selection of audio, you may switch Live's Normalization setting to On (when rendering) to save time.

Render as Loop
Upon first glance, Render as Loop may seem like an insignificant option; however, this is a very important box if you have used any reverbs or delays in your soon-to-be-rendered loop or selection of audio. Normally, any loop with delay or reverb will have a tail, or specified amount of

decay, until the sound completely dissipates. The problem arises in the first few notes of a given loop, where the delay or reverb has not had time to kick in—those early notes are dry in comparison to the rest of the loop. Each time the loop cycles, you will hear the dry notes at the beginning and then a gradual swell in the effects. By activating the Render as Loop option, Live will actually render the file twice—once placing in all the reverb, delay, and effect tails, and twice to actually render the sample(s). You should be aware that this option is not desirable for complete songs. It's doubtful that you would want any sort of tail at the beginning of your compositions.

File Type

When rendering, you have a choice between saving your audio in either AIFF or WAV file format—either of which is capable of being burned to CD. AIFF is usually the preferred format for Apple Macintosh computers, while WAV is the Windows audio standard. When it comes time to actually burn your music onto a CD, you will need to use Apple's iTunes, Microsoft's Windows XP burning utility, or a third-party CD burning utility such as Ahead Software's Nero (www.nero.com), Roxio's EZ CD Creator (www.roxio.com), Cakewalk's Pyro (www.cakewalk.com/products/pyro), or Adaptec's Toast (www.adaptec.com).

Bit Depth

The Bit Depth dropdown menu gives you three choices: 16-, 24-, or 32-bit. Bit depth was discussed in Chapter 2, "Back to School," but I want to reiterate that unless you are short on hard drive space, you should usually render to 24-bit. Why not have a little extra detail to scrape away later if you so choose? Since Live can work with 24-bit files, loops, and samples, any loop you render can be re-imported into Live at a later time. If, on the other hand, you plan on burning the rendered file directly onto CD, you'll want to choose 16-bit, as this is the proper bit depth for audio compact discs. Thirty-two-bit is a new capability in Live 5 and is really only necessary for the most professional and discerning users. If you don't know if 32-bit quality is worth the increased file size for you, it probably isn't.

Sample Rate

Typically, you will only use sample rates of 44,100 (the CD standard rate) and up. 48,000 and 96,000 will provide more accurate sampling at the expense of hard disk space in similar fashion to bit depth selection. The lower sample rates (22,050 and 32,000) will most often be used for creating lo-fi special effects popularized by older first- and second-generation hardware samplers.

Create Analysis File

Each time Live sees a WAV or AIFF file, it has to draw a visual waveform, determine the positioning of the Warp Markers, and analyze the pitch and tempo. To do all this, Live uses a small pertinent secondary file called an *Analysis File* that will retain the master sample or loop's filename with the added file extension .asd. When this setting is activated, Live will also create an ASD file in addition to the rendered audio file. This is helpful when creating loops that will be reimported back into Live. Otherwise, it is really not necessary to create the added file.

Convert to Mono

Tho... this heading is fairly self descriptive, I want to point out its usefulness. Many Live musicians have ... that mono loops/samples are prefer...ble when working in a limited environment such as ... laptop computer setup. The reason is that stereo loops are actually two channels of audio run... ... ... Therefore, they require roughly twice the system resources of a mono file ... ... because Live can forgo all Warp Marker and file analysis since it has already be... ... ... side/channel...

M... ... ... also be a great ... ... loops or samples that you are planning to use ag... in an Ableton Live song. T... ... ... ve more presence than their stereo counterparts. If ... ... you can always ... ... kind of stereo simulation effect to widen the stereo fi... ... sample.

...endering Summary

... this is ... ... official contr... ... ... it helpful to look at the summary provided by Live ... the bottom ... the Render to ... ... Here ... ... will see a description of what you are about to ... ... you might see ... will render the Master output over the chosen length," ... Live will render the Master output over the selected time range [1.1.1-9.1.1]." If you get in the habit of watching this ... ... you may cut down on mistakes in the rendering process.

... ... mix, pay close attention to Live's Master Level meters. They ... ...aking (for an added visual cue, the meters will turn red any ...ut channels will result in a nasty digital glitch or distortion. ...ease) the Master Volume. Don't worry if you see other ... red. Live has an extreme amount of headroom that will allow ...ithout distorting. The only channel you really need to be worried about is the Master.

Rendering Techniques

It is worth pointing out that rendering can be done with any portion of the song, at any time you are working with Live. In other words, if you want to render a loop or section of a song, you can do this from either Session or Arrangement View. Why would you do this? Listed here are some common reasons for rendering a portion of a complete song. What follows is an explanation of how to complete the process.

❋ **Grab a loop:** I often render small loops for later use with a different piece of music, or make a complete file out of several edited clips.

❊ **Submix a section:** Occasionally, you might have added so many plug-ins to a particular section or track that Live can no longer run smoothly. At this point, you may want to consider rendering a single track or a subsection of the song (such as a verse or chorus) in order to lighten the processing load on your computer.

❊ **Export a completed song:** By far, the best feeling is rendering a completed song. This is nearly always done from the Arrangement View.

Grab a Loop

Follow these steps to Render/Save a loop.

1. Determine how long you want your loop or rendered audio section to be. There is no need to render more than one repetition of the audio segment; however, you can often make your music more interesting by embellishing the repeated loop and then rendering both the original and the varied loop as two loops.

2. Determine whether you are going to render in Session or Arrangement View and go to that View.

3. Highlight the clip(s) to be rendered. In Session View, highlight the clips or scenes that you would like to render with the mouse. In Arrangement View, highlight the desired length (on any track) at the appropriate location. Note: Live will render whatever is coming through on the Master Track. If you want to render the loop on Track 3 only, you will need to either mute the other tracks (by turning off the speaker-shaped Track Activator icon) or solo all pertinent tracks, such as Returns and the track(s) you want to render.

4. Press Ctrl(⌘)+Shift+R to call up the Render Options menu; or, you can select File → Render to Disk. Note that in Session View, you will need to type in the length of the file to be rendered determined in Step 1.

5. Here, your choices may vary, but we will recommend for small samples that you do the following: Normalize = On; Render as Loop = On; File Type = AIFF for Mac, WAV for PC; Bit Depth = 24; Sample Rate = 44,100; Create Analysis File = On; Convert to Mono = Off (usually).

6. Click OK or press Enter and select the drive/folder where you want to save your new loop.

Submix a Section

When creating a sub-mix of several tracks or one effect-laden track that is too processor intensive to continually keep playing, there are some slightly different options to select in the Render to Disk menu. Follow these steps to create a track to be reimported into Live.

1. In the Arrangement View, select and highlight the entire track or tracks that you would like to render. This may include several drum and percussion tracks, multiple vocal takes, or the compiled genius of your guitarist pal's efforts.

2. Solo all tracks and sends you are planning to render by activating the Solo/Cue button labeled S in the Arrangement View. You may also mute all other tracks (by turning off their Track Activator icons). Remember: Live will render whatever you hear coming through the Master Track.

3. Press Ctrl(⌘)+Shift+R to call up the Render Options menu. Or you can select File → Render to Disk.

4. Select these settings: Normalize = Off; Render as Loop = Off; File Type = AIFF for Mac, = WAV for PC; Bit Depth = 24; Sample Rate = 44,100 (or the setting you are accustomed to); Create Analysis File = On; Convert to Mono = Off.

5. Click OK, or press Enter, and save the rendered file (and analysis file) somewhere that makes sense with your current song. I suggest saving it in the same sounds folder as the other loops from your song. When you add the sub-mixed track back into your mix, don't forget to mute all of the original tracks, or else you will hear an intense phasing effect.

Export a Completed Song

Finally the time has come to render your completed song. Don't expect this to be a one-time process. You may find that there are subtle tweaks you'd like to make to the mix after burning your song to a CD and listening to it on different stereo systems.

1. On the Master Track in the Arrangement View, highlight the entire length of the song.

2. You may want to place a bit of leader, or space, at the beginning of your track. To do this, use the mouse to highlight the first couple of seconds of your track and then add the leader by selecting Edit → Insert Silence. Remember that you can always clean up the beginning and end spaces on your track in a wave editor.

3. Press Ctrl(⌘)+Shift+R to call up the Render Options menu. Or you can select File → Render to Disk.

4. For a final mix, we recommend setting Normalize = On (Off if you have a wave editing application); Render as Loop = Off; File Type = AIFF for Mac, = WAV for PC; Bit Depth = 24; Sample Rate = 44,100 (or the setting you are accustomed to); Create Analysis File = Off; Convert to Mono = Off.

5. Click on OK, or press Enter, and carefully save the file to a location where it is safe for final mixes.

Summary

I covered quite a lot of topics in this chapter—everything to bring your song from the tiniest musical fragments to fully arranged compositions. It is appropriate, therefore, to summarize the process once more just to help solidify it in your mind.

Here is a *general* idea of how a song is built in Live:

1. You start, for example, in the Session View by making a MIDI Track named Drums. You load an Impulse instrument (Chapter 9, "Live's Virtual Instruments") onto the track and quickly build a drum kit from samples on your hard drive. You program a MIDI Clip for the main groove of your song and set it looping.

2. You might then make an Audio Track titled Bass. You pull out your P-Bass and plug it into the instrument input 1 of your audio interface. You select input 1 of your interface on the Input/Output Routing strip and arm the track. You can now hear your bass blended with the drums, although you're not recording anything. You fool around for a moment on the bass until you come up with a part you like. You click one of the Record buttons in a slot on the track and start playing on the next downbeat. You put down the jam along with the drums. When you're done, you click again on the clip, and it begins to play. You move the clip's right loop marker to the left since you didn't stop the recording on the downbeat (your hands were full playing the bass).

3. You keep recording new clips, such as guitar and MIDI synth parts. You search your loop libraries for things that augment the song. Once you find a good combination, you use Capture and Insert Scene. You now have one scene in your Session.

4. You record a new bass part for the next section of your song. You write some new drum clips. You record the parts of other members in your band. You start tweaking clips with envelopes. You keep building more and more sections and capturing them as scenes.

5. Once you have a pretty good set of scenes to build a song from, you start listening to them and move their order around on-screen into a fashion that starts resembling your song (it's OK if you don't use all the scenes you captured). You enable Record in the Control Bar and start performing the song as it's arranged in the Session View. You can, of course, trigger any scene in any order that you want (you don't *have* to go top to bottom) and can also launch any clip you want individually.

6. You'll have a skeleton of your song in the Arrangement View. You now start making multiple passes over the song to program volume fades, mutes, pans, effect modulations, or any other automation you want in your song. You also edit the clips in the Arrangement, changing their length, volumes, etc., and also split and rearrange them.

7. Throughout this process, you are adding effects to the mix and bouncing the results to new clips when necessary.

8. You then start to experiment with new parts against your Arrangement by launching new clips in the Session View. You try out some new synth loops and record new guitar riffs—they'll all play synchronized with the Arrangement. When you want to hear your original Arrangement again, you click Back to Arrangement.

9. You finalize your song's Arrangement, putting the last tweaks on your mix. You render the final Arrangement to a WAV file. In WaveLab, you apply mastering plug-ins and maximize the quality of your song. You render the results to a 16-bit, 44,100 stereo file, which you burn to CD. You take the CD and put it in your car and drive all around town with it turned up as loudly as possible!

Of course, the process of creation in Live is entirely up to you. You may decide that, instead of building the song from little pieces, you're going to multi-track your whole band playing at once, thus capturing the song in one pass. You then use the creative editing and mixing features of Live to finalize the mix. Afterwards, you may take those large recordings and split them into small clips so you can make a live remix in the Session View. The creative flow is all up to you. Isn't that nice?

6 The Audio Clip

The Audio Clip has been the basic building block in Live since version 1 and is basically a reference to an audio file on your hard drive. When you trigger an Audio Clip to play, it plays the referenced audio file according to the settings contained in its Clip View. The parameters available to you are plentiful yet simple to understand. Using the tools of the Audio Clip, you can make any audio file play back in perfect sync with your song, as well as play them in the proper key. You can also use the Audio Clip settings to mangle your sounds and generate new ones.

Of course, you can also record new Audio Clips from virtually any source. You can use the inputs of your audio interface for recording vocals, guitars, drums, pianos, horns, and synths—anything that can be picked up with a microphone or connected directly to the audio interface is fair game. You can also record from other computer programs, bounce other tracks in your Set, or even re-record Live's own output. All of these recordings can be performed with the precision of Live's Launch Quantizing, allowing perfect loops to be recorded on the fly.

Before you start recording hordes of Audio Clips, take a moment to familiarize yourself with the unique parameters of Audio Clips. Drag an audio file from the Browser into a Clip Slot or load one of Live's Demo Sets, so you can follow along and try tweaking some of the parameters that follow.

Audio Clip Properties

The properties of an Audio Clip are edited through the Clip View (see Figure 6.1a). Double-click an Audio Clip to see its contents at the bottom of the screen. Every clip in Live has common settings, such as those found in the Clip and Launch windows of the Clip View; however, things will start to differ as you look at the windows entitled Sample and Envelope. In a MIDI Clip (shown in Figure 6.1b), the Sample window is replaced with a Notes window, and the Envelope window has different options. These are the areas that make using Audio and MIDI Clips unique. For the duration of this chapter, however, I'll explain those areas unique to Audio Clips alone. You'll get the rundown on MIDI Clips in the next chapter.

Figure 6.1a
The Clip View for an Audio Clip.

Figure 6.1b
The Clip View of a MIDI Clip. Can you see the differences?

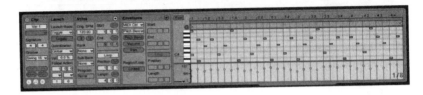

Buttons

In the Sample window (Figure 6.2) is a group of six buttons that are used to load and set playback quality for the sample used in the Audio Clip.

Figure 6.2
The Sample window contains controls concerning audio file playback speed, pitch, volume, and loop region, plus the settings for the Warp Engine.

Edit

Pressing the Edit button will launch the external wave editor you selected in the Default tab of the Preferences. The clip's audio file will be loaded automatically into the editor so you can perform any offline processing you want. When you are finished editing the audio file, close the editing software. It will ask if you want to save your changes. Click Yes, and the new changes will be saved and ready for Live to play.

 SELF DESTRUCT

Unlike every other process in Live, editing the source audio file will result in a change to the original audio file. If this file is also used in another Live Set, the Set will inherit the same edit (both Sets use the same file). Please pay special attention to this when using the Edit button. For safety, first save your Set as Self-Contained. Any edit you perform then will only alter the sound file in the Sounds folder for that project.

EXTRA HINT: If you're super-paranoid about screwing up files, go ahead and Consolidate your clip using Ctrl(⌘)+J before doing your edit. This will make a new copy of the clip's audio file before you do the edit.

Using an offline editor can be helpful when making microscopic edits to audio. Perhaps the vocalist's lips smacked as she began singing the first verse. The lip smack could be silenced easily in the external editor. Furthermore, every clip referencing that same file will have its offending lip smacks removed, too.

An offline editor is also helpful for layering effect plug-ins. While you could build a chain of plug-ins in the Track View and then resample the output, some may prefer to use the offline method to only affect part of the audio file. Furthermore, some audio editors will allow you to use plug-in formats not supported by Live. For example, Sony's Sound Forge supports DirectX plug-ins on the PC, which are not supported by Live. Using Sound Forge as your external editor will allow you to process your Audio Clips with any plug-ins you may have that are DirectX only.

Replace
The Replace button uses a different audio file than your sound source, while keeping all of your clip's playback parameters the same. Imagine having an Audio Clip as a part of a chain of Follow Actions. After listening to the chain, you decide you want to use a different audio file for the third clip. Instead of deleting the clip, loading a new one, and then setting the new clip's Follow Actions to the previous settings, you can click Replace and then choose a new audio file. The Follow Actions, Pitch, Quantize, etc. will remain the same.

DRAG-N-REPLACE

As with almost everything in Live, there's another super-slick way to pull off the function listed above. Dragging an audio file from the Browser (or Explorer on Windows and Finder on OSX) into the waveform display of the Audio Clip will just replace the audio while leaving the other parameters unchanged. (You will have to reassign your Warp Markers, though.)

Save
When adjusting the parameters of a clip, you may want your changes to become part of the audio file. For example, if you have to Warp Mark a certain beat every time you load it into a Clip Slot, wouldn't it be nice if the Warp Markers could be remembered the next time you import the file? By pressing Save, information regarding the playback settings of the audio file will be saved in a special file with the extension .asd. The ASD file contains the peak information of the audio file (used for the Clip View waveform display), but can also contain information regarding Warp

Markers, tempo, tuning, and warp modes. Pressing Save updates the ASD file with the current settings of the clip. Next time you create a clip from the file (dragging it from the Browser), the Warp Markers will already be in place, and the proper tunings and warp modes will be set.

Hi-Q

This button simply switches the Audio Clip between high-quality and low-quality interpolation (used for time-stretching). If this button is on, the clip will play using better pitch shifting and resampling algorithms, but it will also place a heavier strain on your CPU. I recommend leaving this option on (even setting it on in the Default Preferences) and only turning it off when the CPU starts to overload.

Fade

To help an audio file loop seamlessly (no clicks or pops when the file loops around), Live can perform a quick volume fade at the ends of the clip. I recommend leaving this option on (as default, too) unless the downbeat transient seems too quiet. It is possible that the fade can soften the initial attack of the downbeat (for instance, shaving the attack of a one-shot sample), so you may need to turn this off from time to time.

RAM

As I've mentioned before, Live streams audio files from disk as they play. With each additional Audio Clip that plays, the computer will have to stream another file from disk. Your hard disk can only stream a finite amount of data per second, and when Live requires more than the disk can provide, audio dropouts begin to occur (Figure 6.3).

Figure 6.3
When the hard disk is not able to stream the neces-sary amount of audio for playing Audio Clips, the "D" icon in the Control Bar will blink, signaling a disk overload.

To alleviate this, you can load Audio Clips into your computer's RAM memory, which is accessed much faster than the hard disk. Pressing the RAM button for an Audio Clip will cause Live to load the associated audio file into RAM and cease streaming it from the hard disk.

Remember to be conscious of the size of the files you're loading into RAM. If you have five clips that are four minutes long and two clips that are loops of only a few seconds, it would be better to load the short clips into RAM. Even if you're using only 10 seconds of an eight-minute file, Live will still load the whole file into memory if you press its RAM button! Unless you have multiple gigabytes of RAM available on your system, you should try to load only short files into RAM.

> ❋ **A MOMENT OF TROUBLE**
>
> Once when I was performing live, there was a section of the show (one scene to be particular) that had 16 Audio Clips playing simultaneously. The only way my computer could do this was by running a couple of the clips from RAM. Even though the kick drum clip had streamed from disk throughout the performance up until this scene, it was necessary to run it from RAM for this one point in the show, which lasted all of 20 seconds. So, the kick drum clip was set to RAM only in the offending scene with 16 clips. When the next scene was launched, it triggered the kick drum from disk again.

Transpose and Detune

When adding a new Audio Clip to your Live Set, more than likely it will not be in the right key. If you're writing a song in the key of E, but you import a clip that's in B-flat, the new clip will be out of tune with the rest of the set, even though it's playing in sync tempo-wise with the song. The Transpose and Detune controls (see Figure 6.4) change the playback tuning of the clip (without changing its playback speed) to shift it into key with the rest of the song.

Figure 6.4
The large Transpose knob will shift an Audio Clip up or down in semi-tone amounts. The Detune value below the knob can make micro-adjustments to the tuning by moving it up or down within 50 cents (100 cents = 1 semi-tone).

You'll use the Transpose knob to shift the playback pitch of the Audio Clip. In case the Audio Clip is still slightly out of tune, the Detune knob can be used to fine-tune the pitch by raising or lowering it in small steps known as *cents*. Cent means one-hundredth, which is why a centimeter is one-hundredth of a meter. In music, a cent is one-hundredth of a semi-tone.

Gain

The Gain slider is used to adjust the individual volume of a clip. If you grabbed three different drum loops for a song, it's possible that the loop for the bridge is quieter than the other two. Instead of trying to automate a volume change at the bridge, you can simply turn up the volume, or *gain*, of that clip to match the others.

When you adjust the gain, you'll see the waveform display change to reflect the new playback volume. Even though you see the waveform display change, remember that the original file has not changed. You're only telling Live to play the file at a different volume. Keep an eye on your levels as you increase the gain of the clip since it's possible to turn the volume up so much that the clip will begin to distort.

Cranking up the volume also provides you with a way to zoom in vertically on a waveform. You can always extend the Clip View window vertically (see Figure 6.5), but it still may not show enough detail.

Figure 6.5
By dragging the top edge of the Clip View upward, you can see the waveform in better detail.

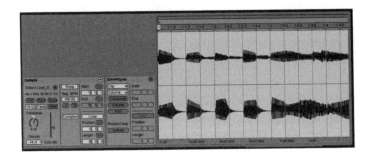

If enlarging the Clip View still doesn't show enough detail, turn up the gain, and you'll have a larger waveform to edit in the waveform display (see Figure 6.6). When you're done editing and adjusting, don't forget to turn the gain back to its original level or the clip will play extremely loud (watch those ears!).

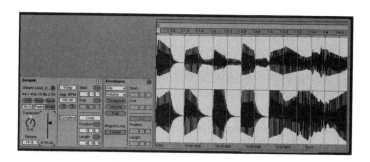

Figure 6.6
The waveform is much
larger after you increase
the clip's Gain setting.

❊ **TWEAK THAT CLIP**

New to Live 5 is the ability to assign MIDI and key controls to various parameters of the Audio and MIDI Clip Views. The method works as you'd expect. Engage either MIDI or Key Map mode, and boxes will appear over various controls in the Clip View. Click the control; then move or press the desired control to link them.

One thing to be aware of is that your MIDI and Key assignments in the Clip View do not stay stuck to a particular clip. Instead, the assignments work on whatever clip, or clips, you have selected. Therefore, if you use a MIDI knob to transpose a clip, you can click on another clip and the same MIDI knob will now transpose the new clip.

Warp Control

Warping is the term used to describe Live's time-stretching and compressing technique. The method of warping an audio file to match the tempo, groove, and pitch of a song is determined by many parameters. The most basic controls are the Warp button and the Original Tempo value.

Live's time-warping features will be available only when the Warp button (see Figure 6.7) is on. If this button is off, the Original Tempo box will be grayed out, and you will not be able to use Warp Markers. With Warp off, the clip plays at the audio file's original tempo and pitch, unless you tweak the speed with the Transpose knob (the tempo and pitch will be adjusted simultaneously, like a record). However, once Warp is engaged, a whole world of possibilities opens. You can change the playback speed and pitch of the Audio Clip independently, as well as make adjustments to its timing and groove.

Figure 6.7
Engage Warp to "open
up" your Audio Clip.

Seg BPM

This value box is similar to the operation of Warp Markers, which I'll explain in a moment. Seg is short for *segment*, which is what Ableton uses to refer to a section of audio between two Warp Markers. When you have multiple Warp Markers (explained below) in a clip, the Seg BPM window will display the BPM from the selected Warp Marker to the next one to its right. If you have four Warp Markers in a clip and you click on the second one, the Seg BPM window will show the tempo between Warp Markers two and three. When you click on the third Warp Marker, another tempo will be displayed that reflects the playback speed from marker three to four.

You'll see when adjusting grid and Warp Markers that the tempo listed here will change. This is helpful because, after setting the Warp Markers appropriately, Live will be able to determine the exact BPM of the clip. Quite often, this is not a round number, like 120 BPM, but more like 119.72 BPM.

This value is used by Live to set the playback speed of an Audio Clip in beats per minute. If the Project tempo is 120 BPM and the clip's Seg BPM is 120, then Live will not change the playback speed of the clip. If the project tempo is 100 BPM, Live would know (from looking at the Seg BPM value) that it needs to slow down the clip so that it will match the rest of the song.

For those familiar with Live 4 or older, you may remember this value as being labeled Original BPM. This is still a good concept to remember. The idea was that if you had only one Warp Marker in the clip (just marker 1 at the downbeat), this box would indicate the original tempo of the audio file being used. If Live happened to auto-detect the tempo of a loop, it would be shown here. If you were matching up a whole song for a DJ set, you'd put the song's BPM here after using the Tap Tempo. The same is still true for the newly named Seg BPM. A rose by any other name...

Half/Double Original Tempo

The two buttons below the Seg Tempo window will either double or halve the tempo of the clip. Pressing the *2 button will multiply every Segment Tempo by two. The result is that the clip will play at half speed. Pressing :2 will have the opposite effect. This is helpful when Live incorrectly guesses the length and tempo of a new Audio Clip. Loops at a drum and bass tempo of 170 BPM will frequently import as 85 BPM clips. A simple click of the *2 button will fix this immediately.

Warp Modes

As mentioned earlier, Live's Warp modes allow for cleaner, more musical warping. The Warp mode affects the way in which Live approaches stretching and pitch-shifting your Audio Clips. Five different Warp modes are available in the Audio Clip's Warp section: Beats, Tones, Texture, Re-Pitch, and Complex. Each mode also features a special set of controls that will appear below it in the form of a Transients dropdown menu, Grain Size box/knob, and Flux box. I will cover these in subsections below. Also, don't forget that you can simply turn off Live's Warp Engine altogether and play the sample at its default speed and pitch. Here's a list of what kinds of different sounds you can expect when switching between these five Warp modes.

Beats

Beats mode is a great mode for rhythmic loops, percussive samples, and even entire songs. You will usually want to use Beats mode with percussion, drums, drum machines, and sounds characteristically containing minimal decay (sustain). When importing songs (or long wave files), the same rules apply. Occasionally, if the sound is too textured or lacks rhythmic definition, you may hear artifacts. Artifacts happen when Live tries to warp a non-percussive file, such as a drone or flute melody. Live's transient settings, just below the Warp mode settings, allow you to zero in on busier patterns or to relax the Warp Engine for more sparse-sounding loops.

❊ **DEFINITION OF TRANSIENT**

The Transient setting is a critical element of Live's beat-warping functionality. But what is a transient to begin with? A transient is the short, sharp attack portion of a sound. An acoustic snare has a huge transient, which is the "crack" you hear (and see, as in Figure 6.8) right when the stick hits the drum. The soft attack of strings has no transient.

Transient

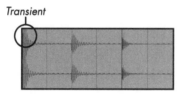

Figure 6.8
Drum parts have easily identifiable transients.

You'll choose the proper setting for the Transient value based upon the rhythm of the audio file. If the beat doesn't have anything smaller than a 1/8-note subdivision, set the Transients to 1/8.

The way Beats mode works is by cutting the file into slices the size of the Transient setting. If you have a one-bar loop with the Transient value set to 1/16, the file will be cut into 16 slices (see Figure 6.9). The positions where these slices are taken are determined by the grid and Warp Markers in the waveform display. If your markers are aligned perfectly with the transients in the file, the Beats mode will be cutting the slices at the appropriate locations. If the markers are out of place, the slice points may be after a transient, making it disappear upon playback.

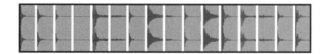

Figure 6.9
A beat split into 16 slices.

If the beat being warped needs to be sped up to match the tempo of Live, the slices will be moved closer together (see Figure 6.10). As this happens, the end of each slice will be cut off by the next slice, which needs to play sooner because of the faster tempo. If your beat only contains transients of the subdivisions you specified, only the tail end of every sound will be getting cut off, which is hardly noticeable.

Figure 6.10
The slices start overlapping as they move closer together. Each slice cuts off the previous one, so the tail end (right edge) of each slice gets shorter.

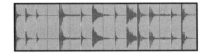

However, if you specify a Transient setting of 1/8 for a beat that has 1/16-note transients, the beat will only be cut into eight pieces. Since a slice is an 1/8-note wide, it will contain two 1/16 note transients each (see Figure 6.11).

Figure 6.11
The same beat in eight slices.

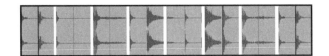

When the slices are moved closer together, the space between the two transients on each slice stays the same, but the distance from the second transient to the first one on the *next* slice gets shorter (Figure 6.12). This means the even timing of the 1/16 notes in the audio file will be lost since the space between *every other* 1/16 note changes. If you do this right, you can turn a straight beat into a swinging beat! Check out the Beats Mode example in the Chapter 6 folder to hear how this is done. I've even included a detailed description of each scene in the Set's Lessons View.

Figure 6.12
1/8-note slices moved closer together. The resulting beat has uneven spacing between the individual 1/16 notes.

The space between these beats has been shortened due to the overlapping slices.

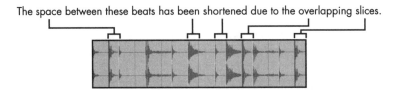

The slicing mechanism in Beats mode is a special form of granular synthesis. Instead of using miniscule "grains" of audio, beats uses large slices. Instead of repeating each grain when filling the space between pieces that are moved apart (slowing down a file), Beats mode only loops the last portion of the slice—the fading sound of the transient. This means that the wrong setting for the Transient value, such as 1/8 for a 1/16-note loop, will have undesired effects as Beats mode will loop the second transient on the slice in an attempt to fill the space, which will sound weird.

Tones

Tones mode is standard granular resynthesis. As a file is played back, it is broken into tiny pieces called *grains*. The idea is that when you loop a tiny grain, you get a continuous tone that represents that sound "frozen in time." By splitting the audio into grains and spreading the grains apart, Live slows down the tempo of the audio playback; however, since each grain is still played at its original pitch, there will be empty space between each grain. By looping each grain to fill the space, granular time-stretching is achieved.

Of course, looping each grain isn't necessary when speeding up playback of a file. As the grains are brought closer together, they will overlap one another. Each grain will therefore cut off the one before it, resulting in a continuous sound, but one playing faster than before. For this reason, you'll probably find that you have better success speeding up loops or transposing them down (both methods use the same process) than slowing them down or pitching them up, which requires looping the grains.

With careful setting of the Grain Size value, you can achieve nearly transparent warping. Tones such as bass guitars, synthesizers, vocals, keyboards, or other long-sustaining instruments will usually sound much less processed when playing in Live's Tones mode. You can adjust Live's Grain Size to help reduce undesirable audio artifacts.

Texture

Texture mode is built for using orchestral samples, field recordings, thick keyboard pads, and similarly dense audio textures. Like Tones mode, Texture mode is based on granular resynthesis. In an effort to cloud the repetitive artifacts from looping grains, a Flux value is added that, when increased, allows Live to randomly change the grain sizes used in the process. This also adds a sense of stereo imaging to mono files.

Re-Pitch

Re-Pitch mode is more like true vinyl DJing—Live will alter the pitch of the sample, depending upon the playback speed. This mode will produce no artifacts, especially if the warped, looped, re-pitched sample is played close to its original tempo. Re-Pitch basically turns off the granular and slice-based resynthesis and merely alters the file playback speed, which results in pitch changes. Since resynthesis is off, you will not be able to use the Transpose adjustments in this mode.

Complex

New to Live 5 is the Complex mode. This is another enhancement aimed straight at the heart of DJs, but has positive repercussions for all types of users. The Complex mode employs a phase-vocoding algorithm to stretch and shift Audio Clips. This requires more effort from your CPU, but the end results are gorgeous. Designed for use on entire songs, such as MP3s, this Warp mode will match the Audio Clip with nearly no noticeable artifacts. It's really that good. I use a Pentium 4 computer with a 3.6GHz processor, so I can afford to use quite a lot of clips in Complex mode. In fact, I've made it my default Warp mode in my Preferences. It sounds great on nearly everything. If your computer is having a tough time keeping up with the added load of the Complex mode, you can use the Freeze Track option from the Track context menu (right-click on PC or Ctrl-click on Mac to open it), or you can resample the warped clip into a new clip that doesn't need Complex mode.

Reverse

Live's Sample Reverse feature is not instantaneous—don't expect it to be. It is, however, a whole lot of fun when used properly.

The process is simple. Click the Reverse button (see Figure 6.13), and Live will calculate a new audio file, which is a reversed version of the original. This new audio file will be named the same as the original, but will have the letter "R" added to the end.

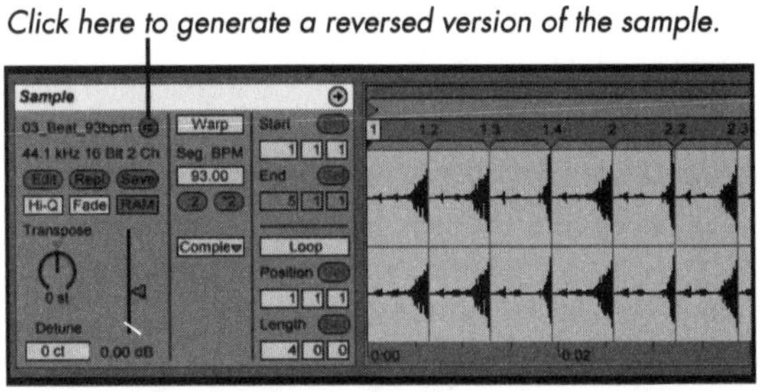

Figure 6.13
That tiny little icon is the Sample Reverse button. You can see the transients of the drum beat are now backwards.

Click here to generate a reversed version of the sample.

OK, so it's not a Reverse button, as in "play the sample backwards." Instead, the Reverse button means "play a backward version of the sample." This means you'll have to wait for the "R" file to be made the first time you Reverse, but from that point on, Live will just choose the original or reversed file to play, allowing you to switch directions almost instantaneously.

> ❄ **ON THE UP AND UP**
>
> When controlling objects on the screen with the mouse, they almost always respond when you release your mouse button, not when you first click on them. The Reverse button is no different. You may think that the reverse response is sluggish because you expect it to reverse right when you click; however, reverse won't take effect until you release your mouse button.

Because of the nature of the Reverse feature, I don't suggest that you use this button during live performances. You'll lose all control while the "R" file is being calculated, and the timing of the reverse isn't tight with the mouse (you can't control it with MIDI Remote, either).

Instead, I recommend you make two clips: one normal and one reversed. Enable Legato mode, and you'll be able to switch between them in the Session View for the same results, with the aid of Launch Quantization if you want.

> ❄ **WAITING FOR R**
>
> When you click the Reverse button for the first time, a new audio file is created on your computer. If you switch the clip back to normal playback, you will technically have an unused file on your computer (the reversed file with the "R" at the end). If you save or quit, Live will ask you if you want to get rid of the unused reverse file. If you say yes, you will have to wait for Live to recalculate the file the next time you click Reverse. If you were just experimenting and don't plan on using the reversed version of the file, go ahead and delete it. Otherwise, keep it so that Live can still switch to the reversed version quickly.

Warp Markers

I've mentioned Warp Markers time and time again throughout this book, so it's about time I explain what they are. The principle behind Warp Markers is simple but still manages to confuse some long-time users; however, using them properly will have a profound effect on Live's ability to lock your Audio Clips together, and they are essential when dealing with live (human) players.

Purpose of Warping

In a nutshell, you use warping to alter the playback timing of an audio file, usually to match the tempo of your song. You've already witnessed how Live can quickly change the playback tempo of an audio file dependent on the Session tempo. When you lowered the tempo, the audio files slowed down immediately. Since Live is performing all its warping in real-time, it can respond to instant changes anywhere during audio playback.

If you have an audio file that has improper timing, such as a drum part where the drummer played a beat late (see Figure 6.14), you can fix the timing by using small changes to the warp parameters. If the snare drum on beat 1.2 is late, playing through the first beat of the file at an increased rate will cause the snare to move earlier. Playing the second beat of the file slower will allow the rest of the file after beat 1.3 to stay in the same place. By adjusting these two speeds, you can correct the timing of individual beats in a file. Fortunately, you don't have to alter these playback speeds numerically. They are computed for you as you manipulate Warp Markers.

Figure 6.14
The snare drum hit on beat 1.2 is late. Damn those human drummers!

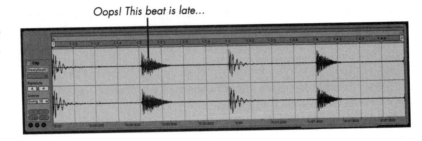

Oops! This beat is late...

Auto-Warping

One occasion that may require you to make numerous Warp Markers is when synchronizing an entire song to your Set. DJs have to do this with all of their files before they can be played in Live. It used to be that this operation required staring at your computer screen for hours while making your hand numb from clicking on all the Warp Markers.

Ableton has responded to the need for automatic Warp Marking with the release of Live 5. Now, whenever you import a long audio file, Live will run it through its Auto-Warping scheme, thus making the file immediately ready for use in your Set (if you don't like this behavior, you can turn this off in the Preferences). The process of Auto-Warping is quite quick, and you can initiate it manually if you desire. Right-click a Marker and select one of the Auto-Warp options from the context menu:

* **Warp From Here:** This tells Live to Auto-Warp the clip starting at the selected Warp Marker and continuing to the right. Everything to the left of the selected marker will remain intact.

* **Warp From Here (Start at *tempo*):** This option is the same as above but uses the current project tempo as a starting point for the Auto-Warping algorithm. If you've already determined the approximate tempo of the audio file using the Tap Tempo, this option should yield good results. The reason this is necessary is because Live can calculate BPMs that are twice as fast or slow as they should be. For example, a 1-bar loop at 62 BPM is the same length as a 2-bar loop at 122 BPM. By providing a starting tempo in the neighborhood of 60 or 120 BPM, Live will know to evaluate the clip as 122 BPM.

* **Warp From Here (Straight):** This mode attempts to set the tempo of the clip using one Warp Marker only. This should only be used when warping electronically produced music that has a fixed tempo.

* **Warp Tempo From Here:** This simply sets the current Warp Marker to the project tempo. If there are any Warp Markers to the right, they will be erased in the process.

* **Warp as X-Bar Loop:** If you already know that the file you're working with is an even bar number in length, you can select this option to automatically turn the clip into an even loop.

The number shown here will be dependent on the current project tempo. If Live determines that it will have to do the least amount of warping to turn the clip into a 1-bar loop as opposed to a 2-bar loop, 1 will be displayed in place of X in the menu item above. If you change the project tempo (increase it by almost double), Live will see that it is now easier to make the clip a 2-bar loop and will suggest that by showing 2 in place of 1 in the menu option.

Manually Creating and Erasing Warp Markers

Click the Sample window Title Bar in the Clip View to view the clip's Markers. The Markers show where Live thinks the beats are in an audio file. The lines that appear with numbers above them are the Grid Markers. The lines with the green handles at the top are Warp Markers. Any Grid Marker can be turned to a Warp Marker by double-clicking its beat number (Figure 6.15). Double-click a Warp Marker to switch it back to a gray Grid Marker.

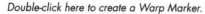
Double-click here to create a Warp Marker.

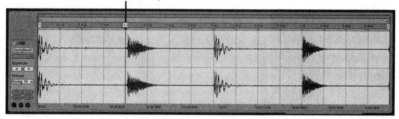

Figure 6.15
There is always at least one Warp Marker in an Audio Clip. It's the Marker at beat 1. You can make others by double-clicking Grid Markers.

The difference between Warp and Grid Markers is that Warp Markers will stay where you place them. When you create a Warp Marker, you can click and drag it to a new location in the waveform display. The Warp Marker will stay in this location even if you move other markers around it. Grid Markers will always stay evenly distributed between neighboring Warp Markers (see Figure 6.16). Moving a Warp Marker will make all the surrounding Grid Markers move as well.

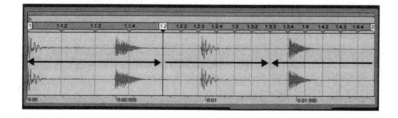

Figure 6.16
As Warp Marker 1.2 is moved right, the Grid Markers to its left spread apart while the markers to its right get closer together.

Correcting Timing Errors

If you turn Grid Marker 1.2 into a Warp Marker and move it right so it's lined up with the beginning of the snare drum, you are telling Live the new location of beat 1.2 in the file (see Figure 6.17). Since you are showing Live that the second beat is later in the file, Live will play the file quicker up until this point to make sure it reaches this later transient on beat 1.2.

Figure 6.17
Creating a Warp Marker and moving it in line with the snare drum will cause Live to play this section of the file in time.

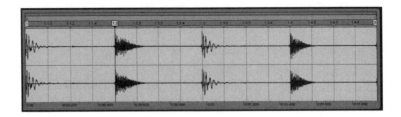

When you move the Warp Marker over to its new location, it causes all the Grid Markers to its right to move as well. This means beat 1.3 now needs to be lined up. Changing Grid Marker 1.3 into a Warp Marker and moving it left to the proper location fixes this (see Figure 6.18). Since the location of beat 1.2 is now closer to beat 1.3, Live will play that section of the file slower so it doesn't arrive at the third transient early.

Figure 6.18
Moving Warp Marker 1.3 into position with the third transient corrects the rest of the file.

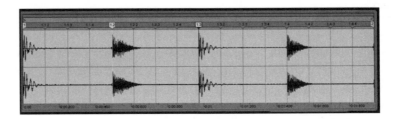

To potentially fix all of the timing errors in a file, you may need to make a lot of Warp Markers (Figure 6.19). In cases like this, you'd probably want to click the clip's Save button so the Warp Markers will be loaded in future imports of the file.

Figure 6.19
You can manipulate Warp Markers down to small subdivisions to correct multiple timing problems.

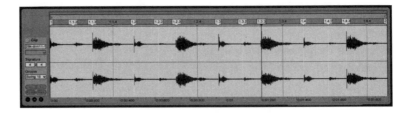

Keep in mind that all the usual editing commands and techniques work here. You can, for example, click on a Warp Marker and press Ctrl (⌘) + A to select all of the Warp Markers. You can then slide them around as a group or delete them. You can also select a range of markers by clicking one of them and then clicking another while holding the Shift key. You can then move or delete only that specific range of markers.

Creating New Rhythms

If you can use Warp Markers to align audio to the proper beat, can you use them to align audio to the improper part of a beat? Of course! You can change your beat by having Live play the snare later in time, perhaps on beat 1.2.2. If you remove Warp Marker 1.2 and create Warp Marker 1.2.2, you can align this new marker to the transient of the snare (see Figure 6.20). By doing so, you have told Live that the snare drum falls on beat 1.2.2. Live will now play the audio file from 1 to 1.2.2 much slower than normal. By playing slowly, the snare won't sound until later—beat 1.2.2, in this case. Since the snare was pushed so far back in time, Live will now have to play quickly from 1.2.2 to 1.3 in order to keep the rest of the file aligned.

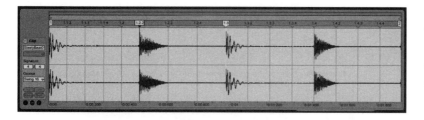

Figure 6.20
Though the waveform hasn't changed, this beat will sound significantly different when it plays back.

Clip Envelopes

The final window in the Audio Clip View is the Envelopes window. Before I go too far, some of you may be wondering what an envelope is. To start with, it's nothing that you will put in a mailbox. Rather, it's a graphical representation of values, such as positions of knobs and faders, which change over time. The envelopes appear as a line graph superimposed over the audio waveform and represent anything from volume and pitch changes to effect tweaks. To understand how envelopes function, it helps to actually manipulate them and hear the results, so play along with me here by opening the Clip Envelopes example in the Chapter 6 folder of the CD-ROM materials.

Volume

The easiest Clip Envelope to understand is the Volume Envelope (see Figure 6.21). In the figure, the envelope is the ramp that rises from the bottom-left corner of the display window to the upper-right corner. When you play this clip (labeled Volume Up in the example Set), its volume will rise over its two-bar length. When the clip repeats, the Volume will immediately jump to silence and will begin to rise again.

Figure 6.21
The upward ramp will cause the clip's volume to rise over two bars as it plays.

To access the Volume Envelope for your clip, press the Volume shortcut button in the Envelope window. The Volume Envelope will superimpose itself over the clip.

When you first make a clip, its Volume Envelope will look like the one in Figure 6.22. Clip Envelopes are always working, so this "fully up" envelope allows you to hear your clip. This means there's no such thing as a clip without a Volume Envelope—it's just set to full level so it appears to have no effect. In other words, all the envelopes are always present, they're just set to do nothing by default.

Figure 6.22
This is the default Volume Envelope for a new Audio Clip.

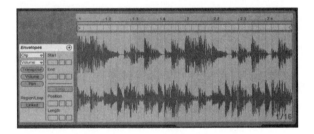

You can freely edit this envelope to hear the effect it will have on the clip. Click on the Pencil tool in the Control Bar so its icon is on. Then click in the Envelope window to create some "steps" like those shown in Figure 6.23. You'll hear Live adjust the volume of the clip according to these steps when you play it.

It's important to realize that the Volume Envelope (as well as any other Clip Envelope) is affecting the playback volume in a relative way. If you look closely at the Gain slider in the Sample window, you'll see a small dot by it that moves up and down along with the volume changes. This dot shows the volume of the clip based on the Volume Envelope. I like to think of this dot as the envelope's "finger" on my controls showing me what it's doing. If you change the Gain amount, you'll hear an overall volume change while the steps drawn in your Volume Envelope continue to incrementally change the volume. You'll notice that the volume didn't jump back up to its

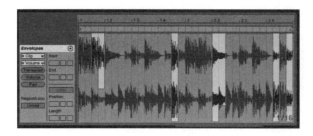

Figure 6.23
These steps will change the playback volume of the clip.

previous location because of the envelope. Instead, the envelope scales its range based on the location of the Gain slider. This is because the Clip Envelopes work relative to a control's current position. This way, you can create repetitive volume patterns but still adjust the overall level of the clip in the mix.

Pan

Another simple envelope to master is the Pan Envelope, which is accessed with the Pan button in the Envelopes window. Instead of seeing a "full up" envelope like you saw for Volume, you'll see a "flat line" going through the middle of the window (see Figure 6.24).

Figure 6.24
The Pan Envelope doing nothing.

Remember how I said that Clip Envelopes work relative to a control's current position? In the case of the Pan Envelope, the flat line down the middle means no panning left or right. If the envelope is above this center line, the pan position of the track will be moved right. The track will pan left when the line is below center. This means creating a ramp from the upper-left corner of the window to the bottom-right (see Figure 6.25) will cause the clip to pan from right to left as it plays. Launch the Ramp Pan Clip to hear this in action.

If you turn the Pan knob in the Session Mixer to the left, you'll hear that the panning doesn't start fully on the right. It now starts partway to the left and continues fully left. This is because the envelope is changing the pan position relative to the current location of the Pan knob. In fact, if you look closely, you'll see a colored indicator appear around the Pan knob as the envelope changes its position (Figure 6.26). This is how the envelope's "finger" is represented on a knob.

Figure 6.25
This ramp will cause the track to pan from right to left during playback.

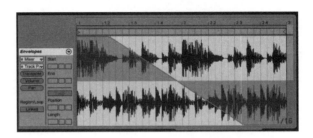

Figure 6.26
The colored section of the Pan knob shows the actual output position as a result of the Pan Envelope.

This track is being panned left by a Clip Envelope

Transpose

The third envelope accessible through shortcut buttons is the Transpose Envelope. This envelope will modulate the location of the Transpose knob, allowing you to program pitch changes, slides, or entire harmonic progressions for the clip.

The envelope begins as a flat line, just like the Pan Envelope. Every line above zero is one semitone up, while every line below zero is a semitone down (see Figure 6.27).

Figure 6.27
This envelope transposes the clip up and down as it plays.

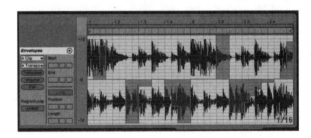

The envelope affects the Transpose knob in a relative way, meaning that after you've programmed in your progression, like Figure 6.27 above, you can still select the root note of the scale with the Transpose knob.

Sample Offset

There are only three shortcut buttons in the Envelopes window, yet there are many more envelopes available for you to program. In fact, there's a Clip Envelope for nearly every parameter of the clip and its containing track.

To select an envelope other than the three available as shortcuts, you use the two dropdown menus at the top of the Envelopes window. These menus work in a similar fashion to the pairs found in the Input/Output Routing section. The top menu will choose the device you want to view, and the bottom menu selects the parameter. One of these additional Clip Envelopes takes a little explaining—the Sample Offset Envelope. This envelope can be found by selecting Clip in the top menu and then choosing Sample Offset in the lower menu. This option is only available to clips in Beats mode. If this option is grayed out, switch to Beats mode or find another clip that's in Beats mode already.

The Sample Offset Envelope (see Figure 6.28) is another one of those "flat-liners" like the Transpose and Pan Envelopes above. It can be thought of as a step sequencer for your beat. Each line above zero is worth +1 1/16 note. Each line below is worth -1 1/16 note. Compare the two clips named Normal and Offset in the example set to hear how the Sample Offset works.

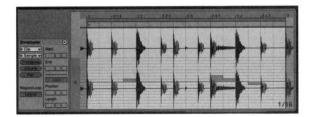

Figure 6.28
The Sample Offset programmed above in the Offset clip will cause the snare drum on beat 1.2 to play on 1.1.4 as well. The snare at 1.4 will play at 1.3.3, 1.3.4, 1.4, and 1.4.2.

Remember how Beats mode splits an audio file into multiple slices? Well, when playback of an Audio Clip reaches a non-zero value in the Offset Envelope, it signals Live to jump to a different slice of the file relative to the current location. In Figure 6.28, there is a value of +1 at beat 1.1.4. When playback reaches this point, Live will play the slice of audio located 1/16 note ahead of the current position, which is the slice for beat 1.2. So, when playback reaches 1.1.4, you'll hear the snare that occurs on beat 1.2. On the next beat, 1.2, the Offset Envelope is zero. This means Live plays the audio slice at its current location. In this case, you'll hear the snare on beat 1.2 again. The additional steps around beat 1.4 will cause two hits before 1.4 and one after. By creating patterns of offset motions, you can rearrange the slices of an audio file into any order you want. Try it—take the pencil and scribble all over the Sample Offset Envelope and listen to the random results.

Since the Sample Offset Envelope rearranges the slices in a Beats mode clip, the Transient setting for the clip will determine the smallest Offset that can be performed. If Transient is set to 1/4, you will be able to offset the beat only on the quarter note. This also means that the finest possible resolution for the Sample Offset is 1/32 (the clip's Transient setting can't get any smaller).

However, if you're looking to do some meticulous micro-editing of your beats, using the Sample Offset Envelope may not be the best solution, but it can definitely get you started. Really tight and complicated edits are still better suited for the Arrangement View (see Chapter 14,"Live 5 Power," for the "Beat Wreckin' Clinic").

Sends and More

Another fun Clip Envelope is the Send Envelope. Select Mixer in the top device menu and then choose Send A in the lower menu. With this envelope, you can control the level of signal sent to the various Return Tracks.

The Send Envelope (see Figure 6.29) is a "full-on" envelope like Volume. This makes sense because the Send knobs are just special volume controls themselves. Editing the envelope will scale the output level of the associated Send knob. In the envelope below, the Send only works on beat 1.4. In the example Set, I've already placed a Reverb on Return A. Turn up Send A on the Drums track and launch the Send a Clip to hear what happens.

Figure 6.29
The Send Envelope sending
on beat 1.4 only.

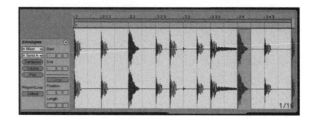

To hear this work, you'll need to have an effect loaded onto the Return Track (see Chapter 8, "Using Effects and Instruments") and the Send knob for the track turned up. Since the Send Envelope is relative, the track has to have its Send turned up at least a little before the envelope can scale the level. The result is that the Send knob will actually send on beat 1.4 only. The rest of the time, it will be muted, even though the Send knob is up.

You'll find even more Clip Envelopes as you explore the dropdown menus in the Envelopes window. In fact, as you add effects to the track (see Chapter 8), envelopes for the plug-in's parameters will also appear in this list so you can modulate them. That's quite a lot of modulation available at your fingertips!

Unlinking Envelopes

Until this point, I've been talking about editing loops of a given length. After all, a loop is, by definition, a repeating sample or phrase. That is just what loops do—they loop. And by default, each envelope in a clip is the same length as the clip itself, allowing you to create repetitive modulation patterns that recur every time the clip repeats itself.

Sometimes you may want to extend a given loop beyond its original borders. For instance, you have a repetitive two-bar drum loop, and you really wish that you had an eight-bar loop to make it sound more lifelike and less repetitive. I'll introduce you to the process of unlinking envelopes. By changing the length of the Clip Envelopes so that they are different than the length of the clip that contains them, you can introduce just this kind of variation to your loops.

Anytime you click the Unlink button (Figure 6.30), the audio peak data is removed from the waveform display. This is because the envelope you create may not occur at the same place in the clip upon every repetition, especially if you set the envelope length to a value other than a multiple of the clip length.

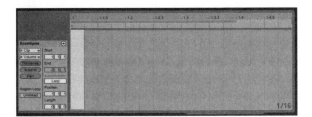

Figure 6.30
Unlinking the Clip Enve-
lope will allow you to
create more "random"
sounding modulations
because the various en-
velopes can repeat at
independent times.

If you have a one-bar clip and you unlink its Volume Envelope, setting its envelope length to three beats will cause the Volume Envelope to repeat sooner than the clip itself. If you've muted the volume at any place in the envelope as in the figure above, this mute will begin to occur at different places as the clip loops. The envelope shown above will remove one 1/16 note every three beats. This means beat 1 will be missing, then beat 1.4 (it's three beats later, see?), followed by beat 1.3 the next time through the clip. The third time through the clip, beat 1.2 will be muted. With the fourth repetition, the pattern starts again. It therefore takes three bars for the Volume Clip to repeat itself, thus the resulting clip also repeats in a pattern three bars long. Launch the Unlinked Clip to hear this firsthand.

To make things more complicated (and fun), other Clip Envelopes can be unlinked and set to their own unique lengths. If a Pan pattern is programmed into an envelope that is set to be 3.3 beats long, it will take seven bars for the pattern to repeat itself. Most of your listeners would probably think the motion was totally random, especially with mutes occurring every three beats.

Breakpoint Editing

In these examples, you edited the envelopes using the Pencil Tool. The Pencil tool creates steps that are as wide as your Quantization setting. Alas, step-style modulation is not always proper for some situations. For example, you may want to make a smooth panning ramp to cause the clip to swirl around your head. These ramps can be achieved by turning off the Pencil tool. With this tool off, you will edit the envelope in "breakpoint style."

When in Breakpoint mode, each "elbow" in the envelope will be marked with a tiny circle or *node*. Nodes are created by double-clicking with the mouse on the envelope. Double-clicking an existing node will remove it (see Figure 6.31). By moving the nodes around, complex modulation curves can be created.

Figure 6.31
Double-click to create and destroy nodes. Click and drag to reposition them. The clip shown here is the Breakpoint clip in the example.

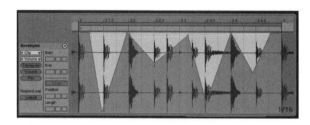

You can also select an area of the breakpoint curve and move all the selected nodes together as one unit. You can also click and drag segments of the envelope, causing its attached nodes to move as well. With a little clicking around, you'll quickly learn how to create your desired ramps.

❄ **CONTROL THE LEVELS**

If you like the timing of your envelope and you just want to change the level of a node or segment, hold down the Ctrl key (⌘ on Mac) while dragging it. Your moves will be restricted to the vertical plane and will also be more precise.

❄ **WARP MODES AND CLIP ENVELOPES**

The behaviors of some of the Clip Envelopes may seem incorrect when in Beats mode. Remember that Beats mode is treating sections of the audio file as independent slices. These slices are not processed through granular resynthesis and are therefore limited in their capabilities.

For example, when transients are set to 1/8, the Transpose Envelope will only have an effect every 1/8 note. Each slice will play at the pitch determined by the Transpose Envelope as the slice starts to play. If the Transpose Envelope changes value during the time when the slice is playing, it will be ignored. The next slice to play will sound at the pitch dictated by the Transpose Envelope at the new point. Therefore, even smooth ramps in the Transpose Envelope will create audible steps when retuning clips in Beats mode. To decrease the size of these steps, increase the clip's Transient setting. To hear a smooth Transpose curve, switch the clip to Tones or Texture mode.

Recording New Audio Clips

Now that you've got a grip on Audio Clips, you can really start putting them to use. While Audio Clips will frequently be created by dragging an audio file into Live from the Browser, you can also record a live audio input directly into a new clip. This means you can pick up your guitar and start throwing ideas into Live to be sorted out later. You can start putting out vocal fragments to begin sketching the structure of a song. You can record multiple clips of percussion to create multi-layered polyrhythms. Since you're recording anything that can be fed into your computer's audio interface, anything you can hear can be a potential piece of your song.

...In the Session View

New Audio Clips can be recorded in the Session View, even while the others are playing. First, select the source you're recording from in the track's Input menus. The top menu lets you select the source device, which includes options such as Ext. In (the inputs of your audio interface), Resample (for recording Live's Master output), ReWire applications (for recording the output of external programs such as Reason), and the outputs of the individual tracks in your Live Set. When you arm the track for recording, all of the Stop Clip buttons in the track's Clip Slots will turn to circles (see Figure 6.32). These are individual Clip Record buttons—click one of them to start recording a new clip in that location. You can stop recording by clicking the clip again, clicking the Stop button in the Control Bar, or disarming the track.

Figure 6.32
Select an active audio input, arm the track, and then click one of the circular Clip Record buttons in the Clip Slot Grid. Recording will commence at the time specified by the Global Quantize setting in the Control Bar.

What's fantastic about recording in the Session View is that Live can create perfect loops from the recordings with ease. Just as a clip will wait for the Launch Quantize setting before playing, clips will also wait for the same setting before recording. If you have Bar selected as the Global Quantize value, Live will wait until the downbeat of a measure before it begins to record. If you click the red Play button in the clip while it's recording, it will stop recording at the downbeat of the next measure. Furthermore, if your default launch mode is Trigger, the clip will immediately start looping when recording ends.

Please keep in mind that recording will stop following the Global Quantize setting only if you click the clip's Play button while recording. If you press Stop in the Control Bar or disarm the track, the recording will stop immediately.

SOUND ON SOUND

Since Live makes recording perfect loops so easy, you can build sections by doing multiple layers of recorded loops. For example, you can begin by recording some congas for four bars. When you stop recording, the clip immediately starts to loop. Move the clip to an empty Audio Track, and it will continue to play. You can then trigger another recording in the first track and play along with the congas. Perhaps you want to record a shaker part for the second loop. When you stop recording, the congas and shaker will both be looping in sync with one another. You can keep layering additional clips in this fashion and then resample the output into one final clip when you're done.

Doing multiple takes (repeated recordings of the same part of the song) is as easy as triggering additional Clip Record buttons in the track. Every time a new recording starts, the previous one will end. You can then go back and listen to each take individually to find the best one. You could then move the clips to the Arrangement View to edit the multiple takes together into one perfect "super-take" that is a consolidation of the best parts of each of the individual takes.

Of course, the nicest thing about this workflow in the Session View is that it allows you to quickly build layers and sections of a song without ever stopping Live. You can then go back and audition all of your new clips and capture scenes to start arranging the sections of your song.

ON THE LEVEL

Before you start recording, check your input signal level to make sure it's not too high or too low. The track's meters will show the volume of any incoming signal as soon as the track is armed. Play the part to be recorded as loud as you plan to while watching Live's meters. If the signal is too loud (the meters reach the top), you may distort, or clip, the recording. If the level is too low, your sound may become grainy when turning it up to match the rest of your song. Even if you're recording a part that should be quiet in your song, always record it as loud as possible without distorting. You can then turn down the part in the mix when you play it back.

...In the Arrangement View

To record an Audio Clip directly into the Arrangement, select the channel input and arm the track just like setting up recording in the Session View. This time, instead of pressing one of the Clip

Record buttons, press the Arrangement Record button in the Control Bar (see Figure 6.33). When you start Live's transport, it will begin recording a new clip into the corresponding track of the Arrangement while playing back the other tracks in the Live Set. Stop the transport, disarm the track, or turn off the Record button in the Control Bar to end recording.

Figure 6.33

I'm recording a new Audio Clip in Track 2 of the Arrangement. You need to arm the track for recording and enable Record in the Control Bar to record new data into to the Arrangement.

❄ **GET READY, GET SET, GO!**

New to Live 5 is the Count In feature, which is found on the Misc tab of the Preferences. When this is active, Live will wait the specified number of bars before recording actually commences. This will only work if the Live transport is stopped when you initiate recording (if the transport is already running, the Count In setting will be ignored). During the count off, the metronome will sound so you can "get into the beat" before it's time to play. This feature will work in both the Session and Arrangement Views.

You can also automate Arrangement recording using the Punch-In/Punch-Out values in the Control Bar. Set the Start and End Markers around the area you want to record. Engage the Punch-In and Punch-Out buttons (see Figure 6.34) and press Record and then Play in the Control Bar. Live will start running but will wait for the Punch-In time before starting to record. Recording will continue until the Punch-Out point is reached. You may, of course, use just the Punch-In or Punch-Out feature by itself if you choose.

❄ **RECORDING EFFECTS**

If a track's monitoring is set to Auto while it's armed for recording, Live will play the incoming audio through the Session Mixer and out to your speakers or headphones. You can place effects onto the track for real-time processing of your input, but Live will still record the part without these effects.

If you want to record the sound of your incoming part *with* the effects, you'll need to use another Audio Track. On the second track, set its audio input to the first track. The sound of your incoming audio will be processed by the effects on the first track, which you can then record on the second track.

Figure 6.34
Live will automatically begin recording on Track 3 at bar 3 and then stop recording at bar 7. This leaves your hands free to play your instrument instead of trying to trigger the recording.

Editing Audio Clips

After you've recorded your new clips, you may need to edit them. Perhaps you rushed a part or breathed too loudly between your vocal lines. There are a variety of ways to alter your clips after they're recorded, and these are a few you'll want to check every time.

Clip Timing and Rhythm

Live's functionality is dependent on your ability to adjust the timing of audio files to match playback of others. Whether an Audio Clip is created by dragging a file into Live or by recording something new, the method for fixing the timing of the file is the same: Warp Markers. After you've recorded your part, look it over and see if it needs to have any warp adjustments made. You may see that you played a few notes a little early with one note late near the end. Whatever the mistakes are, you can quickly fix them with a few clicks using Warp Markers. Then check your Warp mode and set it to something appropriate for the audio file, as explained at the beginning of this chapter. Press the Save button in the Sample window so your markers and tunings are saved with the audio file, in case you use it in another project. Making a habit of doing this now will help keep future creative sessions running smoothly.

Destructive Sample Editing

Some of the mistakes in an audio file may be so minute that they are more appropriate for a detailed offline sample editor like Steinberg WaveLab, Sony Sound Forge, Bias Peak, etc. Within these specialized editing environments, you can make edits more detailed than could be achieved with Live alone. When you save your changes, the new audio file will be ready for use in your clip.

Editing in the Arrangement

While using the Session View to record new pieces of audio, the Arrangement can be used as a "splicing block" for editing multiple clips together. If you want to use the first two bars of Vox A and the last bar of Vox B, you can arrange them as such on an Arrangement Track and then consolidate the clips into one new one (see Figures 6.35a and 6.35b).

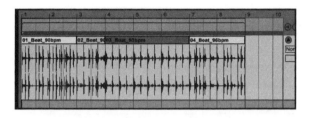

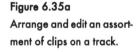

Figure 6.35a
Arrange and edit an assortment of clips on a track.

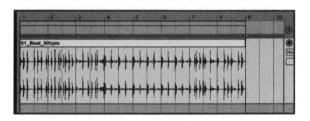

Figure 6.35b
Choose Consolidate from the Edit menu to render the track into one new clip, which can be moved back to the Session View.

The resulting clip will contain the parts from Vox takes A and B all wrapped up in one convenient Audio Clip. You can copy this clip from the Arrangement to the Session View for use in the developing song structure. If you need to change the edit, the original Audio Clips remain, so you can always do it again.

Tips for Great Loops

Looping audio files is an art form all on its own. You're trying to make something that was only played once sound like it's playing over and over again in perfect time with the rest of the parts in your song. While Live does an exceptional job of looping imported files (especially loops that are already cut to the right lengths), there may be times when Live is unable to determine the proper tempo and length of a file, especially in the case of a long audio file (like a whole song). When Live fails to identify a loop, you can quickly tell it where the loop points should be and figure the original tempo. The tools to do this are simple, and the concepts are just as easy:

❈ **Set Warp Marker 1:** Always be sure that the loop is actually beginning on the downbeat of the sample. Zoom in at the beginning of the sample (see Figure 6.36) and make sure there is no silence before the sound starts. If there is, slide Marker 1 over to change the start location.

❈ **Do the same zoom-in check at the end of your sample:** Make sure there is no extra noise from a following beat (see Figure 6.37). Just like above, move the last marker in line with the beginning of this noise if it's present.

Figure 6.36
Make sure there's no dead air before the sample starts.

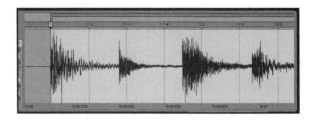

Figure 6.37
Check the end of the loop for any extraneous noise that shouldn't be there.

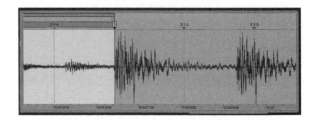

❋ **Check the beats in between:** If the beginning and end markers are in the right place, there's still no guarantee that every beat of the loop will be locked in with the rest of your parts (Figure 6.38). Check all the major beats and be sure that the sounds are lined up properly. Create Warp Markers to compensate when necessary.

Figure 6.38
You can see that the sub-beats of this loop are not lined up, even though the first and last markers are in the right place. Additional Warp Markers will be necessary to fix the timing of this loop.

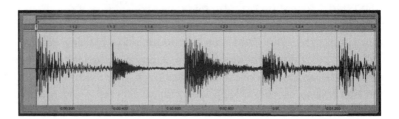

❋ **Make sure that the Fade button is on:** This will perform a quick fade at the beginning and end of the audio loop to remove any "clicks" that can occur at the loop point.

❋ **Experiment with all of the Warp modes:** While Beats mode will be rhythmically accurate, it may cause sonic artifacts that outweigh the rhythmic precision. You may find that some of your loops sound better in Tones mode. Don't forget to check Re-Pitch mode as well—some drum loops will sound better with no Warp processing at all.

✳ **Play with the Warp Markers:** The elastic audio possibilities of the Warp Engine are staggering. While you can fix timing errors with Warp Markers, try messing things up a bit by "shifting" some beats. Is there a Warp Marker on beat 1.2? What happens if you put the 1.1.4 marker there instead? The sound will now play a 1/16 note early! Use this in combination with the Sample Offset Envelope in Beats mode to reorder the slices in your loop. Then layer a Transpose Envelope, then an unlinked Pan Envelope, and then whatever other parameters you dare to experiment with!

proteus

We all have guilty pleasures, don't we? Mine happens to be the song "Toxic" by Britney Spears. I don't care for anything else she's done, but that song totally rocks. When I happened to stumble across a bootleg Psytrance mix of the song, I was quite interested in who pulled it off. The man behind the mix is Fernando Arquines, aka pr0teus. This guy has played all over the world, and here's what he had to say about Live:

The complexity of Psytrance makes a truly live performance difficult to achieve. I've been searching for the best way to perform my music "live" for years. I wanted a way to trigger, layer, and manipulate sounds on the fly, which led me to purchase the M-Audio Trigger Finger. It wasn't until then that Ableton Live came into the picture. I could have sworn the Trigger Finger was specifically designed for Live as I began to notice that they complemented each other perfectly.

Now, I have complete control over my Live Sets. I'm constantly changing my Live setup, but here's a good example of one I used recently: I Warp-Marker all of my tracks and set them aside in a couple muted "queue tracks." I used one of the Trigger Finger's faders to control the crossfader on two main tracks, which I use much like a DJ setup. I have an EQ Three on each of these tracks, which are controlled by computer keyboard assignments. Now the fun starts: I have two loop tracks, which I use for drum, percussion, and synth loops. I use more faders on the Trigger Finger to control the track levels. My main loop track is fed to an EQ Four, Auto Filter, Compressor II, and finally a Chorus. I've got a set of Trigger Finger knobs that are assigned to control the Auto Filter Cutoff and Resonance, and another set of knobs that are assigned to control the Chorus Modulation Amount and Rate. This setup is great for mangling my loops to get weird sounds. I also set up another track to sprinkle vocal samples here and there.

The other main part of my Live setup integrates the 16 pads on the Trigger Finger. I use my last Trigger Finger fader to control the level of a MIDI Track set up to control Native Instruments' Battery. I assign a sound to each pad, grouping them ergonomically for efficient triggering. For example, a group of pads for hand drum samples, another group for staccato FX samples, another for longer spacey samples, etc. Then I just fade it in and jam out with the track, layering whacked-out FX and percussion on top of the mix. One wicked trick is to take a short sample in Battery, such as a snare, and set it to loop. I assign it to one of the Trigger Finger's pads and set the pad's pressure to send its MIDI CC to control the loop length. When I press the pad lightly, it will retrigger the snare slowly. As I press harder, it speeds up to create an insane motor sound. I just go wild! I also use the same MIDI CC to control the pitch of the sample, too. I can then assign one of the Trigger Finger's knobs to control the pan and toss the sound across the stereo field. The possibilities are simply mind-boggling! I've been using Live along with the Trigger Finger for a while now, and I find the two inseparable. I see the difference on the dance floor, and after my set, I hear the enthusiastic response from the dancers. I've only been using Live and the Trigger Finger for just over three months. This is only the tip of the iceberg!

7 The MIDI Clip

As expected, implementation of MIDI in Live is leveraged from the concepts set forth by Audio Clips. Each MIDI Clip is its own, self-contained sequencer with its own data. Just like Audio Clips, every MIDI Clip is independent of all the others. MIDI Clips with the same name can all be edited independently, allowing collections of infinitely varied clips to be generated effortlessly.

The good news is that MIDI Clips are actually simpler to manipulate than their Audio Clip brothers. Ple MIDI Clips don't use any files on the hard drive for playback. Instead, the MIDI data for the clip is saved in the Live Set project file itself. Unlike audio files, MIDI data does not need to be fed through any sort of Warp Engine when matching its playback speed to the project tempo, so you won't have to worry about Warp modes or any of the related settings, such as Warp Markers; nor do you have to worry about Hi-Q interpolation, RAM modes, locating audio files, or hard drive speeds. As a result, there are only a few parameters for MIDI Clips compared to the number required for Audio Clips.

If you've learned anything about Live so far, you'll know that the apparent simplicity of the MIDI Clip actually belies an extreme amount of power. You'll find that tossing MIDI notes and commands at your virtual instruments and external hardware can be just as powerful (if not more so) as Audio Clips, especially since they both behave the same in regard to Launch modes, Launch Quantization, Follow Actions, and Envelopes. For this reason, using a combination of audio and MIDI in a Live Set is not confusing—Audio and MIDI Clips look and respond the same in both the Session and Arrangement Views. The differences aren't apparent until you start digging into the Clip and Track Views. In Chapter 5, "Making Music in Live," I discussed a good portion of the Clip View, such as naming and coloring clips, defining loops, and Follow Actions. These properties exist for both Audio and MIDI Clips. I also covered the additional areas of the Clip View that were unique to Audio Clips in Chapter 6, "The Audio Clip." Now it's time to look at the unique sections of the Clip View for MIDI Clips.

MIDI Clip Properties

The list of unique properties for a MIDI Clip is abbreviated compared to Audio Clips. As explained previously, manipulating MIDI information is not limited to the same constraints found when dealing with audio files. In the MIDI world, pitch is not related to time. You can speed up a MIDI Clip without causing the MIDI notes to rise in pitch. The opposite is also true—you can transpose the notes in the MIDI Clip without changing its playback speed. Because all these changes are possible by editing the MIDI data, there is no need for special functions in the MIDI Clip View like the Transpose and Warp functions in an Audio Clip.

Furthermore, MIDI and Audio Clips approach controlling sound from different directions. While Audio Clips manipulate an existing sound (an audio file), MIDI Clips manipulate ways to actually *make* the sound by triggering another sound-creating device—be it an external device or a virtual instrument. This means the "sound" of a MIDI Clip is based entirely on the sound created by the device that receives the MIDI data from the clip.

> ❋ **BEST OF BOTH WORLDS**
>
> If there is an Audio Clip-specific function that you want to perform on your MIDI part, such as reversing the sound, you can record the output of the MIDI instrument into an Audio Clip in an Audio Track and then tweak this new clip.

The MIDI Clip View is much smaller than the Audio Clip View. The only properties that are unique to the MIDI Clip are the Bank, Sub-bank, and Program selectors (see Figure 7.1). Bank and Program Changes are used to recall particular sounds on the destination MIDI device. Most MIDI devices have the ability to save their settings, such as filter parameters, LFO speeds, modulation sources, etc. These saved settings are referred to as a programs, patches, presets, sounds, or instruments, depending on the manufacturer's nomenclature. Regardless of what the company calls its saved sounds, they are almost always accessed with MIDI Program and Bank Change messages. By setting the Program and Bank values in the Clip View, each clip can recall a different patch from the same instrument when it is launched.

A Program Change is a MIDI message with a value between 0 and 127 (that's no surprise, is it?) and refers to a memory location in your MIDI device's sound bank. The way a manufacturer maps the Program message to the memory slots is entirely up to them, but generally a Program Change of 0 will cause the first sound on the instrument to be loaded. In the case of a General MIDI synthesizer, this will load a piano patch (the General MIDI specification includes a predefined list of standard instruments and their associated program numbers that manufacturers should adhere to). So, using the Program Change message, you can recall a sound from our instrument's 128 choices. But what if your device has more than 128 sounds? That's where the Bank Change

Figure 7.1
The above settings will recall the twentieth sound in the ninth bank of the associated Wavestation instrument. When using the factory default sound bank, these settings will load the Sub Stick sound.

The Bank and Program selectors

message comes into play. A bank holds 128 programs. So, you can recall any sound in your MIDI device by first specifying the containing bank followed by the program number.

Again, the way instrument manufacturers choose to assign sounds to banks and programs is entirely up to them. For example, Waldorf's MicroQ has three banks of 100 sounds. This means that Program Changes 100 through 127 aren't used by the MicroQ. Furthermore, the first sound is labeled as Bank A Sound 01. This means that a Program Change of 0 will recall sound A01. A Program Change of 15 will recall A16. Therefore, if you wanted to use sound B01, you'd first have to send a Bank Change message to switch from bank A to bank B and then issue a Program Change of 0 to recall the first patch in that bank (number 01).

You will probably have to consult the manual for your MIDI instrument to find out how the manufacturer is using the Bank and Program Change messages. Some will even require that the Bank Change be done with two numbers, thus the presence of the Sub-bank setting in the MIDI Clip properties.

While this may sound confusing, figuring out how your MIDI instruments respond to these messages will open up a level of flexibility where each clip in a MIDI Track can "sound" different. This is because a new sound will be loaded when you launch a new clip. When using the Waldorf mentioned above, you can make one MIDI Clip that is a string part, while another clip (in the same track) is an arpeggiated blip sequence. If you do not want to change the patches of your virtual instruments during your song, you can just load the patch you want directly in the instrument's interface, and Live will recall it each time the Set is loaded.

Recording New MIDI Clips

To harness the power of MIDI Clips, you'll need to make some first. The easiest way to make a MIDI Clip is to simply record a part from a MIDI device, such as a keyboard, EWI (electronic wind instrument), MIDI guitar, or a controller, although you can also record the MIDI output of other MIDI Tracks and external sequencers. You'll need to have a MIDI interface (discussed in Chapter 3, "Getting Live Up and Running") to record an external MIDI source. Some audio interfaces include MIDI ports, making them especially handy in this situation. After you have your MIDI device connected and selected in the Preferences, you're ready to record.

...In the Session View

In the Session View, recording a new MIDI Clip is almost identical to recording an Audio Clip. The fact that the procedures are similar means there is less for you to learn and remember when using Live. It makes the composition process more transparent because you'll use the same motions every time you record, be it audio or MIDI.

To begin, make a MIDI Track Ctrl(⌘)+Shift+T. Then specify the MIDI input you'll be recording. This is done in the Input/Output Routing strip, shown in Figure 7.2, by selecting the MIDI input device followed by the channel you want to record. Live has a setting called *All Channels* that will record any MIDI data entering the selected input, regardless of the MIDI channel assigned to the data. If you have only one device connected to the MIDI device you selected, then All Channels will be an appropriate setting. If you have multiple instruments entering the selected MIDI port, you may want to specify the channel you want to record to prevent data from another instrument being recorded in your clip. Of course, in order to hear your MIDI data, you'll need to select an output destination for the MIDI Track. You can simply load a virtual instrument onto the track, or you can specify an external device and channel to play the MIDI.

In the example above, the input and output have been specified for the track, so I can set the track for recording by activating the Arm button in the Session Mixer. With Monitor set to Auto, I'll now be able to play the MicroQ from the Ozonic keyboard (MIDI data enters the track from the Ozonic and is then immediately sent out to the Waldorf). The track is now ready to record.

You'll notice that all the Clip Stop buttons in the track have changed to circles. Clicking one of these circles will begin recording a new MIDI Clip in that slot. Just like Audio Clips, recording will wait for the time specified by the Global Quantize setting. Once recording has commenced, start playing. Everything you do, including pitch bends, aftertouch, knob tweaks, etc., will be recorded into the MIDI Clip. When you're done, click the play icon in the clip to stop recording (if your

Figure 7.2
The M-Audio Ozonic key-
board has been selected as
the MIDI input device.
Since the Ozonic is just a
controller keyboard, I can
tell Live to listen to all incoming MIDI channels. This
track will end up controlling
channel 4 of Waldorf's MicroQ, which is hooked up
to the MIDI Out port of the
Ozonic.

default Launch mode is Trigger, the clip will begin playing back your new recording). You can start recording additional takes by clicking the circles in any of the other Clip Slots.

...In the Arrangement View

If recording MIDI Clips resembles recording Audio Clips in the Session View, you can probably already guess how to record MIDI Clips in the Arrangement View. Indeed, it is the same procedure used with Audio Clips in the Arrangement View. You'll need to set up your MIDI input and output first, as explained in Figure 7.2. You'll also arm the track, but instead of using the circles in the Clip Slots to start recording, you'll click the Record button in the Control Bar. When you press Play in the Control Bar, Live will start playing your Arrangement while recording your new MIDI Clip (see Figure 7.3). If Live is already playing, recording will begin the instant you press the Record button. By arming multiple tracks, you can record multiple clips simultaneously, allowing Live to work as a multi-track MIDI recorder. You can, of course, also record multiple Audio Clips at the same time, too!

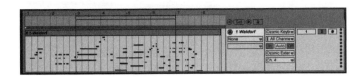

Figure 7.3
Clips are recorded into the
Arrangement when the
Record button in the Con-
trol Bar is activated.

Quantizing Your Performance

Nobody's perfect. We can't always play our instruments with the rhythmical precision of a drum machine; but, with judicious use of quantizing, Live can make you sound like you're dead-on the beat. *Quantizing* is the process of aligning events to a timing grid. In the case of Launch Quantizing used in the Session View, you're making sure your clips start playing on a division of your timing grid. When quantizing a MIDI Clip, you're making sure *every note* is aligned to the grid.

Live, by default, will automatically quantize any MIDI Clip you record. If you record a part and immediately play it back, it will be perfectly aligned to the rhythmic subdivisions currently selected in the Record Quantization menu (see Figures 7.4a and 7.4b). This is great as it keeps you from having to manually quantize every MIDI Clip you make. This is a dream come true when programming drum beats since every recording will be rhythmically tight. The size of the subdivisions used for the Quantize function is set in the Edit → Record Quantization menu. Live can quantize notes to a grid of 1/4 notes, 1/16 note triplets, and everything in between.

Figure 7.4a

Here are some unquantized MIDI notes.

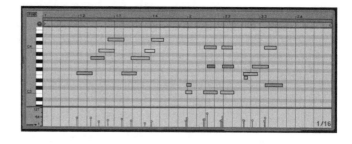

Figure 7.4b

The same notes after quantizing. Notice how each note's left edge is aligned with one of the grid lines.

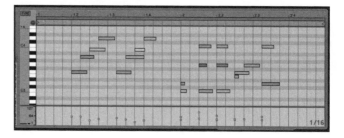

Of course, not every style of music demands strict rhythmic quantization. In fact, many musicians prefer to keep the natural feel of their performances in their takes. You can turn off Live's automatic quantizing by choosing No Quantization from the Record Quantize menu.

If you decide later that you do want to quantize the part, press Ctrl(⌘)+U to open Live's Quantizing dialog box (see Figure 7.5). This new dialog box offers more control over how Live quantizes your performances. The first value at the top sets the quantize grid. You must set this to the smallest subdivision that occurs in the part. If you have played a part with 1/16 notes, you'll need to select 1/16 here. If you select 1/8, the Quantize function will move the 1/16 notes to the closest 1/8 note, therefore screwing up the part.

Figure 7.5
Live's new Quantize dialog box will tailor the method in which Live quantizes your notes.

Below the grid selection are two buttons labeled Start and End. By default, only Start is enabled. This means that Live will only change the start location of a note when it quantizes—the length of the note will remain the same. If you enable End as well, Live will make sure that the note ends on a grid subdivision, too. This is handy for rapid-fire synth bass sequences, as each note will be on beat *and* the same length. If you wanted, you could deselect Start, making Live fix only the end of each note.

The last parameter in the dialog box is the Amount value. Normally, this is set to 100 percent, which makes Live force every note to the nearest grid subdivision. If you set this value to 50 percent, Live will only move the notes halfway to the proper place. The result is a tighter performance, but one that is not completely rigid. This is great for piano parts because there are usually lots of grace notes and other flairs that get destroyed by perfect rhythmic timing.

 THE UNDO TWO-STEP

When Live is set to automatically quantize a recording, you'll still be able to undo the quantizing in case you left it on by accident. The first time you press Ctrl(⌘)+Z after recording, the recorded notes will move to their original, unquantized locations. The second Undo will erase the clip, allowing you to make another.

Overdub Recording

Overdub recording is a function available only for MIDI Clips; it records additional MIDI data into a clip without erasing what's already there. This is an awesome feature when it comes to programming drum beats, since you can build them one piece at a time. You can make a two-bar loop with a hi-hat and then play the additional parts (kick drums, snares, cymbals, etc.) layer by layer as the clip continues to loop.

To enable MIDI Overdub recording, click the OVR button in the Control Bar (see Figure 7.6). When you launch a clip, it will start playing, and its play triangle will be green. After you arm the track for recording, the MIDI Clip will keep playing, but its play triangle will turn red. This signifies that the clip is playing *and* recording at the same time. Anything you play at this point will be added to the current MIDI Clip (it will be quantized on the fly, too, if Record Quantization is enabled), and each iteration of the loop will contain the new data you recorded.

Figure 7.6

MIDI Overdub recording allows parts to be built in layers while a MIDI Clip is playing. Note that recording occurs for any playing clip on an armed track.

Overdub is on.

This Clip is playing and recording at the same time.

This track is armed.

Combined with the drag-and-drop techniques of the Session View, programming variations of beats can be accomplished in moments instead of minutes. You can start with a simple drum pattern (perhaps just kick drum and hi-hat for the intro of your song), drag-copy (use the Ctrl key while dragging) the clip to a new location, and then use the MIDI Overdub to layer the snare hits on top of the kick and hi-hat. You'll now have two MIDI Clips, one with just kick and hats and the other with a snare added. You can drag-copy the new MIDI Clip and layer on an additional part, such as a shaker or congas. Using this technique, you can build a collection of drum variations quickly for your song, which you can then trigger on the fly.

Of course, you can use Overdub recording for more than drums. If a piano part is really tricky, you could record the left hand and right hand parts separately. Perhaps you'll perform the left hand part on the first pass and then overdub the right hand on the next pass.

> ❋ **MIDI ON MIDI**
>
> You can have Overdub enabled when recording new MIDI Clips. When you record a new clip, the process is the same as if Overdub were off; however, once you click the clip to stop recording, it will start looping and immediately enter Overdub mode (the play triangle will be red). You can start layering additional parts immediately without having to stop the music.

Editing MIDI Clips

One of the most attractive features of MIDI is the ability to edit the MIDI data in order to create a perfect part. Recorded notes can be effortlessly transposed to different pitches, extended or shortened, and moved to a different location in time. This can make recording MIDI parts a little easier because you don't have to worry about getting the part *exactly* right. You only need to get it close so you can make final adjustments to the MIDI data.

When you edit MIDI Clips in Live, you not only have the ability to change the notes that are recorded, but also create new ones by hand. In fact, many producers prefer to draw parts directly into the clips instead of playing them. It allows them to create specific performances, such as perfectly repeating 1/16 notes that are all the same duration and velocity. Editing data by hand also allows you to create precise automation, such as perfect volume fades and quantized filter modulations.

Adjusting the Grid

All editing in a MIDI Clip is governed by the timing grid. Anytime a note is created or moved, it will snap to the grid values. If your grid is set to 1/4, you'll only be able to align the MIDI notes to the 1/4 note of the clip. You can, of course, change the grid settings, allowing you to make more precise rhythmic adjustments. You can even turn the grid off completely for free-form editing.

Adjusting the timing grid in the MIDI Clip View is performed in the same manner as changing the grid in the Arrangement View (see Chapter 5). It is accomplished with a set of key commands outlined below. As you execute these key commands, you'll see the quantize value change in the MIDI data window (see Figure 7.7), reflecting your modification.

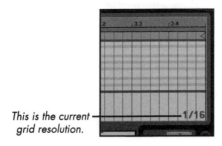

This is the current grid resolution.

Figure 7.7
The current grid setting is 1/16. This means all notes you manipulate will lock to 1/16- note timing.

* **Ctrl(⌘)+1**: This will decrease the value of the grid. If the grid was set to 1/16 before, it will be 1/32 after using this key command.

* **Ctrl(⌘)+2**: This has the opposite effect of the command above. A grid value of 1/16 will change to 1/8 after using this command.

* **Ctrl(⌘)+3**: This key command toggles triplet mode on and off. A previous setting of 1/8 will turn to 1/8T (1/8 note triplet) after pressing these keys. Use this key command again to switch triplet mode off.

* **Ctrl(⌘)+4**: This turns the entire grid on and off. When the grid is off, the grid value display will turn gray. You will be able to place MIDI data anywhere you like while the grid is off. To re-enable the grid, press this key command again.

SHOW ME MORE

Grid size is dependent on your current zoom level. The farther you zoom into a clip, the higher resolution you'll get. You can adjust the resolution standard by right-clicking (Ctrl + click on Mac) and selecting a size from the Adaptive or Fixed Grid settings presented in the context menu. You can also adjust grid settings from the Options menu.

Editing Notes and Velocities

Once you've got your desired grid timing selected, you're ready to start manipulating MIDI notes. Live displays MIDI notes in a style known as a "piano roll." This term comes from the old player-pianos that were programmed using rolls of paper. These rolls had small slots cut into them, each representing a specific note on the piano keyboard or one of the other instruments mounted inside. A note that played for a long time was triggered by a long slot in the paper. As the paper rolled by mechanical sensors, it triggered servos to play notes on the piano.

Viewing MIDI Data

The piano roll view in Live features a lane for each note in the MIDI scale. When looking at Figure 7.8 below, you'll see an image of a piano keyboard at the left side of the window. From each of these keys is a lane extending to the right where notes can be placed. Notes placed in these lanes trigger their corresponding key in the scale.

You can zoom in and out of the vertical piano keyboard, thus allowing you to see more or less of the 128 possible notes in the MIDI scale. You can zoom by moving your mouse over the piano keyboard at the left of the window. When the mouse changes to a magnifying glass, you can click and drag to zoom. Since the view is vertical instead of horizontal, the zooming moves have also been turned on their side. Dragging the mouse left and right will now adjust the zoom, while dragging up and down will scroll through the piano keyboard. If you zoom out too far, the piano keyboard will disappear. Zoom in to see it again.

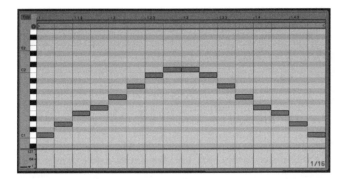

Figure 7.8
The MIDI data here is a C
Major scale. You can see
that only the white keys are
being triggered by the
MIDI notes.

❊ **INTO THE FOLD**

Live's MIDI display has a unique feature that hides any lanes that don't contain MIDI data. When the
Fold button is activated, the display will be condensed, and you'll only see the lanes that contain notes
in the clip. This is perfect for programming drums since many synths and keyboards map their sounds
over a wide range of octaves. You may be using a kick drum sound at D1, while using a hi-hat sound
three octaves higher at E4. So, instead of scrolling up and down repeatedly to see the two parts, you
can press Fold, and you'll see only the lanes for D1 and E4, making editing a snap. Turn Fold off to see
all the lanes again.

Previewing MIDI Notes
Live 5 now includes a tiny little headphone icon right above the keyboard shown in the piano
roll. The headphone icon looks like the Pre-listen icon found in the Browser and has a nearly
identical function. When this button is on, each MIDI note that you click on in the editing grid will
also be sent out to the connected MIDI instrument. This allows you to hear every note that you
add and edit, which can help you keep from editing the wrong note or placing a note in the wrong
lane. Additionally, you can click on the keys at the left edge of the grid to preview the sounds.

Editing MIDI Data with the Pencil
There are two methods for editing MIDI data: with or without the Pencil. When the Pencil is on
(activate it in the Control Bar or press Ctrl⌘+B), you can quickly add notes to the MIDI note
window and set their velocities. Clicking in the grid will cause a note to appear that is the length
of the current grid setting. If you continue to hold the mouse button after you create the note, you
can drag up and down to set its velocity. If you click and drag horizontally (see Figure 7.9), the
Pencil will create a series of notes in that lane, great for hi-hat patterns. (You can also drag up
and down to set the velocities of the whole group.) Clicking an existing note with the Pencil will
erase it.

Figure 7.9
I used the Pencil to quickly draw in a series of 1/16 notes for the 909 HiHat Closed sound.

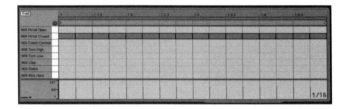

Editing MIDI Data without the Pencil

While writing notes with the Pencil can be extremely efficient, there are a few things that can't be done with the Pencil, such as changing the start time and length of a MIDI note. These advanced edits can be performed by switching the Pencil tool off (click the icon in the Control Bar or press Ctrl⌘+B to toggle it). When the Pencil is off, your mouse will appear as a standard arrow.

To create a MIDI note in this mode, double-click an empty slot. After the note has been made, you can click and drag it to a new location. This will let you change the pitch and time for the note in one maneuver. When you move the mouse to either end of the MIDI note, the mouse will change to a bracket (it will look like "[" at the beginning of the note and "]" at the end). Clicking and dragging in this location will stretch the MIDI note, making it either longer or shorter. Double-clicking the note again will erase it.

To adjust the velocity of a note when you're not using the Pencil requires exposing the velocity lane in the MIDI note window. This lane can be viewed by dragging the lower boundary upward (see Figure 7.10). The velocity of each note is represented by a vertical line with a small circle at the top. The taller the line, the greater the velocity. Since multiple notes can occur in different lanes at one time in a MIDI Clip, it's possible that the velocities for multiple notes will be stacked on top of one another. As you move your mouse over one of the circular handles at the top of the velocity lines, you'll see its corresponding note become highlighted in the upper window, showing you which note you're about to edit. I actually recommend doing the reverse, however, by selecting the note in the upper portion of the window first to ensure you will edit the right velocity. If you do decide to use the Pencil tool in the velocity lane, you will not be able to specify which note to edit when two or more occur at the same time (vertically aligned). Instead, the Pencil will set these notes to the same velocity.

Figure 7.10
By dragging the bottom border upward, I've enlarged the velocity lane.

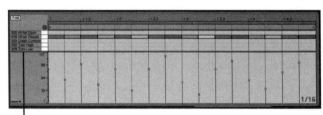

Click here and drag upward.

Another benefit of not using the Pencil is you can select groups of MIDI notes to edit. You can click and drag around the area of notes you want, or you can select them individually by holding Shift and clicking. Once selected, you can perform edits on multiple notes at once. You can drag the notes to a new location, changing their pitch and timing. You can lengthen or shorten them as a group. You can copy them using all the standard Cut, Copy, and Paste commands (even the dragging techniques of the Session View work here), or you can scale their velocities all at once in the lower window.

MIDI Clip Envelopes

After your MIDI notes are straightened out, it will be time to look at your Clips Envelopes. That's right, MIDI Clips have Clip Envelopes just like Audio Clips—some are even identical. These envelopes will be used for creating controller data to be sent to your MIDI devices. When effects and instruments are loaded onto the MIDI Track, the Clip Envelopes will be able to control those devices, too.

MIDI Ctrl Envelopes

In a MIDI Track with an empty Track View, the only category of envelopes that will be available are the MIDI Ctrl Envelopes. These are controllers such as Pitch Bend, Modulation, Volume, Pan, and Sustain, and all are shown as graphical envelopes in the Clip View (see Figure 7.11). These envelopes generate values that are translated to MIDI data and then sent to the destination MIDI device.

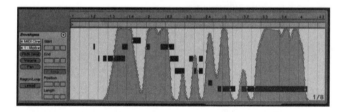

Figure 7.11
The movements of the mod wheel are represented by an envelope that bears a striking resemblance to a roller coaster.

When you look through the list of available MIDI controllers, you'll see some of them have already been named, such as Volume, Breath, Pan, and Expression. This is because part of the MIDI standard defines certain controller numbers for certain musical tasks. Controller 10 is generally Pan. Controller 7 is usually Volume, and so on. Whether these controllers actually have any effect or not will be determined by the MIDI device on the receiving end. If you have an old analog synth with MIDI, it may respond to notes and pitch bend, but it might not be able to do a pan. Others may not respond to Controller 7 for volume. You'll need to look at your MIDI device's manual, specifically the MIDI implementation chart (usually at the end of the manual), to see a list of the MIDI controllers and messages for the instrument.

The MIDI Envelopes are edited in the same fashion as the Clip Envelopes in the last chapter. You can edit them with or without the Pencil tool, and you can unlink them for interesting rhythmical results.

Mixer Envelopes

If you happen to load a virtual instrument onto your MIDI Track, a few more envelope categories will be available for your tweaking. Once the virtual instrument is in place, the track now behaves like an Audio Track. You'll see that you have a Mixer category available with Volume, Pan, and Send Envelopes. There will also be a category for the virtual instrument you loaded. This means you can modulate the parameters of the virtual instrument while it plays. Furthermore, any Audio or MIDI effects loaded into the track will be available for tweaking.

SHORTCUT TO CONFUSION

I found a situation that had me scratching my head in confusion for a moment. I started programming a MIDI Clip on a track with no virtual instrument. (I was triggering an external synth.) I clicked the Pan button and programmed some movements. Everything was good.

Later, I loaded a virtual instrument onto the track. When I pressed the Pan button, I was presented with a flat line! I could hear the part panning around, but I couldn't see the automation anymore.

In a moment, I realized that I was looking at the *Mixer Pan* control. When I originally programmed the Pan, I did so at the MIDI level—I sent MIDI controller 10 messages to the synth. The Pan button had brought up MIDI Ctrl and 10-Pan in the Envelope menus. With the virtual instrument in place, the Pan button was now loading the Mixer and Pan menu selections.

When I manually switched the menus to MIDI Ctrl and 10-Pan, I could see my envelope again. This same behavior is true of the Volume button as well.

Virtual Instruments and Effects

You can draw and edit envelopes for parameters of the Live devices and plug-ins loaded onto a track by selecting them from the Clip Envelope menus. The top menu will select the device or plug-in, which can be an instrument or an effect (both audio and MIDI effects). For each device selected in the top menu, you'll get a list of device-specific parameters that can be edited.

IS THIS THING ON?

All controller values are represented as envelopes in Live. If the parameter you are controlling is a switch, values above 64 usually turn it on and values below turn it off. You'll need to make sure your envelope only passes above 64 when you want your parameter on.

Importing and Exporting MIDI Files

Live stores all MIDI data and parameters for MIDI Clips within the Live Set itself. While Audio Clips must play an audio file stored on a hard disk, the MIDI Clips don't require any sort of external support file that you need to keep track of. When you import a MIDI file, Live copies the data from the MIDI file into the Live Set. Live will never use the original MIDI file again. Should the file be changed or lost, the Live Set will still play perfectly.

Importing Standard MIDI Files

Live imports MIDI parts from Standard MIDI Files (SMFs). SMFs come in two flavors: Type 0 and Type 1. Type 0 won't do you any good in Live—all the parts are squished into one track. Type 1, on the other hand, has the MIDI parts split into separate tracks for each instrument. There will be a track for the bass, some for the drums, and tracks for any other part in the song, all of which will be displayed below the MIDI file when you open it in the Browser (see Figure 7.12). Live lets you import these tracks into new clips by dragging the tracks into your Session or Arrangement like regular clips.

Figure 7.12
This MIDI file has multiple tracks that can be individually added to the Live Set.

If you've got a song in another software, or perhaps something stuck in an older hardware sequencer, and you want to transfer it to Live, Standard MIDI Files will usually take care of the job. The format has been around for a long time, so you can be assured of compatibility; however, SMFs don't retain everything from a computer project. When exporting songs done in other programs, you may have been utilizing application-specific features that are beyond the scope of MIDI. This can include mixer and effect automation, as well as the port and channel assignments of the MIDI Tracks. This kind of information gets saved in the application's native file format but usually won't appear in a Standard MIDI File export. That type of automation will have to be reprogrammed.

Exporting Standard MIDI Files

If you need to take the MIDI part from a clip and send it to another Live Set or a different program, you can export the MIDI data as a Standard MIDI File. Select the clip and choose Export Selected MIDI Clip from Live's File menu. You'll be prompted for the name and destination for the exported data. Choose a location and name and click Save.

Using the Live Clip Format

New to Live 5 is the ability to save your MIDI Clips along with the virtual instrument you used for it, including any MIDI and Audio effects that were in use. This allows you to easily save your MIDI part as a musical idea in your collection of clips. When you add the clip to a new track in another song, it will load up the instrument and necessary effects automatically.

To export this kind of clip, simply click the clip and drag it into a file browser. It will appear there, and you will immediately be able to give the clip a new name. Press Enter when you're done renaming, and the clip will be saved.

You can differentiate these enhanced clips from regular clips by the icon that precedes the clip in the browser (see Figure 7.13). Additionally, these clips have an .alc file extension, which stands for Ableton Live Clip. If you click on the Library icon in a file browser, you'll see a folder named *Clips*. This folder contains a whole collection of these enhanced clips that are ready for you to drag directly into your own compositions. Check them out!

Figure 7.13
You can see that these files have a special icon in front of them, which indicates that these are Live Clips.

Now that you have a handle on the ins and outs of Audio and MIDI Clips and how to arrange them, it's time to start adding effects. The next chapter will show how effects, if used properly, can add another dimension to your music by introducing elements of sound design. You'll also learn how to use virtual instruments and put them fully under hardware control.

8 } Using Effects and Instruments

Effects can have a profound effect on your music. They can be used in a variety of ways: possibly to remove unwanted frequencies from an audio track (EQ); to create the sound of a room for a vocalist (Reverb); or to completely destroy and mangle a sound into something totally new (Distortion). Effects put a lot of power at your fingertips. Those people who are new to these toys will more than likely run hog-wild the first few times they get their hands on them. Hey, effects are fun—I know that. As with all things, practice will help you determine which type of effects will help your mix the most. Don't forget that sometimes having no effect on a sound can be the best decision.

Using Effects in a Session

What are effects and how do they work? In the simplest sense, an effect is a device that takes an input signal—either audio or MIDI data—performs calculations upon it, and spits the result out its other end. For example, a delay effect will take a sound into its input and then wait a specified amount of time before sending it out its output. A filter effect can take a sound, remove all the frequencies below 500Hz, and spit out the result. You can chain multiple effects together for even more power by having the output of one effect feed the input of another, and so on.

The Track View

In Live, the graphical layout of an effect chain is surprisingly simple and logical. Double-click a track name—either at the top of the Session View or at the right side of the Arrangement View—and you will see its Track View appear at the bottom of the Live window. Effects are placed in the Track View side by side to form a chain (see Figure 8.1). A signal enters the left-most device and proceeds through each until it comes out the right-hand side.

Figure 8.1

An arbitrary arrangement of audio effects in the Track View. The input signal is processed by each device in order from left to right.

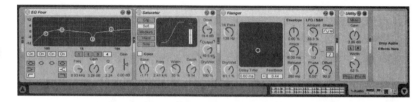

The Effect Browsers

You gain access to your collection of effects through the two Browser icons seen in Figure 8.2. The top icon activates the Live Device Browser (the built-in effects and instruments), while the lower icon activates the Plug-in Device Browser (your external VST and Audio Units effects and instruments).

Figure 8.2

These two buttons are located in the upper-left corner of the Live window. Click the top button to gain access to Live's built-in effects and instruments. The bottom button displays a list of all the plug-ins, both VST and AU, currently available to Live.

The Live Device Browser contains three folders, which can be opened to view the built-in Audio Effects, MIDI Effects, and Instruments, which will be individually discussed later. The folder layout of the Plug-in Browser, on the other hand, will depend entirely on the current configuration of your system and the plug-ins that are available to Live.

Adding a Plug-in to a Track

Adding a plug-in from one of the Browsers is as easy as it gets. In fact, there are three different ways to load these devices onto a track, all of which may be used interchangeably:

* The first method is to click and drag a device from the Browser to the desired track, as shown in Figure 8.3. This will cause the new effect to be added to the right side of the effect chain if there are any pre-existing devices on the track.

...and drag to here.

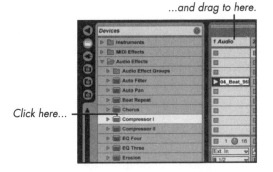

Click here...

Figure 8.3
Click and drag an effect from the browser to the title of a track. When you release your mouse button, the effect will be loaded into the track.

❁ The second method involves first selecting the destination track (click on the track's name) and then double-clicking the desired device or plug-in in the Browser. Just as above, the selected effect will be loaded into the far-right position in the track's effect chain.

❁ The final method involves double-clicking the name of a track to expose its Track View. You may then drag and drop effects from the Browsers directly into the Track View (see Figure 8.4). The benefit of this method is that you may choose where in the device chain the new effect will be loaded instead of always defaulting to the last position, as in the previous two methods. If you decide that you need some EQ before your compressor, you can simply drag it into this location.

Click here...

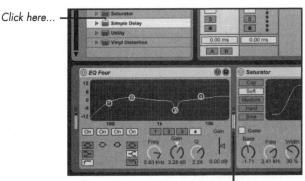

Figure 8.4
By dragging devices straight into the Track View, you can choose to insert them at any point in the chain that you want.

...and drag to here.

All three methods explained above work identically in both the Session View and Arrangement View. Just remember that in the Session View, the track names are found at the top of the window, while the track names are found on the right side of the Arrangement View.

Plug-in Types

There are three types of plug-ins to deal with in Live: Audio Effects, MIDI Effects, and Virtual Instruments. As you would assume, Audio Effects process and alter only audio signals, while MIDI Effects perform calculations on passing MIDI data. It also makes sense that a MIDI Effect can't be used on an Audio Track or vice versa. There is a special case, however, in which MIDI and Audio Effects can exist on the same track—when using the third device type, a Virtual Instrument, on a MIDI Track.

Audio Effects

Audio Effects have existed in Live since the program's first release. Audio Effects can be used to correct tone problems, add ambience to sounds, or shape noise into completely new textures— the possibilities are staggering. Audio Effects include equalizers, delays, choruses, pitch shifters, flangers, compressors, phasers, gates, distortions, and limiters. There may be a few more esoteric effects not categorized here for sure, but the majority of audio plug-ins will be of these types. Live includes a collection of 22 Audio Effects for your perusal, use, and abuse. A complete dissertation on said effects appears in the next chapter.

Audio Effects can be used only on Audio Tracks. An attempt to place an Audio Effect on a MIDI Track will be only somewhat successful. The effect will be loaded, but it will be preceded by a warning message (see Figure 8.5).

Figure 8.5

Here's a Compressor II sitting on a MIDI Track. Notice the Drop Instrument Here message before the device. Do you think something should go there?

Virtual Instruments

When Live tells you to Drop Instrument Here, it's not directing you to drop your keyboard. Instead, it is referring to a *Virtual Instrument* plug-in. While you probably wouldn't consider an instrument an effect, virtual instruments still reside within your effect chain. This is because you can think of an instrument as an effect—it takes MIDI input, like a MIDI Effect, but spits out audio, like an Audio Effect. This allows you to create MIDI data in the Session or Arrangement View and feed it into an instrument to hear the results.

Live comes with three instruments of its own: Impulse, Simpler, and Operator (see Chapter 9, "Live's Virtual Instruments," for the scoop on these), plus supports any plug-in instrument conforming to the VSTi standard. Mac OS X users also have the ability to use Audio Unit

206
✳ ✳ ✳

instruments, too. When you place an instrument onto a MIDI Track, everything to the left of the instrument is MIDI, and everything to the right is audio (see Figure 8.6).

Figure 8.6

I've added Live's Impulse instrument to the MIDI Track. This track will now function properly, and the output of Impulse will be compressed by Compressor II.

By adding an instrument to a MIDI Track, you end up converting it into a hybrid Audio/MIDI Track. The result can be seen when looking at the I/O Routing section of the Session Mixer (see Figure 8.7).

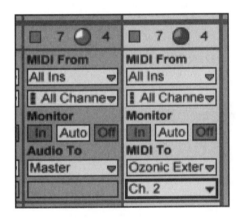

Figure 8.7

The I/O section on the left is for the track in the examples above. Adding the Impulse has caused the router to change the output format of the track from MIDI to audio. The track on the right does not have an instrument loaded, so MIDI is never changed to audio. Thus, the right track still outputs MIDI.

MIDI Effects

The last type of effect used in Live is the MIDI Effect. Placing these on a MIDI Track will alter the MIDI messages being passed through the effect chain. These alterations can range from subtle, such as smoothing out velocity response, to drastic, as when remapping notes to different pitches or using the Arpeggiator. Keep in mind that MIDI Effects do not alter what you hear; they alter what an instrument is told to play. Consider the following information.

You load your favorite piano plug-in onto a MIDI Track. You record a short riff into a clip and set it looping. You then load the Pitch Effect onto the track right before the piano plug-in. As you turn up the Transpose knob on the Pitch Effect, the notes being sent to the piano plug-in are shifted upward. The result is that the piano plug-in now plays the part in a higher register. You'll also notice that as you continue to increase the Transpose knob further, the piano will play higher and higher *while still sounding natural*. This is because you are not shifting the sound of the piano upward, you're moving the MIDI notes used to trigger the piano upward. It's exactly as if you'd moved your hands to a different part of the keyboard and played the part again.

Now, you remove the Pitch Effect and record the piano part into an Audio Clip. As you transpose the Audio Clip higher, there will be a point at which the piano starts sounding artificial. This is the difference between changing pitch in the MIDI and audio domains. The Pitch Effect changes what the instrument plays, which results in a more pleasing transposition.

This distinction also has its "gotchas" that can result in seemingly confusing behaviors for MIDI Effects in certain scenarios. If you use the Pitch Effect (see Figure 8.8) to transpose the MIDI messages sent to the Impulse up two octaves, you will not hear the drums sounding higher in pitch. In fact, you won't hear any drums at all! This is because the MIDI notes being sent to the Impulse are now two octaves above the notes that are used to trigger the samples. If you wanted to play Impulse on your external keyboards, you'd now have to play the notes two octaves lower in order to trigger the sounds. When the sounds are triggered, they will still be at their original pitch. If this situation doesn't make sense, take a look at the MIDI Pitch example provided in the Chapter 8 folder from the CD-ROM. When you first run it, the beat will play normally. Try adjusting the Pitch knob in the MIDI Pitch Effect, and you'll hear the result.

Figure 8.8

The Pitch device is transposing the MIDI data out of the operating range for Impulse. You can see the MIDI data entering the Impulse on its left, but there's no audio exiting on its right.

Third-Party Plug-ins

While Live offers an impressive collection of 31 devices right out of the box, you may still prefer to use plug-in effects and instruments from other manufacturers. Live fully supports the VST and Audio Units (Mac OS X only) plug-in standards, allowing limitless expansion possibilities for your virtual studio.

While all of Live's plug-ins can be edited entirely from their graphical interfaces in the Track View, the nature of VST and AU plug-ins and their fully customizable graphical interfaces requires that a separate window be used to display the effect. When an external plug-in is loaded, a generic

X-Y object will be displayed in the Track View (see Figure 8.9), allowing access to more detailed functions.

Click here to open the plug-in's editor.

Figure 8.9
A VST or Audio Units plug-in shows up as a generic placeholder. Clicking the wrench icon opens up the plug-in's custom graphical interface.

Reordering and Removing Effects

Live allows you to change the order of effects easily within a chain. This ability provides a way to experiment with different device arrangements. Does it sound better to run a vocal through a reverb and then into a delay or the other way around? To find out, just drag and drop the pre-existing effects within the Track View to change their order (see Figure 8.10). The results will be heard immediately. When dragging an effect between existing effects, you'll see a dark line appear, indicating the insertion point for when the mouse is released.

...and drag to here.   *Click here...*

Figure 8.10
Click and drag the Simple Delay to the left side of the Track View. When you re-lease the mouse button, the two effects will switch positions.

> ❋ **WITH OR WITHOUT YOU**
>
> If you want to compare the sound of a track with and without an effect, click the effect's power button located in the upper-left corner of the effect's window. You can toggle the effect on and off without having to delete it. When the effect is turned off, audio will bypass the effect and continue through any others in your chain.

If an effect is no longer needed (perhaps you resampled this track and now wish to remove its effects) or it was loaded by accident, click on the effect title bar to select it and press Delete on your computer keyboard. The effect will disappear, and any effect that may have been to the right will shift to the left to fill any space left behind.

Managing Presets

The handling of presets has been somewhat revamped in Live 5. I say "somewhat" because the changes mostly impact the handling of presets for Audio Units and Live's built-in devices. The way Live handles presets for VST plug-ins remains basically the same as previous versions. I'll cover this first.

Managing VST Plug-In Presets

The preset management scheme for external VST plug-ins is straightforward and similar to the methods employed by other DAW programs. Live can store the current settings of a plug-in using the preset icons at the top of the plug-in's window (see Figure 8.11).

Figure 8.11

Preset management buttons found in each VST plug-in's title bar.

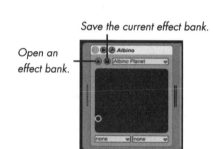

Save the current effect bank.

Open an effect bank.

The dropdown menu in the plug-in window contains a list of previously stored presets for the effect (or instrument), including those provided as starters from the manufacturer (Figure 8.12). Selecting a preset from the menu will cause it to be loaded and will replace the settings currently being used by the plug-in. If this menu is inaccessible, it's because the plug-in's manufacturer has integrated preset management directly into the graphic interface of the plug-in (which you access with the wrench icon in the upper-left corner of the plug-in window).

The icon, which resembles a floppy disk, opens a dialog box for saving and deleting preset banks. This is a normal dialog box that you can use to choose a location and name for the bank.

THE NAME GAME

Giving your presets non-descriptive names will simply waste your time. Some examples of more useful, descriptive names might be "Squashed Drums" for a tough, quick compressor, "Bass Erase" for a hi-pass EQ Four, or "Long Large Room" for a washy and gradually decaying reverb.

Figure 8.12
Choose a preset from the
dropdown menu to load it.

Any saved presets can be recalled in any Ableton Live Set/Song file (ALS) on the same machine because the presets are stored within the Ableton Library located on your computer at:

- ✵ **Mac OS X:** Home → Library → Application Support → Ableton → Library → VstPresets
- ✵ **Windows:** My Documents/Ableton/Library/VstPresets

When collaborating on projects with other artists, you may need to transfer your presets to their computers so they can work with the same collection of tools as you. Simply copy the necessary presets from the folders listed above and include them with the .als file and associated sounds folder. They can then copy your preset into their Library, making them available in their copy of Live 5.

If you are backing up your system or migrating to another machine, it is a good idea to copy the VstPresets folder that contains all of your presets. Better yet, make a copy of the entire Library!

WARNINGS

By using a plug-in, you are incorporating a new piece of program code into Live. This is very much like receiving a kidney transplant—it may work just fine or your body may reject it. Plug-ins are available from a wide range of sources. Waves, Ohm Force, Nomad Factory, and PSP are a few companies that make terrific effects. Native Instruments, LinPlug, GMedia Music, Arturia, reFX, and VirSyn peddle some of the most cutting-edge virtual instruments around. A studious Web surfer can find an even greater offering of plug-ins to try, many of which are available as freeware downloads. In any case, the quality of programming put into the plug-in will determine its effectiveness and stability within Live. It's safer to use plug-ins from major companies because they have the resources to develop, diagnose, and improve their products quickly. Plug-ins developed by some guy in his basement may be the most imaginative of the breed, but commonly suffer from lack of optimization (one plug-in uses a huge chunk of CPU power) and instability (may cause crashes at the most inappropriate times). I am not saying that you shouldn't use these freeware and shareware plug-ins—quite the contrary; I just want to impress upon you the fact that problems may arise in this situation, so be ready (save often!). Most importantly, never use a brand new plug-in for the first time at a gig. Who knows what it may do. Take the time to thoroughly test the plug-in in the safety of your own home before playing live.

Tips

When experimenting with new plug-ins, there are a few precautions to take. These hints can help keep you from losing your work, crashing the system, and destroying speakers.

* **Save your Live Set before loading a virgin plug-in:** Should the plug-in cause Live to instantly crash, you'll be able to load your Set again and continue right from where you left off.

* **Back up the new Set:** Once you have a new plug-in running, save a copy of the set under a new temporary name, possibly the name of the song with -test added to the end. Then quit Live and start back up again. Try loading the test Set to be sure the plug-in initializes properly. I've had a couple occasions where the plug-in worked when added manually, but the program crashed when trying to load the whole Live Set. After you are sure that the plug-in will load dependably, you can then resave your Set under its original name.

* **Watch your volumes:** Anytime you add an unproven plug-in to your Set, turn down your speaker and headphone volumes. A bad plug-in initialization can leave your computer outputting full-spectrum digital noise sometimes, which could rip both your speakers and eardrums to shreds.

* **Organize your plug-in collection:** I like to use the custom plug-in directories (see the "Plug-in Tab" section in Chapter 3, "Getting Live Up and Running") to keep a collection of plug-ins that are confirmed to work with Live separate from the slew of freeware and demo plug-ins that exist in my standard shared plug-ins folders. By only having a small collection of plug-ins for Live to use, you will significantly reduce the boot-up time for Live since the program performs a plug-in scan on every startup. A shorter list is also easier to navigate when drag-and-dropping effects in a live performance.

---

* **CRASH-START**

If you find yourself trying to load a Live Set that keeps crashing, it could be one of the song's plug-ins causing the problem. Try removing (or at least relocating) the plug-ins from your folders one at a time until the song loads successfully. When it loads, Live will tell you that it is unable to load one of the plug-ins (because you hid it), but you'll be able to keep working. Try using a similar plug-in in place of the problem one (i.e., try using Live's Reverb if a third-party reverb gives you problems).

Managing Presets for Audio Units and Live's Devices

The revamp of preset management for Audio Units and Live's built-in devices is significant and intelligent. The upgrade actually makes it easier to access and organize presets, as well as add the additional functionality of Device Groups.

The main difference with device presets is that they are managed directly within the Live Device Browser. Click the Live Device Browser icon and open the Instruments folder by clicking the little triangle in front of the folder. You'll find Impulse, Operator, and Simpler inside. If you look closer, you'll see that there are little triangles in front of these instruments, too. If you click the triangle in front of Impulse, you'll see three folders listed below it: (AL5P Presets), Acoustic, and Electronic. (The AL5P Presets will only be listed if you installed them from the provided CD-ROM.) Open the Acoustic folder, and you'll find a list of 16 different kits. These are 16 of the presets that ship with Impulse—there are more inside the Electronic folder, too.

You'll find that the presets for Audio Units are handled the same way when you open the Audio Units folder in the Plug-in Browser on a Mac.

BROWSE PRESETS BUTTON

There's a little icon in the upper-right corner of the Audio Units and Live Device windows that looks like two arrows in a circle. This is the Browse Presets button (see Figure 8.13). When you click this button, it will turn orange, and you'll see an identical icon appear in the Browser next to the current preset. You can now double-click on another preset to load it into the device.

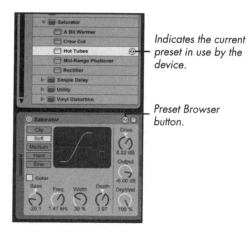

Indicates the current preset in use by the device.

Preset Browser button.

Figure 8.13

Activate this button to link the device to the presets in the Browser.

If you don't have the Browse Presets button turned on when you double-click a preset, the preset will be loaded as a brand new effect at the end of the currently selected track.

SAVING AUDIO UNITS AND LIVE DEVICE PRESETS

The other icon at the far-right of the device's title bar is the Save Preset button. When you've set the device the way you like, click this button and a new preset will appear in the Browser. Type in the name that you want and press Enter. You now have a new preset.

If you make further edits to the preset and press the Save Preset button again, a new preset will be created in the Browser, but with the same name as the previous preset. If you simply press Enter at this point, you'll update the preset with your new settings. If you want to save the prior preset, just type in a new name now.

ORGANIZING AU AND DEVICE PRESETS

You can probably see that the Device Browser is enhanced with the capability to sort the presets into folders within each Device. When you explored the Impulse presets, you saw an Acoustic folder and an Electronic folder. If you right-click (Ctrl+click on the Mac) in the Device Browser, you can choose to create a new folder from the options in the context menu. You can name the folder anything you like, and you can even drag it into another folder after it has been made, thus creating further subdivisions to your preset categories. You can drag and drop presets between the folders or copy them from one to another. These commands, plus deleting and renaming, are all accessed through the right-click context menu. This same organization method is true for Audio Units devices within the Plug-in Browser.

DEVICE GROUPS

Now this is one of my favorite additions to Live 5: Device Groups. This allows you to group together numerous Live Devices to create a "super-device," which you can treat as a single device. For example, you may make a bass sound with the Operator synth and then use some EQ Four to fatten up the bottom end. You can save this Operator instrument with the EQ attached as one single device that you can recall at any time by creating a Device Group.

CREATING DEVICE GROUPS

After you have created a device chain in the Track View that you'd like to save, the first task is to join the individual components in the chain into one group. Select the devices by holding the Shift key while clicking on the devices. When the title bars of the desired section of the chain are highlighted (you don't have to group the entire chain together if you don't want to), press Ctrl(⌘)+G or choose Group Devices from the context menu. You'll see the devices become squished together, and one large border will be created around them.

MANAGING DEVICE GROUP PRESETS

After the Device Group is made, you'll see that there is only one Browse Presets and Save Preset icon available for the whole group. Click the Save Preset button, and you'll see a new preset appear in the Device Browser. You can name it as normal and press Enter. The thing to notice, however, is the icon shown for this new preset. Instead of being a single box, it will be an icon showing the edges of two boxes meeting together (see Figure 8.14). This is the icon for a Device

This is a Device Group.
This is a single device.

Figure 8.14
These are the two types of icons for Live Devices and Device Groups in the Browser.

Group. If you look at the Acoustic presets for Impulse, you'll see that about half of them are actually Device Groups.

To load a Device Group, simply double-click it or drag it into a track as usual. If the Device Group contains a Live instrument, it will replace any other instrument currently on the track. The Audio Device groups (groups consisting only of Audio Devices) will be added to the end of a track (or to wherever you drag it) just as if it were a single effect.

This is one of my favorite additions in Live 5 because it allows me to create and save amazing multi-effects, which I can recall at the drop of a hat. I can create simple effects like a Ping Pong Delay with a touch of Phaser. I can create a Simpler instrument with a MIDI Chord effect in front of it and a Reverb tacked on at the end. I just give them meaningful names so I'll remember what they all are!

 LEFT TO YOUR DEVICES

If you've been getting ahead of me here, you may have already noticed that you cannot include external Plug-in effects within your Device Groups. I guess that's why they call them "Device Groups" and not "Device and Plug-in Groups."

Signal Path

While all signals pass through the Track View from right to left, there are still a few ways you can vary the flow of signals through Live's mixer. Effects can be used as *inserts*, or they may be used as part of a *send and return*. This routing is determined by whether you're placing the effect directly onto one of your Audio Tracks or into a Return Track.

Using an Effect as an Insert

When you use an effect as an insert, you are literally inserting your device into the normal signal flow of your track. In Figure 8.15, an EQ Four has been inserted on Track 1. All of the audio coming from the clips on that track must first pass through the EQ Four before it reaches the volume and pan controls in the Session Mixer.

Figure 8.15

Placing an effect on the Track View of an audio, MIDI, or Master Track creates an insert.

While all of the signals on Track 1 are forced to go through the EQ Four, some plug-ins allow you to set the balance of the original (dry) signal to the affected (wet) signal (see Figure 8.16).

Figure 8.16

The Reverb Device allows you to add only a small amount of effect to your sound, thanks to the Dry/ Wet knob. When the knob is fully clockwise (100% wet), you will only hear the reverb signal generated from the original input. Setting the knob at 25% as shown will allow 75% of the original signal to still pass through.

Use this knob to adjust the balance between the effect and the original sound.

Effects best suited for insert use are EQs, compressors, gates, and filters. When you EQ a signal, for example, you want to modify the frequency content of the whole signal, not just a fraction of it. Using an effect as an insert forces the entire audio stream to pass through the effect, giving you full control of the sound.

Using a Send Effect

Send effects are used when you want to *add* or *blend in* an effect to your sound, as opposed to replacing it like an insert. This is achieved by sending a signal to an effect processor and then blending its output with the Master Track. In Live, you pull this off by using a Return Track (choose Insert Return Track from Live's Insert menu). A Return Track is an abbreviated version of an Audio Track in that it cannot house Audio Clips, but Audio Effects may be added to its Track View. While it may seem weird to use something called a Return Track for send-type effects, the name is properly descriptive of the signal path since you send signal to the input of the track, which then *returns* it to the Master Track via its loaded effects. In Figure 8.17, you'll see a Session with one Return Track. You'll also see a row of Send knobs labeled 1. You can now have up to 12 Return Tracks in a Set.

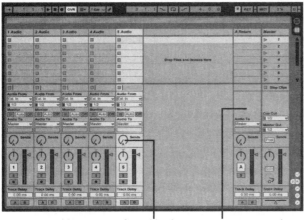

Figure 8.17

When the Return Track was added to this Set, a row of Send knobs was also automatically created.

...yields one row of Send knobs.   *One Return Track...*

You use the Send knobs to dial in the amount of signal you want sent to the input of the associated Return Track. You can add effects to the Track View of the Return Track (double-click the Return Track name) just as you would when adding them to a regular Audio Track. The portion of the signal being sent from the Send knob will be processed by the effects and output to the Master Track via the Return Track's volume and pan controls. You'll see that the Return Track itself also has a Send knob. This allows you to output a portion of the returned effect to another Return Track for layering. The Return Track can also send back into itself, allowing you to create feedback loops (watch your volume!).

❋ PRE OR POST?

On the right side of the Session Mixer, there is a button labeled Post for each Send knob (see Figure 8.10). These buttons determine whether the Send knobs take their signals pre-fader or post-fader. Post-fader is the default setting for each track, which causes the amount of signal sent from the Send knob to be varied by the track's volume slider. If you're fading down a vocal part that is sending to a Reverb, the amount being sent to the reverb will also diminish, causing the Reverb to fade out as well.

The Pre-fader position (click the Post button to turn it to Pre) causes the Send level to remain the same, even if the track's volume is adjusted. This means, in the case of the previous example, you would still hear the vocal reverb even after you had faded the track volume fully down. That could make for an interesting way to end a song.

Keep in mind that the Send knob does not divert signals to the Return Track—it copies the signal to the Return Track. This means that the output volume of the source track will stay the same, regardless of the Send knob position.

So why would you want to use a Send/Return? There are a couple of reasons. First, some plug-ins, such as reverbs and delays, are meant to be blended with their original signals. For example, in order to add reverb to a vocal track, you would place a Reverb Device on a Return Track with its Dry/Wet knob set to 100% wet (every effect on a Return Track should be fully wet). While the vocal is playing, you start to turn up the Send knob. This will start sending a copy of the vocal to the Return Track armed with the reverb. The reverb will generate the proper ambience, based on the incoming vocal, and the result is mixed in with the final mix. By adding reverb in this fashion, your original vocal track remains unchanged; you've simply added in some reverb to your mix.

Another reason for using a send effect is that it allows you to use the same plug-in to add effects to multiple tracks. If you have a lead vocal with three harmony parts, you can send all four vocals to the same reverb. The incoming vocal tracks from the sends will be mixed together as they enter the Return Track. The group vocals will then yield a group reverb, which gets blended into the final mix; therefore, it only takes one reverb to affect four independent tracks, which is great news for your CPU usage.

> ❄ **KEEP 'EM GOING OR CUT 'EM OFF**
>
> Many modern productions, especially in the electronica-influenced genres, employ effect-muting techniques to add emphasis to particular moments in songs. Normally, if you add a reverb effect to a hand clap track, your ears expect to hear the full decay of the reverb, even if you suddenly mute the hand clap track. This is accomplished by placing the reverb on a Return Track and turning up the hand clap's Send knob. When the hand clap is muted, the signal stops being sent to the reverb as well; however, the reverb output remains unmuted, so you still hear the full decay of the reverb.
>
> If you place the reverb effect directly onto the hand clap track as an insert, you can use the Dry/Wet knob to attain a similar balance of hand clap and reverb. Now, when the hand clap track is muted, the reverb will be muted, too, since you're actually listening to the output of the Reverb device on the track (that's why you have to use the Dry/Wet knob to hear the original signal). This can be extremely effective at the end of a build that stops abruptly. Also, give this technique a try with delay effects.

Using Sends Only

There may come a time when you want to combine the CPU-saving method of Send effects with the complete sound replacement function of an insert. Perhaps you want to run a bunch of vocal tracks through one Auto Filter. If you were to place the filter on a Return Track and then turn up the sends on your vocal tracks, you'll only be combining the original unfiltered vocals with the filtered version being output from the Return Track, which will not allow you to completely filter out the vocals. What you need to do is silence the original tracks, while still sending to the Auto

Filter on the Return Track. You accomplish this by setting the output of the vocal tracks to Sends Only, as shown in Figure 8.18.

Figure 8.18

I have silenced the outputs of the vocal tracks by changing their output routings from Master to Sends Only. This keeps all the track functions intact, such as the insert effects (if any) and automation, but disconnects their outputs from the Master Track.

While the original tracks are no longer routed to the Master Track, the sends still remain active so you can funnel your sound over to the filter on the Return Track. You will then use the volume slider on the Return Track to adjust the level of the vocals in the mix.

❄ **MIX TRICK**

Here's a common mixing technique employed by engineers that takes advantage of the routing explained above: Place a couple of drum parts on some tracks, preferably acoustic drums or percussion. Switch the track outputs to Sends Only and use the Send knobs to create a mix of the drums that can be monitored through the Return Track. Once you have achieved a nice blend, load a compressor onto the Return Track and dial up some heavy compression. By heavy, I'd say probably a ratio of 10:1, attack fully counter-clockwise, and a moderate release time of 25ms. Stop the clips from playing and switch the original track outputs to Master. Turn the volume all the way down on the Return Track and start playing the drums again. While the original tracks are playing, begin to slowly raise the volume of the Return Track. The compressed drum parts will start to blend in, with the originals adding beef to the drums.

The reason this is so effective is that right when a transient occurs in the original drum tracks, the compressor on the Return Track kicks in and cuts off the transient (due to the short attack time), leaving only the original waveform in the mix. As the original waveform fades out, the compressor opens up again, thus filling in the space between the transients. This keeps the drums sounding natural, while adding the thickness characteristic of compression. Try this technique with other instruments that may need the assistance of compression while maintaining their original tone.

Control and Automation

As you've probably discovered by toying with a few effects so far, it's fun to tweak the knobs and parameters while audio is playing. Many new layers of musicality can be discovered by carefully manipulating effects during a performance. Live gives you a number of different ways to control plug-in parameters, either with real-time MIDI control or by automatic or preprogrammed automation. MIDI control is by far the most interactive way to control device parameters and offers an excellent way to program automation, too.

Controlling Live's Devices with MIDI

Controlling Live's devices with MIDI is as easy as assigning MIDI control to the Session Mixer and Clip Grid (see Chapter 5, "Making Music in Live," if you missed this). If the device is on-screen, press the MIDI Assign button in the upper-right corner of the Live window. A bunch of colored boxes will appear over the device's controls just like they do for the Session Mixer. Click the control you want to assign; then move the control on your MIDI device. Live will instantly assign the moved control to that effect parameter, and a small box will appear on the control stating the MIDI channel and controller assigned. After you turn off the MIDI Assign button (click it again), the device parameter will now respond to the MIDI control. Piece of cake!

Common things to control with MIDI are the Sample Start and Loop Length in Simpler. You can create a morphing sound by moving through different areas of a long audio file with these knobs. For the Impulse, assigning a control to the Global Tune knob will allow you to tweak the pitch of the entire drum kit on the fly. You can also assign MIDI to the individual drum sounds—try adjusting the decay of the open hi-hat during a song.

Controlling Plug-in Devices with MIDI

Controlling the parameters of a plug-in device, such as a VST audio effect, is a little more difficult, due to the fact that each plug-in has its own unique graphical interface. Because of this, Live cannot superimpose the little squares over the plug-in controls while in MIDI Assign mode. To solve this little problem, Ableton has included a small triangle located at the upper-right corner of a plug-in title bar. Press this triangle, and the plug-in window will expand to the right and show a varying number of horizontal sliders (see Figure 8.19).

Figure 8.19

Pressing the small triangle in the corner of the plug-in window unfolds a collection of sliders, which can have MIDI controls assigned to them.

Click here to gain access to the parameter sliders.

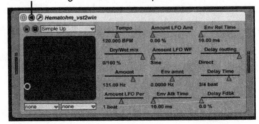

Each slider corresponds to one of the plug-in parameters. Open the plug-in graphical window and move a control. You'll see one of the controls in the Track View move as well. When you press the MIDI Assign button, you will see a box superimposed over the horizontal slider in the Track View. This is where you will make the MIDI assignment. After you have clicked the slider and moved your MIDI control, disable the MIDI Assign mode, and you'll see that the plug-in parameter, including the control in its graphical window, is now under MIDI control.

Modulating Devices with Clip Envelopes

While tweaking the effects live is a blast, creating patterns and predefined movements for the effects can add a new layer of musicality to your songs. Perhaps you want the cutoff of an Auto Filter to follow a sequence of movements that repeats every bar. Or how about a resonator that retunes itself over four bars? Both, and more, are easily accomplished by using the Clip Envelopes.

When I discussed Clip Envelopes back in Chapter 6, "The Audio Clip," you learned that they provide a way to modulate the current settings of their destinations. The same is true for modulating plug-in devices. You will set the controls for the device to one position, and then you will use the Clip Envelopes to add or subtract values from those positions.

The process of creating a Clip Envelope for plug-ins is the same as modulating any other parameter, such as volume and pan. Once a plug-in has been loaded into the Track View, it will be an available selection in the Envelope section of the Clip View in any clip loaded on the track. Figure 8.20 shows an Auto Filter's cutoff frequency being modulated by an envelope.

Use these two menus to select the device and parameter to modulate.

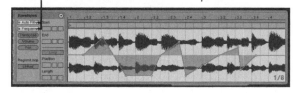

Figure 8.20
Use the two dropdown menus in the Envelope section of the Clip View to select the parameter to modulate.

Automating Devices Within the Arrangement View

Just like the Volume, Pan, and Mute automation I explained in Chapter 5, you can define the exact values for your device's parameters by creating envelopes into the Arrangement View. Every envelope shape you create in the Arrangement View will override the current value of the associated parameter. If you have a sweet effect dialed in, you may want to save it as a preset before drawing in automation so you can retrieve the original settings if you need them.

Just like the process in Chapter 5, effect automation can be created by either entering Record mode in the Transport Bar and performing the desired movements manually or by drawing them into a track using the Pencil tool and Breakpoint editor. Just like their Session Mixer counterparts, any plug-in control with recorded automation will have a small red box in its upper-left corner. If you manually move a control, either with the mouse or by MIDI control, the automation for that control will stop until you press the Return to Arrangement button.

Now that you know how to manage and control your effects, it's time to start sorting through the myriad of plug-ins already available in Live. The next three chapters are a reference section to get you up to hyperspeed with Live's devices.

9 Live's Virtual Instruments

Adding to the plethora of MIDI capabilities in Live are three virtual instruments: Impulse, Simpler, and Operator. These are not run-of-the-mill instruments. They have been designed with careful attention to the working process and creative flow in Live. As such, you'll find many techniques and tricks that are possible with these instruments that cannot be achieved with third-party tools. These are not designed to offer a peek at what is possible with virtual instruments in Live—they are full-fledged, high-quality instruments that will have a place in the most professional of productions. They are also great launching pads for musical ideas.

Impulse

What loop-based production system would be complete without a drum machine? Live's Impulse instrument is a unique take on drum machine design due to its sparse controls but instant usability. Open up the Live Set titled Impulse Demo 1 in the Resources → Examples → Chapter 09 folder on the included CD-ROM so you can follow along as I describe this instrument.

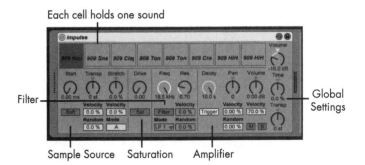

Each cell holds one sound

Filter

Global Settings

Sample Source   Saturation   Amplifier

Figure 9.1
The clean and crisp Impulse interface sports eight cells for samples. Clicking the cell displays the editable parameters for the cell.

Overview of the Interface

The upper portion of Impulse is made of eight squares, or *cells*. These can contain one sample, each of which can be triggered individually—either by MIDI or with the mouse—and edited for customizing the sounds. The editing parameters are divided into five sections below the cells: Sample Source, Saturation, Filter, Amplifier, and Global Settings.

The Impulse Demo 1 Set has eight sounds already loaded into the Impulse. You can play these live with a connected MIDI controller or your computer's keyboard. Try tapping the A key on your computer's keyboard. You should hear a kick drum every time you press the key. Now tap the S key. You should hear the snare drum loaded into the second Impulse cell. As you tap this key, you'll see a small green triangle appear momentarily above one of the sample cells in the Impulse interface. This symbol shows you which cell is playing at the moment. If you want, you can click with the mouse in the same area to trigger the sample.

You can also play Impulse from a MIDI controller. Impulse already has MIDI note assignments for each cell. MIDI note C3 will play the first cell, D3 will play the second cell, E3 is the third cell, etc. In essence, you use the eight white keys on a keyboard controller from octave 3 to octave 4 to play Impulse. Obviously, since Impulse uses MIDI notes to trigger its sounds, it can be played with a MIDI Clip, too. Go ahead and launch the clip titled Simple 1 at the top of the MIDI Track to hear an example of this.

Sample Source

Now that you know how to trigger the samples, let's look at how to change the sound using the playback parameters offered in Impulse. The first section of controls (the Sample Source controls) determines the playback nature of the selected cell. The cell may be retuned, stretched, or shortened and can have its front end cut off. Pitch can be randomized or modulated by input velocity. The Soft button performs a fade at the beginning of the sample to soften its attack.

Click on the cell named 909 Kick. This will select the cell for editing. While the MIDI Clip is playing, click and drag up and down on the Transp dial. You'll hear the pitch of the kick drum change as you tweak this dial. Unlike the Transpose parameter found in an Audio Clip, the Transp control in Impulse does not use the Live Warp Engine. You'll hear that the sample plays for a shorter amount of time as the pitch increases and a longer time as the pitch decreases. If you do want to stretch or compress the length of the sample after you have transposed it, use the Stretch knob. As you increase this value, you'll hear the kick drum being stretched out to a longer length (decreasing it will cause the drum to be shortened). The Mode button found below the Stretch dial changes the method used for stretching the sample. In Mode A (the default), Impulse waits a brief moment before starting to stretch a sample. This ensures that the attack of the sound doesn't get distorted by the Warp Engine. For punchy drum sounds, this is especially important. Mode B, on the other hand, begins stretching the instant the sample starts to play. Since this will distort the attack of the sound, this mode is recommended for sounds that don't have a distinct attack in them, like ambient sounds and effects.

Increasing the Start dial will cause the sample to start playing from a position later in the sample file. In the case of this kick drum, you'll hear that the attack (the initial punch of the drum) is removed. This is because Impulse starts playing the kick drum sample *after* the attack sound of the drum. This can be used as an effect, but also has one other important use: Some of the samples you may want to use in Impulse might have a little moment of silence before the sound. This results in the sample sounding late every time you play it. (Impulse plays the silence before playing the actual sound.) The Start dial can be used to advance the sample start position so that Impulse plays the sample right at the attack of the drum, thus bringing it back into time. This saves you the hassle of having to manually remove the silence using an external wave editor.

The Soft button is somewhat related to the Start dial in that it affects how Impulse plays the beginning of the sample. When Soft is off, Impulse simply plays the sample the instant it is triggered. When Soft is turned on, Impulse will perform a short fade-in on the sample when it is triggered. The result is that the attack of the sample is softened without changing the length of the sound. If you try this with the kick drum, you'll hear that the "snap" at the beginning of the sound is softened, while the beefy punch of the drum remains.

The value boxes below the Transp and Stretch dials do not affect the sound of the sample directly. These values are used to modulate the Transp and Stretch settings based on velocity and randomness, and the value boxes are arranged below the dial they will modulate. To hear how velocity affects these parameters, you'll need to be playing Impulse with a velocity-sensitive MIDI pad or keyboard. If you're using the computer keyboard, you can change its velocity using the Z and X keys, but you'll get the best results from MIDI devices. For simplicity, I've also included a clip titled HiHat Only, which has a lot of velocity changes. Click on cell seven (909 HiHat) to select it and turn up the value box below Transp. You'll hear that the hi-hat begins to change pitch as it follows the velocity. Done in moderation, at about 15%, it adds a subtle touch of additional expressiveness to the hi-hat.

Saturation
The Saturation section is the next, and simplest, of the five sections. Engage the Sat (saturation) button and turn up the Drive to achieve overdriven percussion sounds. If you apply saturation to the kick drum, you'll get a distorted "gabber-house" style kick. Give it a try!

Filter
The Filter section offers a way to perform some additional sound design on a sample after it's already loaded into a cell. Click the Filter button to engage the section. The menu below the Filter button chooses the filter mode. You'll find the usual suspects here: low-pass, high-pass, band-pass, and notch filters. The Freq knob sets the cutoff frequency of the filter, and the Res knob determines the filter resonance. The last two parameters, Velocity and Random, allow you to use incoming velocity or random values to modulate the filter cutoff.

The reason this section follows the Saturation stage is that distorting a sound can yield some unwieldy high-harmonics and noise. If it's too much, you can apply a low-pass filter to the sound to calm it down. Try it with the distorted kick drum and a Freq setting of 745Hz.

Amplifier

The Amplifier section sets the output volume and pan position for each individual cell. The Pan knob can be used to move the hi-hat to one side of the mix while the volume control pulls it down to a quieter level. The Decay knob shapes the tail end of a sample. If the associated button is in Trigger mode, the Decay knob will dictate the fade-out time from the moment the sample is triggered. In Gate mode, the fade-out won't begin until a MIDI note off message is received (when you lift your finger off a key). The Gate mode is fun, as it allows you to control the length of your sounds as you play them, such as a long snare sound on beats 1.2 and 1.4 with a short snare on beat 1.3.2. Switch the snare cell to Gate and set the Decay to 147ms to hear what this sounds like. The two Vel values determine how much the incoming MIDI velocity affects the output volume and pan position.

Global Settings

The Global section contains a master Volume knob, plus Master Time and Pitch knobs. These knobs are begging for MIDI control since they are wonderful performance parameters. The Time knob can be used to shorten or stretch out all the samples at the same time. The Pitch knob will transpose all the samples together as a group. Try tweaking these values during a drum fill for extra expression.

Importing Sounds

By now, you've probably noticed the consistency in design philosophy behind Live. Because of that, you can probably guess how to get sounds into the Impulse cells: You drag them from your File Browsers. Loading up eight drum sounds is super-simple since you can pre-listen to the sounds in the Browser and then drag them directly into the cells. This is a great reason to create a folder on your hard drive full of one-shot drum samples since it makes browsing all of them a snap.

You don't have to use pre-made one-shot samples to make beats, though. A popular source for drum sounds, pioneered by Hip-Hop producers, is to grab them right out of full drum loops. You begin by loading a drum loop into a Clip Slot and isolating the portion of the sound you want to use from the Clip View (see Figure 9.2a) and then dragging the clip into any one of the Impulse cells (Figure 9.2b). I've already placed a drum loop on Track 2 for this purpose.

Figure 9.2a
Isolating a section of the Audio Clip to be loaded into an Impulse cell.

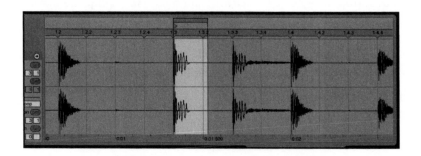

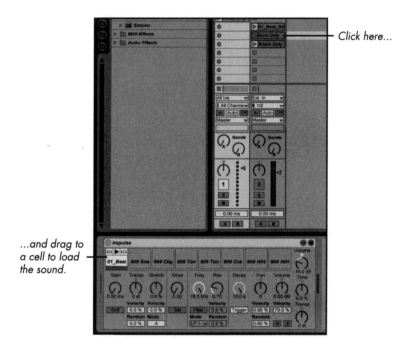

Click here...

Figure 9.2b
Switch back to the Impulse
in Track View and then
drag the clip into a cell.

*...and drag to
a cell to load
the sound.*

Cutting up drum loops for reprogramming has never been easier. If you load a Warped drum loop into the Session View, it is a painless process of isolating portions of the beat since the sample region start and end markers snap to the beats. Isolate the first sound you want (a kick drum) by placing the region markers around it. (I've already done this for you in the Kick Only clip.) Drag it to the first cell of Impulse to replace the 909 Kick sample. Then isolate the next sound (a snare perhaps) in the same clip and drag it to another Impulse cell (again, you can just use the Snare Only clip if you like). Even though you modified the clip that was used for the first cell, the cell's sample will not change after it's been added to Impulse. So, you can repeat the process again and again using the same clip until you populate the Impulse cells with all the parts of the loop that you want. Now, when you play the MIDI Clip, the kick and snare parts will be played by the new samples.

MIDI Control

The MIDI notes assigned to trigger the eight cells are fixed to the white keys between C3 (middle-C) and C4 (one octave above middle-C). However, when editing the MIDI data of a clip driving the Impulse, the normal piano keyboard will be replaced with the names of the samples assigned to each line of the MIDI data. This is the kind of helpful integration that is possible with Impulse but not possible with third-party drum samplers, such as Native Instruments Battery 2 or Fxpansion GURU.

❄ **HAS ANYBODY SEEN MY KEYS?**

If you're using a small MIDI controller, such as the M-Audio O2 or the computer keyboard keys, you may find yourself bashing away on the notes but hearing nothing from the Impulse. This will frequently occur if the keyboard has been transposed to another octave. Try adjusting the octave/transposition of your MIDI controller so it sends notes to the Impulse in the proper octave. If you're using the computer keyboard for MIDI input, the Z and X keys will transpose the keys. When transposing the keyboard, you'll see the current key range listed at the bottom of the screen. You'll want to choose the C3 to D4 range to properly play the Impulse. You can also use C and V to change the velocity output of the computer keyboard. As you press the keys, Live will display the new velocity at the bottom of the window.

The best form of MIDI control for Impulse comes from the use of drum pad controllers. Drum pads are starting to pop up everywhere—you can even find them on controller keyboards like the Korg MicroKontrol. The M-Audio Trigger Finger (mentioned in Chapter 3, "Getting Live Up and Running," at the beginning of this book) is especially suited for Impulse. Preset 10 is specially designed for use with Impulse—two of them, actually. Since the Trigger Finger has 16 pads, you can control two complete Impulse drum machines from this one controller. Create two MIDI tracks, place Impulse instruments on both of them, set both of their inputs to the Trigger Finger, and then set the left track to listen to MIDI Input Channel 10 and the right Track to listen to MIDI Input Channel 11. When you arm both tracks, the lower eight pads of the Trigger Finger will control the left Impulse, and the top eight pads will control the right Impulse. Simple! Assigning MIDI Remote control to the parameters in Impulse follows the same method as any other control in Live. Press the MIDI Map button in the upper-right corner of the screen. You'll see the telltale blue boxes superimpose themselves over the Impulse controls waiting for your assignments. You can still click the individual cells to display their parameters while in MIDI Assignment mode, which makes even extensive assignments a piece of cake.

MIDI Routing

Drum parts are a collection of multiple parts, generally a kick drum part, a snare drum part, and a hi-hat part, all playing together at the same time. Because the beat is comprised of these smaller parts, it may make more sense to you to build the drum parts out of multiple clips, such as a clip for the kick drum, a clip for the snare, etc. Live allows you to do this by routing the output of other MIDI tracks to the input of Impulse.

Let's try adding a hand clap part to the Simple 1 beat in the example Set. First, create a new MIDI Track and set the top MIDI To box to the 1-Impulse track. Next, set the bottom MIDI To box to 1-Impulse, as opposed to Track In, Set this way, the MIDI on the new track will be fed directly to the Impulse instrument on Track 1. If the lower box is set to Track In, the MIDI data will be routed to Track 1 itself—you will have to switch the track's Monitor to In in order to hear the new part. (This would end up muting the Simple 1 clip, which you don't want to do!)

Now, double-click in a Clip Slot in the new MIDI track to create an empty MIDI Clip. Place notes on beats 1.2 and 1.4 of the hand clap lane (see Figure 9.3). When you play this new clip along with the Simple 1 clip, you'll hear an additional hand clap on beats 2 and 4.

Set this way, you can make additional variations of the hand clap part, adding extra claps here and there throughout the clip. Then you can switch between these clips in order to change the hand clap part while the Simple 1 beat plays unchanged.

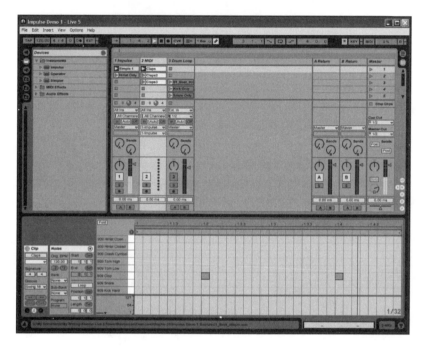

Figure 9.3
The hand clap clips can be played one at a time on top of the Simple 1 beat.

Audio Routing

From time to time, you may want to place an effect on one or more of the drum sounds in the Impulse, but you don't want to affect all of the drum sounds at once. To solve this, each cell of the Impulse has its own dedicated output that can be used as a source for another Audio Track, which can be loaded with any effect you choose.

To see this in action, make another Audio Track and set its Audio From to the MIDI Track containing the Impulse. In the channel selector below that, you'll see a list of not only the Track Output, but the individual drum sounds as well (Figure 9.4).

When one of these channels has been chosen as the input for another track, that sound will cease to be sent out the normal output of the Impulse track (this keeps the sound from being doubled). For this example, select the Snare drum from the channel list and enable monitoring on the Audio

Figure 9.4

Routing individual drum sounds to other tracks is achieved within the Input/Output Routing section.

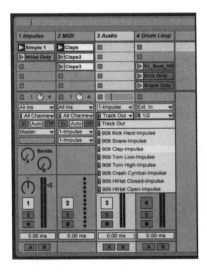

Track. Nothing will sound different, but you'll see that the snare drum is now sounding out of this new Audio Track. Drag the Reverb preset Forest Floor from the Live Device Browser onto this Audio Track, and you'll hear a nice reverb on the snare hits only.

> ❋ **NO STATIC**
>
> One factor that can make your drum parts sound dull is static loops. That is, loops that are exactly the same every time they're played. To create some motion or subtle change in your drum parts, try dropping a Velocity device before the Impulse and have it introduce random variations in velocity. The result will be a more human-sounding part in which each of the drums is played with a slightly different loudness. See Chapter 10, "Live's Audio Effects," for the low-down on how to use the Velocity device.

After creating separate tracks to process the individual sounds of Impulse, it is often helpful to group them back together so that they can be treated as a single drum part. This is done by adding another Audio Track to the Set and enabling its monitor (for clarification, rename this new track to Drum Mix). Once the new track is in place, set the Audio To for both the Impulse track and Snare track to Drum Mix. The outputs of these tracks will now be mixed together and used as the input for the Drum Mix track. You can now use the volume fader of the Drum Mix track to change the volume of the whole drum part at once. Of course, you could also add additional effects to this track (compression comes to mind) to process the drum part as a whole.

After this is done, you'll have four tracks in Live representing one drum part. You can use Live's new Track Width feature to collapse the Snare and Drum Mix tracks to buy yourself some space on your screen (see Figure 9.5).

Figure 9.5
Collapsing tracks can help organize the precious real estate of the Session View.

As a final note, open up the Live Set titled Impulse Demo 2. Here, you'll find a Set utilizing nearly every technique described above to create a house beat. Can you figure out everything I did?

Simpler

When it comes to quick and imaginative sample playback and manipulation, nothing is simpler than Simpler. What is Simpler? It's a simple sampler, silly. However, with the release of Live 5, Simpler has received an upgrade that now offers even more creative possibilities within its humble interface, such as independent pitch, filter, and amp envelopes, as well as portamento.

Overview of the Interface

The Simpler interface (see Figure 9.6) looks quite similar to Impulse, but it has one large sample window instead of eight sample cells. Simpler only works with one sample at a time, and its contents are displayed in this main window. The + and – zoom buttons will allow you to enlarge part of the waveform for setting accurate start and loop points.

Figure 9.6
The Abletons do it again with another deceptively simple interface.

Not one to break with tradition, the Simpler can be loaded with a new sound by either dragging a sample from the File Browser or by taking an Audio Clip from the Session and Arrangement Views. Just like Impulse, Simpler will use only the portion of the sound that is between the Region start and end markers of the imported clip. Since Simpler only holds one sample, any new sound dragged into the instrument will replace the previous one.

Sample Source

There are seven sections in the Simpler interface: Sample Source, Filter, Envelopes, Pan, LFO, Tuning, and Volume. The Sample Source section is where you'll set all the parameters for the sample playback. The effect of the four knobs can be seen and heard immediately as the changes you make will be shown graphically in the Sample Display window. The Sample Play area is shown in dark green, while the Loop area (when the Loop button is active) is shown in light green (see Figure 9.7). As you adjust the knobs, you'll see the green areas change. The first three knobs change the start position, loop length, and end position of the sample. The loop length is based on a percentage from the end of the sample, which allows you to loop the tail end of a sound to extend its length. The Fade knob applies a crossfade to the sample loop points to smooth out any pops you may encounter when the sample starts over. The Snap button will help prevent these pops by forcing the start and end points of the loop area to snap to a zero crossing.

Figure 9.7

Simpler will only play the sound located in the green area of the Sample Display window. Playback begins at the far-left edge of the green section and plays all the way through to the end of the green. If the Loop function is activated, Simpler will then begin repeating the section in bright green until a MIDI note off is received.

Envelopes

The Envelope section (just to the right of the Sample Source section) is where you will shape the sound as it's played. There are three envelopes in the new version of Simpler—Amp, Filter, and Pitch, which can be edited individually by pressing one of the three selector buttons in the Envelope section. Each of these envelopes is hard-wired to the output volume, filter cutoff, and sample pitch, respectively.

Every time a MIDI note on message enters the Simpler, it triggers the envelope generators. As soon as the MIDI note is received, the envelopes enter their attack phase. This is where the output rises from zero to full level. The amount of time it takes for this increase in level to happen is set with the Attack knob, which displays its value in milliseconds. After the attack time has passed and the envelope has reached full level, the envelope drops to the sustain level. The amount of time it takes to drop is set by the Decay knob. The target level is set with the Sustain knob, which shows a percentage of the full level. The envelope will stay at the sustain level until Simpler receives a MIDI note off message (i.e., lifting your finger off of the keyboard). Once the MIDI note off is received, the envelope will drop off to zero in the amount of time specified by the Release knob.

Filter

The Filter section (which is engaged with the Filter button) is used to remove certain frequencies in the sample. As usual, you've got your choice of low-pass, high-pass, band-pass, and notch filters. The Freq and Res knobs are used to adjust the base cutoff frequency and the resonance for the filter. The remaining controls are used to modulate the filter cutoff with the envelope, velocity, key position, and LFO (low-frequency oscillator). All of these modulation sources can be used at the same time for complex filter motions. The Env knob scales the amount of Filter Envelope signal used to change the filter cutoff. As the envelope value rises, the cutoff will also rise. The Vel value will scale the cutoff based on the incoming MIDI note velocity. If the value is 0%, the velocity will have no effect on the cutoff. The Key value is used to change the cutoff value of the filter based on the pitch of the incoming MIDI note. The higher the pitch, the higher the filter cutoff. This helps emulate real sounds, which get brighter as their pitch increases. The LFO knob determines the amount of LFO signal used to modulate the cutoff.

LFO

The LFO (engaged with the LFO button) can be used to modulate the filter cutoff, sample pitch, and output pan. An LFO can be thought of as an automatic envelope that has a repeating pattern. The shape of the LFO is selected in the small dropdown menu right below the Filter button. The Rate knob changes the speed of the LFO, which can be further modified with the Key value (playing higher notes will speed up the LFO when the key value is increased). You can also use the Attack value to have the LFO gradually fade it instead of starting immediately when a key is pressed. This is great for lead sounds where you'd like to introduce vibrato after you've held a note for a moment.

Pitch

The Pitch section has been expanded with the release of Live 5. The Transpose value will (obviously) transpose the pitch of the Simpler up and down—Detune will adjust the pitch in cents (like the Detune in an Audio Clip). The LFO box will set the amount of LFO modulation to apply to the pitch of the sample, also known as *vibrato*. The Envelope box will similarly set the amount of pitch modulation applied by the Pitch Envelope. The Spread knob will perform an automatic detuning of the left and right channels to create a wider sound from your sample.

My favorite addition, however, is the Glide feature. When active, Simpler will bend up or down to each consecutive note that is played. For best results, set the Voices value to 1, which will make Simpler monophonic. The Time value sets how long it takes Simpler to bend from one note to another. When used properly, you can get Simpler to react like a classic mono-synth.

Pan
Another new section in Simpler, the Pan controls specify the output location of the sound (done with the Pan knob), as well as introduce modulations to the pan with the LFO and randomness.

Volume
The Volume box obviously sets the output volume of the Simpler, while the Vel value determines the effect of incoming velocity messages on the output volume. If the value is set to 0%, the sample will play at the same volume no matter how hard a key is played (velocity information will be ignored). There is also an LFO box, which will apply LFO modulation to the sound, which creates a tremolo effect. The Voices box determines the *polyphony* of Simpler. Polyphony is the maximum number of simultaneous notes that can be produced by Simpler. If the value is set to 1, the Simpler will be *monophonic*, being able to only play one note at a time. Any time polyphony is exceeded, a previous note will be cut off in favor of playing the new one. This condition is indicated when the indicator next to the polyphony value blinks. Finally, the R button (short for Retrigger) is used to set whether or not the envelopes retrigger when played polyphonically. When this option is on, the envelopes will restart with every new note played, even if you're currently holding other notes. When this is off, the envelopes will only restart after all the keys have been released.

> **ANALOG PRESETS**
>
> Ableton has provided a number of presets (found in the Presets menu) to get you started. Most are based on small samples that act similarly to the waveforms found in analog synthesizers. Indeed, using a saw wave in the Simpler is the same as using a saw wave in an analog synth. These tones will be great for beefy basses and gnarly leads.

MIDI Control
Simpler will respond to any incoming MIDI note to create sound. Just like the other devices in Live, the Simpler dials and buttons can be assigned to MIDI controls. Press the MIDI Assignment key in the upper-right corner of the screen as usual, click one of the blue boxes superimposed over the Simpler controls, and twist a knob. Assigning the Sample source controls to MIDI

controllers is an extremely expressive performance technique. Altering the loop length and start positions on the fly can change the timbre and tone of the sample in wild ways as well.

> ❄ **SAVING GRACE**
>
> You can save your instruments, be they a Simpler patch or an Impulse drum kit, using the Preset controls found in the title bar of the devices. You can save, rename, or delete presets using the same procedure described in Chapter 8, "Using Effects and Instruments."

I've found that the Simpler presets provided by Ableton offer the best demonstration of what Simpler is capable of. I suggest you inspect each of the presets and experiment with the various parameters to learn how they affect the overall sound.

Operator

Introduced in Live 4.1 (right after I finished the *Ableton Live 4 Power!* book), Operator is Ableton's second product. That is, it's the second piece of software that can be purchased from them. Operator is included in all Live versions after 4.1 (including Live 5.0), but it is available only as a demo. You will need to purchase a separate unlock code from Ableton to use this instrument to its full potential. And believe me, Operator is full of potential.

Part of that potential comes from the fact that Operator is basically three synthesizers in one. You can employ three different types of synthesis to craft your sounds: subtractive, additive, and FM. Before we look at the details of this synth, I will give you a brief explanation of these three different synthesis types.

Waveforms and Harmonics

The simplest sound in the world is known as a *sine wave*. A sine wave is an example of a waveform and is shown in Figure 9.8. Some would classify the sound of a sine wave as being a "pure" tone. To hear what a sine wave sounds like for yourself, open the example Set titled Operator Demo 1 and launch the clip titled Single Sine Wave.

A sine wave is unique in that it contains no harmonics or overtones, just one fundamental frequency. Other waveforms can be characterized by the number of overtones/harmonics they contain and their relationship to each other.

Overtones are frequencies that are integer multiples of the original frequency. Figure 9.9 shows two sine waves—the top sine wave has twice the frequency of the lower sine wave. Notice how it cycles twice as fast as the lower sine wave. These are two sine waves that are an octave apart. To hear how these two waves sound when played together, launch the Octave Sine Waves clip. The higher sine wave is said to be the *second harmonic* (or *first overtone*), while the lower

Figure 9.8
The image of a simple sine wave.

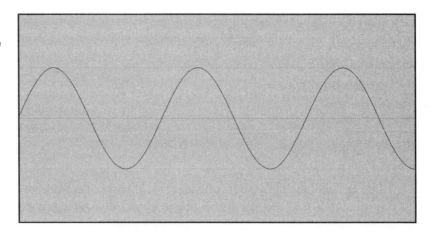

frequency is the *first harmonic,* or *fundamental frequency.* A sine wave an octave above the second harmonic is the *third harmonic,* and so on. What should be noted is that the human ear detects the fundamental frequency as the pitch of the waveform.

Figure 9.9
You can see that the top waveform cycles twice as fast as the lower.

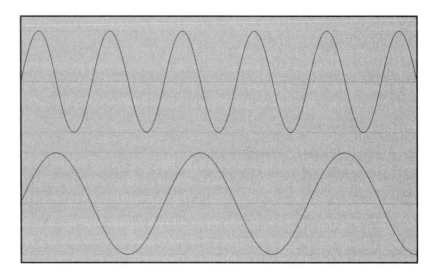

When the two sine waves are added together, it results in the waveform shown in Fig 9.10.

Take a look at what happens when the fundamental sine wave is added to the second-order sine wave, but at half volume. The resulting waveform (Figure 9.11) is similar to the waveform above, but slightly different.

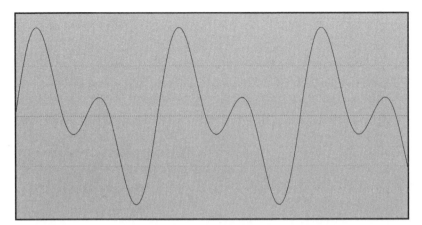

Figure 9.10
This complex waveform is the result of adding two simple waveforms together.

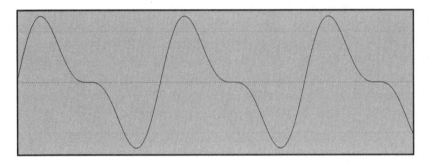

Figure 9.11
It's the same as above, but different.

What is really interesting, however, is what happens when we continue to add additional harmonics, all half the volume of the previous. Figure 9.12 shows four sine waves: the fundamental, the second-order at half-volume, the third-order at quarter-volume, and the fourth-order at eighth-volume.

When these four sine waves are added together, the resulting waveform looks like Figure 9.13.

Does this waveform look similar to one you've seen before? It bears a close resemblance to the *sawtooth wave* shown in Figure 9.14.

If we were to continue adding higher and higher harmonics to our sine waves, all at half the volume of the previous, it would result in an even closer approximation to a sawtooth wave.

So what happens if we add sine waves together that have a different relationship to one another? Let's take a look at what happens when *every other* harmonic is added together. If we take the fundamental, add the third-order harmonic, fifth-order harmonic, seventh-order harmonic, etc., it will result in a *square wave* (see Figure 9.15).

Figure 9.12
A fundamental frequency with three higher harmonics, all half the volume of the previous.

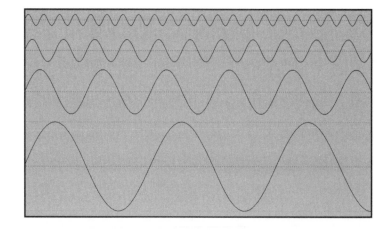

Figure 9.13
Four sine waves added together.

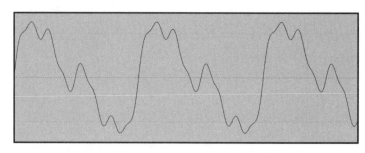

Figure 9.14
A simple sawtooth wave. Can you tell why they call it a sawtooth wave?

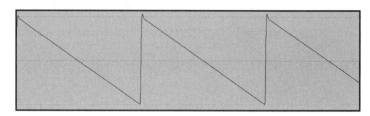

Figure 9.15
A square wave generated by adding a lot of odd-numbered harmonics together.

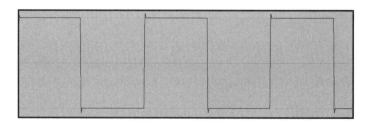

Does this mean that all periodic waveforms are composed of sine waves? Yes, tons of sine waves—all with different volume and phase relationships to one another.

Subtractive Synthesis

Throughout this book, I have referred to filters. I have said that filters remove certain frequencies while allowing others to pass. In the case of a low-pass filter, high frequencies are removed while low frequencies pass.

When a periodic waveform, such as a sawtooth wave or square wave, is passed through a low-pass filter, you can lower the filter's cutoff frequency to a point where some of the upper harmonics of the waveform are removed while the lower harmonics remain, thus changing the sound of the waveform. This is the essence of *subtractive synthesis*. In this process, you start with waveforms that are rich with harmonics and filter out, or subtract, the harmonics you don't want.

In addition to low-pass filters, there are also *high-pass, band-pass,* and *band-reject* (or *notch*) filters, which will remove different frequency ranges from the waveform. High-pass filters are the opposite of low-pass filters, where only frequencies lower than the cutoff are removed, and band-pass filters only allow a small range of frequencies above and below the cutoff to pass. Band-reject is the opposite of band-pass, where a range of frequencies above and below the cutoff are removed while the rest of the frequencies pass.

This means that a standard subtractive synthesizer will have an *oscillator* that generates a waveform (typically a square or sawtooth, though certain manufacturers will offer you more choices for waveforms), a filter that removes part of the sonic content, and some envelopes to control the filter and volume. These synthesizers, such as the Minimoog and Roland TB-303, are deceptively simple to use and offer a wide range of sonic possibilities. Other subtractive synthesizers will feature multiple audio oscillators, multiple low-frequency oscillators (or *LFOs*), multiple filters with variable routings, multiple envelopes, saturators, and other enhancements, all to push the possibilities of subtractive synthesis to the limits. Operator falls into this category.

Additive Synthesis

Additive synthesis works in the opposite manner of subtractive synthesis. Instead of starting with a harmonic-rich waveform and filtering parts of it out, you start with sine waves and build your waveforms from the ground up—no filters required.

This type of synthesis is harder to accomplish because it requires the use of many sine wave oscillators, all of which must be at different frequencies and amplitudes, but also in specific phase relationship with one another. Whew! The benefit, though, is that (provided you have enough oscillators) you can generate *any* periodic waveform you wish. This is a lot of power for a synthesist to wield and takes quite a lot of practice to master.

Even with this potential for power, subtractive synthesis is more popular because it's usually easier to get what you want from it. Comparing additive and subtractive synthesis, I like to use the following analogy:

Additive synthesist says, "Give me two all-beef patties, special sauce, lettuce, cheese, and onions on a sesame seed bun."

Subtractive synthesist says, "Gimmie a Big Mac—no pickle."

FM Synthesis

Another way to generate harmonic-rich waveforms is to use one sine wave to alter the frequency of another. You have heard frequency modulation before—a police siren that rises and falls in pitch at a repeating rate is an example. You can think of this as using a slow sine wave to control the pitch of the siren.

Look in the Live Device Browser and open the Operator → (AL5P Presets) folder. Inside, you'll find a preset named Police 1. Double-click the preset, and it will be loaded into Operator. Now, when you play the Single Sine Wave clip, you'll hear the sine wave's pitch rising and falling.

This is an example of frequency modulation using a low-frequency oscillator. The low-frequency oscillator is the *modulator*, and the siren sound is the *carrier*. With the modulator cycling this slowly, you can hear a distinct rise and fall in the siren's pitch.

Figure 9.16 shows the two waveforms at work in the police siren. The top waveform is a slow sine wave—the modulator—while the lower waveform is the siren—the carrier. As you can see, the frequency of the carrier is much higher than the modulator. When the modulator is used to change the pitch of the siren, you get the third waveform.

Figure 9.16
Three waveforms: a modulator, a carrier, and the result of using the modulator on the carrier.

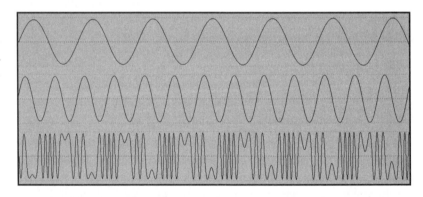

By looking at the third waveform, you can see that there are sections where the pitch increases (the sine wave is squished together) and areas where the pitch decreases (the sine wave is stretched apart). You can see that the squish/stretch pattern follows the shape of the modulator.

In FM synthesis, you use an oscillator that operates within the audio range for the modulator. The result is that the carrier is modulated so quickly that your ears can no longer hear the pattern of rising and falling pitches. Instead, your ears will begin to hear new pitches in the form of *side bands*. These side bands are what construct the harmonic content of a waveform in FM synthesis.

Our ears and brains determine the pitch of a waveform by determining how long it takes for a waveform to repeat itself. When the modulation is slow, like the Police 1 sound, our ears can identify the cycles of the sine wave as it is modulated. When the carrier is modulated quickly, our ears will start to hear the pitch of the modulator repeating its cycle. So, instead of identifying the time from one peak of a sine wave to the next as the pitch, our ears identify the time from the squished section of the sine wave to the next squished section as the pitch. This means that the waveform our ears hear is no longer a simple sine wave, but it's now a crazy squished/stretched sine wave, which has quite a unique sound.

Load the Operator preset titled Police 2 to hear what this sounds like (this preset is identical to Police 1 except that the rate of the modulator has been increased significantly). You'll notice that you can't hear the rise and fall of the siren anymore. Additionally, you'll notice that the new tone created in this method doesn't sound like the original siren tone from Police 1, either, although the same oscillators are still being used. This new tone is the result of applying audio-rate frequency modulation to the original tone, which yields the squished/stretched waveform shown previously.

In FM synthesizers, the oscillators are actually referred to as *operators*. Traditionally, there will be more than two operators provided in an FM synth—Operator has four of them (plus an LFO, which can be goosed up to audio rates), while the legendary Yamaha DX7 was equipped with six. You can use the additional operators to perform further modulations to the carrier, or you can modulate the modulators to create some really complex waveforms.

The way in which the operators interact with each other is determined by an *algorithm*. In essence, an algorithm is a pre-set wiring map for the operators that determines which operators are carriers and which are modulators. You'll see in a moment that Operator provides nine algorithms for you to use in an easy-to- read graphic format.

The use of different terms, such as operators and algorithms, and the absence of a filter can make even seasoned subtractive synthesists scratch their heads in confusion when presented with a traditional FM synthesizer. However, Operator bridges this gap in a thoughtful manner that allows you to employ all of the synthesis techniques described above in an easy-to-learn interface.

Overview of the Interface

Operator represents a slight departure from the user interface scheme set forth by Live. While Operator still conveniently sits within the Track View (see Figure 9.17), it does not display all information and parameters at once. Operator is a deep and complex synth, so many of the parameters have been consolidated into the center window of the interface.

Figure 9.17

The Operator interface has two sections: the center window and the eight "shells" surrounding it.

Looking at the interface, you'll see a large center window, called the *display*, surrounded by eight sections, collectively referred to as the *shell*. The shell sections are (moving clockwise from the lower-left corner): Operator A, Operator B, Operator C, Operator D, LFO, Filter, Pitch, and Global. If you click on one of these sections, the display will change to show its associated parameters. Try it—click anywhere within the Operator A section. The display will show a graphic envelope, as well as a myriad of values below it. If you click on the Pitch section, a different set of information will be shown in the display.

Ableton has placed the most tweakable parameters of Operator into the shell so that they can be accessed at all times. The more intricate details—parameters that you normally "set and forget"—are neatly tucked away within the display. If you'd like, you can even hide the display, only leaving the shell exposed, by clicking the little triangle in the upper-left corner of the interface (see Figure 9.18). Also along the top title bar are the standard controls for recalling and saving presets.

Figure 9.18

Buy yourself some screen space by hiding the Operator display.

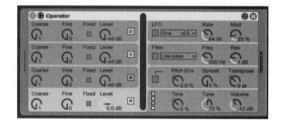

Creating and Shaping Sounds

So how do you operate Operator? It depends on what type of synthesis you're trying to achieve. As mentioned earlier, Operator can pull off both subtractive and FM synthesis, plus it has some additive synthesis features as well. It would therefore make sense to set up Operator to perform your desired synthesis before getting any deeper.

The Algorithm

Click on the Global section in the lower-right corner of the shell. The global parameters will now be shown in the display (Figure 9.19). If you've been clicking around through the other sections in Operator, you'll notice that this display is different than the others. Gone are the graphic envelopes, and in their place is a collection of colored squares.

Figure 9.19
The Global parameters of Operator.

While the term *algorithm* may conjure up images of mind-bending calculus formulas, you'll be pleased to know that Operator provides a simple way to visualize an algorithm using the assortment of colored squares in the display. By default, the upper-left algorithm will be active (its squares are solid color as opposed to outlines). If you look at the operators to the left of the display, you'll see that they have the same colors as the squares in the display. The colored squares are therefore a map, or flowchart, of how the operators interact with each other.

You can read an algorithm from the top down, but I also like to look at it from the bottom up from time to time. If you look at this first algorithm starting at the bottom, you'll see that the bottom square is a yellow A. This is operator A. You'll also see that there is a little yellow line extending downwards from this square. This line shows that operator A will be outputting signals that you can hear.

If you look at the next block above A, you'll see a green square with B inside. This block has a line extending downward from it, too, but it connects to operator A instead of being an output. This means that the waveform created by operator B will be used to change the frequency of operator A, which is output to your speakers. In this arrangement, operator B is a modulator and operator A is a carrier.

Knowing the above, you can now see what parts operator C and operator D play in this algorithm: They are additional modulators. Operator D will modulate operator C, which modulates operator B, which modulates operator A—the carrier. Wow! This algorithm sure offers a lot of modulation!

Click the algorithm below the current algorithm. This new algorithm has the shape of a T. Can you tell what will happen when you use this algorithm? Let's read it and see: Operator A is again at the bottom and has a line extending downward. This means you will hear this operator, just like the previous algorithm. Where this algorithm differs, however, is in the arrangement of the three modulators. Instead of being stacked such that D feeds C, which feeds B, which feeds A, each of the three modulators will work directly on operator A.

Just to the right of the T algorithm is one shaped like a box. When you select this algorithm, you will see the familiar arrangement of operator B modulating operator A. The difference this time is that operator C is now a carrier—you will hear the waveform it generates, as well as hearing the waveform generated by operator A. You can think of this as a dual-FM synth where you can create two unique waveforms simultaneously, which can be used in layers to thicken your sound or to create two independent sounds that interplay with each other.

You should now be able to tell how each algorithm will make the operators interact. One algorithm of special note is the horizontal arrangement found in the lower-right. When using this algorithm, you will no longer be using any of the operators as modulators—they'll all be carriers. This arrangement is one that you would use when using Operator for subtractive synthesis. Each operator will output its own unique waveform, which can be mixer together and filtered, very much like a Minimoog synth.

The Operators

Leave the algorithm set to the horizontal arrangement and click on operator A in the shell. The algorithms in the display will now be replaced with an envelope and additional parameters. These are all of the control parameters for operator A. By default, each operator is set to produce a sine wave with instantaneous attack and release. Try playing a few notes to hear this for yourself.

Tucked away in the display is a parameter named Wave. The option below it is currently set to sin—a sine wave. Click on sin to open a sin menu with all of the operator's waveshapes. Try out a few of them to hear how they sound.

Normally, FM synthesis only uses sine waves. The additional waveforms here, such as the saw and square, can be used as sources for subtractive synthesis. Of course, you can also use them for FM synthesis, which will allow Operator to create sounds unlike other FM synths that only have sine waves. Additionally, the saw and square waves have multiple shapes, denoted by a number after the name. Remember our discussion of how periodic waveforms are composed of multiple harmonics? Well, the number in the waveform name tells you how many harmonics were used to create the waveshape. In the case of Sw3, only three harmonics were used: the fundamental, the second harmonic, and the third harmonic. As a result, the Sw3 waveform still resembles a sine wave more than a sawtooth wave. As you go further down the menu of waveforms, you'll see saws with greater numbers of harmonics. Sw64 uses 64 harmonics to generate the sawtooth wave and therefore sounds like the kind of sawtooth wave you're used to hearing. This same numbering scheme is true for the square waves as well.

A sine wave has no harmonics, so what are the other sine wave variations about? First, notice that the sine wave variations are lettered, not numbered. This helps alleviate confusion regarding harmonics. The sine variations are just that—slight tweaks to a sine wave that emulate the kind of waveforms generated by analog oscillators. You may not be able to hear much of a difference while listening to each of the sine waves directly, but they may cause more obvious changes to your sound when they are used as modulators.

Along with selecting the waveform for the operator, you can also set its tuning and volume. Tuning and volume have a tremendous impact on the sounds resulting from FM synthesis, so these controls have been placed directly onto the shell so you can access them at all times. Furthermore, it is the tuning and volume relationships between the various operators that will define your sound. As such, you can see all of the tuning and volume information for all four operators simultaneously on the shell.

Tuning has two modes: variable and fixed. The variable setting (the default) causes the operator to change frequency based on the notes you play. The fixed setting (enabled by clicking the Fixed box of an operator) causes it to ignore incoming note information and will instead sound at a specific frequency that you set in the shell. When in fixed mode, the two tuning options will be Freq and Multi, which stand for frequency and multiplier, respectively. The operator's frequency is therefore determined by multiplying the Freq with the Multi value. If Freq is 100Hz and Multi is 1, the resulting frequency will be 100Hz (100Hz × 1 = 100Hz). If Freq is 245Hz and Multi is 10, the operator's frequency will be 2,450Hz.

When in variable mode, the operator frequencies are no longer shown. Instead, you are presented with Coarse and Fine adjustments, which express the operator's frequency as a ratio of the base frequency. An operator with a Coarse setting of 2 will sound an octave higher than one with a Coarse setting of 1. An operator with a course setting of 0.5 will sound an octave lower. You can use the Fine adjustment to create ratios that are fractions, such as 1.5 (Coarse 1, Fine 500) or 2.25 (Coarse 2, Fine 250). When working in subtractive synthesis (with the horizontal algorithm), this will create chords where playing one note results in multiple pitches from Operator. However, when using FM, this will create harmonic or inharmonic tones, depending on the ratio.

FM in Action
Enough talk, already. It's time to hear what all of this sounds like. Load up the preset Simple FM from the (AL5P Presets) list in the Operator Browser. Play a note, and you should hear a single sine wave. You are hearing operator A by itself. While holding the note, turn up the level of operator B. You'll notice that instead of hearing a second pitch as you turn up this operator, you will hear the sound of operator A change. This is because operator B is modulating operator A (which you can see if you look at the active algorithm), resulting in side bands. Operator A becomes more and more brilliant (more upper harmonics) as you increase the level of operator B (the level control is essentially the FM modulation amount). If you turn operator B back down again, operator A will revert to a sine wave.

This phenomenon is the reason why FM synthesizers traditionally don't have filters. As I mentioned at the beginning of this section, when a waveform is passed through a low-pass filter, it is possible to remove all the upper harmonics, leaving only the fundamental behind—a sine wave. By turning down operator B, you're also left with a fundamental sine wave. In this case, the level of operator B acts in a similar fashion to the cutoff frequency of a filter. So if your sound is too bright, instead of reaching for a filter, decrease the amount of modulation so that the carrier will stay closer to its original sine waveform.

A moment ago, I mentioned that the ratios of the operators in an FM system will result in harmonic (tuned) or inharmonic (untuned) sounds. The patch you were just playing with used a modulator and carrier that were at a 1:1 ratio—the modulator had the same exact frequency as the carrier. The result, as you heard, was a constant pitch that changed timbre. For your next experiment, turn up operator B again and then play with the Coarse knob. The result will be another constant tone, but one with a different harmonic structure. As you increase the Coarse knob, you will be changing the ratio between operators A and B but keeping the ratio in whole numbers (i.e. 1:2, 1:3, 1:8, etc.).

Things start to get strange, however, when you begin to change the Fine adjustment. Hold a note and slowly increase the Fine setting. Almost immediately, the sound will go "out of tune," or more precisely, will become "without tune." This is because the frequencies of the modulator and carrier are no longer at a whole number ratio. If operator A is at Coarse 1 Fine 0 and operator B is at Coarse 2 Fine 20, then the ratio between the two operators is now 1:2.02, which is not a whole number ratio.

But why does this sound so weird? When performing subtractive synthesis, slightly detuning an oscillator is a great way to fatten up a sound. Why doesn't this same principle work in FM?

The answer lies with the squished/stretched waveform and our ears' ability to detect repetitions. In the examples so far, the modulator completes a cycle at the same point the carrier does. While a modulator might cycle twice for every cycle of the carrier, they will still repeat at the same time. A way to illustrate this is to take a look at the Live Set titled Beat Sync that is provided on the CD-ROM. Launch Scene 1, and you'll hear two drum beats playing together. They are both at 90 BPM. The first drum beat plays one measure for every measure of the second drum beat.

Now, launch Scene 2. You'll hear the same drum beats, but the second beat is going twice as fast as the first. Though the second beat repeats twice for every repetition of the first beat, they are still synchronized together. You can still hear the tempo and could easily play along with this beat.

OK, launch Scene 3. Yikes! What's happening? The two drum beats now sound like a complete train wreck. The difference here is that the second drum beat is now playing just slightly faster than it was before. The result is that the second drum beat now loops just slightly faster than the first drum beat, resulting in misalignment of the individual beats. You'd have a really difficult time playing along with this one.

The relationship between two drum loops playing together is the same relationship of a carrier and modulator. When the modulator has a frequency that is not double (or some other whole number multiplier) the carrier's frequency, it will cycle around at a different point each time the carrier cycles. The result is that the squish/stretch pattern your ears were hearing is now happening at a different point in each of the carrier's cycles. Thus, your ears can no longer determine the pitch of the waveform.

To take this drum beat analogy a step further, launch Scene 4. Things should sound nice again, but you may notice something a little different. While the two drum beats are in sync, one is offset from the other. You can still feel the tempo, but the beat sounds different.

This same phenomenon can be exploited in the FM world by offsetting the *phase* of an operator such that its waveform begins at a different point in its cycle. You'll still get pleasing harmonic tones, but you'll notice that the timbre changes slightly as you adjust the phase. While the difference is subtle, it may introduce a tonal quality that you prefer.

> ✷ **A HIDDEN MODULATOR**
>
> While the Operator algorithms select which operators will be modulators for others, there is another hidden modulation that can be performed with operator D. Click its section to show its parameters in the display. You'll notice that there is an extra parameter here, Feedback, which will change the waveform of the operator. This uses the output of the operator as a modulation input for itself. If you turn the Feedback parameter up to 50%, the result will be nearly identical to a sawtooth wave. Of course, if you have a waveform other than sine selected, the result will be extremely strange. Try it out!

The Envelopes

So far, the experiments with FM have only concentrated on designing a waveform using a modulator and carrier. All of our examples have been fairly static sounds—press a key and hear the sound; release the key to stop the sound. The envelopes in Operator will help bring the synthesizer to life by offering ways to automate and animate the waveforms over time.

Each operator has its own volume envelope. The LFO also has its own envelope. The Filter and Pitch sections also have their own envelopes. That's seven envelopes for a single voice! That's quite a lot compared to Simpler, which only had three envelopes per voice.

You heard in the experiments above how the volume of a modulator would affect the timbre of the carrier. Therefore, using an envelope to change the volume of a modulator will allow you to change the harmonic content of a sound as it plays, like using a filter envelope in subtractive synthesis.

Load the Operator preset titled Simple Bass and play some notes. This sound now has some motion to it—it has an aggressive attack that quickly decays into the fundamental sine wave. Played in low octaves, this is a great bass sound that sounds similar to a subtractive bass synth. Click on operator B and look at its envelope. It has a quick attack with a fairly fast decay and a sustain level of −infinity. This makes operator B play at full volume when you strike a note, but it quickly fades out after the initial attack. This is what creates the harmonic complexity at the beginning of every note.

This is a pretty simple implementation of the envelope—just attack and decay. However, the Operator envelopes are much more powerful than this, even more powerful than the envelopes in Simpler. Most synthesizers use ADSR envelopes, which stands for Attack, Decay, Sustain, and Release. This is the type of envelope used in Simpler. The Operator envelopes, on the other hand, are composed of six parameters: Initial level, Attack time, Peak level, Decay time, Sustain level, and Release time (IAPDSR). This offers much more flexibility when designing your sounds because you can break many of the constraints set forth by an ADSR envelope. For example, it is possible for the Sustain level to be higher than the Attack level. In an ADSR envelope, the Attack always reaches maximum level, and the Sustain can only be set to this same level or lower.

Furthermore, the Operator envelopes can be looped, either based on time or based on the tempo of the current Live Set. This means that you can use the envelopes as pseudo-LFO sources as well, since you can create a modulation that can repeat again and again. The ability to synchronize the repeats to the tempo of the song allows you to create interesting rhythmic patterns with ease.

How easy? Click on the Operator B section and switch the Loop parameter to Beat. Now hold a note. You'll hear your bass sound retriggering every 1/16 note! You can of course change the loop rate by changing the Repeat value. Furthermore, the looping will follow the Song Tempo if you change it in real-time. If you really want these repeated notes to be locked in with your composition, select Sync as the Loop mode. When active, you can play notes at any time you'd like, but the envelope will only repeat in sync with the beats in your song (this will only work while Live is playing, of course). This will ensure that this triggered bass sound plays in time no matter if you're late or early when you play it.

The remaining parameters in the display for an operator govern how velocity and key-follow will affect its pitch and level. For starters, the Vel parameter will modulate the operator's volume based on velocity—positive values will cause the operator to increase in volume as you play harder, while negative values will attenuate the operator the harder you play. If you use this setting on a modulator, it will have a similar effect to applying velocity scaling to a Filter envelope in subtractive synthesis. The harder you play, the more FM modulation will result, thus causing a brighter sound. The Key parameter will cause the operator to play louder or softer (depending on the value you use) as you move into the higher registers of your keyboard. This is similar to the "key-follow" found in the filter sections of many subtractive synths.

The Osc<Vel parameter determines the impact of velocity on the tuning of the operator. Playing harder will cause the operator to increase in pitch, provided you use a positive value. Of special interest is the Q button next to this value. When active, the incoming velocity will only affect the

Coarse tuning of the operator. This is handy because it will ensure that you have a harmonic interval (a whole number ratio between the modulator and carrier), no matter what velocity you play. If you turn this button off, your velocity will affect the Coarse tuning *and* the Fine tuning, resulting in tunings that can have inharmonic results.

The final parameter, Time<Vel, is really great for adding expressiveness to your sounds. When set to a positive number, it will cause the envelope to run faster as you play with heavier velocity. Set to a negative value, the envelope will run slower as your velocity increases. This can be used to mimic the performance of acoustic instruments whose envelopes change naturally as a result of dynamic changes.

I've covered quite a lot so far, so much that you actually have enough knowledge to create some killer FM tones, even though I haven't even touched on the sections on the right side of the shell (save the algorithm setting).

The LFO

Moving on to the right side of the Operator interface, we find the LFO section right at the top. On a synthesizer, an LFO is used to create repetitive automations to other parameters of the synth. On a subtractive synthesizer, LFOs will often be used to modulate the filter cutoff or the volume. The LFO of Operator can do this and much more.

For starters, the LFO (which you know stands for low-frequency oscillator) is not relegated to low- frequency operation in Operator. You can actually goose this one up into the audio range, thus making it available as another audio oscillator for your FM experiments. This is done with the tiny dropdown menu next to the waveshape. The options are L for low-frequency mode, H for high-frequency mode, and S for sync. After that, select your rate and mod amount with the dials in the shell.

In order for the LFO to work at all, you'll need to turn it on with the little box to the left of its waveform menu in the shell. Once active, you'll see all the parameters light up in its display. The display looks like the other operators, except that the waveform and phase parameters have been replaces with Destination boxes. By default, the four operators will all have their pitches modulated by the LFO. You can turn these off individually, and you can also use the LFO to modulate the filter cutoff.

If you're using the LFO at audio rates to modulate the operators, you'll probably want to turn up the Rate<Key value to 100%. This will make the LFO track the keyboard so that you will have consistent harmonic results for every key you play.

Other than those parameters above, the remaining settings for the LFO function like the settings for an operator. The envelope will control the modulation amount of the LFO (whose upper limit is set with the Mod dial in the shell) and the Loop parameter can be used to retrigger the LFO envelope. With this arrangement, you can create an envelope loop that will modulate the LFO while it runs at audio rates—the looping envelope essentially becomes another LFO!

The Filter

So here we are: an FM synth with a filter. With all the tonal control possible by adjusting the modulation amounts of the operators, why would Ableton put this here? The best explanation I can offer it that it offers something familiar to those new to FM synthesis. Coaxing your desired tone from an FM synth is not easy, especially for beginners. However, generating a complex waveform with FM is easy. The filter therefore allows you to treat this complex FM waveform as the starting waveform for subtractive synthesis. Thanks to Operator's FM capabilities, your subtractive experiments won't merely be based on simple waveforms like sawtooth and square. Your arsenal of waveforms is nearly limitless. Once you get a complex wave you like, you can then run it through the standard rigmarole of filters and envelopes you're used to using.

Another reason for the filter has to do with bandwidth. As I explained in Chapter 2, "Back to School," digital audio has a limited frequency range determined by the sampling rate. According to the Nyquist theorem, the highest frequency recordable by a digital system is equal to half the sampling rate. If the sample rate is 44,100Hz (which is the CD standard), the highest recordable frequency is 22,050Hz. In practice, however, this top frequency is usually limited to roughly 20,000Hz (which is the upper limit of human hearing). FM synthesis is capable of producing hundreds of side bands, some of which could exist above the 20,000Hz limit. If these frequencies are left unchecked, they will create foldback frequencies that will distort the sound. The filter, therefore, allows you to remove these high frequencies so that they will not interfere with the limits of digital sampling.

Like the LFO, the filter must be turned on before it will have any effect. Do this by clicking the box just to the left of the filter-type menu. Once active, you'll see the center display spring to life with color, indicating that the filter is active. The filter contains the same six-parameter envelope as the operators and LFO that will modulate the filter cutoff frequency. The amount of envelope modulation is set with the Envelope parameter. The other parameters in the display will determine how key position and velocity will affect the filter.

The filter types available are as basic as they come: low-pass, high-pass, band-pass, and notch. They're all 12dB/octave filters, so the resulting tone is smooth without being overly squelchy. The Ableton manual describes that the notch filter is not really a notch filter, but rather a single-band parametric EQ with negative gain. The Res dial will adjust the width, or Q, of the EQ where higher values result in a narrower bandwidth.

The Pitch Settings

Below the Filter section is the Pitch section, which contains an envelope, as well as some other unique pitch-related controls. Not only will you have to switch on the pitch section to make the envelope work, but you'll also have to turn up the Pitch Env dial in the shell. You can use both positive and negative values here, so it's possible to reverse the effects of the envelope.

As with the LFO, you can choose which operators will be modulated with the Pitch Envelope. Often times, it's not necessary to modulate all the operators. Of course, if you don't modulate them all, inharmonic results can occur. However, this can be desirable on the attack of a sound, such as when making drum sounds.

The Spread dial in the shell will instantly turn your synth creations into stereo patches by using two voices instead of one, each panned to either side of the stereo field and detuned slightly. This is similar to the fattening technique on analog synths where multiple matching oscillators are all slightly detuned from each other. The result is a full, lush sound similar to a large group of singers, which is why this effect is sometimes referred to as "chorus." Since Operator must create two slightly detuned tones when using Spread, your CPU load will be much higher as a result (nearly double). Therefore, use this control wisely.

> ### ❋ ALL THINGS BEING RELATIVE
>
> Many people have asked me how I create such a wide stereo field in my recordings. They assume that everything they're hearing must be in stereo or that I've done some sort of phase trick. This is not the case. In order for your ears to perceive a sound as being stereo, it helps to play the sound against sounds that are mono. This makes the difference between what is mono and stereo much more apparent to your ears. If there is no mono material in your recording, there will be no point of reference for your ears to say, "Wow, that sound is really wide." Therefore, don't hesitate from recording or mixing certain parts as mono. Their contrast against the stereo parts will not only make the stereo material sound wider, but it will also help clean up your mix because you won't have every sound filling up the same stereo space.

Next to the Spread knob is the Transpose knob, which will shift the pitch of Operator up or down by the specified number of semitones. This is a real-time control, so you can tweak it while a sound is playing.

There are two important pitch parameters in the display that haven't been discussed yet. The first is PB Range, which determines the amount of modulation resulting from using the pitch wheel on your MIDI controller. By default, this is set to +5 semitones. This means that a pitch of C will be bent up to F if you turn the pitch wheel all the way up. The same C will bend down to G if you move the pitch wheel downward.

The last group of settings are the Glide parameters, found in the lower-right corner of the display. These only work when used in conjunction with the Voices parameter on the Global Settings display, which is explained in the next section. I'll therefore get back to this one in just a moment.

The Global Settings

The last section of Operator contains global settings for the instrument. You're already familiar with the algorithms contained there, but there are still a few more things you should know about.

First, the Time control. This knob adjusts the speed of all of the envelopes in Operator simultaneously. You can slow them down dramatically or speed them up to a point where you hardly notice them. I've found that after I dial in a tone, I can get a sound that I like a little more by adjusting this parameter. Also, if you make a sound whose envelopes are timed to the tempo of the song, you can adjust their timing as a whole should you change the tempo of the song. Other than that, this can be a great dial to tweak while Operator is playing a programmed synth pattern—it can add additional expressiveness beyond tweaking the oscillators and filters.

To the right of the Time knob is the Tone knob. This knob will behave like a low-pass filter, even though it's not. This knob can be used to reduce the amount of high-frequency overtones being generated in FM. Often, a sound will sound OK at one pitch but may sound strange when played an octave or two higher. This is because at the higher pitches the harmonics of the sound cross the theoretical limit imposed by the Nyquist theorem. Those high overtones then fold back into the regular audio spectrum, which can sound unpleasant. The Tone knob can be used to keep those high harmonics in check.

The last control in the shell is the Volume knob. If I have to explain what this does, then you should probably put down this book and step away from your computer (or any piece of technology for that matter).

Within the display for the global settings, below the algorithms, are seven more parameters. The three parameters on the right are merely used to set the pan position of Operator's output. The Pan value lets you position the sound in a specific location of the stereo spectrum. The Key value is used to make the key-position influence the pan. When this is used, your sound will pan to the right as you play higher notes, as if you were sitting in front of an acoustic piano. The last value, Rnd, will cause the pan position to change randomly with the specified depth.

To the left of the Pan parameters is Time<Key. This parameter is also helpful in mimicking acoustic instruments in that the envelopes can be set to run faster (or slower if you use a negative value) as you play higher notes. If you think about a piano, you'll know that the low notes can sustain much longer than the higher notes. This setting will cause Operator to behave in the same way.

Continuing left, we come across the HiQ parameter. This is the same as the HiQ found in the Audio Clip View and determines the quality of interpolation used when Operator renders its sounds. Turning this on will result in a more polished sound, but at the price of CPU load.

The RTG button sets the Retrigger mode for the envelopes. If this is on, the envelopes will reset to their initial values every time a note is played. So, if you play a note that has a long release phase, playing the note again before the release has completed will cut it off abruptly as the envelope jumps back to its initial value. If this button is off, retriggering the same note will cause the envelope to enter its attack phase, but starting from the current level of the release phase. This is most useful for pad sounds where there should be no abrupt changes in volume as notes are played.

The last parameter at the far left of the display is Voices. This setting determines the maximum number of notes that Operator can play at once. When set to 2, you'll only be able to play two notes at the same time. If you play a third note while still holding the other two, the oldest note will be replaced by the new note, a technique referred to as "voice stealing." By default, this value is 6, which is usually sufficient. However, if you are using a sound that has a long release time, it becomes quite easy to have more than six sounds playing at once, even if you aren't holding any notes. The voice stealing will cause the oldest note to immediately stop in favor of the newest note. This will ensure that you hear every note you want to play, but it can sound strange if you keep hearing these beautifully sustained notes being cut off by the voice stealing. In this case, you'll want to increase the number of voices. Be careful, though, as each simultaneous voice requires additional CPU processing!

The other way to use the Voice parameter is to set it to 1, which turns Operator into a monophonic synth that can only play one note at a time. If you play one note followed by another, the first note will be stopped in order to play the second. While this may not sound like such a hot feature, it definitely heats up when paired with the Glide parameters mentioned in the previous section. If you engage the Glide function (click on the G in the pitch), notes will now automatically bend to each new note as they are played. This only works when playing in a legato fashion, where each note is started before the previous ends. If you're playing in a staccato fashion, Glide will have no effect as there are no overlapping notes. The Glide Time, also found in the Pitch Section display, sets the time it takes for Operator to bend to the new note after it has been triggered. This effect is also known as *portamento* and is quite useful for synth leads and bass lines.

That's it! You now know everything about all the controls of Operator. However, knowing is only half the battle—it's time to put that knowledge to use making some sounds.

Synthesis Examples

This section is not intended to be an exhaustive tutorial on sound design using FM, additive, or subtractive synthesis. That topic alone would warrant a separate book of its own. Instead, this section is provided to "get you going" with your own sound design experiments. It will introduce you to a few standard concepts and techniques, which you can then use as the basis for further sonic exploration. I'll start with examples of how to make simple bass and drum sounds, followed by leads, pads, and effects. It's crucial that you try these examples as I describe them—don't just read about them. For convenience, I've provided all of the sound examples below as presets in the Operator → (AL5P Presets) folder.

Bass

Let's start with the easy sounds first: basses. These are traditionally simple sounds with minimal harmonic content and strong fundamental frequencies that act as the foundation of your songs. If the sound is too ripe with harmonics, the tone will become muddy and indistinguishable. Therefore, you won't be using a whole lot of FM here, just a touch where needed.

> ❄ **BASS ON THE SIDE**
>
> As mentioned earlier, FM synthesis creates harmonic content known as *side bands*. Note that these are not called "over bands" or "overtones." The reason for this is that the side bands can manifest above *and below* the current fundamental frequency. This happens quite often when a modulator is at a non-whole number ratio with the carrier.
>
> You must pay special attention to these lower side bands when creating your bass sounds as they may exist below a frequency where you can hear them. Although they can't be heard, their power is still in the sound and can cause difficulty during compression and mixdown.

The simplest of all bass tones is a sine wave. It's also the easiest to make with Operator. Simply load a new instance of Operator onto a MIDI Track, and it will already be set to play a sine wave with operator A. Transpose this down an octave or two, and you'll have the gut-shaking bass so popular in hip-hop and techno. The Sine Bass patch is a perfect example of this, with a little bit of envelope added to operator A for flavor.

While sine waves are great at shaking bass bins, they can be hard or impossible to hear on small speakers. This is because the sound contains no upper harmonics that would lie in the range of the smaller speakers. In order for this bass tone to be heard on more than just a pair of 15" subwoofers, you can blend in some more tone using some modulators. The Harmonic Bass patch is an example of this where I've used the other three operators to each introduce a small amount of harmonics to the sine wave. Try turning off the operators one at a time to hear what each one adds to the overall sound. Because this uses the vertically stacked algorithm, turning off operator B, for example, will also remove the modulations performed by operators C and D. Therefore, start by turning off D, followed by C, etc.

I'll now add some character to this bass tone, making it more appropriate for techno styles of music. I'll do this by increasing the amount of modulation performed by operator D, which in turn causes greater amounts of modulation all the way down the line of operators due to the vertical arrangement of the algorithm. Furthermore, I will modulate the volume of operator D using its envelope such that the extra modulation only occurs at the attack of the note. See Techno Bass to hear what this sounds like.

This bass sound is definitely getting more interesting, but there are still a lot of things that can be done to the sound as I've left the entire right half of Operator unused so far. For my next enhancement, I want to add some LFO to create rhythmic modulation. However, instead of using the LFO as a low-frequency modulator, I will switch it to high frequency and loop its envelope to create the repetitive modulation. Check out Engine Bass to hear how this sounds.

Above is an example of an FM bass. Let's switch gears and check out a subtractive bass. Load up the Saw Bass preset and play some notes. This bass is made from a single operator using the SwD waveform passing through the filter. I've added some velocity modulation to the filter and envelope times for expressiveness. This bass is reminiscent of a TB-303 style bass, so I even switched it to one voice with Glide. Try playing multiple notes to hear how this works. The Square Bass preset is the same exact program, except that a square waveform is used in place of the sawtooth. The sound is more beefy, but a little "hollow," too.

I'm using the algorithm that allows you to hear the output of every operator. So, for the next bass sound, named Layer Bass, I've added two more operators all tuned to different intervals. The result is a layered chord sound when you hit the keys with a decent velocity. If the velocity is too low, the filter will not open up, therefore suppressing these higher tones.

You can see that making bass is pretty easy using FM or subtractive synthesis. Indeed, you will be able to create many more bass tones of your own in no time. The two bass tones I created all had sharp attacks, but you may want to try some with slow attacks. This works especially well if the modulator has a slow attack, therefore introducing modulation after the note is played. This style of bass is popular in the drum 'n bass communities, and you'll find it here in the DnB Bass preset. This is an example of using FM to generate two waveforms (look at the algorithm) and passing them through a filter in a subtractive manner.

Kick Drums

Next on the list of essential sounds is the kick drum. These, like basses, are really easy to program. In fact, kick drums are just very short versions of bass sounds.

Let's start with the hallmark of hip-hop kick drums: the TR-808. This drum machine was released in the early 80s and used analog synthesis to generate its drum sounds. As a result, you can mimic the sounds using regular analog synths. The kick drum in particular was nothing more that a sine wave controlled by a volume envelope. Check out the 808 Kick preset to hear this for yourself.

When playing this preset, the first thing you'll notice is that it doesn't matter what key you play— it always sounds at the same pitch. This is because I have switched operator A into Fixed mode. Secondly, you'll hear that there is a little "snap" at the attack of the drum. This was achieved by adjusting the phase of the sine wave so that it starts partway through its cycle, which causes the volume to jump abruptly from silence to a mid-point of the sine wave every time you strike a key. Turn Phase to 0 to remove the snap.

While this is a great bass drum for rap music, you may want something a little different for your song. One of the parameters on the TR-808 allows you to alter the decay time of the kick drum. You can use the Time dial in the Global section of Operator to shorten the kick's envelope (lower the time value). Doing so, however, removes a lot of the "beef" in this tone, making it sound weak and thin.

In order to get a punchy kick drum sound, you'll need to employ some other techniques. The first is to change the envelope on operator A. Load the Fat Kick preset to see an example of this. In this patch, I have created a long attack stage where the volume of the sine wave remains at full volume before quickly dropping off to silence. I have also removed the snap generated with the phase control. The result is a big "poof" of bass tone, which is now ready for additional modulations.

What I'm going to do next is to use the Pitch Envelope to rapidly change the pitch of this drum over the short duration of its sound. I engage the Pitch section and crank up the Pitch Env knob to 100%. This means that the Pitch Envelope will have full control of the pitch. Second, I change the initial and peak levels of the envelope to +24 semitones. Third, I set the sustain level for 0 semitones and the decay time to about 300ms. The result is that the pitch of the drum starts two octaves higher and drops two octaves within 300 milliseconds. Load up the 909 Kick preset to hear what effect this has.

Wow! What a great dance kick! The sound is quite similar to the kick drum found on Roland's other famous drum machine, the TR-909. We can add some more punch to this sound now by employing some FM. I'll use operator B with a short envelope to add some harmonics to the attack of this sound. The result can be heard in the Hard Kick preset.

Now this kick drum is becoming extremely dance-worthy. To really push it over the edge, I'll add another stage of modulation using operator C. Using the current algorithm (the vertical stack), operator C will modulate operator B, which is being used to add the extra attack. With this additional modulation, the attack will be super-extreme, as heard in the Killer Kick preset.

Toms

The sound of a tom drum is not much different than a kick drum, except that it is higher in pitch and usually has a longer decay. Additionally, since a tom usually has two heads, we need to create a more harmonically complex tone to emulate the sound.

The TR-808 drum machine didn't do this very well. Its tom sounds were nothing more than sine waves at higher pitches (the congas were the same tones even higher with shorter decays). The TR-909, however, was a little closer in that the waveform used was more complex, yet it was still light years from sounding like a real tom.

Like the second kick drum example, toms usually drop in pitch a little after they have been struck. You should therefore try to emulate the same drop in pitch using the Pitch Envelope. Check out the Eighties Tom preset to hear it in action.

Snare Drums

Snare drums are similar in nature to a tom. A snare drum is like a tom in that it has two drum heads that create a tone when played. In addition to the heads, the drum is also equipped with a snare, which is a set of wires stretched across the bottom head of the drum. When the bottom head vibrates, it vibrates the snares against the head, giving the drum its characteristic high-frequency buzz or hiss.

To emulate a snare drum with a synthesizer requires creating two sounds: the tone of the drum and the noise of the snare. The Tom patch already gives you the tone, so you only need to add noise to the patch to make a snare. This can be done in a couple of ways. The TR-808 and TR-909 drum machines merely blended in some white noise to create their snare sounds. The presets named 808 Snare and 909 Snare are examples of this. In addition to adding the white noise with an operator, the length of the drum has also been shortened (the snares on the bottom of the drum choke the sound, as well as adding noise).

Hi-Hats

What is a hi-hat? Put simply, it is two cymbals smashed together that, when struck, create a short, crisp burst of metallic noise. The force with which the two cymbals are held together is governed by a foot pedal. If the drummer lifts his foot off this pedal, the cymbals will be spread apart, resulting in a longer noise.

Take the tone away from a snare drum, and you'll just be left with the noise. Shorten the envelope decay on this noise to make a closed hi-hat sound (preset Simple CHH), or increase the decay to make an open hi-hat sound (preset Simple OHH). To make the sound less like a burst of noise and more like a tinny hi-hat, use a band-pass filter to narrow in on the higher frequencies only. A little filter resonance can add some character to the hi-hat as well (preset Rezzy Hat). I don't recommend using a high-pass filter on your hi-hat sounds, especially when using FM as the source. This is because FM can create extremely high-frequency side bands, all of which will be able to pass when using a high-pass filter. The band-pass filter will not only remove the undesired low frequencies, but it will also pull out the super-high side bands, which will protect your ears and reduce fatigue.

Once you've built yourself a collection of drum sounds, you can record them into new Audio Clips, which you can then use to build a drum kit in Impulse. Check out the Operator Kit presets to hear the above examples compiled into a nice unit.

Leads

With drums and bass covered, you now have the essentials for building the foundation of a song. Naturally, your song will consist of more parts than this, so you'll need to coax some more sounds from Operator, such as a *lead*. Leads are instruments with prominent pitch used for playing melodies in a song. Often times, leads are monophonic (meaning you can only play one note at a time) and used for solos. Building a lead is pretty simple—you start with a pure tone, like a sine, square, or saw wave, and find interesting ways to morph the sound without affecting its playability or pushing it into inharmonic territory. This is a simple task for Operator, quite similar to the process of creating a bass sound.

Classic lead sounds can be made using subtractive synthesis—they got their start on classic mono-synths years ago. The Lead Simple preset is a basic sawtooth lead with a smooth filter envelope. If you hold the note long enough, some vibrato will be introduced by the LFO (it has a slow attack). You can simply change the waveform used for operator A to change the sound of this lead.

Of course, Operator is capable of more than just subtractive synthesis, so you can create leads that use FM as well. The Lead Grow preset is an example of this—a sine wave is used for the base of the tone, and two additional operators provide some color. Operator B adds a slight sense of attack to the first note you play. If you hold the note long enough, operator C will swell in volume, changing the timbre of the lead.

Pads

Pads are sounds that generally have slow attack and release phases and are used for playing chords—they can add a chord bed, or "pad," for your song to be built upon. Since these sounds are usually sustained, they are typically thinner in sound so they don't mask the frequencies of the other parts in your music.

Many synthesists explore ways to add constant motion to their pads so they don't become stale and boring if they're played for a long time. Operator's envelopes (especially the looping feature) can add all sorts of motion to pads as they sustain.

I've included two pad presets for you to look at. Pad Stringy is a fairly typical pad sound that uses sawtooth waveforms, which makes it sound reminiscent of a string section. By frequency modulating the sawtooth waveform, this patch can create some pretty intense high-frequency overtones. This is where Operator's Tone control comes into play. I've turned this all the way down to keep the overtones from folding back (because they exceed the sample rate) and creating low-frequency harmonics. Try turning this up to hear all the grit that ensues.

The other preset, Pad Space, reminds me of a pad sound I had ages ago on my ASR-10 sampler. This one is made from sine waves, so turning down the Tone control isn't as necessary. One interesting point of motion is culled from the Pitch Envelope, which creates a brief bend up to your notes each time you play. You'll also find that if you hold the notes for a while, a rhythmic pulsing will start to be heard. This is operator D with a looped envelope. The reason it takes a moment for operator D to take effect is that operator C has a long attack phase (if you look at the algorithm, you'll see that operator D modulates C).

You'll find many more presets within the (AL5P Presets) folder, as well as those provided by Ableton. As always, the best way to learn about synthesis is to work through existing presets and see how each setting contributes to the overall volume of the sound.

10 } Live's Audio Effects

When you perform a *mixdown*, you are attempting to create a sonic picture, a three-dimensional landscape of sound in which every instrument, voice, and noise has an individual place, yet blend together in a cohesive fashion. This is not a simple task, as there are many obstacles to overcome in the process. Instruments may have similar timbres and occupy the same area of the frequency spectrum, making them hard to differentiate from one another. Some parts may vary in volume so greatly that they are inaudible at times while overpowering at others. You may be suffering the consequences of poor gear choice—cheap mics, audio interfaces, cables, and more could all be contributing to the degradation of your recorded sound. Audio engineers, being the clever people that they are, have devised a number of tools over the years in the form of signal processors and effects to overcome these problems and help you achieve the ultimate mix.

Effects first manifested themselves as hardware boxes that could be connected to a mixing console. Normally, when dealing with hardware effects, you only get to use each box once. If you use an effect processor to generate a reverb, you will need to find another hardware box to generate a chorus. This can become quite costly if you need to use a large palette of effects in your mix. In fact, you've probably seen pictures of large recording studios with walls of rack-mounted devices for this very reason. Thanks to the increasing power of computer processors, it is now possible to re-create these effects using software. Software effects, commonly referred to as *plug-ins*, are extremely useful since one effect program may be used multiple times in a project.

On a computer, you can use multiple *instances* of effects with ease. This means if you use a reverb plug-in to add some space to a voice, you can use another instance of the plug-in to create a different reverb for a snare drum. In fact, you can use as many instances of the plug-in as you want as long as your computer's CPU can handle the work.

The number of effects available to those with a modest computer system can be staggering. There are truly hundreds, perhaps thousands, of effect programs available from a myriad of developers and hobbyists. The quality of those plug-ins can be astounding; many software emulations rival their hardware counterparts. For convenience and power, Ableton has included a suite of effects integrated into Live to help bring your projects to life.

As you go through these explanations, please don't just look at my pretty pictures and take my word for it—drop these effects on a track and listen to how they alter your sounds. You will learn by doing.

I now present you with the ultimate guide to Live's built-in Audio Effects, all 22 of them.

EQ and Filters

The first batch of effects I'm going to dive into are the *filters* and *equalizers* (EQ for short). These types of signal processors are used to *attenuate* (reduce in volume) and *amplify* (increase in volume) only specific frequency ranges within an audio signal. Engineers will use filters and EQs to finely craft the frequency distribution of their mixes, resulting in beautiful, rich, and detailed masters (final mixes). Of course, these tools can also be used to radically distort sound, creating unique effects in their own right.

EQ Four

A parametric EQ is a powerful frequency filtering and timbre-shaping tool. While most hardware and software mixers usually have some variant of this equalization available on every channel, you will need to add an EQ plug-in manually to a track any time it's needed in your Live project.

The goal when using an EQ is to either boost or diminish certain audio frequencies, or a range (bandwidth) of frequencies, within a given sound to overcome problems arising from poor recordings and mics, reduce muddiness from overlapping frequencies in other sounds, or to emphasize certain characteristics of the sound to make it cut through the mix. The frequencies are often referred to as lows, mids, and highs, or other subdivisions such as low-mids or high-mids. High frequencies are found in the register called *treble,* while low frequencies are referred to as *bass.* Low-mids, mids, or high-mids make up the middle section (from left to right) of the sonic spectrum. Live's EQ Four features up to four adjustable *bands* (frequency ranges) of equalization represented by the green-illuminated 1, 2, 3, and 4 buttons in the middle region of the plug-in pictured in Figure 10.1. With EQ Four's separate and selectable multiple bands, you will be able to meticulously sculpt the audio frequencies of your parts.

Many engineers like to *shape* or *carve* a sound's frequencies in a particular way for each song (or mix of a song). For instance, if the meat of a sound is in the bass, such as a bass guitar or synth, the part's high content and even high-mids may be uncomplimentary to the rest of the mix. Since you only have a finite number of frequencies to work with (anything between 20Hz and 20kHz), you may want to save the song's high-frequency content for your singer's lovely voice or your drummer's hi-hat. In this case, you'd want to use EQ to reduce the highs (everything above 4kHz) and boost the lows (everything below 100Hz) in the bass track. An example of this can be seen in Figure 10.2.

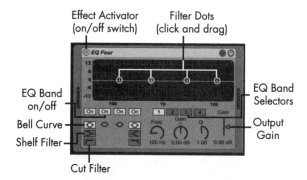

Figure 10.1

Here is Live's powerful, if unassuming, EQ Four.

Effect Activator (on/off switch)

Filter Dots (click and drag)

EQ Band on/off

EQ Band Selectors

Bell Curve

Shelf Filter

Output Gain

Cut Filter

Figure 10.2

Here's an example of how an EQ curve would look when boosting the bass and cutting the highs. The graph shows low frequencies on the left and high frequencies on the right.

Another frequency-shaping example would be to *shave* (remove) the mids and lows off a crash cymbal sample (primarily a high-frequency sound) so that no extraneous noise, such as mic or stand rumble, is heard. Therefore, some engineers may choose to *roll off* (eliminate) the lower frequencies using an EQ, as shown in Figure 10.3.

Figure 10.3

Here's an example of a low-shelf curve, which is often used to reduce background noise and rumble from audio tracks.

With EQ Four, each band specializes in treating certain audio frequencies by applying particular grades of slope, called *curves*. Bands 1 and 4 provide the option of using one of three different curves: bell, shelf, or cut. Actually, the last mode has a couple of names, such as cut, roll-off, and high/low-pass. Filter bands 2 and 3 are simpler in that they are only bell curves.

A *bell curve* is a parabolic-shaped boost or cut of a given range of frequencies (see Figure 10.4). To change the grade or steepness of the slope, use the Q setting. To change the height or depth (the boost or the cut), alter the EQ band's Gain setting.

Figure 10.4
This bell curve demonstrates a swell of the high-mid frequencies.

As mentioned, you can zero in on specific frequencies by altering Q setting on each EQ band. Figure 10.5 shows a steeper, more acute frequency cut, accomplished by increasing the Q of a bell curve.

Figure 10.5
Notice the steep V-shaped cut in this instance of EQ Four. This is good for pulling out strange resonant frequencies.

A *low-shelf* or *high-shelf*, possible with bands 1 and 4, respectively, provides an easy way to cut or boost all of the frequencies below or above a certain point, specified by the frequency setting of the EQ band. Figure 10.6 shows an example of a low-shelf and high-shelf curve being used at the same time.

Figure 10.6
The low and high shelves are being used to boost the bass and treble, a sound many people like for their music.

❋ KICK ME! (PART 1)

Here's a little something that gets pulled out of the ol' bag of tricks time and time again: how to get "that sound" for your kick drum. First, let me state that this is best for an acoustic kick drum, one that you may have recorded yourself. Synth kicks are a different species and don't suffer the same tonal complexities of a real bass drum, but this trick may help with them, too. Also, if you're using a kick drum from a sample library, it may have had this trick applied to it already.

Many people will try to add bass with an EQ to get it to cut through the mix—it is the "bass" drum after all! This actually makes things worse by adding even more level to the bass frequencies, which can cause operating levels to clip. The end result is that you end up feeling the kick more (your subwoofer will really be bumpin') but not really hearing it cut through any better. The reason the drum is muddy in the mix is because it is occupying the same frequency bands as other instruments in the mix.

To get that deep yet punchy tone that will slice through the mix, try the EQ curve shown in Figure 10.5. Each bass drum is different, so you'll have to sweep the frequency around a bit. Around 150–200Hz, you'll hear a particular tone of the kick drum disappear, leaving behind that awesome kick sound we all love. The resonant tone that you pulled out may not be very strong on your kick, so experiment with the amount of gain you're removing—you may not need to cut all of it. By cutting this tone from the sonic space of the bass, it now occupies its own space (the low frequencies where you feel it and the high frequencies where you hear it) and cleans up the sonic image (the range from 150Hz to 250Hz can be extremely problematic in many mixes). Apply some compression (see below) and you've got your kick tone.

❋ GAIN

While boosting and cutting various frequencies, you may notice that the overall volume has changed. Use the Gain slider to make up for any reduction in volume from serious cuts or to pull back on extreme frequency boosts, especially in the bass frequencies.

To edit the filter curve, click and drag one of the filter dots in the X-Y view. Horizontal movement changes the filter frequency, while vertical movement adjusts the filter gain. To adjust the filter Q, hold down the Alt (PC)/Option (Mac) modifier while dragging the mouse. You can also use the numbered filter selector buttons to select a band for editing; then edit parameter values with the Freq, Gain, and Q dials (or type specific values into the number fields below each dial).

❋ DOUBLE STACK

For more drastic cuts, boosts, and effects, try stacking EQs by assigning the same parameters to two or more bands, or use more than one EQ Four on the same track.

> ※ **POWER MISER**
>
> Ableton suggests that you turn off any unused EQ bands to save CPU (processing) power. To do this, simply disengage (click) the On/Off button corresponding to the band not in use. For example, the first band is the first On button, the second band the second, and so on.

EQ Three

While EQ Four specializes in precision frequency crafting, the EQ Three is designed for more drastic EQ effects. Modeled after the EQ banks found on many DJ mixers, the EQ Three allows you to "cut holes" in the frequency spectrum and make broad adjustments to the overall sound of a track.

The EQ Three is only concerned with three frequency bands: lows, mids, and highs. You can see in Figure 10.7 that the EQ Three has three main dials, GainLow, GainMid, and GainHi. The frequency range of these dials is determined by the FreqLow and FreqHi knobs at the bottom of the effect. The GainMid knob will boost or cut all frequencies between FreqLow and FreqHi. The GainLow will adjust all frequencies below FreqLow, and the GainHi knob will handle everything above FreqHi.

Figure 10.7

Lows, mids, and highs are under your complete control with EQ Three.

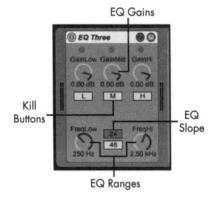

What makes the EQ Three uniquely different from other EQ plug-ins, including the EQ Four, is its ability to completely remove, or *kill*, entire frequency ranges from your audio. You'll see that as you turn the Gain knobs down—they'll eventually reach infinity, meaning the frequencies are completely cut. If you want, you can use the green *kill buttons* (labeled L, M, and H) located below each Gain knob to toggle that frequency range on and off with ease.

The 24 and 48 buttons determine the slope, either 24dB/octave or 48dB/octave, at the edges of the frequency bands. This setting will be most apparent when using the kill feature of the EQ Three on a full song. For example, drag a whole song (an MP3 with lots of bass) into a Clip Slot and place an EQ Three on the track. Click the 48 button, place the FreqLow control at 200Hz, and kill the low band—you'll hear the bass disappear from the song. Now try clicking the 24 button. You may notice that you can now hear a little more bass.

When set to 48, the EQ Three is reducing the volumes of all the frequencies below 200Hz at a rate of 48dB per octave. If your song has two tones in it with matching volumes at 100Hz and 200Hz, the 100Hz tone will sound 48dB quieter with the EQ Three settings above. Reducing a sound by 6dB results in the sound being half as loud as it was originally, so cutting a sound by 48dB nearly removes it entirely. When you switch the EQ Three to 24, it will now only reduce the 100Hz tone by 24dB, thus making it slightly more audible than before.

Using the kills of the EQ Three when set to 24 will result in a smoother-sounding cut, while the 48 setting will sound a little more abrupt and synthetic. You can use whichever setting suits your taste.

The EQ Three is especially useful on the Master Track in Live. Assign MIDI controllers to the EQ Three's controls and have fun sucking the bass out of the mix right before a huge drop, or slowly remove the upper elements of the music until only the gut-shaking bass is left.

 SONIC JIGSAW PUZZLES

Try placing three different drum loops on three different tracks, each armed with an EQ Three. Then isolate the bass in one track, the mids in another, and the highs in the remaining track. You'll now have one hybrid beat consisting of kicks, snares, and hi-hats from different loops. Try swapping or automating the kills for other rhythm combinations.

Auto Filter

One of Live's greatest live performance effects, Auto Filter (seen in Figure 10.8), is a virtual analog-style filter with four selectable classic filter types (high-pass, low-pass, band-pass, and band-reject). Each of these can be controlled via the effect's X-Y controller and modulated by envelopes, rhythmic quantization, and any of three different LFO shapes. As you may have gleaned from the EQ Four explanation, suppressing certain frequencies allows you to carve out specific problems or overcooked frequencies so your mixes sound more professional. The Auto Filter can do this as well, but it can also accentuate the cutoff frequencies for groovy effects.

A common DJ trick is to mix two beat-matched songs, one with a low-pass filter and the second with a high-pass filter (one on each turntable). The result is more than simply mixing two songs—the creation of an entirely new song is made from the combined frequencies (highs from one, lows from the other) of the two tracks. Without cutting some of the frequencies, the two songs could sound like a jumbled mush when played simultaneously. Keeping the best frequencies does require some practice and will vary, depending upon the musical content. If you are new to this concept, it can be a huge ear opener. See the following note called "Filter Frenzy."

Figure 10.8
Here is Live's Auto Filter device. If you've just been reading so far, you really need to get up and try this one. No, really.

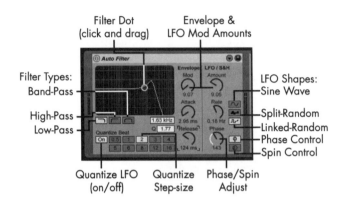

Filter Dot
(click and drag)

Envelope &
LFO Mod Amounts

Filter Types:
Band-Pass

High-Pass
Low-Pass

LFO Shapes:
Sine Wave

Split-Random
Linked-Random
Phase Control
Spin Control

Quantize LFO
(on/off)

Quantize
Step-size

Phase/Spin
Adjust

❄ FILTER FRENZY

Low-pass, high-pass, band-pass, band-reject...what does it all mean?

Low-pass simply means that the low frequencies pass through the filter, but nothing else does. For instance, your bass guitar and kick drums will be heard, though a little dulled out from the lack of highs. Some sounds will be gone completely, such as hi-hats. Conversely, a high-pass filter will allow shimmering cymbals and sparkly guitars and synths to pass but will suppress basses and any other instruments in the lower frequency range. How low is up to you. Band-pass filters are basically high-pass and low-pass filters put together; thus, only frequencies falling between the two filters will pass, sounding similar to a telephone at times. Band-reject filters work opposite of band-pass—only audio lying outside of the cutoff frequency can pass.

To get going with Live's Auto Filter, you will want to select a filter—low-pass is a good starter—then use the X-Y controller to dial in Frequency (X-axis) and Q (Y-axis). The frequency range for the Auto Filter is adjustable between 46.2Hz and 12.5kHz. The Q control (also called resonance or emphasis) can range from .20 to 3.0 and will affect the volume of the filtered sound. I like to think of Q as the intensity of the filter, where low Q values will generate broader, less dynamic curves, and higher Q values will result in a more narrow, direct, and in-your-face kind of sound. If you really crank up the Q, you'll get those super-squelchy, screaming techno sounds as the filter begins to resonate. This can be lots of fun, but watch your volumes when this happens!

To the right of the X-Y controller are two strips of controls: Envelope Mod and LFO/S&H. The Envelope Modulation section determines how Auto Filter's sound-activated envelope changes the filter frequency. In other words, it directs how much of the filter's variance or movement is audible and how the changes are applied. Attack and Release work in tandem to determine the speed of the modulation. The shorter the attack, the quicker the modulation will be heard once the signal is present. Longer attack times will be slower to shift the filter. Similarly, small (quick) release parameters will tend to cut the modulation in and out more often. Long release will hold the modulation more steadily.

Hint: start out with quick Attack (5 milliseconds) and a medium amount of Release (200 milliseconds). Then gradually increase the modulation effect (Mod) to your liking. You will hear the sound get steadily brighter and louder.

✲ **FILTER DEFINITIONS**

Envelope: A signal (used to be electric) that evolves over time to shape the timbre and amplitude of a sound.

LFO: Low-frequency oscillator generates a periodic waveform that affects the envelope filter—usually adding vibrato-type movement to it.

Modulation (oversimplified): The act of changing a sound using another signal. An example of *modulating the amplitude* would be turning up the volume of an amplifier with your hand (the control signal). More common modulations, as in Live's Auto Filter, involve using an LFO to modulate oscillator pitch. Frequency modulation is the use of a control device to change the frequency of a sound.

S&H: Sample & Hold uses randomly generated pulse waves (square waves of varying values) as modulators. The middle wave (on the right side of Live's Auto Filter) looks like a filled-in random pulse wave and is actually two independent (left and right channels) non-synced random pulse modulators. The third (lowest) button is a single (L/R-synced) random pulse modulator. When using the S&H modulators, the Spin and Phase functions are not relevant; thus, they have no effect.

You will also want to check out the Quantize Beat section at the bottom of the Auto Filter effect. The default position is off, so you will need to click the switch on to hear Auto Filter modulate your filter to the 1/16 note step size of your choice. Depending upon the rhythmic quality of your sample, you may or may not want to use the Quantize Beat settings. Short times can sound very choppy, while longer times can have strange shifts that may or may not make musical sense. Each loop will react differently, so try to listen closely to how the filter moves.

LFO stands for low-frequency oscillator (see the "Filter Definitions" Note) and can help add further expression and movement to your original filter in an imprecise but rhythmic fashion. The Amount knob controls LFO's effect, while the Rate control designates the speed of the oscillation (movement)—the range is .01 (slow) to 10.0 (fast). Next to the Rate knob are three separate waveforms from which to choose. The top is a sine wave and will dictate fairly smooth sailing in terms of frequency modulation. The second and third waveforms are Sample and Hold variations—the middle wave is mono, while the bottom wave creates different values for the left and right channels.

To help rein in the wild waves created thus far, the selectable Phase/Spin knob (located at the bottom right half of the plug-in) will add stereo dimensions to your frequency modulation. Phase will keep both right and left side LFOs at the same frequency. Of course, you can then gradually knock them out of phase by turning the knob towards 180 degrees. The Spin setting, which trades places with the Phase knob when activated, offsets the right and left channel LFOs, so that each channel is filtered at a different frequency.

Dynamic Processing

What are dynamics again? Dynamics refers to the volume or amplitude of a sound. More specifically, it refers to the *change* in volume of a sound. The sound of a drum kit can range from quiet ghost notes on a snare drum up to the thundering sound of the kick drum and toms, and it is therefore considered to be more dynamic than a distorted guitar, which primarily plays at one volume only.

It therefore makes sense that dynamic processors will alter the volume of signals passing through them. But why would you want to do this? Like EQing above, dynamic processing can be used to compensate for problems arising in the recording process. It can also be used to help parts stick out from a mix. It can also be used as an effect of its own.

Auto Pan

The simplest dynamic processing effect to understand is the Auto Pan (shown in Figure 10.9), one of the new devices in Live 5. It will automatically pan the position of the track from left to right in cycles. It does this by alternately turning down the volumes of the left and right sides of the channel. When the left side is turned down, the sound will be heard from the right, thus making it sound panned to the left.

Figure 10.9

The Auto Pan has a surprising number of controls for such a simple device... could it be that this effect has a few surprises locked inside?

The Auto Pan interface is split into two sections. The top section contains a graphical representation of the volume pattern being applied—it is for display purposes only. The Auto Pan is adjusted by using the knobs and buttons on the lower half of the interface.

When the device is first loaded, it will have a flat line through the middle of its display, and you will hear no effect. This allows you to add the device and set it *before* using it on your sound, making it easier to use during a live performance. The reason you hear nothing is because the Amount knob is set to 0%. As you increase this knob, you'll hear the sound begin moving left and right. The higher you set the Amount knob, the "wider" the left to right movement will be.

As you increase the Amount knob, you'll also see the graphic begin to change on the Auto Pan interface. When the Amount reaches 100%, you'll see two sine curves on the screen in different colors. The blue curve represents the left channel, and the orange curve represents the right channel. What this curve tells you is that, when the left channel is at full volume (the highest point of the blue curve), the right channel will be at its lowest volume (see Figure 10.10). As the left channel drops in volume, the right channel rises and vice versa. The button below the Amount knob will swap the left and right pan assignments when activated (you'll see the colors of the two sine curves change).

Figure 10.10
By looking at the picture in the Auto Pan window, you can see the relationship of the left and right channels over time.

The Rate knob next to the Amount knob will change the speed of the left-right motion created by the Auto Pan. You'll see that as you turn up this knob, not only does the left-right speed increase, but you'll also see the graphic waveform change in kind. You'll appreciate this control-graphic relationship even more as you start tweaking more of the Auto Pan's controls.

Below the Rate knob are two selection buttons. By default, Hz is selected, meaning that you will define the rate of the Auto Pan in terms of cycles per second. So, if you set the Rate knob to 1Hz, the Auto Pan will complete one left-right cycle within one second. If you increase the value to 2Hz, the left-right pattern will happen twice every second. If you click on the button that looks like a 1/16 note, you will be able to define the Auto Pan cycle time in terms of beats. For example, when set to 1/4, the left-right pattern will repeat every quarter note. If you change the tempo of the Live Set, the Auto Pan will also change to maintain the cycle-per-beat relationship.

❊ **To Pan or Not to Pan**

I want to immediately avoid any confusion that may arise from the use of the Auto Pan effect. You should understand that the Auto Pan does not automatically move the track's Pan control the way the Pan automation envelopes do. You'll notice that there is no change or movement of the Pan control while Auto Pan is running. This is because the Auto Pan applies itself directly to the signal passing through the track. The added benefit is that you can use more than one Auto Pan on a track. You'll see why this is important in just a moment.

Next on the list of Auto Pan controls is the Phase knob. If you move this knob while watching the waveform graphic, you should get a pretty good idea of what it does. The knob simply adjusts the phase relationship of the left and right curves, or the position where the waveforms start. When set to 180 degrees, the two curves are out of phase, meaning one channel is at full volume while the other is silent. If you twist this knob down to 0 degrees, the two curves will now be in sync (you'll now only see one curve), resulting in the left and right channels changing volume in sync. The result of this is that the Auto Pan no longer pans the signal from left to right—it simply turns the volume of the whole signal up and down! This is where the Auto Pan device begins to function beyond what its name implies. I'll show you how to take advantage of this in a couple ways in just a moment.

There are a pair of buttons below the Phase knob. When you click the bottom one, the Phase knob turns into a Spin control. What this does is alter the rates of the left and right waveforms. With Spin at 0 percent, the left and right run at the same speed. As you increase Spin, you'll see that the right channel begins to increase in rate compared to the left channel. When using this feature, the sound will no longer appear to pan back and forth between the left and right. Instead, a strange wobbly pattern will result.

Before I get into the tricks, though, let's finish looking at all of the Auto Pan's controls. Below the Phase knob is the Offset knob. This is essentially a "global phase" knob, as it changes the phase of both curves in relation to the song. This is extremely helpful when the Rate is synced to the song tempo. When you start the song and the offset is at 0, the Auto Pan will only output the left signal. You may, instead, want the pan to start in the middle at the beginning. To do this, turn the Offset knob until the graphic display shows the two waveforms crossing at the left edge of the window, as shown in Figure 10.11, which should be 90 degrees.

Figure 10.11
The start of the Auto Pan waveform has been offset so that the pan is in the center at the start of the song.

The last knob on the Auto Pan is the Shape knob. As this knob is turned clockwise, the waveform will slowly morph into a square wave. When set to 100%, this will cause the Auto Pan to flip-flop the audio between the left and right channels—there will be no motion through the center. Of course, setting this knob at an amount less than 100% will allow you to hear some of the left-right transition.

In real terms, I use this knob to make the pan "stall" at the left and right extremes. Sometimes, even though the Amount knob is set to 100%, it doesn't sound like the sound is fully panning from left to right, especially when being mixed in with the other parts of the song. This is due to the fact that the sound is panned fully left and right for only an instant before the Auto Pan begins to pan it back again. Increasing the Shape knob results in flat lines at the top and bottom of the waveform, therefore causing the pan motion to sit at these extremes for a moment before panning back to the other side. The result is a more pronounced panning motion that can be heard better over an entire mix.

The final controls of the Auto Pan are the waveform selection buttons. You've been using the sine waveform thus far, so try clicking on some of the others to see what they look like. The button in the upper-right is for the triangle waveform. As the name suggests, the waveform looks like a triangle at the top and bottom. When using this waveform, the left-right pan motion is linear—the left-to-right speed remains constant. This is different from the sine waveform where the pan motion would slow down as it reached the left and right extremes. The button in the lower-left is for the sawtooth, or ramp, waveform. This is a unique waveform in that it does not create a smooth side-to-side panning motion. Instead, it will pan a sound in one direction (determined by the Normal/Invert button) and then immediately reset before panning again. This means that the motion goes from left to right and then immediately to left before panning to the right again. The last button in the lower-right is for a random waveform where the volumes of the left and right channels are changed at random. You'll notice that when this waveform is selected, the Phase knob changes to Width. This knob will adjust the left-right deviation of the randomness. When set to 0 percent, the random pattern will influence the left and right volumes identically, resulting in random changes of the sound's volume. When set to 100 percent, the difference between the left and right volumes will increase, resulting in random panning patterns.

So what were all those secrets and tricks I was alluding to earlier in this section? The secrets involve using the Auto Pan for something other than panning. This stems from the use of the Phase knob. When Phase is set to 0 degrees, the Auto Pan will simply turn the volume of the sound up and down. Try this out: Load a song onto a track, place an Auto Pan on the track, and set its Rate to 1/8, shape to 100 percent, Phase to 0 degrees, Offset to 270 degrees, and Waveform to sine. As you increase the Amount knob, you'll begin to hear the track volume jump up and down in 1/8-note steps in sync with the song. Turn up Amount to 100%, and you'll have magically chopped the song into tiny slices!

Now that you've got the "strobe" effect going, start playing with the Rate knob to change the speed of the strobe. Reducing the Shape knob below 100% will also reduce the abruptness of the strobing. For a real crazy effect, try slightly altering the Phase knob. When the two waveforms are just slightly out of phase, you'll hear each strobe "zip" across your speakers as one side is turned on just slightly before the other.

This strobe effect is great to use during a DJ set, especially when mixing between two tracks. You can use it to remove all of the sound between the beats (set the Rate to 1/4, and you'll only hear the 1/4-note beats), making the transitional mix smoother. This can also be a great effect to use on vocals from time to time.

Compressor I

Compression can add clarity and power to your mixes if done properly. Done wrong, it can suck all life from what once was a brilliant track. For audio engineers, compression is one of the hardest things to learn to use properly and is one element that separates the big fish from the little guppies.

What is a compressor and what relates it to our discussion of dynamic processors? In brief, a compressor is a device that will automatically turn down the volume of sound passing through it. For example, have you ever noticed how the commercials on TV are louder than the show you're trying to watch? This isn't your imagination, it's true. They play the commercials louder as a way to get your attention. For most of us, it just makes us reach for the remote or run from the room. Wouldn't it be great if you could buy something that would turn down the TV whenever something loud came on? It would keep the commercials at the same volume as the TV show, and it would also keep loud things like car explosions from blasting your neighbors awake in the middle of the night. Well, that something that you'd buy would be a compressor.

So you go out and you buy this compressor for your TV. You hook it up, but there are a few settings you have to choose before it will work. The first one is called Volume Trigger. You set this one to the volume where the box should start killing the volume. You set this to a point just slightly louder than the TV show you're watching. This guarantees that the compressor doesn't turn down your show at all. However, when a commercial comes on, it will be louder than the Volume Trigger, thus the compressor will engage.

The next control you're supposed to set on this thing is the Kill Amount. The deal is that, when the compressor engages as a result of the Volume Trigger being exceeded, the volume will be turned down by the Kill Amount. Setting this to infinity makes the compressor turn down the volume to match the Volume Trigger. Thus, the commercial is turned down to the volume of the TV show.

The third setting is the Cut Out Time. This setting sets the time the compressor takes to turn down the volume once the commercials start. If this value is set to a long time, like five seconds, the compressor will take five seconds to turn down the volume when the commercial comes on. The point here is to cut the volume on the commercial the moment it comes on, so you set the time to 10 milliseconds. Now, the commercial is turned down within 10 milliseconds of coming on.

The last value is Back In Time. This is the opposite of the Cut Out Time, where you now specify how long it should take for the compressor to turn the volume back up again after the commercials are over. You don't want to miss any of the dialogue when the show starts, so you set this to one second.

So that's it, you've now mastered the compressor. It turns down commercials that exceed the volume of your TV show within 10 milliseconds and then returns the volume to normal one second after the commercials are over. Nice.

See, many people believe that a compressor makes sounds louder. This is not true. As you can see in the illustration above, a compressor makes loud sounds quieter. Still, engineers do employ compressors as part of a technique for making sounds louder. Imagine the TV scenario above, except that you're watching your show on a TV with really small speakers. You're trying to listen at high volume, but every time the commercials come on, they're so loud that the speakers begin to pop and distort. To keep from distorting, you have to turn down the volume to a point where the loudest commercial still plays without overdriving the speakers. Now your TV show is too quiet. How do you make the TV shows louder without killing the speakers with the commercials? You put the compressor on it. This time you plug the output of the compressor into another volume control before it goes to the speakers. You can then turn up the new volume control to a point where both the commercials *and* the TV show play loudly—in effect turning up the quiet TV show without turning up the commercials.

As I explained in Chapter 2, "Back to School," you have a limited amount of dynamic range, or *headroom*, when dealing with digital audio. There is a limited range in the analog world, too, but analog equipment is a little more forgiving when headroom is exceeded. Digital distortion, the result when exceeding digital headroom, is harsh and abrasive. Even one millisecond of this type of distortion can make a perfectly good take unusable. Compressors can be used to keep a sound recording from exceeding the ceiling (notated as 0db in the digital world), thus saving our ears and our takes. Compressors can also be used to keep a wily vocal part in check. Got a singer who likes to switch from a delicate whisper to a death yell within the same verse? No problem. A compressor will allow the nuances of the whisper to pass through unaffected but will turn down the scream to keep the listener's head from being ripped off. As you're about to see (and hear— you're playing along at home, right?), compressors have a number of uses and many ways to abuse them.

If you've looked at a compressor at all, hardware or software, you know that I've replaced the real names of the controls with fake, yet more descriptive, names above. Here's the decoder: The Volume Trigger is really the Threshold control. The Kill Amount refers to the Ratio. Cut Out Time and Back in Time refer to Attack and Release, respectively. The second volume control above is known as Make-Up Gain. You will see most of these controls on Live's Compressor I device, shown in Figure 10.12.

It's not too hard to understand what a compressor does or what the various controls are supposed to do. What is difficult is to determine if compression is needed and how to set the compressor when it is. One of the first tasks is to determine if a sound actually needs to be compressed at all.

Figure 10.12

Live's Compressor I device.

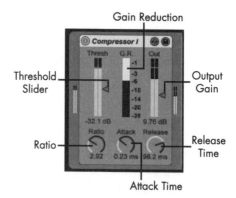

Gain Reduction

Threshold
Slider

Output
Gain

Ratio

Release
Time

Attack Time

You may have a hard time hearing the part in the mix, but sometimes the fix is simple, like a little boost of an EQ band, or sometimes simply turning up the part. Remember, a compressor is a dynamics processor—it controls volume. You therefore do not want to use it to fix problems that are related to frequency. For example, if you can hear the low tone of a bass guitar but can't hear the picking in the upper frequency ranges, use an EQ, not a compressor, to boost only the frequencies that you can't hear.

Compression is useful in two main situations, keeping wily transients under control and smoothing out the overall dynamic content of a part over a length of time. Examples of parts with lots of transients are drums and vocals. The "crack" created when a drum stick hits a drum can be extraordinarily loud in comparison to the lingering tone of the drum. Vocals also tend to have sudden transients in the form of plosives, which are bursts of air that strike the microphone while the person is singing. Put your hand an inch from your mouth and say, "Peter Piper picked a peck of pickled peppers." You'll feel those bursts of air every time you pronounce something with a "p." While they don't feel like much, those soft bursts are like gale-force winds when striking the sensitive diaphragm of a microphone.

A compressor can turn down the volume quickly when these transients are detected, thus keeping them from distorting a recording or popping out of a mix. The compressor attenuates the transients but leaves the rest of the sound untouched.

How do you properly compress a sound with a lot of transients? The technique involved is nearly identical to the process used to set the compressor for the TV in the example above. You need to identify the volume at which you want to start compressing, how much to compress once the volume reaches that point, and how quickly the compressor should respond. In order to set the Threshold to the proper level, you'll need to be able to see the point where the compressor starts to work on your sound. To do this, set the Ratio to the maximum, reduce the Attack to its minimum, and set the Release to 500ms. Place the Threshold at its highest setting and start playing the sound. With the Threshold at maximum, the sound will not exceed this level, and the compressor will never engage. As you start to move the Threshold downward, there will be a point where you notice that the Gain Reduction meter starts to respond. This means you've found the Threshold at which some of the transients are loud enough to trigger the compressor. As you keep moving the Threshold slider downward, the Gain Reduction meter will begin to respond more often and will also show a greater amount of attenuation.

If you keep reducing the Threshold, there will come a point where nearly every element of the sound you're compressing, the transients and the quieter tones, will all be beyond the Threshold, thus causing the compressor to work nonstop—always in some state of gain reduction. If you reach that point, the Gain Reduction meter will always be showing some sort of level. This is a sign that you are probably using too much compression, as nearly every element of the sound is being attenuated. Back off the Threshold to a point where only the heavy transients are triggering the Gain Reduction.

The compressor's Ratio control determines the amount of compression expressed as a ratio of the input volume to the output volume. For instance, 2 to 1 compression means that when a sound increases by 2dB going into the compressor, you will only hear a 1dB increase at the output. And 4 to 1 would mean that for a 2dB increase, only a ½dB change would be heard at the output. You may also notice that for larger Ratio settings, the sound may become muffled or muted sounding as a result of the volume squashing that is going on. As you dial in your compression for a given track, you will want to watch the downward-spiking red indicator on the Gain Reduction meter. Extreme gain reduction, such as −12dB and below, will often cut the life out of your sound—although you may occasionally want to overcompress an instrument as a special effect.

The compressor's other two controls, Attack and Release, determine how soon after a sound crosses the Threshold the compression will begin to work and how long the compression remains active after the sound has dropped below the Threshold. Ableton's manual recommends that using a small amount of attack time (5–10 milliseconds) is best for retaining some sense of dynamics (varying degrees of loud and soft in the music). Short attacks are great for instruments like drums and percussion, as well as vocals. Longer attacks are most often used with horns, bass, and longer sorts of sounds where the volume increase (crescendo) is also slower.

In contrast, a compressor's release settings are often better (less noticeable) when long. Basically, a long release time means that the compression continues to work for a given length of time (in milliseconds) after it has been engaged and the signal level has dipped back below the Threshold. Typically, a short release time will force the compressor to repeatedly engage and disengage (start and stop), and a listener will be more apt to hear the repeated contrast (sometimes referred to as *pumping* or *breathing*), as well as low-frequency distortion. Short release times can still be a cool-sounding effect when used on drums and diced-up pieces of audio (where the signal repeatedly crosses the Threshold).

❊ KICK ME! (PART 2)

After you've used the EQ Four to dial in a nice kick drum tone, place a Compressor I on the track. You'll use the compressor to shape the amplitude of the kick sound just like using an ADSR envelope on a synth (see Chapter 11, "Live's MIDI Effects," and the Simpler).

The setting for the Ratio dial is dependent on the amount of attack already present in the kick sound. If there's already a decent amount of punch, a ratio of 4:1 may be all that's necessary. If the kick is flat and has no life, a 10:1 ratio may be in order.

A fairly short attack time will need to be used, somewhere in the neighborhood of 5 to 20 milliseconds (ms). If the attack is too short, the drum will sound short, snappy, and clipped.

A slightly longer release time, 25 to 50ms, is used, depending on the length of the bass drum. If the drum has a long tone (perhaps there was no padding inside the drum), a longer release will keep the tail end of the tone from popping up in volume after the loud transient of the drum has passed. If, on the other hand, the drum has a short tone or if the drum is played quickly, a short release time will allow the compressor to fully open before the next drum hit. If the release time is too long, only the first kick drum hit will sound right, while the others that follow shortly after will not sound right because the compressor is still attenuating the signal.

The Threshold should be at a point where every kick played at normal volume will trigger the compressor. If it's too low, the compressor will squash the volume and never let go!

❊ A LITTLE GOES A LONG WAY

Compression can create its own kind of special effect but can sound unnatural when overapplied. Like EQ, a little goes a long way when adding compression.

Compressor II

Compressor II (see Figure 10.13) works the same as its predecessor but has additional controls that allow you to be more specific with your compression and timing.

Figure 10.13

Compressor II gives you even finer control over your compression parameters.

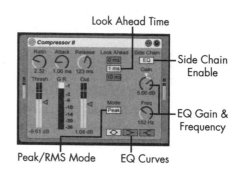

Look Ahead Time

Side Chain Enable

EQ Gain & Frequency

Peak/RMS Mode

EQ Curves

❊ ❊ ❊

One of the additional sections added to Compressor II is the *side chain*. This allows you to specify the frequency range that will trigger the compressor. For example, if you're trying to compress a snare drum, but you've got the sound of a kick drum bleeding through onto the same channel (this usually can't be avoided when miking an acoustic drum kit), you can specify the snare frequencies as the trigger signal for the compressor. This is done by using the EQ on the right edge of the device. If you focus the EQ on the high frequencies, Compressor II will start attenuating the signal when the amplified frequencies exceed the threshold. Please note that the side chain only determines what the compressor hears—the output signal will not be processed by the EQ.

Another frequent use of the side chain is for *de-essing*, which is the process of softening the sharp "sss" sound that can occur in vocal parts. By focusing the frequency control of the side chain on these sibilant frequencies (8kHz and higher), the compressor will drop the output volume any time a strong "sss" escapes the vocalist's lips. The rest of the vocal content below the side chain frequency will not cause the compressor to kick in.

You'll also see that Compressor II has a Look Ahead amount, which allows the compressor to start reacting to sounds that are 1ms or 10ms in the future. This will help tame extremely sharp transients because the compressor will already be attenuating the signal before it arrives at the input.

The last control, simply labeled Mode, switches the compressor between Peak and RMS detection. Peak detection is best used on audio tracks with lots of transients, such as drums. It will cause Compressor II to react to the loudest moments of the sound. RMS, on the other hand, calculates an average amplitude based on the incoming audio and uses that to control the compressor. This smooth type of compression is best suited for vocals and strings, as it will generally keep the audio levels in check while still allowing brief transients (consonants, string plucks, etc.) to pass through the compressor unaffected.

✳ **VOCAL COMPRESSION**

Pay attention class, this is how to compress a vocal for a pop song. This works for rap, rock, R&B, grunge, electronica, or anything else that's got a nice full musical arrangement.

Drop a Compressor II onto your vocal track. Crank the Ratio knob up all the way and then twist both the Attack and Release knobs fully left. Engage Peak mode and disengage the side chain. Start with the Threshold knob all the way up and start the vocal track.

As the vocal plays, begin to turn down the Threshold knob. Once the input level of the vocal passes the threshold, you'll see the Gain Reduction meter start to move. Keep reducing Threshold to a point where the compressor is reducing only 1dB or so from a normal voice. A whispered voice should not make the Gain Reduction meter register at all. A loud passage, on the other hand, will make the compressor squash the vocal. Since the attack and release times are nearly instantaneous, the compressor kicks in immediately when the vocal passes the Threshold level. It then opens up again right when the vocal is back to normal levels. This means that the vocal will always be at a full level, allowing it to sit nicely in the front of your mix.

Gate

Gates can be thought of as backwards compressors, and therefore the two are often discussed (and used) together. Where compressors focus on reducing volume spikes above a certain threshold, Gates help weed out low-level noise beneath a certain threshold. The result of using a Gate is usually a cleaner, less cluttered, and overall more pleasing audio signal. Gates are a tool for reducing quiet hums, microphone bleed, and background noise (like your singer yelling for you to turn up his headphones). That said, Live's Gate device is an excellent utility for this kind of work.

A Gate effect operates just like it sounds. Certain audio can make it through the Gate, while other audio cannot. The threshold, or minimum requirement, to get through an audio gating effect is set by the Threshold slider. Any incoming sound quieter than the threshold will cause the Gate to close, thus attenuating the signal. Gating can be an excellent effect to apply when attempting to eliminate excess noise, hiss, hum, or undesirable reverb decay. You may find that a slight Gate effect can really clean up your drum loops. Many producers use Gate on drums like toms or snares so that they can capture the essence of the instrument at its highest volume point and eliminate all weaker background sounds. Figure 10.14 shows Live's Gate effect.

Figure 10.14
Live's Gate effect.

The small triangle next to the Threshold bar can be dragged with the mouse to set the minimum level of output (required to pass through the Gate). The lower the threshold, the more sound gets through the Gate. As sound passes through the Gate, you will see the small circular LED light flicker.

❋ **ALL OR NOTHING?**

So far, I've only discussed a Gate as a tool for completely removing quiet audio signals from your tracks. From time to time, you may desire more of a semi-gate where some sound still gets through even while the Gate is closed. This is commonly used for toms, so that part of the decay and tone from the toms still sits quietly in the mix even after the initial attack has passed. If the Gate closes completely, it may sound like the toms are overdubbed or pasted into the composition as they pop in and out of the mix. To remedy this, the Gate has a numerical value right below the Threshold slider. The default setting is −40dB, which means the Gate will reduce the incoming sound by 40dB when it's closed. Try raising this value while the Gate is closed, and you'll hear more of the input signal bleed through. Of course, if you're looking for a brick-wall gating effect, reduce the range to −inf.

The Attack, Hold, and Release settings determine how the Gate is applied. For instance, a sharp/short attack will make the Gate open quickly when the threshold is exceeded, sometimes resulting in harsh audible clicks. A longer attack will sound more relaxed as the Gate takes longer to close on sound crossing the volume threshold. Be aware that having a long attack time may cause the Gate to open after the initial attack of the sound has already passed. Use this setting judiciously.

Similarly, the Hold and Release functions affect how long the Gate remains open after the signal has fallen below the threshold. Think of Attack as how quickly the Gate will open, and Release and Hold as relating to how quickly the Gate will close.

Delay Effects

Ableton's delay effects group may just be their most creative effects ever. Each effect features solid tools for both assembling new rhythmic variations and creating innovative textures with repeated long sounds. While many of the delays have similar Feedback, Lowpass/Highpass filtering, and Dry/Wet controls, each delay is also somewhat of a specialist that features one or two particular kinds of controls. As you explore them one by one, don't be afraid to do lots of experimenting and get lost in your own creativity.

Simple Delay

While you may think I am starting simple, Live's Simple Delay (seen in Figure 10.15) is still a formidable stereo, tempo-synchable delay, with a rhythmic beat division chooser.

Looking at the device, you can see two separate beat division choosers—one for the left channel and one for the right. If you are in Sync mode—where the small sync box is illuminated in green—each boxed number represents a multiple of the 1/16-note delay time. For instance, choosing a 4 would mean a four 1/16-note delay, or a full quarter-note hold before you would hear the delayed note sound. An 8 would be two beats, and 16 would be four beats—typically an entire measure. In either of the beat division choosers, you can choose from 1, 2, 3, 4, 5, 6, 8, and 16 times 1/16-note delay times.

Figure 10.15

Live's Simple Delay plug-in.

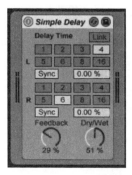

As mentioned, this beat dividing works only if the green Sync button is depressed for that channel (R or L). Sync means that the delay is set to synchronize with the song tempo (beats per minute). If you disengage the Sync, you can manually set up the delay time up to $1/100$ of a second by click-dragging (up or down) on the Time field box. Note: You may also click-drag the Time field box with Sync engaged, but note the percentage (%) indicator. This means that you are slowing or speeding up the delay below or above the current project tempo (that you are synchronized to). In other words, you can add a little slop, or even approximate a triplet, if your delays are sounding too strict.

> ❄ **DELAY RELAY**
>
> By setting extremely short delay times (less than 30 milliseconds with the Sync off), you can create some wild thickening, phasing, and metallic-sounding results. Try setting both delay times to 1, 10, and then 30 milliseconds, with the Dry/Wet set at 30 percent and Feedback set to 70 percent, to hear what I'm talking about. Although these effects may not result in a lingering discernible delay, these flaming, buzzing, and biting sounds can be a creative playground.

The Dry/Wet knob determines how much of the effect versus original sound you hear. *Dry* is the term audio engineers use to refer to the original sound, while *Wet* is the delayed or affected sound. A setting of 12 o'clock (or 50 percent) for Dry/Wet will create a delay signal that is at the same volume as the original. A 100 percent Wet setting means that you will no longer hear the original sound and will hear only the delay effect.

If Dry/Wet controls the volume of the delay, Feedback controls the intensity. By increasing the percentage of Feedback, you raise the effect's signal output to its own input, in sort of a rerouting to continue the delay's effect. The circular signal created by Feedback will radically shape the delay, from flanging disharmonic swells (small percentage of feedback) to a wild echo chamber potentially spiraling out of control (with large amounts of feedback). If your delay does get out of control, reduce the Feedback below 80 percent or less. For example, 100 percent Feedback will deliver an unbelievable noise—or perhaps a cool effect?

 ALL WET

When effects plug-ins are located in one of the Return Tracks, it is generally a good idea to set the effect Wet/Dry setting to 100 percent wet. Since the original source sound is likely still being heard through Live's mixer, there is no need to route this signal again through the effect.

Ping Pong Delay

Like a game of Ping Pong, Ableton's Ping Pong Delay (pictured in Figure 10.16) plays a game of stereo tennis with your sound by serving it up from left to right. In looking at this device, you may notice that many of the controls are similar to the Simple Delay covered earlier. Like Simple Delay, Ping Pong Delay is a stereo delay with built-in tempo synchronizing ability and sports the same delay-time beat-division chooser boxes, as well as the same Dry/Wet and Feedback controls; however, Ping Pong Delay is a little more creative in terms of what frequencies actually get delayed (repeated). You will find a band-pass filter, complete with an adjustable X-Y controller axis to adjust both the cutoff frequency and the width of the frequency band (the Q). You can select between 50Hz and 18kHz and a selectable Q of .5 to 9dB.

Figure 10.16
Live's Ping Pong Delay bounces signal from left to right.

Notice that the same Sync and delay time boxes are also present in Ping Pong Delay. When Sync is activated, Ping Pong Delay will rhythmically synchronize your audio delays—from left to right—according to your beat-division chooser. Once you deactivate the Sync, you can set the delay time manually from 1 to 200 milliseconds.

For those of you who have used Live for a while, you may have missed the update to the Ping Pong Delay—a tiny little button labeled F. This button is the Freeze button. When active, it will cause the Ping Pong Delay to repeat indefinitely without fading away and without adding new audio into the loop. Therefore, you can "freeze" what is repeating by activating this button. When you deactivate it, the Delay will continue to decay and repeat as normal.

❅ **RUB-A-DUB**

Thanks to the band-pass filter in the Ping Pong Delay, it's possible to simulate old tape-style delays. Every time a sound feeds back through the Ping Pong Delay, it passes through the filter and has part of its sonic character changed.

Set the filter frequency to about 200Hz; then set the Q to somewhere around 5. Crank the feedback up all the way and send a single sound, a snare for example, through the effect and listen to it bounce back and forth. As the sound is repeatedly delayed, you'll notice that it gets darker and darker. This is because the filter is removing the high-frequency character of the sound as it repeats. Try automating the band-pass filter as it repeats for more dub-style goodness.

Filter Delay

Next in Live's group of delay effects is the powerful Filter Delay. This effect is actually three delays in one: one stereo delay and two mono delays—one on each stereo channel. Individual delays can be toggled on/off via the L, L+R, and R boxes on the far left, seen in Figure 10.17. Similarly, each high- and low-pass filter can also be switched on/off via the green box labeled On (default setting) in the upper left-hand corner next to the X-Y controllers.

Figure 10.17

Live's Filter Delay.

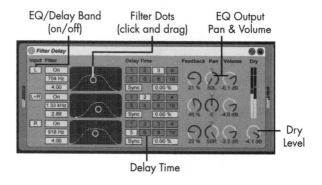

EQ/Delay Band (on/off) Filter Dots (click and drag) EQ Output Pan & Volume

Dry Level

Delay Time

The Filter Delay device is basically a mating of three Ping Pong Delays. Filter Delay's X-Y controllers work in the same way as the Ping Pong Delay described earlier. The Y-axis determines the bandwidth (Q), while the X-axis shifts the frequency. Each delay also features its own beat-division chooser with tempo-synchable delay times.

On the right-hand side of the plug-in, you will see Feedback, Pan, and Volume controls specific to each delay. Each feedback control will reroute the delayed signal back though that delay's input (just like all Live Delays). Interestingly, each delay's panning settings will override their original predisposed location. For instance, if you pan the L delay (top delay) to the right side (with the top panning knob), you will hear it on the right. Volume controls the wet signal or delayed signal for each delay. Finally, a lone Dry control knob is located in the upper right-hand corner. For a 100 percent wet signal, turn the Dry setting to zero.

> ✳ **SUPER SPACEY ECHO**
>
> To achieve truly cosmic delay dispersion, set the filter on the L delay channel to approximately 7kHz, the L+R channel to 1kHz, and the R channel to 140Hz. Set all Qs to 2.0. Pan the L channel hard-left, the R channel hard-right, and the L+R channel in the center. Choose the same delay value for all three channels, but offset the L channel by −1 percent and the R channel by +1 percent. Leave the feedback at zero for all channels at this point.
>
> Now, when a sound is fed into the Filter Delay, the resulting slap-back will happen in stereo. The L channel, which is only high-frequency content, will sound first from the left speaker. The L+R channel will happen next, providing the mid-range component from both speakers. The R channel will follow all of this by giving us the low-frequency content on the right. This makes the delay image in stereo, plus the image moves from left to right as it happens.
>
> Try experimenting with different time offsets to intensify the panning effect. Increasing the feedback on the channels will cause the delay to trail off in three different directions.

Grain Delay

Grain Delay is among Live's more complex, and therefore more creative, effects. The Grain Delay is the same as Live's other delays in that it has many of the same controls—Delay Time, Feedback, Dry/Wet mix, and Beat Quantize settings. While the other delays we've seen so far had a filter at the input stage, the Grain Delay has a granular resynthesizer instead. The basic concept is that Grain Delay dissects audio into tiny grains, staggers the delay timing of these grains, and then opens up a toolbox full of pitch, randomized pitch, and spread (called *spray*) controls for some far-out sound design results. While all the common delay controls exist in this device, the lion's share of the Grain Delay interface (seen in Figure 10.18) boasts a large parameter-assignable X-Y controller.

Figure 10.18
Live's Grain Delay takes audio apart and randomly reassigns the pitch before replaying the sound.

With Grain Delay's X-Y interface, you can quickly control two parameters of your choosing (one for X and one for Y) to allow for some wild interaction. Make sure you choose two different modifiers to achieve the maximum tweak factor. Hint: I like to use Feedback on one axis and then choose either Random P(itch), Pitch, or Frequency on the other.

Frequency

This is the second parameter in the delay interface, but its setting impacts all the others so I'll explain it first. In Ableton's Grain Delay, small grains of sound are quickly dispersed. The frequency setting determines the size and duration of each grain that will be subsequently delayed and can range from 1 to 150Hz. The default setting of 60Hz means that the incoming audio is divided into grains 60 times per second, resulting in 60 grains every second. This means that a low setting creates a large grain, while larger frequency settings create smaller grains. High-frequency settings (lots of small grains) will help keep sounds with rhythmical timing (such as drum loops) intact through the resynthesis process. Low-frequency settings will sound more natural for long sounds like textures and pads. If you are having trouble getting a desirable setting out of the Grain Delay, set the frequency to 150 and work backwards from there.

Spray

The Spray parameter roughs up the average delay (like those in Ping Pong and Simple Delay plug-ins), adding noise and garble to the delayed signal. This setting will allow the Grain Delay to choose a random delay offset amount for each grain. If the frequency setting above is a high value, the effect of spray will be more pronounced, as there are more grains to randomize every second. The delay time for spray can range from 0 to 500 milliseconds. Small values tend to create a fuzzy sounding delay effect, while a larger spray setting completely takes apart the original signal.

Pitch versus Random Pitch

Like the Spray parameter, random pitch tends to throw sound around. The amount of randomness can range from 0 to 161 in terms of intensity (0 being none). The plain old Pitch parameter ranges from 12 to −36 half steps, while allowing for two-decimal point interim values. In other words, fine-tuning a delayed signal's pitch to an actual, discernible tone would be best suited for the Pitch control; trying to eliminate, destroy, or add movement to a pitched signal is the strength of high Random Pitch values. You can use both Pitch and Random Pitch in tandem for some robotic and wild pitch modifications. As with the Spray control above, the higher the frequency setting, the more pronounced the random pitch effect will be as there are more grains to be resynthesized.

Putting Grain Delay to Use

Now that you get some idea of just what kind of mischief the Grain Delay is up to, it's time to get familiar with using Grain Delay's X-Y interface.

Along the X (horizontal) interface, lining the bottom portion of the effect, you will see the boxes for Delay Time, Spray, Frequency, Pitch, Random Pitch, and Feedback. The vertical Y-axis can be set to control Spray, Frequency, Pitch, Random Pitch, Feedback, and Dry/Wet controls. Each parameter's current value will be displayed in the respective boxes on the left hand side of the device, regardless of which axis is set to adjust them.

Any parameters set to correspond to X or Y can be controlled by moving the yellow circle. Vertical moves affect the Y-axis, while horizontal moves alter the X-axis. Exactly which parameters you control are up to you. To set Feedback to be controlled by the Y-axis, simply click on the vertically aligned box labeled *Feedback* just above the Dry/Wet setting. To enable the X-axis to control the delay time (in terms of beat-division), click on the *Delay Time* box while Sync is activated. To control actual delay time, disengage (click on) the Sync button, and you can set the delay from 1 to 128 milliseconds.

 SHIFT MY PITCH UP

One of the more straightforward applications for the Grain Delay is to provide an echo that is at a different pitch. Leave the spray and random pitch values at zero and choose your delay time normally. If the pitch value is at zero, the Grain Delay will be working like the Simple Delay in that it only delays the incoming signal. Change the pitch setting to cause the echo to be transposed to a new note. For example, choosing a pitch setting of 12 will cause the delayed signal to come back an octave higher than the original. This can be pretty fun on vocal parts.

❋ **CHAOS IS GOOD**

Another way to use the Grain Delay is to mangle a sound beyond comprehension. This is best achieved when using an impulse sound—something short like a drum or cymbal hit, the last word of a vocal, or a horn stab. Place a bunch of random values into the Grain Delay; then feed it your impulse sound. The Grain Delay will spit out something that is a rearrangement of all the little grains in the impulse sound. Increasing the frequency setting will cause even more randomness to be added to the mix. Try automating some parameters as the Grain Delay runs its course for more movement.

Chorus

When you listen to a group of people singing (commonly called a *chorus*), each member of the group is singing something slightly different from the others. They may be singing the same words with the same melody, but each person will have slightly different timing and intonation. By having all these slightly different voices singing the same thing, the result is a large and lush vocal sound caused by the slight imperfections in all of the voices.

The Chorus effect attempts to re-create this phenomenon by taking the input signal, delaying it varying amounts, adding a touch of random pitch shift, and then blending the results with the original. In other words, chorus effects assume that two sounds are better than one. It is common to run synthesizers, guitars, vocals, and strings through a chorus. The doubling, or even tripling, effect of a chorus makes solo voices sound more powerful, takes up more space in a mix, and therefore sounds more present.

Live's Chorus (see Figure 10.19) features two parallel delays that can be set for .01 to 20 millisecond delays or linked by activating a teeny tiny equal sign (=).

Figure 10.19

Live's Chorus effect. Note the tiny equal sign (=) between the two delays. This button syncs the two delays.

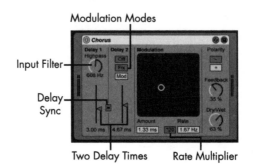

Delay 1

The effect's first delay will always be active when the Chorus is on. To adjust the delay's timing, slide the fader. The adjustable high-pass filter knob allows you to bypass chorusing low frequencies, which can often become muddier and less defined when doubled. The definable range is 20Hz to 15kHz. Delay 1 can be used on its own or in parallel with Delay 2.

Delay 2

Chorus' Delay 2 can add even more thickness and intensity to your sounds. Delay 2 can run in two separate modes, Fix and Mod, and can be bypassed by selecting the top visible button labeled Off. Fix mode will force Delay 2 to the timing specified by its slider. Mod mode will allow the delay time to be modulated by the effect's Mod source.

Modulation

The Chorus' Modulation section is where the effect gets its movement. This section controls a sine wave oscillator (an LFO), which can be used to change the timing of the two delays. Whether you are going for completely unrecognizable new sounds or just looking for a little more stereo spread, you will want to spend some time fiddling (click-dragging) with the Modulation X-Y controller. Horizontal moves change the modulation rate from .03 to 10Hz, while the vertical axis increases the amount of modulation from zero to 6.5 milliseconds. So, if Delay 1 is set to 1ms and you have a modulation amount of 1ms, the LFO will continually change the delay time between 0 and 2ms. The modulation rate changes the speed of the LFO from subtle movements to bubbly vibrations. You also have the option of typing in values by simply clicking on the box, typing a number within the allotted range, and pressing the Enter key.

The LFO will modulate both delays in stereo. This means that the delay times used for the right and left channels will be different, which increases the stereo intensity of the effect. This also means that if both delays are being modulated, there will be four different delay times at any given moment. How's that for fattening up a sound?

If you are looking for radical sonic redesign, the *20 button multiplies the Chorus' LFO rate by 20. While this may not sound great all of the time, the *20 multiplier will push the envelope of the dullest of sounds.

Feedback, Polarity, and Dry/Wet

For increased intensity, the Feedback control will send part of the output signal back through the delays. The more feedback you elect to add, the more robotic and metallic your sounds will become. The positive and negative polarity switch determines whether the signal being fed back to the delays is added to or subtracted from the new input signal. To hear the greatest contrast between the two polarities, you should use short delay times and increase the Chorus Feedback. The results are often frequency and pitch related; a low-frequency sound becomes a high-frequency sound, a pitch may shift by as much as an octave, and so forth. Finally, the Dry/Wet control determines the amount of original versus chorused signal going to output.

Phaser

The Phaser (see Figure 10.20) is another new device in Live 5 that introduces phase shifts in the frequencies of a sound. When this effect is in motion, it has a sort of "wooshing" sound that can give your sounds a smooth sense of warmth and motion. It can also be cranked up to a point where it seems to cut into your sounds, thanks to some unorthodox controls.

Figure 10.20
Star Fleet insists that you never leave the house without a trusty Phaser at your side.

Poles

The Phaser uses a series of filters to create the phase shifts you hear in the sound. The Poles control sets the number of filters, or notches, that are used in the Phaser. If you use a low number of Poles, the Phaser effect will not be as pronounced as when you use a larger number of Poles.

Color and Mode

The button below the Poles knob sets the mode for the Phaser. The button toggles between Earth and Space. The Live Manual is pretty ambiguous about what differentiates these modes, except to say that these adjust the spacing of the notch filters. The Color control will further change the relationships of the filters when Earth mode is active.

Dry/Wet
You should know what this knob does by now—it changes the mix between the original dry signal and the phased signal. Blending the two together can soften the effect of the Phaser.

Frequency and Feedback
The large X-Y area in the middle of the Phaser is for adjusting the center frequency and the feedback amount. Move the dot on the screen left and right to adjust frequency (you can also use the number box at the lower-left corner). Vertical movement will adjust the feedback (whose number box is in the lower-right corner). You normally won't find a feedback control on a typical Phaser, but it's a control that Ableton added to their Phaser to help emphasize the phase effect.

Envelope
This section is identical to the Envelope Follower you'll find in the Auto Filter device. It works by using the volume of the incoming signal as a means to modulate the frequency of the Phaser. The speed at which the Envelope Follower responds to changes in input volume is governed by the Attack and Release knobs. Use the top knob to increase the Envelope's influence on the Phaser frequency.

LFO
Again, this section is a duplicate of the LFO section found in the Auto Filter. You'll use the Speed controls to set the LFO rate either in relation to the current tempo or freely in Hertz. The relation of the left and right LFOs are set with the Phase/Spin controls. Finally, the LFO's overall influence on the Phaser frequency is set with the Amount knob.

Open the Phaser example in the Chapter 10 folder and launch the first scene. You'll hear two loops playing simultaneously: a drum loop and a hi-hat from Operator. Both of the sounds are being run through Phaser devices in their Track Views. The hi-hat track is using the LFO to slowly modulate the phase over two bars. The Drum Loop track has its Phaser controlled by a Clip Envelope. Listen to each track individually and toggle the Phaser devices on and off to compare with the original sounds. Also, try adjusting the Feedback and Poles of each Phaser—the results can be fairly pronounced as these parameters are increased.

Flanger
The Flanger bears an extremely close resemblance to the Phaser, both in design and use. A flanger works by taking a sound, delaying it by a slight amount, and blending it back with the original sound. This introduces constructive and destructive interference between various frequencies in the sound, producing a characteristic comb filter effect. The Flanger has a much more metallic edge compared to the Phaser. Its sound can become quite abrasive when used with high-feedback settings, as you'll see in a moment.

Figure 10.21
Flanging was first performed by playing two identical recordings on tape machines, then touching the flanges of one of the tape reels to subtly shift the timing of the two recordings. Live's Flanger sure makes the same effect easier and cheaper to achieve.

High-Pass Filter

As mentioned above, the Flanger will be making a copy of the input signal and mixing it back in with the original after being briefly delayed. This will result in flanging throughout the entire frequency spectrum of the sound. Often, this can product inharmonic (unpitched) results, which can make melodic parts "muddy." To alleviate this effect, you can pass the input signal through a high-pass filter. When the delayed signal is mixed back in with the original, the Flange effect will only happen on the higher frequencies, leaving the low frequencies intact.

Dry/Wet

You know this one already.

Delay and Feedback

This looks quite similar to the X-Y control in the Phaser, doesn't it? Functionally, it's the same—horizontal movements adjust the Delay Time, while vertical movements increase the Feedback. Because the Flanger uses a delay, there will be a "pitch" to the effect, which is related to the Delay Time parameter. As the Delay Time is shortened, the pitch will seem to rise. When you crank up the Feedback, the pitch will become even more pronounced.

Envelope and LFO

These two sections are identical to the Phaser and Auto Filter above except that they modulate the Delay Time of the Flanger.

To hear the Flanger in action, open the Flanger example in the Chapter 10 folder. This is the same Set as the Phaser example above, except that the Phasers have been replaced by Flangers. I think you'll agree that this sound is a little more metallic and aggressive. To push things to the max, switch the Feedback polarity of the Flangers by clicking the small + button next to the Feedback number box at the bottom-right corner of the X-Y control.

Reverb

Reverberation occurs when sound bounces off a surface, usually many surfaces, several times. In the process of reflecting, the original sound dissipates, becoming diffuse and muddy and eventually disappearing altogether. Depending upon the shape and reflective qualities of the room, various frequencies will be more pronounced than others in the reverberated sound or *tail*.

While Ableton's Reverb device, added in version 1.5, may not be a full-fledged delay, it is certainly from the same echo-related family. The number of controls may seem daunting, but as I step carefully through the signal path, you will see that each knob and X-Y controller is there only for your benefit. Before I get carried away, take a quick look at Figure 10.22.

Figure 10.22

Live's feature-laden Reverb plug-in.

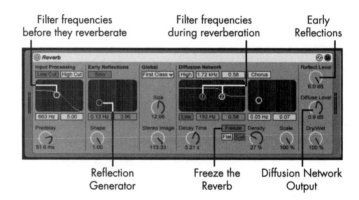

Input Processing

The first link in Reverb's signal chain is the Input Processing section. Here you have on/off selectable Low and High Cut filtering, as well as a Predelay control. The Low Cut and High Cut X-Y interface allows you to trim your input's frequencies before they are reverberated. Similar to Live's other delays, the horizontal X-axis shifts the frequency of the cut (50Hz to 18kHz), while the vertical Y-axis changes the bandwidth (.50 to 9.0). You can also turn each filter off by deselecting its green illuminated box. I recommend spending some time playing with this filter each time you use this effect. Think of these filters as altering the acoustic characteristics of a room. For instance, a concrete room may not reproduce low frequencies as well as an acoustically engineered studio room. Each room will favor completely different frequencies.

Also, check out the Predelay control for adding milliseconds of time before you hear the first *early reflections*, or delayed sound, of the forthcoming reverberation. While the Predelay can range from .50 to 250 milliseconds, to simulate a normal sounding room, it is best below 25 milliseconds. For large cannons, go long, baby.

Early Reflections

Early reflections are the first reverberations heard after the initial sound bounces off the walls, floor, or ceiling of the room—yet they arrive ahead of the full reflection, or tail. At times, they sound like slapback delays, or mushy portions of the whole reverberated (diffused) sound. The Reverb houses two early reflection controls: Shape and Spin. Spin's X-Y interface controls, depth (Y-axis) and frequency (X-axis), apply a subtle modulation to early reflections. Results may range from shimmering highs to whirligig panning flourishes. For quicker decay of early reflections, try increasing the Shape control gradually towards 1.00. Lower values will blend more smoothly with the normal reverb diffusion.

❆ **YOU WANT IT WHERE?**

Because Reverb is Ableton Live's most robust (processor-intensive) effect, I recommend that you use it on a Return Track instead of inserting it onto individual tracks. This way you can use the same reverb (instance) for multiple tracks. The added bonus with this strategy is that by using the same reverb, it will sound as if all of the instruments were in fact played in the same room. Of course, this may not be the best idea for every song, so use this technique at your discretion.

Global Settings

In Reverb's Global Settings section, you can select the quality level of the Reverb: Economy (default), Comfort, or First Class. The three settings will demand small, moderate, and large processor power, respectively. You may also determine the apparent volume of the room via the Size (of the imaginary room) control, which ranges from .22 (small/quiet) to 500 (large/loud). A Stereo Image control allows you to select from 0 to 120 degrees of stereo spread in the reverberation. Higher values will be more spread out, while lower ones approach a mono sound.

Diffusion Network

The Diffusion Network is by far the most complex-looking area of the Reverb effect. These controls help put the final touches on the actual reverberation that follows closely behind the early reflections. From here, you will be able to decorate and control the finer points of the reverberated sound. To begin with, high and low shelving filters can further define your imaginary room's sound. By shaving off the highs, for instance, your room may sound more like a concert hall or large auditorium, while brightening up the diffusion (raising the high shelf) will approximate a "bathroom" reverb. Similar to X-Y interface controlled filters, each filter's X-axis determines frequency, while Y-axis controls bandwidth. Turning these filters off will conserve some system resources.

Beneath the high and low shelving controls, you will find the Reverb's Decay Time settings, which range from an extremely short 200 milliseconds to a cavernous 60-second–long tail. Long reverbs are mesmerizing but can make audio sound muddy and jumbled if used profusely. Use with care.

To test the coloring and sonic quality of your reverb, you can use the Freeze control. Any time you press Freeze, Reverb will indefinitely hold and reproduce the diffusion tail. This frozen Reverb can be a handy diagnostic tool for shaping your overall sound or a creative trick to make new sounds from a piece of reverb. Typically, I will freeze the reverb when I am first setting it up and then stop all other loops and sounds. After analyzing the reverberated sound for a moment, I often tweak parameters to weed out extreme or obnoxious low or high frequencies, or change the Reverb's modulation.

When Flat is activated, the low- and high-pass shelving filters will be ignored. In other words, your frozen Reverb tail will contain all frequencies. An active Cut command prevents further audio from being frozen, even if it is passing through the Reverb. For instance, you may want to analyze the tonality of the Reverb tail. To do this, you play your audio through the Reverb, then press Freeze, and then press Cut (to cut off future audio from snowballing into a wall of useless noise). Even if you stop playback, the frozen Reverb sample will continue to play. While frozen, you can make adjustments to the diffusion network settings and more acutely decipher their impact. Try starting and stopping audio a few times to analyze the differences between your project's audio and the reverberating audio. Is the Reverb tail adding unwanted mud?

The second X-Y interface in the Diffusion Network, labeled *Chorus*, can add subtle motion or wobbly effect to the overall reverb tail diffusion. When not in use, deactivate the Chorus button to save system resources and turn the Reverb's Chorus effect off.

The final section in Diffusion Network controls the density (thickness) and scale (coarseness) of the diffusion's echo. The Density control ranges from .1 percent (a lighter sounding reverb), to a 96 percent rich and chewy reverb, while Scale can run from 5 to 100 percent, gradually adding a darker and murkier quality to the diffusion. A high Density setting will diminish the amount of audible change made by Scale controls.

Output

The Output section is the final link in the Reverb signal chain. At this stage, just three knobs, Dry/Wet, Reflect Level, and Diffuse Level, put the finishing touches on your Reverb Preset masterpiece. Dry/Wet controls the ratio of original unaffected sound to affected reverberated sound that you hear coming from the effect's output. When using Reverb in one of Live's Return Tracks, I recommend using a 100 percent wet setting, as opposed to using Reverb on a regular track, where settings between 10 and 45 percent sound more natural.

The Reflect Level control knob adjusts the amplitude (level) of the early reflections specified in the Early Reflections box from −30 to +6 dB. The louder you make the early reflections, the more you will hear an echo of the true sound (which will sound even more like a slapback delay as opposed to a reverb).

In similar fashion, the Diffuse Level controls the amount of diffusion network level in the final Reverb output. A low diffusion level will diminish the tail of the Reverb, while a high amplitude of diffusion network will increase the presence of reverb in your mix.

Resonators

Here's a fun device for techno-heads and sound designers, the Resonators (see Figure 10.23). When sound is fed through the Resonators, it will cause the virtual resonators to start "vibrating" or creating a tone at their set pitches and volumes. This effect is best understood when heard, so open up the Resonators example Set and try it out yourself.

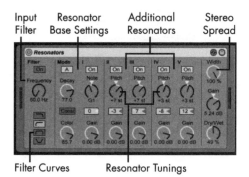

Input Filter   Resonator Base Settings   Additional Resonators   Stereo Spread

Filter Curves   Resonator Tunings

Figure 10.23
The Resonators device will start generating pitches based on an input signal.

To begin, crank the Dry/Wet mix knob fully clockwise to isolate the sound of the Resonators. Turn off the Input Filter so a full-range sound is feeding the device. Adjust the settings for Resonator I first, since the other four Resonators base their tones and pitches from number 1. You'll see that you have control of the decay of the Resonators (best heard on sparse percussion tracks), as well as the color and pitch. Once the first resonator is set, engage the other Resonators and use the Pitch knobs to set their frequencies relative to the first. This makes it simple to create chords using multiple Resonators and then transpose them all using the first Resonator's Pitch knob.

Resonators II & III and IV & V can be panned apart from each other by increasing the Width knob. This can help create a lush tonal pad that blends well with a mix. You can also use the input filter to remove frequencies that may be overpowering or saturating the resonator banks. The Gain knobs are used to achieve a blend between the various Resonators, allowing you to emphasize certain pitches over others.

❈ **TUNED REVERB**

Try adding a Resonator right after a Reverb effect on your vocalist's Return Track. Build a chord with the dials on the effect and set it fully wet. Now the Reverb effect will cause the Resonators to ring in tune with the song, adding an ethereal sound to the voice.

Distortions

This brings me to the third group of Ableton's devices: the Distortion effects. While each of these effects can quickly and drastically alter your audio content, taking time to learn the ins and outs of these babies can take your mix to a whole new level.

Saturator

I'll start with the new Saturator device (see Figure 10.24) as this is the most straightforward type of distortion. This is a distortion based on overdriving the input signal, which is a common effect to apply to guitars, drums, and even vocals.

Figure 10.24

Just call the Saturator effect "Instant Fatness!"

Shape

The top of the Saturator interface is dominated by the Shape select buttons and display. These buttons determine the characteristic of the Saturator, and you can gain insight into how it's modifying your signal by looking at the resulting curve in the display.

The Clip shape maintains a linear relationship between input and output volumes, but this ratio is ramped slightly upward such that the signal will reach maximum level a little sooner than normal. This type of distortion is fairly transparent and usually adds crunch only to the heavy transients in a sound (those sounds that exceed the output headroom).

The Soft shape is a step up from the Clip shape. You can see in the display that this shape is a little more curved and that the middle section of the curve is sloping upward even steeper than the Clip shape. The result is that mid-level sounds will now be amplified more than before. The distortion will become a little more pronounced with this setting and will also start to take on a touch of lo-fi grunge now that the input and output levels are no longer in linear relation to one another.

Moving down from the Soft button is the Medium button. The shape display says it all: This is a steeper version of the Soft shape. The resulting sound is now more distorted because quieter signals are now being amplified into the distortion range.

The Hard button is the gnarliest distortion of all. You can see that this shape reaches maximum amplitude very quickly. As a result, at least half of the signal will be in the distortion range.

The Sine shape has a unique sound to it that I would describe as "squidgy." Transients sound sort of sci-fi with this distortion, reminiscent of a ring modulator. Ableton recommends this setting for special effects, and so do I.

Drive

On a dynamic distortion unit such as this, the Drive knob is where you'll demolish your sound. The higher the Drive amount, the more the input signal is amplified. This forces more of the signal into the distortion range, therefore slaughtering the sound at high levels. Of course, if you're getting too much distortion, you can reduce the Drive into negative amounts, so that only a slight portion of the signal is distorted.

Output

As you increase the Drive amount, you will consequently be increasing the volume of the distortion, quite often to a point where it overpowers the other instruments in your mix. Pull the Output down a bit to bring the sound back into check where it should be.

Color

These controls are similar to the tone controls on a guitar amp. The Base knob will increase or decrease the amount of bass being distorted by the effect. The last three knobs control a high-frequency EQ whose Frequency, Width, and Depth (gain) can be set specifically by you.

Open the Saturator example to hear how the Saturator demolishes both a drum loop and a bass sound. Try the other shapes while the loop is running to become familiar with their sounds, and don't forget to check out the sounds with the Saturators turned off.

Erosion

Similar to the concepts of subtractive-synthesis and frequency filtering, deconstructing a sound can also be a creative endeavor. Live's Erosion is Ableton's most unique effect in this regard. Erosion gives you three possible methods for sonic degradation. You can choose from Noise, Wide Noise, and Sine by selecting one of the three buttons beneath the X-Y interface as pictured in Figure 10.25.

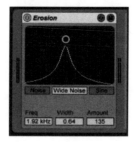

Figure 10.25
Live's Erosion device. Erosion's screen is primarily taken up by its unusual X-Y field.

Depending upon which mode you currently have active, Erosion will use one of three different sounds (one of two filtered noises or a sine wave) to modulate the sound. Noise, Wide Noise, and Sine all have different characteristics, so you will want to experiment switching between the three.

To control the degree of Erosion's effect on a sound, move the Y-axis (vertically) to change the amount or level of the modulation signal. Horizontal moves along the X-axis allow you to control the frequency that you are affecting. To change the Width with the X-Y interface, hold Alt (option) and click on the yellow dot, and move the mouse forward and backward. You can also drag any control vertically or manually type in a value in Freq, Width, and Amount.

❄ **RING TONE**

Live's Erosion effect is a ring modulator when in Sine mode. Ring modulation, a very popular decimation technique, is achieved by multiplying the incoming signal with another one, an internally generated sine wave in this case. This makes the incoming signal adapt some of the pitch characteristic of the sine wave. The noise modes multiply the incoming signal with white noise signals, which you can tune in the X-Y area of the plug-in. This causes the incoming signal to adapt some of the noises' characteristics.

Redux

While you're digging into new tools for sonic decimation, you will definitely want to check out Live's Redux device. Redux (see Figure 10.26) is a bit-depth and sample-rate reducer that can make even the prettiest of guitars, or anything else for that matter, saw your head off. Of course, results need not be this drastic if you are capable of restraint. In fact, reducing the fidelity of a sample is like a tip of the hat to old Roland, Emu, and Akai 8- and 12-bit samplers—or even old 2- and 4-bit computer-based samples (Commodore 64, anyone?).

Figure 10.26
Live's Redux is a talented sample-rate and bit-depth reducer.

The controls for Redux are split into two tidy sections, with a Bit Reduction knob and On/Off switch on top, and a Downsample knob and Hard/Soft switch on the bottom. The default position for Bit Reduction is 16-bit (off). As you reduce the bits, you will hear an increasing amount of noisy grit infect the sample. The numerical setting will indicate the bit-depth (i.e., 8=8 bit, 4=4 bit). For extremists, try trimming it down to 1-bit—ouch, that hurts!

When it comes to sample rate reduction, the settings are a little more inexact. In Hard mode, Downsampling will stick with whole integers such as 1, 2, 3, up to 200 for dividing the sample rate, while in Soft mode, you can adjust from 1 to 20 to the nearest hundredth of a point (1.00 or 19.99). A setting of 1 means you are not hearing any sample rate reduction—oddly, the higher the number, the lower the resulting sample rate.

For a quick course, spend a minute perusing the Ableton factory presets, such as Old Sampler and Mirage. This will give you a basic template to work from. Also, try toggling back and forth from Hard to Soft Downsampling with different settings (while you are in playback mode) for a cool effect.

> ❋ **REDUXION CRECENDO**
>
> You can create an ear-ripping build-up by piping your tracks through a Redux and lowering the bit depth at the build. The Redux chops off the tops of your audio and then normalizes it, which makes it louder and more distorted at the same time.

Vinyl Distortion

The imperfections of vinyl have actually become quite lovable these days. Whether you are missing the dust pops and crackles of an old record or the warped vinyl sound of a record left out in the sun, vinyl has a certain retro charm. Though CDs and digital recordings are great, they are hopelessly clean and free of these impurities (which is also their strength). Of course, Ableton thought about this, too, and as a result: Vinyl Distortion (Figure 10.27).

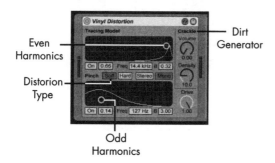

Figure 10.27

Live's Vinyl Distortion effect hopes to make you miss your turntable just a little bit less.

Vinyl Distortion is divided into three separate sections: Tracing Model, Crackle, and Pinch effect. While the controls for Tracing Model and Pinch effect look identical, each section generates a totally different sound. Also note the Soft/Hard and Stereo/Mono switches are also a part of the Pinch effect. If Pinch effect is off, these controls will remain grayed out (inactive).

Tracing Model adds a subtle amount of harmonic distortion to your audio as a means of simulating wear and tear on vinyl or an old stylus. To adjust the intensity of the distortion, increase the drive by moving the yellow circle along the Y-axis (range from 0.00 to 1.00). The frequency of the harmonic can be altered via the X-axis (range of 50Hz to 18kHz) and can also be input manually by typing in the box. To adjust the size of the bandwidth you are affecting, hold down ALT (Option) and click-drag forward or backward on the yellow circle.

The Pinch Effect section of Vinyl Distortion is a more drastic and wild-sounding distortion at the input level. The resulting richer stereo image is from Pinch effect's 180 degrees out-of-phase harmonic distortions. Like the Tracing Model, you can increase the intensity of the distortion through the Y-axis. The X-axis will configure the Frequency range. You will want to pay special attention to the Soft/Hard boxes to the right of the X-Y interface on the Pinch effect. Soft mode is engineered to sound like an actual dub plate (acetate), while Hard mode will sound more like a standard vinyl record. Also, the Stereo/Mono switch correlates with Pinch effect only.

No vinyl simulator would be complete without a vinyl pop and crackle simulator. Crackle provides two simple controls: Volume and Density. Volume is obviously the level of the hiss and crackle in the mix. Density adds a thicker amount of noise to the output. Note that you will hear the crackle and hiss whether Live is in playback mode or not, because effects are always running. If you forget this, you might just take a screwdriver to your audio interface trying to figure out where all the noise is coming from!

Miscellaneous Tools

This last section of devices covers two of Live's more esoteric plug-ins, the Beat Repeat and Utility. These devices aren't necessarily effects as they don't really change the sound that passes through them. The Beat Repeat will simply repeat certain segments of the sound as it passes through, while the Utility device will offer us some basic gain and phase adjustments.

Beat Repeat

Techno heads, rejoice! Ableton brings you the Beat Repeat device (see Figure 10.28). Now the stereotypical beat-stutter can be performed by you with just a few simple gestures—you can even program repeats to happen automatically.

Repeat

Open up the Beat Repeat example Set and launch the first scene, titled Manual. This will start a drum loop running. The beat will play without being repeated. Go ahead and click the Repeat

Figure 10.28
Th-Th-Th-This dev-v-v-v-ice is
sw-ee-ee-ee-ee-t!

button in the Beat Repeat interface. Woo-hoo! There it goes repeating away. Click the Repeat button again to turn it off, and the regular beat will resume. Obviously, the Repeat button is named well.

Grid and Variation

The size, or length, of the repeated segment is set with the Grid knob. Turn on Repeat and try tweaking this knob. You'll hear the Repeat size change in real-time—an awesome effect for remixing. The No Trpl button will remove the triplet values when scrolling through the Grid sizes—handy if you want to keep all the rhythmic repeats in sync.

The Variation knob just to the right of the Grid knob is used to introduce randomness to the Grid size. When set to 0%, the Grid will always be what you've set with the Grid knob. As this value is increased, Live will automatically change the Grid based on the mode selected in the pop-up menu below the knob. When set to Trigger, a new Grid size is selected any time the Repeat function is started. It will hold the Grid size until the Repeat is stopped or retriggered. The 1/4, 1/8, and 1/16 settings will change the Grid setting at the specified time interval. The Auto setting will change the Grid size after every repeat. This can get really hairy as you can have a single repeat of 1/64 followed by a repeat of 1/6, followed by 1/16, followed by 1/2 (full-size), etc. The results are truly unpredictable!

Mix, Insert, and Gate

These three buttons control the output mode of the Beat Repeat. So far, you've been using the Insert mode. When using this mode, the original drum beat is silent while Repeat is on. Click on the Mix button and try using the Repeat button. In this mode, you'll hear the original drum beat while the Repeat is occurring—the two are being mixed together. The final mode, Gate, will only allow sound to pass when Repeat is on. When Repeat is off, the output of the device will be silent. This mode is useful when you've placed the Beat Repeat on a Return Track, especially if you've chained additional effects after the Beat Repeat.

Volume and Decay

The Volume knob sets the volume of the repeated sounds. Note that the first repeat is always at the original volume. I find that I like to decrease the volume a little bit so that the music comes back in heavier after the repeat. It's almost necessary to turn this down when you're using small Grid sizes, as the repeats become so fast that they start to make a tone of their own.

The Decay knob will cause the volume of each consecutive repeat to be quieter than the first. This means that your repeats will slowly (or quickly) fade away to silence each time Repeat is triggered.

Pitch
The pitch controls can be used to introduce pitch shifts into your repeats. The Pitch knob will simply transpose the repeated sound down by the specified number of semitones. The Pitch Decay knob works similarly to the Volume Decay knob above, except that it makes the pitch drop further and further with each consecutive repeat. When used, it's possible to make the repeated sound drop so low in pitch that it becomes inaudible. This is a neat tool to use in conjunction with the volume decay because you can make your repeats drop in pitch and fade away at the same time.

Filter
This filter functions in the same way as the filter in the Ping Pong Delay, except that the repeated sounds are not fed back through this filter. When Repeat is on, you can engage the filter and choose a specific frequency range for the repeats. This can give your repeats a lo-fi sound in comparison to the normal part. You can even change the filter frequency and width while Repeat is running for even more animation.

Chance and Interval
So far, I've been showing you how to use Beat Repeat in a completely hands-on fashion, which is how you'll use Beat Repeat in a live situation. However, as I alluded to earlier, you can set Beat Repeat to perform repeats automatically. This is the purpose of the Chance and Interval knobs.

In your experiments so far, the Chance knob has been set to 0%. This means there is no chance that the Beat Repeat will automatically trigger itself. If you turn this value up to 100%, Beat Repeat will automatically trigger at the rate specified with the Interval knob. If the Interval is set to 1 Bar, Beat Repeat will activate itself every bar. If you set the Chance to 50%, there will only be a 1 in 2 chance that the Beat Repeat will trigger.

Offset and Gate
These last two knobs determine when an automatic repeat will start and how long it will last. When Offset is set to 0, the repeat will start the instant it is called by the Interval and Chance knobs. If you turn this knob clockwise, you'll see it count up in 1/16 notes—with the knob turned up halfway, the value will be 8/16. This means that the beat repeat won't start until the third beat of the bar. You'll also see the Repeat markers move in the display as a visual aid.

The Gate knob sets how long the repeats will last once triggered. If set to 4/16, the repeat will last for a 1/4 note. If set to 8/16, the repeats will last for half a bar. Therefore, using Offset and Grid, you can specify any location in the audio to repeat, as well as how long to do it.

To hear all these properties at work, launch the Automatic scene. This will play the same drum beat, but through a Beat Repeat on another channel.

Utility

The Utility device (see Figure 10.29) gets a section all its own. This device isn't so much an effect that will make your audio sound weird. Instead, it will provide subtle changes to the audio for adding the right touch to a mix.

Figure 10.29
The simple Utility interface provides easy access to simple tools.

The first two options may seem redundant: Mute and Gain. You already have a Track Activator and Volume slider on each track, right? Well, the Ableton folks aren't stupid, While you won't use it often, you may find it handy to have this type of control sitting on the Master Track. Have you seen a Mute button on there lately? I didn't think so. In fact, this is a great device to place on the Master Track for numerous reasons. When doing a mix, especially for TV, it is a good idea to check for mono compatibility. When the sound of the left channel of your mix is blended with the right channel, certain frequencies may start to interfere with one another. In some cases, guitars may not sound as full when heard in mono. Sometimes, the vocals will sound too loud. In the most extreme cases, some of the parts may completely disappear from the mix! To hear what your track sounds like in mono, take the Width knob down to 0 percent.

If you do run into phase-cancellation that completely removes a part from the song when in mono, try placing Utility on that track and engage one of the Phase buttons (labeled Phz-L and Phz-R). This will invert the phase of one side of the track, bringing it back into phase with the other side. If you're not worried about mono compatibility, you'll find that kicking one side of a track out of phase from the other will make the resulting audio sound amazingly wide, almost as if the sound was coming from behind your head. This can really make a part jump out of a mix or at least sound separated from the other parts. If you're looking to widen your sound only a little, you can turn the Width control clockwise past 100 percent to a level that suits your taste.

The L and R buttons are for using only one side of the input channel as the output for both sides. For example, if you press the L button, the sound entering on the left side of the channel will be mirrored on both left and right at the output. This is not the same as reducing the Width control to 0 percent. When Width is reduced, both the left and right signals are blended together, resulting in a summed mono sound. When using the L and R buttons, only one side is used, while the other is turned off.

✳ WHO'S USING LIVE?

Shawn Pelton

Chances are, even if you don't know his name, you've already been rocked by the rhythms of super session drummer Shawn Pelton. If you've seen Saturday Night Live within the last 13 years, you've heard him play—he's been with the band longer than any other member. On top of this steady gig, you'll also find him backing up artists such as Bob Dylan, Rod Stewart, Bruce Springsteen, Sheryl Crow, Edie Brickell, The Brecker Brothers, Buddy Guy, Joan Osborne, Hall & Oates, Celine Dion, Billy Joel, Luciano Pavarotti, Spice Girls (another guilty pleasure—sorry...), Loudon Wainwright, Peter Frampton, Robert Palmer, Bruce Hornsby, Adam Sandler, and Vanessa Williams.

I was fortunate enough to speak with Shawn while prepping this book, and he gave me the inside scoop on what he's doing with his current project, House of Diablo (www.houseofdiablo.com), which is an eclectic three-piece composed of Brian Mitchell on vocals, keyboards, and electronic voodoo, Edward Potokar playing homemade analog tone generators and jewel-encrusted gizmotrons, and Shawn on his drums and "electrified swamp water."

"House of Diablo has been described as deep-fried swamp music mixed with abstract noise and groove electronics," says Shawn. "Imagine if Booker T. and the MGs crashed into Dr. John's backyard in 1968 with King Tubby at the grill, then they woke up in the year 2013 with DJ Shadow's cousin in the band and subtonic transmissions from Saturn."

To achieve the ultra-dubby sound for the group, Shawn uses Live to create layered beats, which he can feed through sets of delays all controlled from three footpedals and an Evolution UC-33e fader controller. An image of his Live Set is shown below.

"The first seven faders on the UC-33 correspond to the first seven tracks in Live, which all contain various rhythmic elements and loops. The three knobs above each fader are used to control the effect sends on each track, which are tied to three delays with different rhythmic settings—1/16 note, 1/8-note triplet, and dotted-1/8 note. The three knobs above the eighth fader control the feedbacks of the three delays, while the fader itself is assigned to Live's crossfader.

"I also have three pedals set up near my hi-hat, which are assigned to Live's Start, Stop, and Tap Tempo. This allows me to start and stop the backing rhythms and also change their tempo at will. The resulting tempo is then transmitted via MIDI to any of the other cats in the band who need it."

11 } Live's MIDI Effects

MIDI Effects, like Audio Effects, allow you to alter data as it's passed from a clip to the track output. MIDI Effects can be used by themselves on a MIDI Track whose output is some external MIDI sound device, or they can be used before a virtual instrument in the Track View. It's important to understand the place of the MIDI Effect in the chain of events that occurs on a track. MIDI data in a clip is played through the MIDI Effect, which alters it in some way. The altered MIDI data is then sent to the MIDI destination, which is either an external MIDI device or a virtual one loaded in Live, which then reacts accordingly. It is important to understand that MIDI Effects do not change the sound that is produced by an instrument the way Audio Effects do. MIDI Effects change the notes playing those instruments, resulting in an entirely new part. This is why, for example, the Pitch MIDI Effect won't change the pitch of the drums coming from Impulse. If this doesn't make sense right off the bat, don't worry—if you're like me, we learn by doing. So pop open the Chapter 11 folder in the Library and check out the Live Sets in there as I reveal the wiring behind the six MIDI Effects in Live.

Arpeggiator

Since I feel like doing the headings of this chapter in alphabetical order, I get to start with the coolest, gnarliest, sickest, most highly anticipated MIDI device of them all, the brand new Arpeggiator. An arpeggiator is a device that came into existence in the early days of monophonic synthesizers. *Monophonic* means "only able to play one note at a time." When synthesizer technology was in its infancy, that's all you could hope to get out of a synth—just one note. Playing one note at a time isn't much of a problem if you're playing a lead or melody part. The trouble arises when you try to play a chord (two or more notes at once), which a monophonic synth is incapable of. The solution devised was an arpeggiator that would quickly play all the notes you held on the keyboard in series or other repetitive patterns. The result is, even though the notes don't play simultaneously, you can "hear" the chord being played because the notes are played in such quick succession. You *really* have to play this one to understand it, so go ahead and open the Arpeggiator Set from the Chapter 11 examples provided with this book.

After the Set loads, press a key on your MIDI keyboard, or just use the computer keyboard to play a note. What is this? You hold down a note and a steady stream of 1/8 notes comes out. Now try holding down two notes. Instead of hearing both notes playing 1/8 notes, Live will play each of the notes alternately. Now try holding three notes. Live will now play each of the three notes in series and repeat. That's the Arpeggiator at work (see Figure 11.1), intercepting your played notes and turning them into a sequence of notes before being handed over to the Simpler loaded in the track.

Figure 11.1
The Arpeggiator on this track is creating instant sequences from the MIDI notes it receives.

There are many ways to tweak the performance of the Arpeggiator. You can change the note order employed by the Arpeggiator, the speed at which the notes are played, the length of each note, and quantization in relation to the grid of the current Set.

Style

The Style dropdown menu is used to select the note-order pattern employed by the Arpeggiator. The default setting is Up, which means that the Arpeggiator plays each of the held notes in sequence, starting from the lowest note and working up to the highest before repeating. The Down option is the exact opposite—the Arpeggiator starts with the highest note and works down before repeating. The UpDown and DownUp patterns are simply hybrid patterns made from the individual Up and Down patterns. The UpDown style will make the Arpeggiator play up the note sequence and then back down again before repeating. The DownUp style does the opposite. The Up & Down and Down & Up modes are the same as the UpDown and DownUp modes, except that the top and bottom notes of the scale are repeated as the Arpeggiator changes direction.

The Converge style works by playing the lowest note followed by the highest note. It will then play the second lowest note followed by the second highest. The pattern will continue by playing the third lowest note followed by the third highest note, etc., until all the notes in the scale are exhausted. The pattern will then repeat. The Diverge style is the opposite of Converge, and Con & Diverge are the two patterns placed end-to-end.

The Pinky and Thumb styles are interesting in that they alternate the note order with the highest and lowest note played, respectively. For example, when using the PinkyUp mode, the Arpeggiator will play the lowest note followed by the highest note (the "pinky note"). It will then play the second lowest note followed by the highest note again. The Arpeggiator will continue to work up the scale of held notes, alternating each with the high pinky note until the pattern repeats. The ThumbUp mode works in the same way, except that the lowest held note (the "thumb note") gets inserted between each step of the scale.

The Play Order style is nice in that the Arpeggiator works through the scale of held notes in the exact order as you played them. For example, if you play the notes C, E, G, and A, the resulting pattern will be C E G A C E G A C E G A.... If you play the notes in a different order, like E, C, G, then A, the pattern will be E C G A E C G A E C G A....

The Chord Trigger style breaks away from the traditional arpeggiator methodology in that this style results in more than one note being played at a time. In fact, it repeatedly triggers every one of the notes you held down. The result is that you get a stuttered chord.

The final style options are random options that will yield unpredictable patterns from your held notes. The Random mode simply chooses a note at random from your held notes for each step it plays. In this mode, it's possible for Live to choose the same note repeatedly—it's truly random. The Random Other pattern is a little more controlled. It will create a random pattern from your held notes, play it, and then create another random pattern and play it. The result is that you have fewer repeated notes as Live must play all the notes at least once before it creates a new pattern. The Random Once pattern is like Random Other, except only one random pattern is built. After the Arpeggiator plays the random pattern once, it will play it again identically. The result is a new random pattern every time you play new notes, but a pattern that repeats while you hold the notes. Pretty cool, huh?

Groove

The Groove menu is identical in function to the Groove setting found in the Clip View. Choosing a groove here will cause the Arpeggiator to offset its note as the Groove Amount is increased. This will allow you to create swinging arpeggiations on the fly!

Hold

The Hold button will automatically latch, or sustain, the notes you play so that you don't have to continually hold notes while a pattern plays. Switch this on and try playing a chord. When you release the notes on your keyboard, the Arpeggiator will continue to play. Now, play another chord. The Arpeggiator will stop the old pattern and will start the new one when it receives your new notes.

Offset

This dial is used to offset the start point of the Arpeggiator pattern by the specified number of steps. For example, if the style is set to Up and you play a C-Major triad, the resulting pattern from the Arpeggiator will be C E G C E G.... If you then set Offset to 1, the pattern will be E G C E G C.... The start point of the pattern has been shifted to the right by one step; therefore, the pattern begins on the second note of the chord (E) as it plays.

Rate and Sync

These next two parameters are related to one another. The Rate knob is used to set the speed at which the Arpeggiator plays each step of its pattern. By default, 1/8 note is selected. When the neighboring Sync button is on, the Rate will be constrained to note values. If you turn Sync off, the Rate will now be running free of the current project tempo and will play at the exact rate specified here in Hertz. You'll find that you can get the Arpeggiator running quite fast when you turn Sync off, even to a point where the individual notes in the scale are blurred. This is a neat special effect and is also reminiscent of SID-based synth music, like that of the Commodore 64 of yore.

Gate

This dial is used to set the length or duration of each note played by the Arpeggiator. By default, this value is set to 50 percent, which means that the notes are only half as long as the rate at which they are played. Therefore, with the Rate set to 1/8, the notes are only 1/16-note long. If you set this to 25 percent, each note will only be 1/32-note long. This is a great parameter to tweak while the Arpeggiator is running.

Transposition Controls

Grouped together into a column near the center of the Arpeggiator are the Transpose controls. These parameters will allow the Arpeggiator to shift the pattern in pitch as it repeats. Start by turning the Steps knob to 1. Now play a single note. You'll no longer hear a single note being repeated. Instead, you'll hear two notes: the note you're holding plus a note one octave higher. This is because the Distance knob is set to +12 semitones, which is an octave. By turning Steps to 1, you've instructed the Arpeggiator to shift its pitch by the Distance amount once for each repetition of the pattern. Turn Steps up to 2 and listen to what happens. Now the Arpeggiator plays three notes for each key you press. This also works when holding multiple notes—so the Arpeggiator will play the pattern once and then play it again for each step indicated, transposing by the Distance amount each time.

Now try this: Set the Steps to 8 and the Distance to +1 semitones. Now when you hold a single note, the Arpeggiator plays nine notes chromatically. If you hold C, the Arpeggiator will play C C# D D# E F F# G G# and then repeat. This is because the Arpeggiator is shifting the pattern (which is only the one note you're holding) eight times after it has played the original pitch, transposing it one semitone each time. Change the Distance amount to +2 and listen to what happens.

Obviously, you can create some transposition patterns that will fall outside of the key you're working in. To remedy this, there are two menus that can be used to constrain the notes to those of a selected key and mode. With the top Transpose menu, choose Major or Minor. After this is selected, you can choose a root note with the Key menu below it. For example, set the Transpose menu to Minor and change the Key menu to D. Now press and hold D. The resulting pattern will have all its notes transposed to the nearest note within a D-Minor scale.

Retrigger

The Retriggering parameters can be used to cause the Arpeggiator to restart its pattern when triggered with a new note or in rhythm with your song. The default Retrigger mode is Off, which means that the Arpeggiator will never restart its pattern, even if you play new notes while the Arpeggiator is running. The pattern will only restart when you stop all notes and play new ones. If you set this to Note, the pattern will restart any time a new note is played. Therefore, if you're holding three notes and play a fourth note, the Arpeggiator will immediately restart, now including the fourth note in its pattern. The last mode, Beat, will cause the Arpeggiator to automatically restart at the rate specified with the neighboring knob. By default, this value is set to one bar. If you hold a three-note chord while this is on, you'll hear the Arpeggiator pattern start over on every downbeat of a bar.

Repeats

By default, Live will arpeggiate the notes you play for as long as you hold them. This is because the Repeats amount is set to Infinity by default. If you change this knob to a numerical value, the Arpeggiator will only run its pattern the specified number of times before stopping. Setting this to a low value, such as one or two repeats, while setting the Rate to a quick setting will cause the Arpeggiator to "strum" the notes of your chord. That is, they'll play quickly and then stop. This little burst of arpeggiation is reminiscent of old video game soundtracks.

Velocity

The final controls in the Arpeggiator are for modifying the velocity of notes as they play. Normally, these functions are off, which makes each note of the arpeggiation pattern sound at its played velocity. That is, if you press C lightly while striking G hard, the resulting pattern will have quiet C notes and loud G notes.

The purpose of the velocity controls here is to create a pseudo-envelope for the volume of the arpeggiation. Of course, this will only work with sounds that are velocity sensitive. When you turn velocity on with the top button, the Arpeggiator will modify the velocities of the notes as they repeat. The bottom dial sets the Target velocity, and the Decay knob above it determines how long it takes the Arpeggiator to modulate from the original velocities to the Target. For example, if you set Target to 10 and Decay to 1000ms and play a note with full velocity, the Arpeggiator will reduce the velocity of each consecutive note it plays to 10 over one second. You can invert this, of course, by setting a high Target velocity and playing quiet notes—the velocity will increase to the Target over the specified Decay time.

The Retrigger button will cause the velocity scaling to restart with each new note that is added to the chord. Otherwise, new notes will be constrained to the current values of the decaying velocities.

Chord

The Chord device (see Figure 11.2) will generate new MIDI notes at pitch intervals relative to an incoming MIDI note. This will allow one MIDI note to trigger a chord on the receiving instrument.

Figure 11.2

The Chord device allows us to build a multi-note (up to six notes) MIDI chord from one input note.

When the Chord device is first loaded, it will have no effect on incoming MIDI notes—they will pass straight through. If you move the first Shift knob, it will become active. The knob sets the interval in semitones for the new MIDI note. Setting the Shift 1 knob to +4 and playing a C will cause both a C and E note to be sent from the plug-in. Setting Shift 2 to +7 will create a C-Major chord when you play just the C note. Playing G will result in a G-Major chord (G, B, and D). You can define up to six notes to be added to the incoming note using the dials. Just below each dial is a percentage value, which determines the velocity of the new note. You can use this if you don't want all of the notes in the chord to be the same volume. If Shift 1 is set to 50 percent, the E in the resulting chord will only have a velocity of 64 when the incoming C has a velocity of 127. Try slowly changing this value while playing repeated notes to hear how the additional note fades in and out of the chord.

❄ DANCE CHORDS

Chord stabs and pads are a staple of electronic music. Originally, these fixed chords were created by detuning some of the oscillators in a synthesizer so that they sounded at musical intervals (usually +7— a perfect fifth) against the base oscillators.

The Chord effect can create the same sound on instruments that don't have individual tunings for their oscillators or when using samples by sending the actual chord information to the instrument for you. There are a number of chords already built for your use in the Preset menu.

Pitch

The Pitch device can be confusing to someone not familiar with MIDI. It would seem that this effect would change the pitch of your track. In a way, it does, but it doesn't do it by shifting the audio from the track. Instead it transposes the MIDI notes sent to an instrument, resulting in a higher or lower part.

The Pitch effect (see Figure 11.3) is the best way to change the pitch of a MIDI part since no warping or resynthesis is involved. We're just telling our instruments to play different notes. The result is that the track sounds shift up or down but still sound natural. When dragging in new MIDI parts from the Browser, it's quite possible that they will be in the wrong key. This effect will transpose the track to the appropriate key in the same way you use the Transpose knob to retune an Audio Clip.

Figure 11.3
Twist the Pitch knob to transpose the MIDI data passing through the effect. Easy, huh?

There is a situation in which the Pitch effect will have improper results—when transposing MIDI used to play drum parts. It is a standard convention to assign drum sounds to individual notes of a scale. By transposing the MIDI notes going to a drum instrument, you are assigning MIDI notes to new instruments. For example, if a kick drum sound is loaded into the first cell of the Impulse instrument and a snare is loaded into the second pad, MIDI note C3 will trigger the kick and D3 will trigger the snare (see the "Impulse" section in the Chapter 13). So, if MIDI data is programmed into a MIDI Clip for the kick drum, the clip will contain a pattern of MIDI notes, all C3. If we run this through the Pitch effect with the Pitch knob set to +2, the MIDI notes will be transposed up to D3, so the kick program will trigger the snare. So, instead of pitching up the kick drum, the Pitch effect transposed the kick information up to the snare key range.

This situation may also arise when using patches on synthesizers that have splits. If you try to transpose the MIDI information out of the appropriate keyzone, the synth will start playing the notes with the patch assigned to the other zone.

❄ **MIDI RANGE**

The two values at the bottom of the Pitch device set the range of notes that can be used with the effect. If the bottom value, labeled "lowest," is set to C3, only MIDI notes C3 and higher will be allowed to enter the effect. The Range value determines, by interval, the highest note that can enter the effect. So, if the range is set to +12, notes C3 through C4 will enter the effect. Only after the incoming notes have passed the range test will they be transposed up or down.

Random

As the name suggests, the Random device will randomize the incoming MIDI notes. We can determine how liberal Live is with its randomization using the controls seen in Figure 11.4.

Figure 11.4

The Random MIDI device will shift the pitch of incoming notes a different amount every time.

The first control in the effect is the Chance value. This knob sets the odds that an incoming MIDI note will be transposed. At 0 percent, the effect is essentially bypassed because there is no chance a note will be transposed. At 100 percent, every MIDI note will be subject to randomization. At 50 percent, roughly every other note will be randomized. Once a note is chosen by the effect to be transposed, it will be shifted using the rules set up with the three remaining controls. The three parameters make up part of a sort of formula that determines the transposition.

The Choices parameter determines the number of random values that can occur. If the value is set to 3, the Choices parameter will generate values of either 1, 2, or 3. This value is then passed on to the Scale knob. The value of this knob is multiplied by the random value from the Choices knob. The resulting number is the semitones to shift the MIDI note. So, if the Scale knob is set to 2, the resulting random transpositions will be either 2, 4, or 6 semitones. The final variables in the formula are the Sign buttons. If Add is selected, the resulting random value will be added to the MIDI note, causing it to move up in pitch. Sub will subtract the random value from the current note. The Bi setting will randomly choose between adding or subtracting the value. The indicator lights on the plug-in panel will show when the note is being transposed up or down.

Let's run some quick examples to make sure we understand the math behind the plug-in:

1. If the Choices knob is set to 1 and the Chance knob is set to 50 percent, about half the time a transpose value of 1 will be generated by the Choices knob. If the Scale is set to 12 and the Sign mode is set to Add, the incoming notes will be transposed up one octave half of the time.

2. If the Choices knob is set to 4 and the Chance knob is set to 100 percent, a transpose value between 1 and four will be generated for every MIDI note. We then set the Scale knob to 3 and leave the Sign mode on Add. In this situation, every note will be transposed (Chance at 100 percent) by one of the following semitone amounts: 3, 6, 9, or 12 (1[Choices]×3 [Scale]=3, 2×3=6, 3×3=9, and 4×3=12).

3. If the Choices knob is set to 2, the Scale knob is set to 12, and the Sign mode is set to Sub, the resulting transposition will be either 1 or 2 octaves down (1×12=12 and 2×12=24).

Scale

The first time I played with this effect, the only thought I had was how much fun it would be to sneak this in on an unsuspecting keyboard player. Scale allows an incoming MIDI note to be mapped to another one. I can tell the plug-in that I want every incoming D# transposed up to E. I can also tell it that I want incoming Es to be taken down to Cs. Remapping pitches like this would leave a keyboard player scratching his head, wondering what had happened to his keyboard.

While Scale is perfect for practical jokes, it has practical uses as well. Don't play keyboards well? Don't know your scales? The Scale device will transpose all the wrong notes you play to the proper pitches for the appropriate key. This mapping is achieved with a 12 ×13 grid of gray squares. The columns in the grid refer to the input notes, while the rows refer to output notes. The Base knob determines the note in the bottom-left corner of the grid. If the Base note is C, then the first column on the left is the input for C notes. The next column over is the input column for C# notes, etc. The row on the very bottom of the grid is the output row for C notes. The next row up from it is the output row for C# notes.

If you look at Figure 11.5, you'll see that the bottom-left grid square is on. This means that when a C note enters the far left column, it runs into the orange indicator in the last row, which is the C output row. So, in this case, all entering C notes will still exit as C notes. The next column over is the input column for C# notes. As you look down the column, you run into the indicator light on the third row from the bottom. If the bottom row is the output row for C notes, then this third row is the output for D notes. This means that when a C# note enters the Scale effect, it leaves as a D note.

You can use the grid to create musical scales. The pattern of indicators on the grid in Figure 11.5 is that of a major scale. C is chosen as the Base, so you are working with a C-Major scale. Any attempt to play a black key on the keyboard will result in the MIDI note being transposed up to its nearest neighbor in the scale. Changing the Base control to G will change the scale to a G-Major. Every key played on the keyboard will now be forced to one of the pitches in the G-Major scale.

Figure 11.5
The Scale effect lets you remap MIDI notes using a unique grid interface.

Incoming MIDI notes are fed into the columns...

...then exit on the rows.

❋ NO SCALE?

So you're just starting out and don't know all your musical scales? No problem. Ableton included the patterns of common scales in the Presets menu of the effect. You can load one of the patterns and then use the Base knob to adapt it to your working key.

The Transpose knob does what the Pitch effect does. In fact, both the Pitch knob and Range values in the bottom right of the plug-in are lifted straight from the Pitch device. Jump back a few sections if you have forgotten what these controls do.

❋ IN SCALE

The Scale effect can keep you in key, and it can also keep the results of a Random effect in key, too. If the Random plug-in is generating too many notes that are out of key, load up a Scale effect and set it to the appropriate scale. Any stray note from the Random effect will be knocked into key by the Scale plug-in.

By combining a Random and Scale plug-in, a random arpeggiator can be made that arpeggiates the pattern of notes entering the chain.

Velocity

The previous four MIDI effects in Live are concerned with controlling MIDI pitch information. Velocity, on the other hand, deals with (can you guess?) velocity data. It's very much like a compressor or scale plug-in for velocities. The grid display is like the display used in the Scale device (see Figure 11.6). Input velocities are mapped across the X-axis (the bottom of the grid), while output velocities are on the Y-axis (the right edge of the grid).

In its default setting, there is a straight line from the bottom left corner of the grid to the upper right corner of the grid. This means that every input velocity maps to the same output velocity.

Increasing the Drive knob will cause the line in the grid to begin to curve. This new shape shows that low input velocities (near the left edge of the grid) are mapped to higher output velocities.

New velocities exit on
the right edge.

Figure 11.6
The grid of the Velocity
effect shows the effect of
adjusting the various pa-
rameters in real-time.

Velocities enter along the
bottom of the graph.

This will raise the volume of notes played quietly while leaving the loud notes basically unchanged. Decreasing the Drive knob below zero has the opposite effect, causing loud input velocities to be mapped to lower output velocities. Only the loudest input notes will still leave the plug-in with high velocities.

The Comp (compression) knob is like the Drive knob except that it creates two curves instead of one. Turning this knob up past zero makes quiet notes quieter and loud ones louder. Lowering the Comp knob below zero has the opposite effect. Be aware that, like the Pitch effect, the Velocity effect is changing the notes fed into an instrument. Because of this, increasing the Comp knob will not make the part sound compressed as it would if a Compressor II were placed after the instrument. It will merely limit the velocities sent to the instrument, while the instrument continues to output an uncompressed sound.

The Random knob defines a range of randomness that can be applied to the incoming velocities. As this knob is increased, a gray area will form on the grid, showing all the possible velocities that may result from the random factor.

The Out Hi and Out Low knobs determine the highest and lowest velocities that will be output from the effect. The Range and Lowest values work like their counterparts in the Pitch and Scale effects. The Clip, Gate, and Fix buttons determine the action taken when an input velocity is outside of the operation range set by the Range and Lowest values. In Clip mode, any velocity outside of the range will be bumped into range. The Gate mode will only allow notes with velocities within range to pass. Fix mode will force every incoming velocity to be set to the value determined by the Out Hi knob.

❋ **BREATH OF LIFE**

Velocity randomization can add a human breath of life to a programmed drum part. Humans can't play with the same consistency of a machine, so randomizing the velocities of the drum parts can make the beat sound less repetitive. This is especially effective on high-hats and shakers.

12 } ReWire

While Live is an amazing audio production environment, you still may want to use other software tools at your disposal for generating sounds. Virtual instruments and plug-in effects give you access to a plethora of third-party programs. But what do you do if the program you want to use is "bigger" than just a plug-in or effect? What if you want to harness the power of another computer program? Well, you just ReWire them together!

What Is ReWire?

Power users have been synchronizing sequencers and computers for years, as it was the only way they could produce the number of sounds they needed. The limited hardware solutions of yesteryear required that many be used simultaneously to achieve a fully orchestrated sound. Most of the first synthesizers were monophonic (they could only play one note at once), so multiple units were necessary for achieving chords and other simultaneous sounds.

Synchronizing multiple computer systems is common as well. One computer can be playing back audio files through effects while another computer is running virtual instruments. One could be a Mac, and the other could be a PC if you wished. The point is that each system doesn't provide the entire solution on its own and has to be augmented by another.

With the wide variety of music-making software, there are bound to be some applications that have their own unique features, workflow, and sound—Live is no exception. But do you have to run Live on one computer and the other program on another? With the advent of ReWire, the answer is no. ReWire will allow you to run both programs on the same machine simultaneously. But ReWire does much more for you than just allow multiple applications to run. It will keep the applications in sync with each other and allow audio and MIDI to pass from one to the other.

Masters

In a ReWire setup, there's actually no wiring that you have to be concerned with. ReWire functions transparently between compatible applications, allowing operation to be as seamless as possible.

In any ReWire setup, there is always one program designated as the *ReWire Master*. The ReWire Master is the program that will be communicating with the computer's audio hardware and will accept audio streams from other ReWire applications. You must open the ReWire Master application before any of the other programs you want to use.

Slaves

Only one application can be ReWire Master, so all the other programs running will be *ReWire Slaves*. Slaves don't actually communicate with the computer's audio hardware at all. Instead, their audio outputs are routed to the ReWire Master application. This rerouting of audio happens automatically inside the computer after a program is launched as a ReWire Slave. Since the audio is being passed through the Master application, you will not hear the Slave application unless the Master program is set to pass the Slave's audio to the computer's audio hardware.

Using ReWire with Live

Live can act as both a ReWire Master and a ReWire Slave. Not all programs have the capability to function in both modes. For example, Steinberg Cubase SX 3 can only function as a ReWire Master. Propellerhead Reason 3.0 can only be used in Slave mode. So, if you wanted to use Live and Cubase together, Cubase would be the Master and Live would be the Slave. When using Reason, Live would be the Master and Reason would be the Slave. How does the operation of Live differ when running as Master or Slave? Since ReWire was designed to be transparent for the user, little will change in Live's operability either way. There are a few differences, of course, which will be explained next.

Using Live as a ReWire Master

When Live is used as a ReWire Master, it will operate exactly the same as when using Live by itself. When Live is the only ReWire application running, it will be in Master mode. This is true of any ReWire application that is capable of Master mode. Because of this, you'll define your Master application by opening it before any of the others.

When Live is hosting a ReWire Slave application, the Slave's audio outputs will be available as inputs into the Session Mixer (see Figure 12.1). In the Input/Output Routing section, you'll be able to choose the ReWire application in the first box and the desired channel(s) from that program in the second box.

Once you have selected the ReWire source for a channel, it will behave exactly like any other audio channel with an input selected. You can hear the audio from the ReWire source by switching the channel's monitoring to On or by arming the track for recording with monitoring set to Auto. You can record the audio from the external application as a new clip in the track, either by recording a clip in the Session View or by pressing Record in the Control Bar and recording directly to the Arrangement. This is the exact same process for recording any other audio source on an Audio Track, as explained in previous chapters.

Figure 12.1
Here I am using outputs 1
and 2 from Reason as
inputs for Track 1 in the
Session Mixer. I can hear
the audio output from
Reason by switching Moni-
tor to On.

If you don't want to record the ReWire Slave as audio, you can still incorporate its audio streams in a Live mixdown when selecting Render to Disk. If the ReWire Slave applications are running and their channels in the Session Mixer are being monitored, their audio will be mixed in with the rest of your Live Set when rendered. Running the ReWire applications in real-time is often preferred for laptop owners who have fast CPUs. Since laptops generally have slow hard drives, it's easier for the computer to run the ReWire applications, as opposed to streaming their audio from disk.

While audio can only flow from the ReWire Slaves to the ReWire Master, it is possible for MIDI to flow in the opposite direction. This allows you to control compatible ReWire Slave applications in the same manner you would control a virtual instrument in Live. Just as you can select a ReWire Slave application as an input to an Audio Track, a Slave can also be selected at the output of a MIDI Track (see Figure 12.2). You can select the Slave application with the upper box and the destination channel/device in the lower box.

A destination channel will only be listed if there are devices or elements in the Slave application that are active and able to receive MIDI messages. For example, if you load an empty rack into Reason, there will be no output devices listed in the lower box. If you create a few devices, like a Subtractor, Redrum, and NN-XT sampler, these devices will be individually selectable in the lower box of the MIDI Tracks Input/Output section.

Not all ReWire Slave applications are capable of receiving MIDI input from the Master application. If a program is not able to receive MIDI, it will not be listed as an available output destination in the MIDI Track.

Remember, in order to hear the results of your MIDI messages sent to the ReWire Slave, you'll need to have an Audio Track set up to monitor the return signal from the Slave. So, instead of

Figure 12.2

These three MIDI Tracks are being routed to the Subtractor, Redrum, and NN-XT modules in Reason. They can now be programmed and automated using the power and convenience of Live's clips.

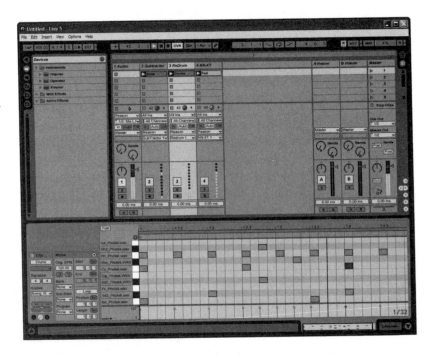

the MIDI Track outputting the audio (as would happen when a virtual instrument is loaded onto a MIDI Track), you'll need another Audio Track to hear the results. This means that the MIDI info leaves on one track, and the audio returns on another.

Using Live as a ReWire Slave

Opening Live as a ReWire Slave will depend partly on the ReWire Master application you use. In some cases, you may need to enable ReWire channels before the ReWire Slave program is launched. Be sure to check the ReWire Master's manual on how they recommend doing this. Generally speaking, though, you'll launch the Master first and launch Live second. When launching Live second, it will detect the presence of the Master application and therefore automatically load itself into Slave mode. (You'll see a little message about this on the Live splash screen during boot-up.)

When using Live as a ReWire Slave application, you'll notice many subtle differences in available options throughout the program. The first thing to be aware of is that like all ReWire Slave applications, Live will be communicating with the ReWire Master program instead of the computer's audio hardware. Because of this, Live's Audio Preferences will not be available and will instead be replaced with the message seen in Figure 12.3.

Also missing from Live in Slave mode is MIDI output (see Figure 12.4). Only the MIDI inputs will be available as usual for remote control and playing virtual instruments.

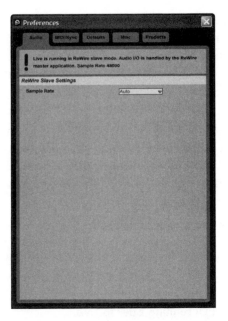

Figure 12.3
Live's Audio Preferences tab is telling us that Live is in ReWire Slave mode and therefore has no audio controls. It does, however, report the current sample rate of the ReWire Master.

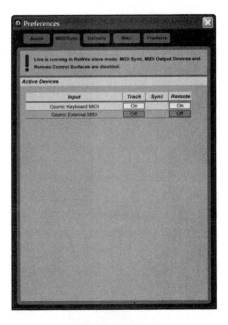

Figure 12.4
The right half of the MIDI Preferences is missing in ReWire Slave mode. Only the MIDI inputs are active.

Another difference will be the available output routings for audio in the Session Mixer. When looking at the Master Track output assignment, you'll find that the list is populated with Mix and

Bus names instead of the outputs of your audio interface. These buses are the pathways that lead from Live into the ReWire Master. The ReWire Master will receive the busses individually, allowing you to route one Live Track to a channel of the Master's mixer while routing a different Live Track to another channel of the Master's mixer. You can then process the channels separately in the Master application however you wish.

The biggest difference in Live when it runs as a Slave is that you will no longer have access to any of your external VST or Audio Units plug-ins. Your plug-ins will only be accessible through the ReWire Master. This is only somewhat inconvenient because, if you really need to use them, you can route a track from Live into the Master and then process it with all the plug-ins available there. You just won't be able to automate these plug-ins using Live—all automation will have to be done on the Master.

When I said above that some ReWire Slave applications do not accept MIDI, I was partly referring to Live. You won't be able to send MIDI information to Live from the Master application. Only the computer's MIDI inputs can be fed into Live. Of course, if you really needed to route MIDI back into Live from the Master application, you could route MIDI out of a hardware interface and receive MIDI back into Live through a hardware interface as well. Connect the output to the input with a MIDI cable, and you'll have MIDI running back to Live.

ReWire Power

When multiple applications are running together using ReWire, they're basically joined at the hip. What I mean is that the transport controls and song locations are kept in perfect sync throughout all of the applications. When you press the Play button on one of the applications, all of the programs will start to play together. If you press Stop in another program, they'll all stop. Furthermore, if you change the start location to bar nine in one application, they'll all begin playing from that same location. It doesn't matter if you use the controls of the Master or Slave applications, they'll all respond as if they're one and the same.

Since the transport functions of the programs are synchronized, changes to the tempo in one program will affect all of the others. In the case of Live with its MIDI-assignable tempo control, this real-time feature can be used to change the tempo of programs previously unable to do so on their own. Changing the tempo in Live will cause Cubase and Reason to respond accordingly. In this way, the programs inherit functionality from the others.

> ❄ **GROOVE BY YOURSELF**
>
> While the tempo control in Live will have an effect on all ReWire applications, the Groove setting is solely for the use of Live. Increasing the Groove will cause Live to start swinging while the other applications remain straight.

Since Reason 3.0 doesn't allow the automation of its tempo, running the program in Slave mode with Live as the Master will automate the tempo of your Reason project. The programmed change of tempo in Live will also change the tempo in Reason, resulting in the desired automation.

Using ReWire Slave applications with Live gives you an expanded list of sound sources to create with. Frequently, you just may want to create some audio loops in a ReWire Slave application, record them in Live, and then close the Slave program. The real-time nature of Live loads ReWire Slaves, uses them, then closes them, all while Live remains playing—without glitches. This makes ReWire a viable live tool since it can be loaded and unloaded during a performance. Of course, as with all other procedures in Live, be sure to try this out a few times before a show to confirm that your computer can handle the workload of multiple audio applications running at once.

Many users flock to Live because of its ability to operate as a ReWire Slave. The unique loop-based and time-compression tools of Live can be used in unison with standard production programs like Digidesign Pro Tools. While having Live feeding into Pro Tools, you can use Live to audition loops at the Pro Tools tempo. You can add drum loops or MIDI parts quickly that remain under user control. You can add Warp Markers to takes done with Pro Tools to fix timing problems. Once all the correct parts are made, the results can be rendered as audio into Pro Tools.

In this chapter, I have looked at the most common ways to use ReWire with Live and other ReWire Slave and Master applications. ReWire is an incredibly exciting, creative, and fun aspect of Live. Many musicians and producers I have met come to Live because of its ability to ReWire. Rest assured, once you begin linking software applications, you will be hooked. Take time to explore your favorite ways of linking Live. As new applications become ReWire enabled and CPUs become increasingly faster, you may soon be linking computers via LAN or even the Internet in similar ways to ReWire. In the next chapter, I will explore some of my favorite power tips for working with Live.

* **WHO'S USING LIVE?**

Dykehouse

Michael Dykehouse blends guitar-based rock with swirling atmospheres and lush electronic production www.ghostly.com/1.0/artists/dykehouse/). He has released two albums, *Dynamic Obsolescence* (2001 Planet Mu) and *Midrange* (2004 Ghostly International), both to critical acclaim.

"My musical interests began with garage bands and four–track–based bedroom production," explains Michael. "As my tastes began turning away from more traditional rock leanings, I began using hardware electronics to flesh out my ideas. Over the last five years, I began the gradual implementation of software."

Mike now uses Live for both composition and performance. "As a Mac user, I have used most of the DAWs available over the years, and none hold a candle to Live's ease of use, power, and flexibility. The fact that Live 4 (which was the first version I became familiar with) seemed infinitely more stable and intuitive than either Pro Tools or Logic was the impetus of my switch. There aren't endless windows cluttering up the screen, on-the-fly arrangements are a dream, and the program seems much more efficiently coded (meaning less of a pull on my CPU) than its competitors."

Dykehouse frequently makes use of Live's ReWire capabilities during production and performance. "I use Live with Propellerhead's Reason, as both are rock solid in their compatibility. Furthermore, I can't live without the Warp functions (and now Auto-Warp!) of Live. No other OS X program performs this function with the ease and flexibility that Live does. Live is a permanent fixture in my studio. Thank you, Ableton!"

13 } Playing Live...Live

Most books written about music production software would not include a chapter like the one you're about to read. It's not because the writer of this book is deranged or just trying to be different. It's because Live can actually live up to its name in a live performance. As you will discover, it's a true treat to use the same software to create your music *and* perform it. You won't have to worry about converting songs from the type of media used by your composing software into something Live can use. You won't have to worry about transferring effect and instrument settings. The same tools you use to write can be used to play—just like any other instrument. After all, should the two processes really be that different?

Because of its flexible control methods and instant response to user input, Live is the perfect companion for a gigging musician. Live performs wonders in all types of scenarios, ranging from DJ gigs to improvisational jazz and theater. Regardless of what type of musician you consider yourself to be, I recommend reading all the information presented in this chapter. Any technique relating to the use of Live is pertinent information—innovations can be made by taking ideas from one musician's style and applying them to your own style.

DJ

DJ or not, every one of you reading this book should study this section. Using Live to DJ exploits some of the unique (and potentially confusing) features of the program and extends them to the *n*th degree. You already know that Live can sync loops together using its Warp Engine. DJs use this powerful mechanism to sync *entire songs* together. They'll also use an array of clips to manufacture new arrangements of the songs, literally creating their own remixes right in front of the dancing masses. By learning the techniques employed here, you'll achieve a firmer grasp on warp marking and real-time control.

Assembling Your Audio Files

The process of DJing with Live is two-fold: First comes the work of ripping and warp marking your songs (prepping the files); this is followed by the joy of putting it all together (performing). One of the greatest additions for DJs in Live is support for importing MP3 files. No longer do you have to keep a hard drive full of uncompressed versions of the tracks you want to spin. Now you can just bring your MP3 collection along. Of course, you can still use any of the other formats supported by Live to DJ, too.

Ripping

If the song you want to use is on a CD, you will need to copy the music from the CD to your computer using a process known as *ripping*. There are many programs that do this, quite a few of which are free. While you can find a deluge of programs to try by typing "CD Ripper" into a Google search, I recommend Apple's iTunes (www.iTunes.com). It's available for both Mac and PC, it's free, and it has a number of features that will prove helpful when building your DJ music collection. I'm going to use iTunes in my instructions, but you can use your favorite ripping program instead with the same results.

❄ TAKE IT WITH YOU

Before I get too far, I thought it would be appropriate to mention external hard drives. If you're a DJ compiling a collection of audio files for your performances, a big hard drive (maybe two!) is a good thing to have. It will keep all of your music in one place. And if you have multiple computer systems that you use (a desktop at home and a laptop for gigs), you won't have to store the collection on both systems. The hard drive will become your virtual record case.

Before you start ripping CDs, there are a few setup options for the ripping software to consider. First, you should check the ripping format. Many programs these days default to MP3 or a similar compressed format for ripping, so you can transfer the results to a portable player such as an iPod or Nomad Jukebox. This is perfect now that Live supports compressed formats. There still are a few options that you may want to consider before ripping your whole CD collection. First, MP3 compression has different quality settings. Since MP3 is compressing your audio, it's throwing away bits that it thinks you can't hear. The lower the quality settings on the MP3 converter, the more info will be thrown away, eventually becoming noticeable to your ears. The most important quality factor for making MP3s is the *bit rate*. I personally recommend converting your songs to MP3 with a bit rate of 192kbps or higher. When setting the bit rate, you normally have an option for specifying *constant bit rate* (CBR) or *variable bit rate* (VBR) compression. CBR is a little bit safer than VBR as nearly every MP3 player (software or hardware) will read CBR files. Some programs and hardware will have difficulty with VBR. Live will handle both just fine, but I recommend CBR for the widest compatibility. Secondly, VBR compression takes longer to perform. This is because the encoder must first analyze the entire song before it begins compressing. CBR, on the other hand, will begin compressing immediately.

In iTunes, you'll find the compression options under the Importing tab of the Preferences (see Figure 13.1). iTunes provides a number of preset compression settings—I use the Higher Quality (192 kbps) setting. You can also choose Custom from the Setting menu to gain access to all of the compression options (including VBR). For programs other than iTunes, you should be able to access these settings from their preferences or options menus. Check the program's documentation if the location of these parameters is not immediately evident.

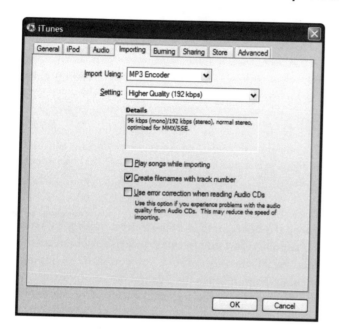

Figure 13.1
The iTunes Importing options allow you to specify MP3 as your preferred file type. You can also select the compression quality with the second dropdown menu.

Now that you've specified the format for ripping your files, you still need to tell your ripping program where to put them. Some programs will ask you for a location to save the files each time a song is ripped. Others will have you select a destination directory for the audio files. Regardless of the method employed by your software, I do recommend making some sort of logical arrangement of your songs in your collection. For example, you can make a folder called "Breaks" and store all your breakbeat tracks there. You could make another folder called "DnB" and store all your drum 'n bass cuts there. Whatever method you choose, it should be easy for you to navigate during a show. You don't want to be left searching for a song when the song currently playing ends!

iTUNES NOTE 2

iTunes can organize your music in folders for you automatically. Click the Advanced tab/button in iTunes Preferences. The first window shows the location where iTunes will maintain your library. You can use the Change button to specify a new location, such as your external hard drive. Next, make sure the first two check boxes are checked. This will cause iTunes to maintain the library and also move any imported songs into this location (in case the songs already exist elsewhere on your hard drives).

When you examine your iTunes music folder, you won't see any music files. Instead, you'll find a list of folders with artist names. Inside each of these artist folders are additional folders for albums. Open the album folder, and you'll find all the songs you ripped from that album. When accessed through Live's Browser, it makes locating a song a snap.

Now that your audio programs are properly configured, it's time to start ripping. When you insert a CD, the program will identify it and usually allow you to select specific tracks in case you don't want to import the entire CD. After you've selected your tracks, you can start the ripping process. For iTunes, you'll right-click on your selection to expose the context menu (if you're on a Mac with only one mouse button, hold the Ctrl key while clicking) and choose Convert selection to MP3. Now sit back and wait.

iTUNES NOTE 3

When connected to the Internet, iTunes will automatically search for the information on the CD you've inserted. It will usually find any retail CD and load the artist's name, album name, plus all of the track names for the CD and fill them in for you. iTunes is not the only program that can do this, but you may have to enable the feature manually in other applications. If you don't have an Internet connection, it's best if you manually type in these names so the program will rip the tracks with the proper filenames.

Converting

With the rise in popularity of online music stores, such as Apple's iTunes (really, they're not paying me) or Bleep (www.bleep.com), you may already have the song you want to play as a digital music file on your computer. Perhaps the song is so hard to find that you're only able to buy it as a download. While these purchased downloads are in a compressed format that can be played by Live, many of them are protected with DRM (Digital Rights Management). This ensures that you, the buyer of the file, are the only person who can play them. In order to play these files, you'll need to use a program that can deal with protected files. Unfortunately, Live does not have provisions for these protected files, so you will not be able to play them natively. The solution for this is to burn the files to a CD (which iTunes will allow you to do, even with protected files) and then rip the CD back into iTunes. The downfall to this procedure (other than it takes a long time and uses up CDs) is that the audio quality of the files will be slightly diminished compared to the original. This is because you'll be burning a compressed file to the CD (a compressed file doesn't sound as good as an uncompressed file) and then ripping the audio from the CD and recompressing it (this will cause further degradation to the sound). If you want to maintain the audio quality of the CD-burned song, rip the CD back into your computer using an uncompressed format, like WAV or AIFF.

Recording

If you don't have your song on CD or as a digital music file, you'll have to import it the hard way. If the track you want is on vinyl, you'll need to connect your turntable to your computer's audio interface. This will probably require that you go through a DJ mixer or home preamp, since most audio interfaces do not allow for a direct connection of turntables. Once you've got your signal entering a channel on Live's Session Mixer, you can record the song as a new Audio Clip (see Chapter 6, "The Audio Clip," if you forgot how to do this). The resulting Audio Clip will then be in a format ready to use with Live (obviously). Live cannot record directly to MP3, so if you want your recorded song in that format, you'll need to convert the file to MP3 using iTunes after you've recorded it.

❄ **WARP ON THE FLY**

Did you know you can add Warp Markers to an Audio Clip that is recording? Simply press the Tap button along with the song, and Live will insert Warp Markers with your tapped beats. This is great when recording tracks that have a varying tempo, such as a song that was recorded without the assistance of computers or metronomes.

Warp Marking Your Songs

Now that you have your songs in AIFF or WAV format, you're ready to begin the second step of prepping a file for DJing. In order to have Live keep the song in time with any others that you may be playing, you'll need to place Warp Markers in the file to indicate the location of beats in the track. Warp marking an entire song can sound like quite an undertaking, but you'll quickly gain a rhythm that will let you complete a song in only a minute or two (maybe less).

Auto-Warping

Live 5 now includes an Auto-Warping algorithm that will analyze any long file you import into your Set. Therefore, prepping your MP3s can be as simple as dragging them into Live. Live will convert the MP3 into an uncompressed format (which it stores in the Decoding Cache of the Ableton Library) and then perform the analysis. When complete, your song will be ready to play. Furthermore, in the future, Live will only have to decode the MP3—the Warp Markers will be stored automatically in the adjoining .asd file.

While I wish that the Auto-Warping algorithm was the ultimate solution for prepping files, there are many times when it won't work properly. To be fair, Live usually only screws up the *phase* of the song. That is, it will get the overall tempo of the song right, but will not put Warp Marker 1 on the first downbeat of the song. In this case, your song will play in sync, but offset from the proper downbeat. It will then be up to you to manually shift all the Warp Markers into the proper location. This can normally be done by clicking on a Warp Marker (to select it) and then pressing Ctrl(⌘)+A, which is the key command for Select All. This will select all the Warp Markers, allowing you to drag them right and left as a group. If you don't shift all the Warp Markers, you'll only correct the timing from the first Warp Marker to the second. From that point on, the song will still be out of sync because you haven't corrected any of the other markers.

> ❄ **THE NUDGE**
>
> If you don't have time to correct a phase error as described above, you can offset the clip using the Nudge buttons found in the bottom left corner of the Clip View. Each time you click one of these buttons, the current play position will be offset by the current Global Quantize amount. That is, if Global Quantize is set to 1/4, each click of the Nudge buttons will offset the clip by one quarter of a bar (one beat).
>
> If you need to make an extremely minute adjustment, set the Global Quantize to None. Now each click of the Nudge buttons will result in a slight shifting of the clip.

Manual Warping

Even with Live's new Auto-Warp technology, I must admit that I still warp mark my tracks by hand. There are two reasons for this, one being that the songs I'm spinning are electronically produced (they have a consistent tempo) and the other because I demand extremely tight synchronization between songs when DJing. By warping the songs manually, I can place only as many markers as are required to get the tempo correct, and I can place the markers perfectly in line with the transients in the song (something the Auto-Warping technology doesn't do too well).

The best way to begin warp marking a song is by determining the original tempo of the song. Start by turning off the Warp button in the Clip View. This will make the clip play at its original speed regardless of the tempo of your Live Set. Launch the clip and begin tapping along with the song using the Tap Tempo button (I recommend using a key assignment for this instead of clicking with the mouse). After you've tapped some beats, Live's tempo will start to settle around the song's tempo. Since Live's Tempo display is accurate to two decimal places, you'll probably get tempos like 125.82BPM or 98.14BPM instead of round numbers like 110.00BPM or 85.00BPM.

Chances are, however, that the tempo is actually a round number, especially if the song was created by a computer or sequencer. So, if Live says the tapped tempo is 102.15BPM, it's probably just 102.00BPM. Go ahead and double-click the Tempo display and type in the rounded tempo; then activate the Warp button in the Clip View. Live will place the tempo of the project in the clip's Seg BPM box (on the rare occasion that this doesn't happen, you can type the tempo into this box by hand).

Now that the tempo has been found, you need to align the grid with the first beat of the song. Zoom in to the waveform display and move Warp Marker 1 into position with the first beat of the file. Don't worry if you don't find the first downbeat until later in the song (perhaps the song has an ambient intro that drops into the beat further in), since the grid also has negative values (grid lines to the left of Marker 1). You can still place the Start Marker before Marker 1, so starting on bar −16 is starting 16 bars before the beat drops (see Figure 13.2). This is especially cool because you can play a song start with a completely nebulous, rhythmless intro, yet drop on the beat perfectly 16 bars later. Try that with a record!

You can place the Start Marker at a location before Warp Marker 1.

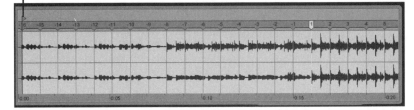

Figure 13.2
Even though you don't hear the first drum beat until bar 17 of this song, you can place Warp Marker 1 at this location and start the song from bar −16.

Once the tempo has been determined and Marker 1 has been placed at the first recognizable downbeat of the song, the remaining grid markers to the right should be pretty close, if not dead on the beats. Turn on Live's Metronome and listen to the track against the click. The song should start out perfectly aligned with the click. If the track stays in time all the way through, then the clip is ready to go; however, chances are that the song will start to drift ahead or behind the click as it plays. This is due to slight differences in BPMs between Live and the song. Perhaps the song is actually running at 101.98BPM (even computers can be a little off). After a few minutes, the discrepancy will add up to a complete misalignment with the beat, seen in Figures 13.3a and 13.3b.

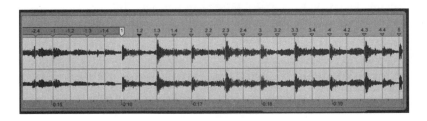

Figure 13.3a
The beginning of the song looks like it's aligned properly...

Figure 13.3b
...but as you look later in the file, you can see that the grid is no longer aligned.

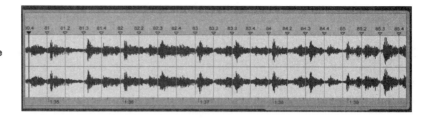

To compensate for the "drift" you may encounter, you can place additional Warp Markers to keep the clip synchronized to Live. Placing a Warp Marker every 32 bars is usually sufficient. To make the process as easy as possible, turn on Loop in the Clip View and use the Region/Loop Markers to inspect small sections of the song one at a time. For example, create a two-bar loop and place it at the beginning of the clip. Launch the clip and listen to the two bars against the click. If the beats are aligned with the click, move the loop region to the right to bar 32. Listen to the loop around these two bars. Here, you may notice that the clip doesn't line up exactly with the click anymore. Create a Warp Marker in the middle of the loop area (at bar 33) and move this marker to properly align it with the beats in the clip (see Figure 13.4). You should now hear bars 32 and 33 looping in time with the click. Furthermore, everything between bar 1 and bar 33 should be perfectly aligned as well. You repeat the process by moving the loop region to the right another 32 bars (bar 64). Check this new loop area and adjust if necessary. Repeat the process to the end of the clip.

Figure 13.4
I was inspecting various sections of the song two bars at a time. When I was listening to this section, I had to create a Warp Marker to align the song to the beat.

I added a Warp Marker and adjusted it to line it up with the beat.

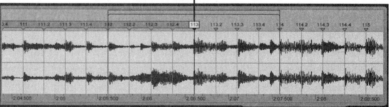

After you've placed your Warp Markers to ensure proper timing, press the Save button in the clip. This will save the location of the Warp Markers so they'll be recalled the next time you import the clip from the Browser. You can also check the Warp mode to make sure that you're using the most effective method for time stretching. Complex mode is usually the best, but you may want to use Beats or Tones mode if your CPU is overburdened.

Now that you know the process for warp marking long files, sit back, grab a frosty beverage of your choice, and start clicking away. You'll want to have every file in your collection saved with the correct Warp Markers so that the songs will play in time every time you use them in a set.

> ❄ **SLOP INTO SOLID GOLD**
>
> With the ability to time-align audio files, many DJs are incorporating songs into their sets that weren't recorded to a steady tempo. Things like old Grateful Dead songs or Led Zeppelin tracks can be warp marked to the point where they will play back perfectly alongside a rigid dance beat.
>
> The process is the same as described above, except that you'll be making many more Warp Markers for these types of songs. Instead of placing a Warp Marker every 32 bars through the track, you'll probably want to place a marker every two bars. If the band was moving wildly in and out of time, you may need to be even more meticulous.
>
> The payoff is worth the extra work. You can really mess with your audience by infusing this old music into your set. Furthermore, traditional DJs will be trying to figure out what you're doing since this is beyond the capabilities of their turntables.

Organization

The new features of Live's Browser—the ability to drag multiple clips to the Browser and recall entire tracks into your Set—open up a whole new world of convenience for DJs. One thing you can do is create multiple clips for a single song. After you've warp marked a song, duplicate this clip a couple of times and set the Start and Loop points of the clips to useful areas of the song. For example, the first clip in the track can be the whole song. The clips below it can be the first verse, first chorus, second verse, breakdown, or any other sections you want. You can then grab all these clips at once and drag them to the File Browser. At this point, a new Live Set will be made, and you can give it the name of the song you're editing.

While performing your DJ set, you can import this Live Set instead of just the single MP3 file. What will happen is that you'll end up loading all of the clips you made so you'll have instant access to various sections of the song. You can jump directly to a chorus, loop the breakdown for an intro, or extend verses. If you make additional variations during your performance, you can drag the clips back to the Browser as a Live Set so you can use them again at your next show.

Another side effect of importing an entire track from a Live Set is that Live will also load the effects assigned to the track. For this reason, I spend a little extra time with each song using an EQ Four to shape the frequency content of the track. Often, when I record a song from vinyl, the bass is not as present as a song that is ripped from CD. Therefore, I use the EQ Four to boost the bass and make any other appropriate adjustments so that the song will sonically match any others that I might be spinning at the time. If the song is really old, I'll even add a Compressor II to the Track View to beef up the song—the brick-wall limiting used in today's CD mastering makes old tracks sound completely weak by comparison. With these effects in place, all I have to do is drag the track to the Browser to save it. Next time I load the track, it will sound great next to anything else I might be playing, thanks to my preset EQ and compression.

Performance Techniques

Now that you've got your warp-marked files ready, I am going to discuss the techniques used for cueing and mixing songs. I will start by looking at traditional DJs, their equipment, and their performance methods. You'll see how Live can be used to do the same things, plus a few never possible before.

Beat Matching

The whole concept of DJing revolves around blending one great song into another great song, without interrupting the flow or rhythm of music. Quite often, this requires aligning the tempos of the two songs so they play in sync with each other, a technique known as *beat matching*. A DJ using turntables or CD decks will use their Pitch Adjust sliders to slow down or speed up a new song to match the tempo of one that's already playing. Once the tempos are matched, the DJ will start the new song and begin to fade it in, usually with the crossfader on his mixer. Since the tempos are matched and the DJ started the track at the right moment, the beats of the two songs will be playing on top of each other. The beat will remain constant as the old song is replaced by the new one. While performing this mix, the DJ will probably have to make minute adjustments to the playback speeds of the records or CDs in case they begin to drift out of sync.

The process of beat matching two songs in Live involves nothing more than having files with proper Warp Markers. Once Warp Markers are in the right place, Live will know how to play that file at any tempo. So any song can be matched in tempo with any other simply by loading the two clips and launching them—this is no different than importing drum loops of different tempos into the same Live Set. Using Launch Quantization, Live will start the songs in sync so you'll never have to worry about making tiny adjustments to keep the songs from drifting. Just fire and forget. Easy!

The DJ Mixer

The whole DJ setup centers around the DJ mixer, a specialized mixer with controls specific for DJ use. The DJ's audio sources (turntables and CD players) are connected to the mixer, and the output is connected to the sound system. The mixer has audio channels with EQ, the ability to pre-listen to tracks (cueing), and a crossfader for mixing between audio sources. Some advanced mixers will also have effect loops, allowing external processing boxes to add beat-synced delays, whooshing flanges, and other tweaks to the mix. To emulate a DJ mixer with Live, you'll use features of the Session Mixer, which will be discussed in a moment. But most importantly, you'll want a MIDI control device to offer you the same tactile control DJs are accustomed to.

I briefly mentioned some MIDI controllers in Chapter 3, "Getting Live Up and Running," and a good portion of them can suit a Live DJ quite well. Evolution's X-Session and Faderfox's Micromoduls will give you just the right assortment of controls for getting the job done. The most important things are a crossfader control (for assignment to Live's Crossfader), at least two controls to adjust the volumes of the tracks you'll be mixing (these can be faders or knobs), six knobs for using as EQ controls, and some keys or buttons for triggering mutes, EQ kills, and effects. Since Live will allow any MIDI knob or button to be assigned to a control, you could certainly use a different type of MIDI controller from the ones mentioned here for the same tasks. For example, you could use a vertical fader on your device as a crossfader, as long as you can get used to the vertical orientation (you probably won't be pulling off any flares, crab scratches, or cuts with this, but it still works for smoothly blending between tracks). Even though Live displays its volume controls as vertical faders, you could use the knobs of your controller to adjust volumes (there are some DJ mixers that actually use knobs instead of sliders for a vintage feel). If worse comes to worse, you can still achieve a great mix just by using your mouse and computer's keyboard; the point is to make sure you have adequate control of your mix so you can shape it at will.

In Figure 13.5, I have set up Live's Session View like a standard 2-channel DJ mixer. There are two Audio Tracks each assigned to different sides of the Crossfader. There are EQ Threes loaded onto each of the Audio Tracks, plus a Compressor II on the Master Track. Two Return Tracks are in use for Ping Pong Delay and Reverb Devices, but you can load any kind of effects you'd prefer.

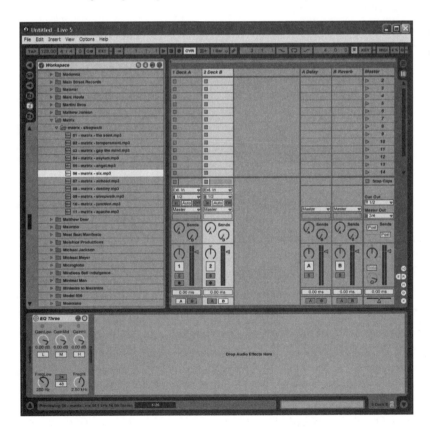

Figure 13.5

A simple Live Set ready for DJing.

In order to cue or preview tracks, you'll need an audio interface with four outputs—two outs for the main mix and the other two to feed your headphones. Some audio interfaces, such as M-Audio's FireWire series and Echo Audio's Indigo cards, have built-in headphone amps, which are perfect for this application. In the Master Track, choose outs 1/2 for Cue and 3/4 for Master (you may need to enable these outputs in Live's Audio Preferences if they aren't available in the menus). Connect outputs 3/4 to the speakers or sound system and plug a pair of headphones into the audio interface. If your interface doesn't have a built-in headphone amplifier, you can use an external amplifier, such as a home stereo or small mixer, or purchase a small headphone amp box from your local music store.

To make Live's Cue system work, click the Solo button just above the Preview Volume knob (see Figure 13.6). The button will change to Cue, and you'll see small headphone icons in the buttons where the solos used to be in the Session Mixer. This button will switch only if you've assigned the Cue and Master to different outputs as explained above. Clicking a headphone icon will route that track to the Cue bus, thus allowing you to hear it on your headphones. Please note that enabling Cue on a track does not remove it from the Master Output. You'll need to turn off the Track Activator button so only you may hear it. Once the track is properly cued, engage the Track Activator to send the track back to the Master Track and out to the dance floor.

Figure 13.6

To enable Live's Cue function, click the button above the Preview Volume knob. The solo buttons in each track will change to headphone icons.

The Solo buttons will change to Cue buttons.

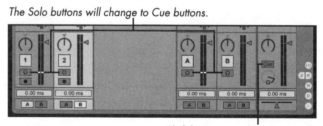

Click here to switch to Cue mode.

To prevent the chance of mistakes caused by forgetting to deactivate the Track Activator, I've made a variation on the setup of the Session by adding another Audio Track whose Track Activator is always off (see Figure 13.7). By leaving it off and leaving Cue on, any Audio Clip placed in this track will be heard in the headphones only. Once your cueing is done, simply drag the clip from this preview track over to one of the main audio tracks in the Set.

If you've been trying this out while reading this, then you'll know that you can only hear your Cue Track in the headphones. What if you want to hear the main tracks in your headphones, too? You could simply click their Cue buttons, thus adding their signals to your headphones, but you have no control of their volume in relation to the Cue Track. Instead, make another Return Track. In Figure 13.8, you'll see that the new Return Track is letter C and has been labeled "Cue Mix." Both of the main tracks have their Send C knobs fully clockwise, thus feeding their signals into Return Track C. The trick is in the Input/Output Routing section: The Track Output is set to

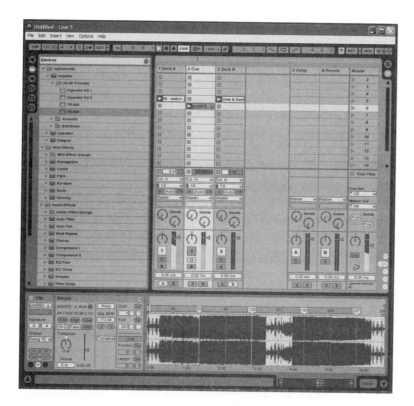

Figure 13.7
This DJ setup features an additional Cue Track. You can place any Audio Clip you want on this track for private headphone tweaking before dragging it onto one of the "live" tracks on either side. You don't have to switch any Track Activators or Cue buttons with this method.

Ext. Out 1/2, which are the headphone outputs. As you turn up the volume slider on this track, the main tracks will blend in with the Cue Track in your cans. You can even pan the main mix over to one side of your phones by panning the Cue Mix track.

You're probably starting to see how Live can be made into a DJ mixing machine by some thoughtful use of tracks and signal routing. To get your hands on the fun, start assigning controls of your MIDI controller. You can set up your system any way you like, but I have a few recommendations:

❄ **The Crossfader:** Even if you don't have a horizontal slider on your MIDI controller to mimic the movement of a real crossfader, assign something—be it a vertical slider or a knob—to this control in Live. Even twisting a knob to perform a crossfade can feel smooth and musical, even if not "true to form." Another option for crossfader control is to select the Crossfader with your mouse and then use your computer keyboard's right and left arrow keys for smooth crossfades.

❄ **The Track Volumes:** While you may think that mixing two tracks should be as simple as setting their volume sliders to the same position and just using the Crossfader, you'll find that some

Figure 13.8

By using another Return Track, you can create a mix for your headphones. Isn't the routing flexibility of Live handy?

songs you play are just louder than others. This could be due to different mastering techniques and sonic content. Regardless of the reason, you'll want to have easy access to the volume of each track; as you begin crossfading, you may need some extra play in the volumes to keep the mix even.

❋ **EQ Kills:** As I mentioned above, EQ Threes are loaded onto each of the live tracks. Assign MIDI buttons (Ctrl⌘+M) or keys (Ctrl⌘+K) on your computer's keyboard to these buttons so you can "cut" frequencies on the fly. When you deactivate the low band of an EQ Three, it will remove almost all the bass and kick drums. The other two buttons, Mid and High, will have the same effect on their own frequency bands. Try taking out the Low from one track while taking out the High from the other. How many three-band combinations can you make?

❋ **Tempo and Groove:** Assign two knobs to these controls—you'll be able to change the speed and feel of your mix at will. Your records have turned into sonic rubber bands!

Looping
New to Live 5 is the ability to define Clip Loop points on the fly by using the Set buttons for the Loop Position and Loop Length parameters in the Clip View. While a clip is playing, you can press

the Set Position button, and Live will move the Loop Start Marker to the closest downbeat. When you press the Set Length button, Live will place the Loop End Marker here and will immediately begin to loop the file. Thanks to an improvement in the MIDI and key mapping structure of Live 5, you can also assign MIDI notes or keys to these Start buttons in the Clip View, allowing you to define loops from an external controller. Furthermore, the mappings will work on whichever clip you have selected, which keeps you from having to reassign the MIDI and key commands every time you load in a new clip.

Impulse

Thanks to the fact that you warp marked all of your audio files, you can create MIDI drum parts to augment the beats in your DJ mix. Load Impulse onto a MIDI Track and build a kit of your favorite drum sounds. As your songs are playing, you can record MIDI Clips and overdub rhythms that will be perfectly aligned with the main tracks. Even if you launch a new song, everything will stay perfectly synced together. In Figure 13.9, I've added the Impulse track and have an assortment of MIDI grooves to play stacked in the Session View. I save these clips as part of my DJ Setup.als file, so they'll be ready to go at my next gig.

Figure 13.9
There's nothing better than a kick drum part or extra hi-hat pattern for adding emphasis to your mixes. It also helps maintain continuity when fading between tracks—your beats stay solid on top, making the transition sound surprisingly transparent.

Live Remix

Remember above when I mentioned saving clips for various sections of the song? Having these on hand will allow you to create live remixes on the fly. When you move the clips into a live track (see Figure 13.10), you'll be able to launch the clips in any order you want, literally remixing the arrangement of the song right in front of your audience. How many clip variations can you make for your remix?

Figure 13.10
The six clips in Track 1 are sections from a larger song. You can jump from the intro to the first verse to the second verse, skipping the chorus. You can then come back and play the chorus twice instead of once—whatever you feel.

Effects

To spice up your DJ set, don't forget to utilize Live's great assortment of Audio Devices. A few of them, such as Beat Repeat, Auto Pan, Auto Filter, and EQ Three, are perfect for augmenting rhythms, emphasizing breakdowns, or smoothing over transitions. While I like to have EQ Threes on each of the track in my Set, I'll usually place the Beat Repeat, Auto Pan, and Auto Filter on the Master Track so they'll affect the entire mix. Don't forget that almost all of the Live Devices will synchronize to the current project tempo, so you'll be able to do things that are perfectly in sync with the songs you're playing. Have fun!

Band

Many gigging bands are using some form of accompaniment, either prerecorded tracks or beat boxes, to embellish their sound. Many times, the bands feature multi-instrumentalists that write more parts for a song than can be played at once. When you have the multi-tracking capabilities of Live at your disposal, you can easily compile the parts you need for accompaniment and break them into scenes. As you perform, you can move through the scenes, or you can record an Arrangement to be played again during a gig.

Click Track

In order to stay synchronized with Live, one or more members of the band may want to listen to a *click track*—which is a metronome sound synchronized with the parts in your song. Usually, this amounts to nothing more than turning on Live's metronome and setting the Cue output to a pair of headphones (like I did in the DJ example above). The drummer will usually be the one begging for the click. He'll play along with the metronome in the headphones, and the band will play along with him. As a result, you all play together with Live.

Of course, since everything is tempo-synced in Live, you could use a regular drum loop as the click track. Instead of turning on the metronome, load a drum loop onto a track and send it to the headphones. Many musicians will find it easier to play against a drum loop, as opposed to the generic metronome sound.

If needed, don't hesitate to let other members of your band hear the click. A simple earphone run up the back of a shirt will suffice. The more members of the band who are locked in with the click, the tighter the sound.

Tap Tempo

Along with playing to Live's click track, you can make Live play to *your* click track. Assign a MIDI button or key to Live's Tap Tempo button. As your band plays, you can tap in your tempo, and Live will follow it. A drummer can assign an electronic trigger to the Tap Tempo and then tap a few beats here and there to keep Live in sync. This is exactly what Shawn Pelton does when he plays with House of Diablo.

 COUNT OFF

Give Live four taps as you count off the beginning of your song. Live will start on the downbeat along with the rest of your band, and it will continue playing at the tempo you tapped.

Live Effects

Besides being a flexible backup player for your band, Live can also act as a sound engineer. To add an echo to your lead singer's vocals, run his mic into an input on your computer's audio interface and select it as an input on an Audio Track. Switch the track's monitoring to On and place a Simple Delay on the track. Your singer's live vocals will pass through the delay, which you can control with MIDI or your mouse. You can also record automation for the effect and play it back as part of the Arrangement. You can program Live to turn the delay on and off at specified times, change the feedback, and so on. This can help emphasize choruses and breakdowns. So you don't completely freak out the sound guy, you can set the output of the vocal processing track to an independent output of your audio interface (see Figure 13.11) and run a cable to the engineer so he can still control the overall mix of the show.

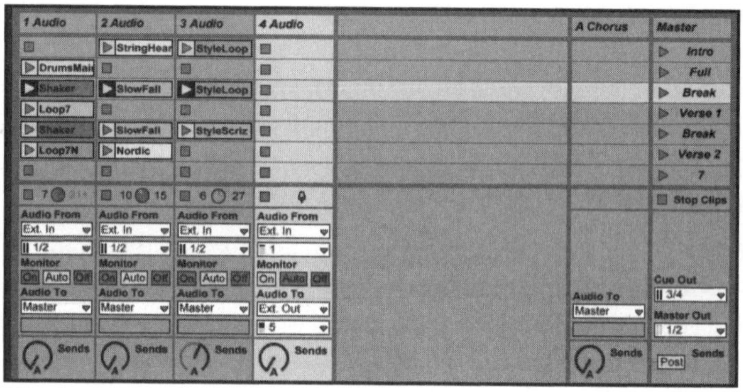

Figure 13.11
Track 4 is processing the live vocals. The affected vocals are being sent to output 5 of the audio interface (outs 3 and 4 are feeding the drummer's headphones).

Jazz Improvisation

Many jazz musicians shy away from computers, especially in a live situation, because they feel they are too constricting for their type of music, one that is built upon the idea of improvisation. Many jazz pieces have a loose structure; certain sections of the song will be explicitly defined (the entrance, ending, and main musical ideas), while others will be completely nebulous (the solo sections). You can see how a traditional sequence may hamper this freeform approach.

Elastic Arrangement

You've heard me refer to the results of Live's Warp Engine as "elastic audio," allowing you to stretch and pitch audio files any way you'd like. The same thing can be said of a musical arrangement in Live—you can jump around and change the length of any sections of the song on the fly. This is accomplished by arranging your clips by song section within the Session View (see Figure 13.12). You can then launch scenes as you progress through the song.

As I've said before, it's not necessary to move through the scenes in a straight top-down order; it's just easier to visualize your song that way when writing. You can set up the scenes any way you like, but just make sure that you have the ability to launch them quickly. Instead of using the mouse to launch the scenes, I recommend using keyboard keys or assigning MIDI notes to a controller. One of the most intuitive methods involves assigning the scenes to buttons on your guitarist's pedal board. He can then switch sections of the song as easily as he changes guitar tones. Or your keyboardist can have command of Live. It doesn't matter who controls the Arrangement, Live's universal MIDI mapping can allow any MIDI device to control Live. If necessary, you can even trigger scene changes from an EWI (Electronic Wind Instrument).

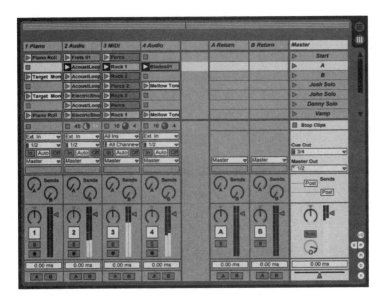

Figure 13.12
The sections of the song are just waiting to be launched. Launching them live, as opposed to playing to an Arrangement, will let you determine the course and speed of the song as you play it.

The important thing to realize is how easy it is to control Live during a performance. If your sax player is performing the greatest solo of his career, you can extend his solo without doing anything at all. As long as the slips in the Solo section are set to loop, they will repeat indefinitely until he signals to move on to the next section. Once he gives the signal, you can trigger the next scene. There's no need to do anything to extend a section; it will happen naturally as you allow Live to loop. All you have to do is launch the various sections of the song when you're ready for them.

New to Live 5 is the ability to place location markers within the Arrangement View. You can assign MIDI notes or keys to these markers, allowing you to jump to different locations of the Arrangement on the fly. This is similar to using scenes, except you're still working within a linear layout. With this feature in use, you can jump back or ahead to different sections of the song at will—the jumps will even follow the Global Quantize setting to ensure there are no rhythmic anomalies when bouncing between the various markers.

Real-Time Loop Layering

Using Live's recording functions within the Session View, you can easily record new clips and set them looping on the fly. This is excellent for creating "sound on sound" layers during a show. A guitarist can play a simple bass line and loop it, and then he can layer a rhythm part on top of it. He can then improvise on top of his new loop creations, making a song right before his audience's eyes (and ears).

The method for achieving these layers is best accomplished with a MIDI pedal board, like the one explained above. You can control Live with your feet, while leaving your hands free to play your instrument. The pedals will each be assigned to the relative MIDI controls in the MIDI Assignment mode. Tapping a pedal the first time will start recording a part; tapping again will begin looping what you just recorded. If you have eight pedals and eight Audio Tracks, you can grab eight different loops and play them at the same time. For more control, you may want to have a MIDI fader box, like Doepfer's Pocket Fader or Evolution's UC-33e, for adjusting the mix of your loops.

Live's relative mapping controls are only visible while in MIDI or Key Assignment mode. When these modes are active, you'll see another row of play boxes appear above the Input Output Routing Strip (see Figure 13.13). When you assign a MIDI note or key to these play buttons, they will individually trigger the clips in the selected scene. In the example, pressing "q" will cause the Beat2 clip in the Bridge scene to play. If the Scene Highlight is moved to the Chorus scene, pressing the "q" key will launch the Break7 beat instead.

Figure 13.13

The relative play controls trigger individual clips from a selected scene. These relative controls will disappear when you exit MIDI or Key Assignment mode, but they will still be active.

These buttons stop the clip in their track.

This button launches the selected scene.

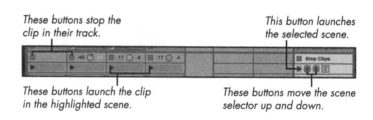

These buttons launch the clip in the highlighted scene.

These buttons move the scene selector up and down.

This relative mapping also works for tracks that are armed for recording (see Figure 13.14). When "q" is pressed now, Live will begin recording a new clip in the empty slot. When you press "q" again, Live will stop recording and begin playing the looped clip. By assigning each pedal to one of these relative slots, you can fire off recordings with the push of a pedal. You can also assign pedals to the stop boxes located right below the relative play controls. You can then stop any playing clip in a track by pressing one of these pedals.

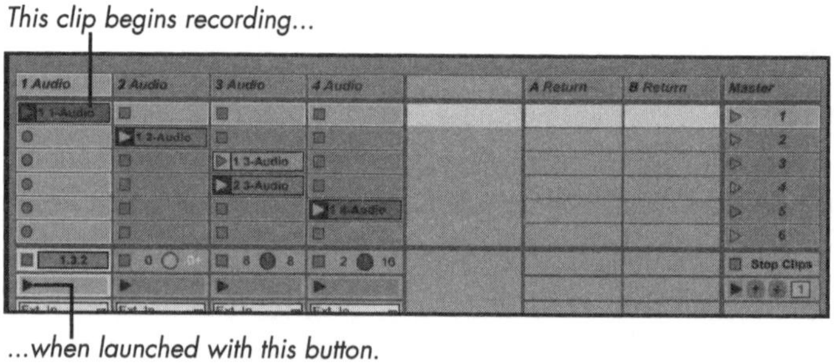

Figure 13.14

Here, clips can be recorded using the same relative buttons by arming the tracks for recording. The stop boxes will stop the playing or recording of any clip on the track.

This clip begins recording...

...when launched with this button.

Theater

Sound cues are one of the most important elements for adding realism to a stage production. Even though an actor may drop a glass on stage, it is usually accompanied with a breaking-glass sample from the theater's sound system (this ensures everyone in the back hears the glass break). Other sound effects, such as wind, rain, thunder, city traffic, church bells, and crying babies, will also be played through the house system. For small theater companies, musical scores will also need to be played back when there's no room (or budget) for a live orchestra. Live performs wonders in this environment, being able to add all of these elements instantly, all with just the push of a button.

Sound Effects

In order to instantly play a sound when using Live, you'll need to turn off any Launch Quantization that may be on, either in Live's Control Bar or individually in your clips. You don't want to trigger a sound and have Live wait for the quantize time before playing it. By switching these quantize settings off, Live will play the clip the instant it is triggered. Whenever possible, I also recommend that you switch off Warp so the sample will always play at its original pitch and speed.

One-shot sound effects would include things such as the breaking glass, a gunshot, doorbell, clock chime, or phone ringing. These sounds happen once and do not loop. For these types of sounds, simply turn off the clip's Loop button. The sound will then play only once every time it's triggered.

For other atmospheric effects, such as rain, traffic, and wind, you will need to loop the sound so it can play for an undetermined amount of time. With the clip's Loop button engaged, you can launch the clip and then slowly fade it in. The sound will stay there until you turn it down again, usually at the end of a scene. Remember, if you need more than one sound effect playing at a time (perhaps someone gets shot in the streets on a rainy night in Chicago), you'll need to have them all on individual tracks.

PERFORMANCE SOUNDS

Contemporary theater companies and performance artists are starting to utilize sensors on their actor's bodies to trigger sounds. Each movement they make can generate unique MIDI messages, which Live can use for triggering clips. A sensor could be used to trigger a gunshot sound when the actor pulls the trigger of his prop gun, thus adding more realism to the performance.

Music Cues

Along with adding sound effects, Live can also be used to play the musical score for the show. Each song, or section of a song, can be made into a clip, allowing you to trigger it at the right moment. You can vary the speed of the music by adjusting Live's tempo. You can even transpose a musical part to another key if your singer's voice is in a different range.

In essence, each musical piece is treated just like the one-shot sound effects explained above; however, to maintain tempo control, you'll want to have Warp turned on in these clips. As you fire off the clips, you can tap a new tempo to keep the music in time with the production. You can even count off the piece with four taps, just like a conductor counting off the beginning of a song. If a piece of music calls for a hold before proceeding to the next section (perhaps there's some dialogue between the verses), split the song into two clips (see Figure 13.15). The first clip will play the song up to the hold and stop. The second clip will begin right after the hold and continue through the end. You can do this for as many holds as there are in the piece.

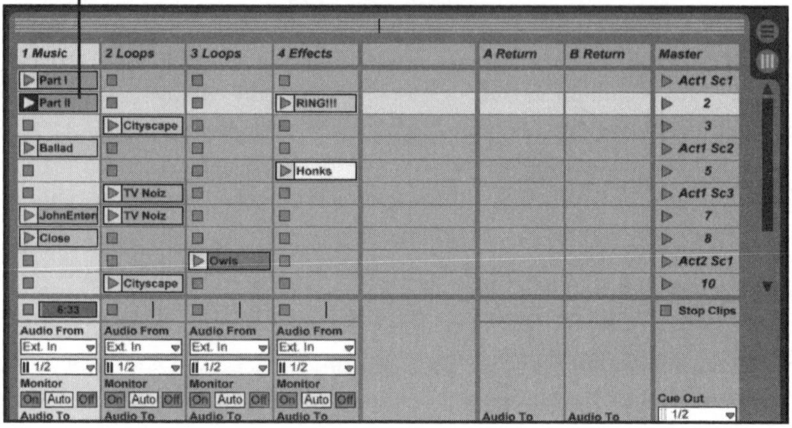

Figure 13.15

The clips in Track 1 are actually the same song. The first clip starts at the beginning of the song, while the second clip starts at the beginning of the second verse.

Part II is launched after the dialogue on the telephone.

Whatever your purpose, either DJing a party, playing at a bar, or performing a stage show, Live can support your endeavors in creative ways that are limited only by your imagination. Since Live is always responding to your input, you will be in control through the entire performance. As you read these sections, we hope you found some interesting applications that you can use in your own performances.

✳ WHO'S USING LIVE?

Gauss Control

Gauss Control is Andrés Criado, a brilliant producer and DJ from Spain who also runs the Undress Records label. I first heard of this guy while listening to some DJ mixes I'd downloaded from the Internet. His mix stood out from the rest due to his excellent choice of songs, but also due to the fluid method in which he mixed the tracks together. After listening to the mix a few times, I decided I needed to find out the names of the tracks he was spinning. I jumped over to www.gauss-control.com and, to my surprise, I found Ableton Live staring right back at me! Andrés loves Live so much, he actually designed his Web site to look like Live. It was there that I found out that all the tracks in his mix were actually written by him—all original productions. Things finally came into focus: Andrés is an artist who uses Live exactly the way it should be used. He uses it for composition all the way through to live performance. Additionally, since he composed his songs within Live, he has intricate control over the arrangements of his tracks because he mixes them part by part while performing Live.

"When I saw Live for the first time, I knew immediately that this software was made to perform and work properly on the stage," explains Andrés. "I prefer a simple layout and new approaches to programming as opposed to a perfect simulation of an old machine. I love the layout of Live—made for functionality while being beautiful and useful. That's why my Web site looks like Live.

"When I started using Live, I always found solutions for my sequencing problems immediately—it is so intuitive and easy to use. I do use Live for sequencing tracks, but not only Live. Live is not a closed production environment like other applications. I use Live for sequencing loops, hosting virtual instruments, and for mastering, too. I think Live is the only one that can do all. It's great to play live sets with the same software used for sequencing the tracks because I don't have to learn a new program again and export files, effects, etc.

"Another good point about Live is that it is giving producers a place on the stage. Not too long ago, producers were closed away at the studio. Now, we have chance to play out regularly like a DJ."

14 } Live 5 Power

You've covered a lot of ground since setting Live's Preferences in Chapter 3, "Getting Live Up and Running." You've learned how to record and modify clips and how to arrange them in the Session and Arrangement Views. You're a master of quantizing and warp marking, and you can spiff up your mix with effects.

Everything up to this point has been left-brain oriented, so I'm now switching gears and will focus on the creative, right-brain things you can do in Live. I'm going to look at how a little "misuse" of some of the tools, such as Warp Markers, can allow you to morph beats into new ones. I'll also show how Follow Actions can make your performance tasks a whole lot easier. You'll even learn how to sync two computers together, as well as learn some final optimization techniques. More than anything, you'll see how thinking "outside the box" can help Live continually adapt to your working style.

More Warp Markers and Envelopes

I cannot stress the importance of understanding Warp Markers enough—they are the essence of Live. The amount of groove massaging made possible by Live's Warp Markers is truly limitless. At first, you may be frustrated by how to specifically adjust a beat or loop to make it sound the way you're hearing it in your head or to get it to align properly within your audio project, but with a little practice, you will develop an intuition for how Warp Markers gradually shift a pattern's events. In the following list, I have outlined a few of my favorite techniques to get you started. After you master the examples, take time to experiment with Ableton's powerful Warp tool. There really are no rules, so go for it!

* **Feel:** The trouble and triumph of loop-based music is that "feel" often becomes stagnant, unwavering, monotonous, and uninspired. It's why dance music is often for dancers, and not always for classically trained musicians. To combat the static element in loop-based music, it is important to add a little variety from time to time, even if the results are basically imperceptible to the untrained or unsuspecting ear. There are several methods for doing

this, but the easiest I've found is to subtly (not randomly!) change the volume of some beats in a few of the repetitions. For instance, you are working in Live's Arrangement View and you have played four measures of a loop. On bar 4, you might try attenuating (reducing) the volume with a Clip Envelope (shown in Figure 14.1). Though a drummer tries to play like a machine, the strength with which he hits the drums will vary slightly throughout his performance. By adjusting the volumes slightly, you can replicate this variability. Remember, it's best to play with the volumes of subdivisions (hi-hats and percussion), not the main beats (such as the kick and snare drums).

Figure 14.1
Altering the volume here and there can add realism to loops.

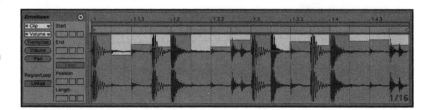

* **Ahead of and Behind the Beat:** Drummers and bass players have developed a unique relationship through the years. An artist's "feel" is often as important as what is being played. You will often hear musicians or critics say it's not what musicians play, but "how they play it." One musical dialogue common to the tradition of drummers and bassists (including organ and synth bass) is that of playing ahead of the beat and behind the beat. The idea is that the bass player (and the rest of the band) plays on the beat, while the drummer plays slightly behind the 2 and 4 snare hits. Generally, you want your kick drum to remain in the same place, meaning squarely on the beat. To play on top or ahead of the beat, the drummer ever so slightly rushes the hit on the snare and even the hi-hats and cymbal parts. This can give the music a rushed or more energetic feel, which is popular in many dance styles. In Figure 14.2a, I have provided a simple drumbeat. Notice that the beats line up perfectly with Live's Warp Markers. In Figure 14.2b, I have pushed a few Warp Markers to the left to make the snare hits feel sluggish or behind the beat, while in Figure 14.2c, I have pushed the same Warp Markers slightly to the right of the snare for a more rushed feel—ahead of the beat.

Figure 14.2a
Simple drum groove aligned with Ableton's Warp Markers.

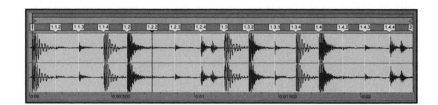

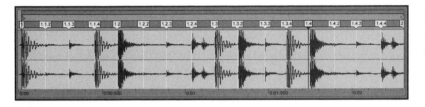

Figure 14.2b
Moving the Warp Markers to the left to make the beat more laid back.

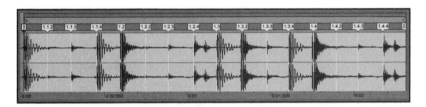

Figure 14.2c
Moving the Warp Markers to the right makes the groove feel "on top."

❋ **Extending One-Shot Style Loops:** Sometimes a looping sample will play too often. Examples such as a single drum hit firing every 1/8 note instead of every 1/4, or a horn section blast on every downbeat instead of every measure comes to mind. If you wanted the blast (seen in Figure 14.3a) to happen on every measure, you can use a Volume Envelope. By unlinking the length of the envelope and stretching it to a bar in length, you can mute beats 2, 3, and 4, resulting in the blast only being heard on beat 1 (see Figure 14.3b).

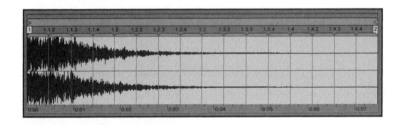

Figure 14.3a
The one-beat long horn blast. Listening to this loop gets annoying really fast.

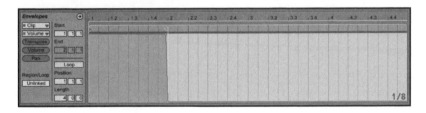

Figure 14.3b
Ah, much better. I've muted the last three beats so I only hear the horns once a measure.

Beat Wreckin' Clinic

Making breakbeats, funky drum patterns, and fills is often best done via trial and error—especially since so much of the music made on computers is programmed in this fashion and not played.

That said, here are a few ideas for making your looped drum and percussion grooves freak the beat.

❋ **Slice 'n' Dice**: Take any drum loop in Arrangement View and use Live's Split command—Ctrl(⌘)+E—at common rhythmic subdivisions (1/4, 1/8, and 1/16-note settings), as shown in Figure 14.4a. Then, rearrange the order of the newly made clips. I like to do this in the track below the original track as shown in Figure 14.4b. You can copy a slice multiple times if you want, and you can leave others out. If you just do this randomly, many a "happy accident" will occur. With practice, you'll work in less random fashion and begin doing edits on purpose. As always, if you are pleased with your results, consolidate the parts into a new loop.

Figure 14.4a
Repeatedly split any clip.

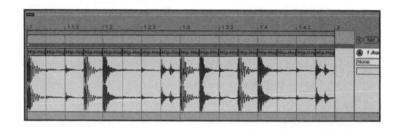

Figure 14.4b
Rearrange and copy the components as you like.

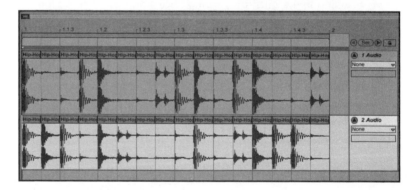

❋ **Double for Nothing**: Another quick trick for adding rhythmic variety to stale loops is to use Live's double and halve original tempo buttons (shown in Figure 14.5). Try sectioning off a 1/4- or 1/8-note section of a loop by using Live's Split command and then double or halve the tempo of the smaller section.

In Figure 14.6, I have halved the last 1/4-note section of the larger loop to give it a slight change in feel. Experiment with other subdivisions and double the groove as well for the best results.

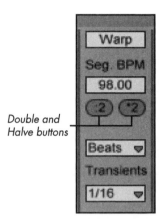

Double and
Halve buttons

Figure 14.5
Use these buttons to halve
or double a small section of
a loop.

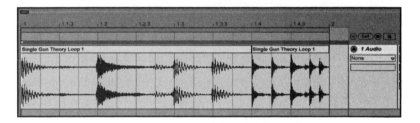

Figure 14.6
Split the loop and then
halve the new segment to
create a fill.

❈ **From the Start**: Topping the list of my fave tricks is to take any of the preceding examples and change the Sample Start for a freshly made loop segment. In Figure 14.7, I have taken the section I halved in 14.6 and moved the start time to 1.2.3. For this particular drum groove, it creates a very realistic and normal sounding drum fill or groove variation.

❈ **Controlling with Clip Envelope**: To take this to an even higher and more complex level, try creating a Clip Envelope to control a loop's Sample Offset. To do this most effectively, make sure you are in Beats mode and then select the Sample Offset Envelope in the Clip Envelope dropdown menu. After you see the flat red line, use Live's Pencil tool to scramble the beat as you like (see Figure 14.7). With some practice you will learn how to reshape loops as you like. Note: Each horizontal line represents a single 1/16 note offset from the Now time.

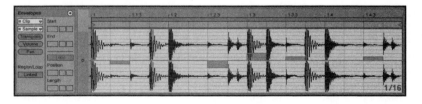

Figure 14.7
Move the clip's play
position using the Sample
Offset Envelope to create
variety.

* **The Rhythmic Microscope:** When trying to line up a loop's feel with other loops and record-ings, try working with smaller sections, one at a time. I find this trick helpful when working with varying degrees of swing or unusual syncopations. In other words, I will work with the first half of the loop until it feels like it complements the feel of the song and then move to the second half.

* **Programmable Slices:** While cutting a beat into tiny slices that you can rearrange is a great way to create micro-edited beats, you can also load these individual slices into the pads of the Impulse instrument by dragging them from the Session or Arrangement View into the cells of Impulse. You can then use the slick precision of the MIDI editor to program patterns of these slices that you can launch at will.

Harnessing Follow Actions

It may sound silly, but even with all the wonderful enhancements in Live, the thing I like the most is the Follow Actions. Can anybody say hidden genius? Really, the Follow Actions section of the Clip View should be in huge, obnoxious flashing letters because this is some serious stuff.

I've said it before and I'll say it again: The power is in the simplicity. The carefully thought-out rules governing Follow Actions allow you to do innumerable things, limited only by your imagi-nation. My favorite uses revolve around enhancing my live performances with them.

* **Mini Song Structures:** If you want to play one clip for three bars followed by another clip for one bar, you could copy the two clips to the Arrangement, extend the first to be three bars, and then tack the second clip on the end (see Figure 14.8). You could then consolidate the clips into a new one, which could be dragged back to the Session.

Figure 14.8
This four-bar arrangement gives us three bars of the BeatA clip followed with a bar of FillA.

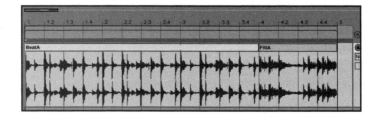

With Follow Actions, you can create the same arrangement in the Session View without ren-dering any new clips. By stacking the two clips on a track, you can set the Follow Actions, as shown in Figure 14.9. The top clip will play for three bars and then trigger the clip below it. The bottom clip will then play for a bar and trigger the top clip, starting the cycle over again.

* **Loop Variations:** I've tried to suggest ways to spice up your loops to keep them from getting too stale, and here's another one. This involves a collection of parts that are subtly different

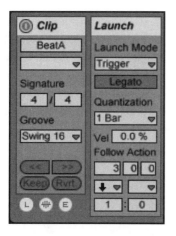

Figure 14.9
By setting the top clip to the settings shown on the left and the bottom clip to those shown on the right, the same arrangement will be played as that in Figure 14.8.

from one another. One example is two drum clips that are the same, but where one has an extra snare hit in it. Set the Follow Action of the first clip to randomly trigger the second one from time to time. You'll set the second clip to retrigger the first. The result is that you get a constant beat that has an additional snare hit thrown in from time to time, mimicking the way a real drummer will modify his beat on the fly. When you set up your Follow Actions, make sure one of the options triggers another clip and that the other option is set to Play Again. Play Again ensures that the Follow Action will be performed again in case Live chooses not to trigger the other clip (check out the Follow Action section in Chapter 5, "Making Music in Live," in case you forgot this little stipulation).

✳ **Pickup Notes:** You know, not every musical phrase starts on the downbeat of a bar. Some start just a few notes before. Take the song "Happy Birthday to You," for example. The two syllables in "hap-py" take place before the downbeat—the word "birthday" happens on the downbeat. Normally you would have to trigger this clip a bar before you wanted it to start. The clip would play silence until it reached the first word (see Figure 14.10). While this does work, it doesn't always feel right to trigger a clip that early before you want to hear it. The second way is to start the clip right on "happy" and change its Launch Quantize setting to 1/4 so you can launch it on the right beat. The downside is that you no longer have the "comfort zone" of the Bar Quantization.

With Follow Actions, you get the best of both worlds: You can launch the clip with the accuracy of a low Quantize setting, while being assured that the part will continue on the beat. To see what I mean, take a look at how "Happy Birthday" is now set up using two clips (see Figures 14.11a and 14.11b). The first clip is "happy," while the second clip is "birthday to you, happy birthday..." and so on. The second clip has a Launch Quantization of Bar. No matter what happens, this clip will start on the downbeat and play in time. The first clip, however, has a Quantize setting of 1/16. Its Follow Action will trigger the next clip after only one 1/16 note (its Follow Action Time is set to 0.0.1). So, 1/16 after the "happy" clip is triggered, the main clip is triggered; however, the main clip will not start immediately since it has to wait for its Quantize setting. This means that if the pickup ("happy" clip) is played a little early or late, the rest of the song will still play in time. This can be a neat tool if your pickup phrase is a whole bar in length. You can trigger it at a bar, half bar, one beat, or any amount and still have the rest of the phrase in time. You'll just hear more or less of the first clip, depending on when you launch it.

Figure 14.10
The clip needs to play all the silence at the beginning in order to come in at the right place.

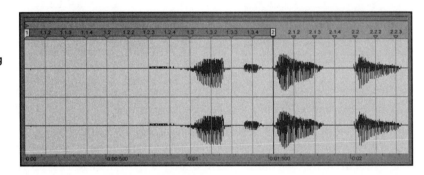

Figure 14.11a
This is the "happy" clip. It is set to trigger the next clip, the "birthday" clip, only one 1/16 note after it is triggered. Since Live won't let you type in a value of 0.0.1 into the boxes, click and drag down on the time value to reduce it to 0.0.1.

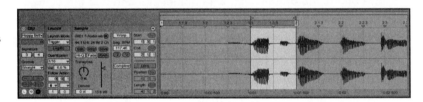

Figure 14.11b
The clip on the right, however, will not play until the downbeat because its Quantize is set to an entire bar.

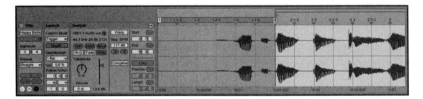

❋ **Drum Fills:** This is my favorite of them all. Triggering drum loops during a live show is so fun, but I don't like having to retrigger the main beat once I'm done with my fills. Follow Actions allows me to play all sorts of beats while Live makes sure to restart the main beat when I'm done. Figure 14.12 shows a stack of drum parts, which happen to be MIDI Clips playing an Impulse. The top clip is the main beat. Every clip below it is a variation or drum fill. Each of these variations has Follow Actions settings matching the ones shown in the figure. By having each of the fill clips trigger the main beat right after it starts, I'm guaranteed that the main beat will start on the next bar (the main beat clip is set to Bar quantization). In fact, since each of the fill clips has a launch quantization of only 1/16, I can launch multiple clips one after the other, literally piecing my fill together in real-time. I always make sure to have a clip with straight 1/16 notes on the snare and another with 1/16s on the kick. These are really effective when dropped in the fill.

Figure 14.12
The top clip is set to Bar quantization, while the others are set to a 1/16. Each fill clip will launch the first, so the beat always kicks in after the fills.

Don't just try this with beats, try it with musical parts, too. Create multiple clips and treat them with different effects and parameter tweaks. Set them to Legato mode so that the playback position is traded off as you switch clips. It will sound like you're performing crazy processing on the part as you switch between the clips. Most importantly, assign these fill clips to MIDI notes for playability!

❄ **Drum Wreck**: Take the previous concept and make dozens (hundreds?) of variant clips. Set them all to Legato with an Any Follow Action. Set the Follow Action time to something pretty short (1/8 or 1/16) and let it rip. Live will start randomly jumping between all your variations at light speed. Render the results so you can grab a great part when it happens.

Minimizing Performance Strain

Effects guzzle plenty of valuable CPU juice. To combat the ill effects of, well, too many effects, I frequently rely on the following tips and workarounds (listed in order of preference):

❄ **Freeze Track**: This new feature in Live will render everything on the track into launchable clips. Simply right-click (Ctrl+click for Mac) on the track's name and choose Freeze Track from the context menu. Live will calculate new clips for each clip in the track and then will disable all of the devices running on the track. The result is that your available CPU will jump up, and the used CPU % will go down. The cool thing is that you are still free to launch the frozen clips at will as if the track weren't frozen at all. The only thing you won't be able to do is make any adjustments to the effects or instruments. If you do need to do this, unfreeze the track, make your changes, and then freeze the track again. You will still be able to change mixer settings such as effects sends, track volume, track pan, mute, and solo while the tracks are still frozen.

This is also a neat way to transfer songs to a friend. If you're using instruments and effects that your friend doesn't have, you can freeze the tracks before saving the Live Set. Once saved, you can give the Live Set to your friend. He'll open it up and find the tracks still frozen. He can trigger these frozen clips any way he likes, so he can still rearrange the parts you've given him.

❄ **Streamline Effects**: Many of Live's included effects contain sections or modules that can be turned off. I've mentioned that by deactivating unnecessary bands of Live's EQ Four, you can shave a couple of points from your CPU meter. Live's Reverb functions in three separate "quality" modes—Economy, Comfort, and First Class modes can be chosen under the Global tab. Other sections of the effects that will save processing power when omitted (if you don't need them) are Reverb's Filtering, Spin, Diffusion, and Chorus Activation buttons, Chorus's Delay 2 Portion, Filter Delay's L, L+R, or R delays or filters, Vinyl Distortion's tracking model or pinch effect, and Redux's bit reduction. In Figure 14.13, I have turned off Reverb's Spin and Diffusion EQ options, and I'm using Reverb's Economy setting. The difference is about five percent less CPU drain.

❄ **Sends and Returns**: In Chapter 8, "Using Effects and Instruments," I recommended taking advantage of Live's Return channels. Simply take any effect that you have created on more than one track and instead "share" it on a Return Track. For example, if you are using several

Figure 14.13
Turn off modules of an effect plug-in to save power.

instances of Live's Reverb on several different tracks, try consolidating by placing one Reverb on a return and then turn up the Send knobs on each of the tracks to be affected. You can then delete the multiple Reverb plug-ins for each track and save a virtual ton of processing power. If the sound changes too dramatically for you, try using the Sends Only output on the channels (as seen in Figure 14.14). You can have up to 12 sends and returns in a given ALS (Ableton Live Set).

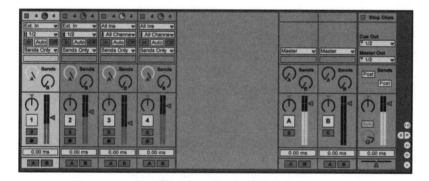

Figure 14.14
Route a track's output to Sends Only to simulate the effect at the channel level, like an insert.

❄ **Render Audio with Effects:** Sometimes, using the returns or streamlining the effects just doesn't do the trick. If this is the case, you may ask yourself if all the effects are absolutely necessary (often the answer is no); however, sometimes you do need all of the effects to achieve the sound you're going for. In this instance, you can render the effect-laden loop(s) (or scenes in Session View) into individual clips. In other words, you'll make a permanent copy of the loop/sample and use this file in place of the CPU-intensive effects and original dry loop(s). After doing so, you can delete the original files and effects from your Live song and save the Set with a new name to ensure that you can always view the originals. In Figure 14.15a, I have selected a scene with several loops running through multiple audio effects plug-ins. In Figure 14.15b, I have rendered that scene and imported the clip and can now play the rendered scene from a single clip with dramatically improved CPU efficiency. You could do this for each scene in a song if you were concerned about crashes or dropouts.

Remember that once you have rendered a scene, you will no longer be able to adjust levels of its individual components—they've all been mixed together in the new clip. Make a habit of saving the original mix so you can always return to the original in case you change your mind.

Figure 14.15a
Several heavily effected clips playing in Live.

Figure 14.15b
After a file is rendered as a single loop, you will no longer need original effects and loops.

Templates

Live lets you save only one template, and it is loaded every time you launch the program; however, with all the different uses for Live, chances are that you won't be able to create a "one-size-fits-all" template to handle every situation. You can, however, create a collection of templates by saving empty Live Sets. Load up Live, set the track count, effects, instruments, tempo, MIDI and key assignments, etc. as desired; then save the Set. When you need to use the template, load the empty set and start working. I recommend making a directory or folder on your computer for saving these various setups. Examples of some templates may be Basic DJ Setup, DJ Setup with Impulse, Multi-track Recorder, Fav MIDI Instruments, etc. The DJ templates may resemble those shown in Chapter 13, "Live Playing...Live." The Multi-track template may have eight Audio Tracks already set to the individual inputs of your audio interface. The Metronome may also be on and pre-routed to the Cue output. The Fav MIDI Instruments template may load virtual instruments that you always use, such as Linplug Albino, NI Pro-53, and GMedia impOSCar. Anytime you start a new song, you can load the template that will get you going quickly.

RENAME ME!

When loading an empty Live Set as a template, immediately save it under its own name. This will prevent you from accidentally overwriting the template with your current project, such as when pressing Ctrl(⌘)+S.

Sample Editing

Now that you have a good basic working knowledge of Live, you may discover that your audio content (samples and loops) could use a little extra cleaning up, examination, or processing. This kind of detail work requires additional software, such as a specific audio waveform/sample editing application (see the "Which Audio Editor to Use?" section later in this chapter). Whether or not you decide to purchase specific audio editing software, I'm going to teach you a few more tricks and tips for getting the most out of your sounds—the fuel for your Live songs. In my experience, these techniques and concepts are some of the least talked about, yet fundamentally the most important and relevant concepts for any computer-based musician or producer to understand. Specifically, I am talking about professionalizing your sound and fixing the digital audio challenges that every producer faces.

Earlier in the book, I pointed out the Launch Sample Editor button located in Live's Clip View (seen in Figure 14.16). If you have not already designated a sample editor in Live's Preferences, pressing the Launch Sample Editor (Edit) button will bring up the message: "No sample editor application has been selected. Would you like to select one now?" Press OK to call up the folder browser and then locate the application (or application's shortcut). After you have done so, you can quickly open any clip in your audio editor by pressing Edit. If your wave editing application isn't already open, the Edit button will launch it and open the AIFF or WAV file. Once you are done working with the file, save and close it. Live will automatically reopen the new file (with any changes) after you revisit your Live session.

Figure 14.16
The Launch Sample Editor button found in Clip View.

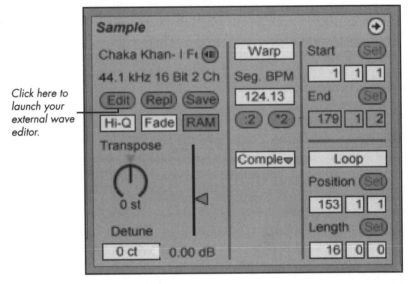

Click here to launch your external wave editor.

※ **WAVE OF WARNING**

Be especially careful when saving audio files from an audio editing application. Any edits done will be destructive, or permanent, once they are saved. Live, on the other hand, invariably saves all Live Set files (ALSs) as non-destructive, or changeable, and therefore keeps all of your original samples intact. This is especially important if you plan to use an edited audio file in another project. To protect yourself, always save your song as self-contained before doing any wave editing.

Which Audio Editor to Use?

At the time of this writing, there are several exceptional, versatile, and professional audio editor applications (also called *wave* or *sample editors*) on the market. Most pro-level audio editors are also fairly expensive (roughly $250 to $500 US), or as much as twice the cost of Live. With this in mind, I put together a list so you can choose your audio editor quickly and confidently. Be aware that most companies make several versions at various prices and in various configurations, ranging from limited to full-feature sets. For example, make sure your audio editor can handle 24-bit audio—Peak DV, a limited version of Peak, cannot. The following list compares the professional versions of each application.

❋ **Adobe Audition (www.adobe.com):** A good deal cheaper than the competition and an excellent value but, unfortunately, PC only. Adobe Audition is also a multi-track recorder that hosts a variety of fun and inspiring features.

❋ **DSP-Quattro by i3 (www.dsp-quattro.com):** Originally available as a shareware application called D-Sound Pro, DSP-Quattro is an inexpensive yet fully featured audio editor for both Mac OS 9 and OS X. This audio editor appears to be an excellent value and has a downloadable demo.

❋ **Goldwave by Goldwave (www.goldwave.com):** Inexpensive (around $45), and a little bit ugly, Goldwave will get you up and running (on a PC only) if you are saving your pennies for a more robust application.

❋ **Peak by Bias (www.bias-inc.com):** Peak users are a loyal crew, and for good reason. The interface is slick, the features are deep, and the sound is amazing; however, if you are composing your music on a PC, you will be left wondering—Peak is for Macs only. Also, Peak's pro version is as expensive as Sound Forge or Wavelab (see next).

❋ **Sony Sound Forge (www.sonypictures.com):** Sound Forge is an expensive, comprehensive, and widely used PC-based audio editor. You can obtain a "lite" version of this product, but keep in mind that these versions don't support higher and more professional sample rates and bit depths.

❋ **Spark XL by TC Works (www.tcelectronic.com):** Comparable with Peak, Spark XL is a professional grade audio editor for Mac OS 9 and OS X. Spark includes many powerful effects and features. While Spark XL is no longer supported by TC Works, a patch for keeping Spark XL 2.8.2 compatible with OS X Tiger (10.4) is available at www.tcsupport.tc.

❋ **Wavelab by Steinberg (www.steinberg.net):** Steinberg's Wavelab is a favorite among DJs who choose to digitize their vinyl and is priced around the $500 mark. Wavelab is available for PC only.

❋ **Soundtrack Pro by Apple (www.apple.com):** Soundtrack Pro is Apple's latest multi-track audio editing solution for Mac OS X. It comes complete with Audio Units and support, video playback support, and a slew of high-quality effects that were previously only found in Apple's Logic Pro.

❋ **SOUND INVESTMENT**

While I am only touching on some basics in this chapter, each of the aforementioned wave editing applications is outfitted with hundreds of features for editing any sound (music, voice, or effect), audio mastering, and CD burning/ripping. You can think of a wave editor as sort of a Swiss Army knife of multimedia. If you are a professional musician, engineer, or producer, you should consider investing in a professional-grade wave/sample editor.

Wave Editor Tips

Like sampling, editing audio waveforms has become both a craft and an art form. Though you will not master it in a day, I find that a basic understanding helps a great deal when working within Live. After some initial practice, working with visual audio, aka waveforms (see Figure 14.17), can be a whole new way of developing, working with, and designing new sounds. If this sounds vaguely familiar, it is because I touched on the concept of visual audio back in Chapter 2, "Back to School." Now would be a good time for a review if you need it.

Figure 14.17

A basic waveform.

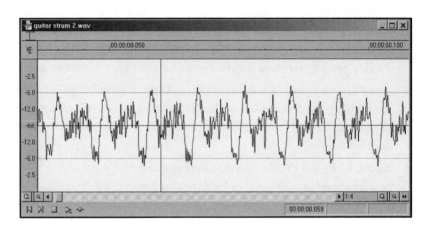

Sprucing Up Your Loops

Wave editors are great for diving deeper into your loops and samples. Like looking under the hood of a car to check out a mysterious noise, you may be surprised to pop open an audio file and discover volume inconsistencies, clicks/pops, and other digital maladies. And similar to a car, you may not be entirely sure what you are looking at.

In this section, I will look at a couple of gain-maximizing tricks (including normalizing), how to de-click your digital audio, and a couple of musical ideas related to audio editing. Since these tips will only be a taste of what any decent wave editor is capable of, you might need to spend some extra time with that application's manual (or relevant tips/tricks book) to take your digital noise to the next level.

Normalizing

Remember, nothing exposes the lack of audio engineering professionalism quite like quirky volume levels. Too much gain during the recording process or excessively boosting audio with a filter or EQ can cause level peaking, which in the realm of digital audio is just plain ugly. Conversely, a signal level that's too low often sounds wimpy and feeble and can weaken an otherwise perfect mix. Other times, audio will develop a combination of the two problems, with great peaks and deep valleys, providing an ultimately unsettling experience for the listener. For these reasons, audio engineers rely on a process called *normalization*. Live musicians (or artists using other loop-based applications) should also take great care to normalize loops and samples.

Normalization is the process of raising the level of an entire audio file so that its loudest parts are as close as possible to the maximum level possible without peaking. In other words, the entire file is made to behave as a "normal" file should. This is great for extended tracks, where the volume may fluctuate a great deal; however, keep in mind that when you normalize, you increase the bad along with the good, and that normalization is not the same as audio compression or limiting (discussed in the "Volume Maximizing" section of this chapter).

❋ **NO WAVE EDITOR? NO PROBLEM**

Even if you haven't yet made the leap and purchased a wave editor, you can still normalize like all the cool kids. Normalizing is actually a built-in feature of Live's rendering options. So, if you are having trouble making levels match up, turn back to Chapter 5.

In Figure 14.18, I have opened the Normalize dialog box in an audio editor (Sony's Sound Forge 6.0). As with many audio editors, you can normalize in terms of percent of maximum dB, where 100 percent means that the highest peak in your waveform will be brought to the brink of the digital maximum. You can also determine more advanced settings, such as how the application looks for the highest gain values and how peaks are handled. I typically normalize only problem loops/samples (too quiet) and all of my finished mixes, but some musicians normalize every single sample. The latter technique will provide more consistency but may also be less urgent if your original recording levels are closely monitored. For loops to be used in Live, I usually normalize at 95 percent and up, while for finished mixes, closer to 100 percent (depending upon the dynamic nature of the material)—it is important for the more dance- and radio-oriented pieces to be maximized in terms of volume.

Figure 14.18

Sound Forge's Normalize dialog box.

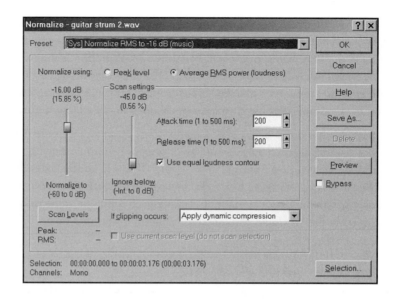

Volume Maximizing

To further support your volume consistency efforts, most audio editors feature at least one compressor, one or two limiting options, and often one volume maximizing (mastering) tool. Each of these effects can help volume peaks and valleys appear less dramatic but can also remove some of the dynamic (loud to soft) musicality of your sample's performance. You may also want to maximize your small, one-shot audio samples (as well as loops). For instance, a single drum hit, such as a kick or snare, might sound good compressed, but a jazz drum set or guitar rhythm might become more sterile sounding with an even dynamic range.

De-Clicking

Clicks and pops are an unfortunate occurrence in digital audio. They occur for a variety of reasons, including cutting off a sample midway through the wave cycle, system strain (CPU, RAM, or hard drive), or inadequate audio interfaces/drivers. Manually removing these annoying little guys can range from simple to next-to-impossible; however, there are several existing click-removal applications for both PC and Mac—although most that I have tried tend to dampen, or diminish, audio clarity for the rest of the audio, as well as take out the clicks. So try the demo before you buy the plug-in/application.

Often times, manual removal is your best and only option. Let's take a look at how to do this.

1. First, you must locate the offending click. To do this, open the sample in your audio editor and loop a small section of audio to see if you can zero in on exactly where the pop is sitting inside the waveform. Occasionally, I will make a marker where I hear the pop occurring during playback (which in Sound Forge can be done by pressing the shortcut key M).

2. Zoom in on the waveform to a magnification that makes sense with the audio you are working on. See Figure 14.19 as an example of a pop I found and zoomed in on in the waveform.

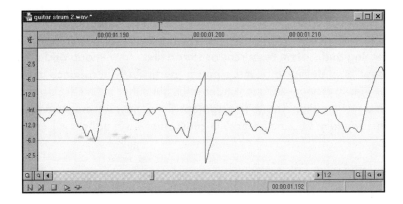

Figure 14.19
By zooming in on the click/pop, you can prepare to fix it.

3. Activate your audio editor's Draw tool and carefully round out the harsh angle or jag that is most likely giving you the pop. If you accidentally draw too much or make some other mistake, undo your last action. The shortcut for Undo is almost invariably Ctrl(⌘)+Z.

4. Check your work. Play the same looped section in step 1 to hear if the click is partially or completely gone. Listen for any other ill effects, such as a muffled sound, additional clicks, or other sonic problems. Sometimes you can make things worse in a hurry by drawing on the waveform. If it does get worse, consider starting over and drawing a less-severe curve or fix.

❋ **FADE IN AND OUT**

The most common clicks in digital audio occur when slicing a sample at a point other than where the waveform crosses the middle horizontal line (often called the zero crossover). If you hear a click at the beginning or end of your sample, you will know that this is your culprit. To rid yourself of these kind of glitches, create a very small (less than 5 millisecond) fade-in at the beginning and a fade-out at the end of your sample.

Streamlining Loops for Live

Laptops are often limited versions of their desktop brethren. They may be a little short of RAM, extra hard drive space, or processor speed, but they are designed as a sleeker, more portable stand-in for your desktop (as opposed to the fully featured multi-processor computers that are common in most recording studios). Since many Live musicians will be porting their music from rehearsal to club to recording session on a laptop, here are a few tips for streamlining audio loops and samples for maximum musicality and minimum system drain in these situations.

Stereo or Mono?

In a typical club, a true stereo field will be experienced by only a small percentage of listeners. Some clubs or performance halls will not even support stereo (right and left) channels. Mono files require roughly half the processing and system resources as stereo files. Also, mono audio files will tend to sound more "present" and deliver a bit more punch (particularly in a dance music environment). To convert your files to mono, you can render each file either in Live (using the Render as Mono option) or in a wave editor. The following steps detail how we create a mono file from a stereo file using Sonic Foundry's Sound Forge 6.0—most other wave editors will contain similar features.

1. Open the loop by clicking on Edit in Clip View.

2. Once the wave editor is open (Sound Forge in this case), select File → Save As and choose Mono in your Save options (see Figure 14.20). Most wave editors allow you to grab one side of the audio waveform (to make a mono loop stereo), but be warned that this is not the true stereo image made mono. For example, if you have a stereo drum track with several different pan settings, grabbing one side only will disproportionately represent your original recording.

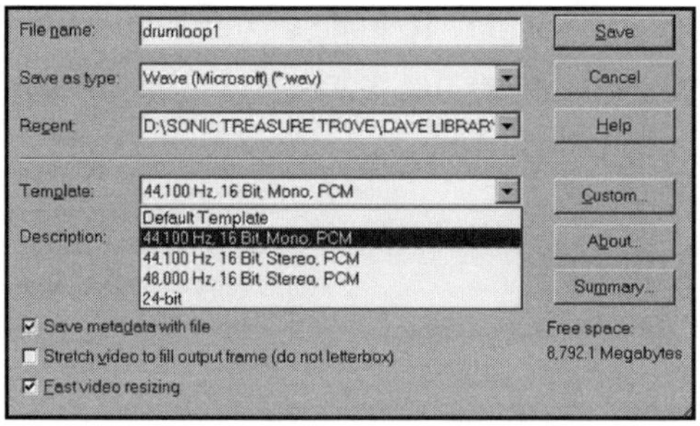

Figure 14.20

Select Mono in your wave editor's Save options—note the highlighted bar in the Description dropdown menu in Sound Forge's Save As options.

3. Since you have created a new file, you need to take advantage of Live's replace (Repl in Live) command, conveniently located in Live's Clip View next to the Edit button (seen in Figure 14.21).

4. Save your newly configured set as self-contained.

Once you have made your stereo loops mono, your Set should demand significantly less CPU power. You will also likely need to readjust your volume, panning, and some effect settings since the new loops/samples will have changed.

Figure 14.21
The Replace/File Locator button calls up the Chooser (Explorer on the PC) so you can swap the files.

Linking Two Computers

In earlier chapters, I explored several ways to synchronize Live with your software applications (using ReWire) and with your hardware (using MIDI). For my last tip, you will combine the two sync concepts by inviting your friends over to jam. Simply decide whose computer will be the master, establish a MIDI link (master computer's MIDI output to slave computer's MIDI input), set up the master to send Beat Clock and the slave to receive it, and go. Inexpensive MIDI splitters and multiple outputs can make the number of players limitless, although some musical orchestration (organization) is recommended. You might assign one musician to cover the drum and percussion loops, another the synths, and another sound effects. You might have two Live musicians playing within the same band or add a singer for a futuristic improv trio. The future of Live may just include two, three, or more musicians getting together, patching their laptops into the MIDI chain, firing up a ReWire application or two, and then jamming the night away. For added fun, try recording the output to some kind of multi-track recorder.

As you can imagine, there are many more tricks and tips still waiting to be discovered in Live. As you spend time experimenting with new ways of working, you will certainly discover what works for you. Also, check out Ableton's user forum, which now features a section called *Tips & Tricks*. I encourage you to share your ideas and interact with other Live users. It's a great community to be a part of. I learn something nearly every time I drop by.

In closing, I would like to sincerely thank you for reading my book. I spent months learning, inventing, and testing the procedures outlined in this book. Should you stumble onto a tip, trick, or scrap of info that doesn't quite do what we said it is supposed to do, there is most likely an update waiting for you at www.ableton.com (click on downloads) or a note at this book's Web page at www.courseptr.com. This book was based on version 5.0.1 and 5.0.2b5 and was tested on both an Apple Macintosh PowerBook G4 1.5GHz with 1.25GB of RAM running OS X 10.4.2 and a Dell Inspiron 5150 3.06GHz (with 512MB of RAM) running Windows XP.

I can attest to the fact that Ableton Live 5 is a stable, elegant, musical, forward-thinking, dynamic, and inspirational software application. I hope you find it to be the same and enjoy many hours of making your own musical vision a reality.

✳ WHO'S USING LIVE?

Steve Tavaglione

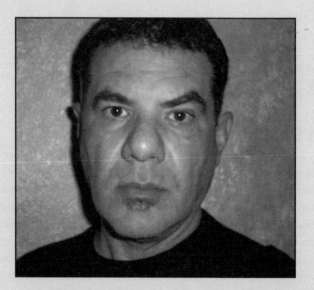

Steve Tavaglione is a woodwind, flute, and electronic wind synthesizer (EWI) player, as well as a sound designer for movies, TV, and records, whom I've had the pleasure of meeting during my tenure at M-Audio. His movie credits include *Finding Nemo, American Beauty, Lemony Snicket's Series of Unfortunate Events, Road to Perdition, Cinderella Man, Jarhead,* and many others. For TV, he has worked on *CSI: Las Vegas, CSI: New York, Charmed, Lois and Clark,* and *Supernatural.* Record credits and performances include work with Roger Waters, Michael Jackson, Sergio Mendes, Chaka Khan, Sly and the Family Stone, John Patitucci, Vinnie Colaiuta, Dave Weckl (one of my favorite drummers), Frank Gambale (a fellow Musician's Institute alumnus), Luis Miguel, and scores of others. Here's what this prolific musician had to say about Live:

"Since I started using Live, which was day one of its first release, possibilities I could have only previously imagined became realities for me. I tend to approach music from an almost childlike place in the first moments, then let the project at hand shape my sense of play into a workable scenario.

"With Thomas Newman, I create soundscapes to handshake with normal and very eclectic acoustic instruments. Since we layer sound and rhythm together, I find that Live is the perfect solution for both.

...any, we are working in and check the tempo and then acoustically ...r directly into Live. After recording the lick, I will copy and paste the ...s into different clips and change the pitch of the licks into harmonies. ...ure, and I will be hearing interesting passages within minutes. If the ...ony of the clips.

...lip dry, then reverse the sample and add reverb. I then resample it ...ample. What I get is a backwards reverb leading to a forward-played

...er samples with newer ambiences that I have made to create new ...ew samples. In that way, my sample library continues to evolve as I ...s and tempo and pitch warping. Every day is a new creative day for

...Evolution or M-Audio keyboard controller along with the full gamut ...Instruments plug-ins, Gigastudio, Propellerhead Reason, and others."

Appendix

CD-ROM Resources

Example Sets

In *Ableton Live 4 Power!*, I had to resort to words and images to explain the concepts of Live. This time around, you get to not only read about what I'm describing, but you also get to actually use the very Live Sets I'm using in my illustrations—hearing exactly what I'm hearing. The CD-ROM contains a collection of little Live Sets that are all designed to showcase some unique features or uses of Live. Please see the end of Chapter 1, "Live 5," for instructions on installing these Sets.

Content Providers

The samples and loops in the examples on the CD-ROM were lovingly provided by a couple of artists I have had the pleasure of meeting over the past couple of years. While their styles differ, they're both Live users. Let's learn a little about these people.

Diavola

Casey Kim, the producer behind the "Mechanically Separated" M-Audio ProSessions sample CD, is a sound designer obsessed with the synthesis of organic and electronic elements. Her classical training and passion for technology have earned her guest appearances and remixes on a number of albums nationwide. Casey currently produces her own breed of electro-acoustic industrial alchemy from her studio in Los Angeles, California. Find out more at www.diavolaonline.com.

Rdizzy

Raul Resendiz, aka Rdizzy, is a hip-hop producer residing in Pasadena, California. He began his venture into the music business working for the nation's largest music store, Guitar Center. There he gained valuable hands-on experience and knowledge on every product available, such as keyboards, sound modules, recording software, microphones, and pro-audio live sound reinforcement. After almost three years of service, Rdizzy left his six-day a week schedule at Guitar Center to join the team at Midiman, which, shortly after, changed its moniker to M-Audio. There he is a software testing engineer and Pro Sessions veteran. He produced three of the M-Audio Pro Sessions CDs titled "Hella Bumps," which are volumes 9, 10, and 48 in the ProSessions library. These volumes have been the number-one selling sample libraries from M-Audio since their release. Stay tuned, because he is currently writing a book dedicated to all the aspiring hip-hop producers out there. Check out www.MySpace.com/3rdegreeProductions for more information.

Web Resources: Where to Get Plug-Ins

While Live includes an extensive collection of fine effects and versatile instruments, you can enlarge your collection by obtaining additional plug-ins—both effects and instruments—from third-party developers. The Web offers access to many of these exciting companies, some of which offer downloadable demos or free versions of their plug-ins. Here's a list of places to investigate when you're looking for some new toys.

Commercial Plug-In Developers

* **www.cycling74.com:** With over 100 plug-ins for $199, Cycling 74's Pluggo effect pack is the perfect example of "bang for the buck," and it's now available for Windows, too!

* **www.tritonedigital.com:** Tritone Digital is a company that uses Pluggo (as mentioned above) to run its plug-ins. HydraTone and ValveTone are reasonably priced analog emulation EQ plug-ins that many users swear by.

* **www.pspaudioware.com:** This is Poland's first software company but one of the world's finest audio developers. For cool "tube" simulation, check out Vintage Warmer and MixPack, or for crazy delay effects (quite unlike Ableton's own brand), try out the Lexicon PSP 42 (or 84) and their new 608 MD.

* **www.steinberg.net:** The inventors of VST technology offer several effects plug-ins and instruments. The GRM tools get a lot of use in my compositions.

* **www.native-instruments.com:** Amazing instruments and effects with a refined look and feel. Expensive, but you get a lot for your money.

* **www.wavearts.com:** Quality equalizers, dynamics, and reverb plug-ins are the specialty at Wave Arts. Their effects are some of the most CPU-efficient plug-ins available, not to mention very affordable.

❈ **www.audiodamage.com**: Do you want it to sound a little nastier? The name "Audio Damage" says it all. They have a lot to offer by way of modular delay, dubbed-out tape delay, distortion, and dark reverb effects. And they definitely won't put a hole in your wallet.

❈ **www.u-he.de**: Urs Heckman makes some of the most stable, intuitive, and intelligent synth plug-ins available. If you'd prefer modular flexibility, his Zebra synth should suit you fine. Or if you just want an exceptionally warm filter, synthesizer, and equalizer collection, look no farther than the Filterscape bundle.

❈ **www.ohmforce.com**: If aesthetics alone determined the quality of their plug-ins, Ohmforce would be the king of cool. Maybe not for everybody, but some wildly interesting effects can be found here.

Web Resources: Free Plug-In Developers

Though the saying "you get what you pay for" certainly holds merit, the Internet was built on freeware, shareware, and try-before-you-buy business models. If you are pinching pennies or just looking for a quick batch of new sounds, the following list should keep you busy for a while:

❈ **www.db-audioware.com**: Dave Brown is the self-proclaimed first third-party developer to post VST effect freeware plug-ins on the Internet. He still provides the original free plug-ins that started his business.

❈ **www.mda-vst.com**: MDA generously provides 23 (at the time of this writing) plug-ins, which, I might add, aren't too shabby. Let's see, 23 times zero is still zero! What a bargain.

❈ **www.funk-station.co.uk/effect.htm**: Some funky little effects.

❈ **www.smartelectronix.com**: DestroyFX, Magnus, and other plug-in makers live here. You'll find some stable, interesting, and experimental effects. Check out the Supa Trigga remixing plug-in—this is one of my favorites.

❈ **www.alphakanal.de**: Known in the past for the free synths, Buzzer and Buzzer 2. Alphakanal's OS X Audio Unit-only Automat synthesizer is right at home in Ableton Live. The synth is constantly updated, and the latest version of Live is used as the primary source for testing Automat before new updates, so you know that compatibility and CPU performance is paramount.

❈ **www.digitalfishphones.com**: Lots of compressors and saturators with a good bit of character.

❈ **www.tweakbench.com**: More free instruments and effects than you can shake a stick at, for PC only.

Web Resources: Staying Informed

Since the Internet changes every second, staying current can be a full-time job. Here are a couple of pit stops that I have found helpful over the last couple of years for keeping up-to-date on the latest happenings.

* **www.ableton.com:** For any serious Live user, the Ableton Forum is not to be missed.

* **www.kvr-vst.com:** This site is updated daily with new instrument and effect plug-in information. Just follow the links.

* **www.osxaudio.com:** This is a great site for Mac OS X users looking for the latest plug-ins and general compatibility talk.

* **www.hitsquad.com:** Hit Squad can be difficult to surf but is informative.

* **www.harmonycentral.com:** This site is packed with music news of all shapes and sizes. Still, we recommend it for VST and software development news.

* **www.gearslutz.com:** Talk audio hardware and software with other gearslutz.

Don't forget to check your favorite search engines as well. I found some way-out-there plug-ins by searching for "freeware vst plugin" on Google!

Where to Get Loops

The following list is a sampling (pun intended) of my favorite loop purveyors. Nearly all of their Web sites feature downloadable demos or even free content for you to play with. If you happen upon a collection of samples that really works for your project or sound, most sites will also recommend other titles, similar to the way Amazon.com recommends books—if you liked this, then try that.

* **Bigfish Audio** (www.bigfishaudio.com)

* **East West** (www.soundsonline.com)

* **Electronisounds** (www.electronisounds.com)

* **Ilio** (www.ilio.com)

* **M-Audio** (www.m-audio.com)

* **Q-UP Arts** (www.quparts.com)

* **Sony Media** (www.sonymediasoftware.com)

* **Sample Craze** (www.samplecraze.com)

* **PowerFX** (www.powerfx.com)

Internet Resources

If you just can't wait for a sample CD, or if you prefer to shop via the Internet, there are several established and professional sample houses that offer downloadable sample wares. You can preview the files first and download the ones you like (for approximately two or three bucks per loop). This can be a convenient and inexpensive way to shop, considering that some sample CDs will only provide you with a few loops that give you what you are looking for.

- ❆ **Sonomic** (www.sonomic.com): One of the most respected pure online sample retailers on the Net, Sonomic will even store your sounds for you on a secure drive in case you need to access your sounds from the road.

- ❆ **Sound Dogs** (www.sounddogs.com): While Sound Dogs specializes in movie and television sound effects, their online database will turn up several quality loops of virtually every musical style. Also, you might be amazed at what a little "spaceship rumble" might do for your next ambient dub jam.

- ❆ **PowerFX** (www.powerfx.com): PowerFX sells both CDs and loop download packs from its Web site. Download packs, usually in the $10 range, provide a solid batch in a given style (for example Hip Hop, Techno, etc.).

- ❆ **Platinum Loops** (www.platinumloops.com): Platinum Loops offers 9,000 original loops and samples for download or in DVD and CD formats.

By doing a couple of Google searches, you will stumble across many other pros, hobbyists, and startup sample making companies. The next two caught my eye.

- ❆ **Loop Kit Pro** (www.loopkit.com)
- ❆ **Acid Fanatic** (www.acidfanatic.com)

> ❆ **ZIPPING ALONG**
>
> Often, loops and samples are zipped or stuffed in order to save you download time. Zipping and stuffing files is a form of compression, and upon download, the files will need to be opened (uncompressed). To do this, you will need to download a free helper application called *WinZip* (for PC), which can be found at www.winzip.com, or *Stuffit* (for Mac), located at www.stuffit.com. After you have downloaded and installed the helper application, any zipped or stuffed file can be opened and their contents extracted to your hard drive.

Index